MANCHESTER MEDIEVAL LITERATURE AND CULTURE

REBEL ANGELS

Manchester University Press

Series editors: Anke Bernau, David Matthews and James Paz

Series founded by: J. J. Anderson and Gail Ashton

Advisory board: Ruth Evans, Patricia C. Ingham, Andrew James Johnston, Chris Jones, Catherine Karkov, Nicola McDonald, Sarah Salih, Larry Scanlon and Stephanie Trigg

Manchester Medieval Literature and Culture publishes monographs and essay collections comprising new research informed by current critical methodologies on the literary cultures of the Middle Ages. We are interested in all periods, from the early Middle Ages through to the late, and we include post-medieval engagements with and representations of the medieval period (or 'medievalism'). 'Literature' is taken in a broad sense, to include the many different medieval genres: imaginative, historical, political, scientific, religious. While we welcome contributions on the diverse cultures of medieval Britain and are happy to receive submissions on Anglo-Norman, Anglo-Latin and Celtic writings, we are also open to work on the Middle Ages in Europe more widely, and beyond.

Titles Available in the Series

12. *Annotated Chaucer bibliography: 1997–2010*
    Mark Allen and Stephanie Amsel
13. *Roadworks: Medieval Britain, medieval roads*
    Valerie Allen and Ruth Evans (eds)
14. *Love, history and emotion in Chaucer and Shakespeare:* Troilus and Criseyde *and* Troilus and Cressida
    Andrew James Johnston, Russell West-Pavlov and Elisabeth Kempf (eds)
15. The *Scottish Legendary: Towards a poetics of hagiographic narration*
    Eva von Contzen
16. *Nonhuman voices in Anglo-Saxon literature and material culture*
    James Paz
17. *The church as sacred space in Middle English literature and culture*
    Laura Varnam
18. *Aspects of knowledge: Preserving and reinventing traditions of learning in the Middle Ages*
    Marilina Cesario and Hugh Magennis (eds)
19. *Visions and ruins: Cultural memory and the untimely Middle Ages*
    Joshua Davies
20. *Participatory reading in late-medieval England*
    Heather Blatt
21. *Affective medievalism: Love, abjection and discontent*
    Thomas A. Prendergast and Stephanie Trigg
22. *The politics of Middle English parables: Fiction, theology, and social practice*
    Mary Raschko
23. *Performing women: Gender, self, and representation in late-medieval Metz*
    Susannah Crowder
24. *Contemporary Chaucer across the centuries*
    Helen M. Hickey, Anne McKendry and Melissa Raine (eds)
25. *Borrowed objects and the art of poetry:* Spolia *in Old English verse*
    Denis Ferhatović
26. *Rebel angels: Space and sovereignty in Anglo-Saxon England*
    Jill Fitzgerald

Rebel angels

Space and sovereignty in Anglo-Saxon England

JILL FITZGERALD

Manchester University Press

Copyright © Jill Fitzgerald 2019

The right of Jill Fitzgerald to be identified as the author of this work has been asserted by them in accordance with the Copyright, Designs and Patents Act 1988.

Published by Manchester University Press
Altrincham Street, Manchester M1 7JA
www.manchesteruniversitypress.co.uk

British Library Cataloguing-in-Publication Data
A catalogue record for this book is available from the British Library

ISBN 978 1 5261 2909 3 hardback
ISBN 978 1 5261 5592 4 paperback

First published 2019

The publisher has no responsibility for the persistence or accuracy of URLs for any external or third-party internet websites referred to in this book, and does not guarantee that any content on such websites is, or will remain, accurate or appropriate.

Typeset by
Servis Filmsetting Ltd, Stockport, Cheshire

For Jeremy (and our little one on the way) with love

Contents

List of figures viii
Acknowledgements ix
Abbreviations xii

Introduction 1
1 Lands idle and unused 23
2 The anxiety of inheritance 71
3 Rebel clerics, monastic replacements 114
4 The angels' share 157
5 A homeland as a possession 197
6 A new *praedestinati* in Wulfstan's *Sermo Lupi ad Anglos*? 231
Afterword 275

Bibliography 281
Index 312

Figures

1 Oxford, Bodleian Library, MS Junius 11, fol. 3r
  (© The Bodleian Libraries, The University of Oxford). 33
2 Oxford Bodleian Library, MS Junius 11, fol. 16r
  (© The Bodleian Libraries, The University of Oxford). 35
3 Oxford Bodleian Library, MS Junius 11, fol. 10r
  (© The Bodleian Libraries, The University of Oxford). 37
4 London, British Library, Cotton, MS Vespasian
  A. VIII, fol. 2v (© The British Library Board) 138

Acknowledgements

I am pleased to be able to express my heartfelt thanks to the many kind people who helped make this book a reality. I am grateful to all those who have read and commented on parts of this manuscript, as well as those who have simply listened to me talk about my ideas – and my struggles and triumphs as a writer – for many years. My greatest debt is to Charlie Wright, who is responsible for whatever good qualities I may possess as a scholar. Charlie has always provided meticulous feedback, saved me from errors, and supplied me with the mental energy to develop my ideas (sometimes in very short spaces of time). But the greatest gift Charlie has given me is the example he sets; he has shown me what I should be striving for as a scholar, a teacher, and a mentor. I also wish to thank Renée Trilling, who helped this project through its early days and always had exciting suggestions about new directions it might take.

There are of course many friends and colleagues I would like to thank here, too many to list by name, though I hope they all have a good sense of how very much they are appreciated. I have enjoyed the many benefits of a wonderfully supportive group of colleagues in the English Department at the United States Naval Academy, who have enriched my life and thus my work. In my first years as a new professor, I had the good fortune of sharing the same halls with John Hill and Richard Abels. Their continued friendship (even in their happy states of retirement) has helped me bring this project to completion. For their guidance and enthusiasm, I am forever grateful. I count myself lucky to have the support of many other generous colleagues, many of whom have read and thoughtfully commented on various portions of this book, most especially Thomas Ward, Mike Parker, Audrey Wu Clark, Naida Garcia-Crespo, Derek Handley, Noah Comet, Allyson Booth, Calina Ciobanu, Charlie Nolan, Jason Shaffer, Michelle Allen-Emerson, and Christy Stanlake. Conversations with colleagues and mentors in the field of medieval studies over the years – even some of the most fleeting – have reshaped and sharpened my thinking, ultimately greatly enriching this book. I wish to thank Martin Camargo and Dan Anlezark for their early feedback on the project. I am also grateful to Dave Johnson (who was kind enough to share unpublished work with me), Johanna Kramer, Roy Liuzza, Andrew Rabin, Stacy Klein, Fred Biggs, Nicole Marafioti, Jill Hamilton Clements, Stephane Clark, Shannon Godlove, Lindy Brady, Brandon Hawk, Ben Weber, Stephen Pelle, Stephen Hopkins, and Carl Kears. I am fortunate to have been able to work with and learn from such gracious individuals.

This book has also benefitted from institutional support in the form of Naval Academy Research Council Grants that provided me with steady summer research funding. I am also appreciative for the support I received from United States Naval Academy Faculty Development Funds and Fluegel Funds, which allowed me to travel to various domestic and international conferences to present my work.

I also wish to thank my anonymous readers with Manchester University Press for their constructive suggestions that helped strengthen the manuscript and Meredith Carroll for her editorial support from the very beginning and throughout the publishing process. I also thank Alun Richards for his assistance in guiding the manuscript to print.

I would be remiss if I did not express my sincere thanks to the many midshipmen I have had the pleasure to teach at the United States Naval Academy, who have always been curious as to what I was doing with a clutter of books and notes around my desk. They continue to awe and inspire me and I owe a good deal to their sharp minds and even sharper wits. Second Lieutenant Tom Doughty (USMC), in particular, meticulously (and with more excitement than I could have possibly imagined) checked early drafts of each of my chapters for inconsistencies and transcription errors while he awaited a call-up from Quantico. To the many midshipmen that have brought me such professional purpose and joy over the years – I forever wish you fair winds and following seas.

My deepest gratitude goes to family. My parents, Christopher and Judith Fitzgerald, always taught me to love reading and learning and have shown me steady support and inspiration from the very beginning. In the end, this book is dedicated to my husband, Jeremy, who has lived with this project for its entirety. He is

Acknowledgements

my dearest friend and most trusted sanctuary, a heroic source of patience, love, and support.

Annapolis, United States Naval Academy
October, 2018

Abbreviations

ACMRS	Arizona Center for Medieval and Renaissance Studies
ASC	*Anglo-Saxon Chronicle*
ASE	*Anglo-Saxon England*
ASPR	Anglo-Saxon Poetic Records, ed. G. P. Krapp and E. V. K. Dobbie, 6 vols (New York: Columbia University Press, 1931–42)
Bosworth-Toller	Joseph Bosworth, *An Anglo-Saxon Dictionary, Based on the Manuscript Collections of the Late Joseph Bosworth Toller*, ed. and enlarged by T. Northcote Toller (Oxford: Clarendon Press, 1882)
CCCC	Corpus Christi College, Cambridge
CCSA	Corpus Christianorum, Series Apocryphorum (Turnhout: Brepols, 2012)
CCSL	Corpus Christianorum, Series Latina (Turnhout: Brepols, 1953–)
CH	*Ælfric's Catholic Homilies*, ed. Peter Clemoes and Malcolm Godden, 3 vols (Oxford: Oxford University Press, 1979–2000)
CSASE	Cambridge Studies in Anglo-Saxon England
CSEL	Corpus Scriptorum Ecclesiasticorum Latinorum (Vienna: Hölder-Pitchler-Tempsky, 1866–)
CPG	*Clavis Patrum Graecorum*, 5 vols, ed. Mauritius Geerard (Turnhout: Brepols, 1974–87)
CPL	*Clavis Patrum Latinorum*, ed. Eligius Dekkers and Aemilius Garr (Steenbrugge: Turnhout, 1995)

Abbreviations

DOE	*Dictionary of Old English: A to H Online*, ed. Angus Cameron, Ashley Crandell Amos, Antonette diPaolo Healey, et. al. (Toronto: Dictionary of Old English Project, 2016)
eDIL	*Electronic Dictionary of the Irish Language*, www.dil.ie
EETS	Early English Texts Society
os	Original Series (London: EETS, 1864–)
ss	Supplementary Series (London: EETS, 1970–)
ES	*English Studies*
HBS	Henry Bradshaw Society
JEGP	*Journal of English and Germanic Philology*
LSE	*Leeds Studies in English*
MÆ	*Medium Ævum*
MGH	Monumenta Germaniae Historica
MP	*Modern Philology*
Neophil	*Neophilologus*
N&Q	*Notes and Queries*
NM	*Neuphilologische Mitteilungen*
OED	*Oxford English Dictionary*
PG	*Patrologia cursus completus, series Graeca*, ed. Jacques-Paul Migne (Paris: Garnier Frères, 1857–1903)
PIMS	Pontifical Institute for Mediaeval Studies
PL	*Patrologia cursus completes, series Latina*, ed. Jacques-Paul Migne, 221 vols (Paris: Garnier Frères, 1844–91)
PQ	*Philological Quarterly*
RES	*The Review of English Studies*
S	Sawyer
SASLC	*Sources of Anglo-Saxon Literary Culture*
SEEH	Studies in Early English History
SEMA	Studies in the Early Middle Ages
SP	*Studies in Philology*

Introduction

Sometime in the eighth century, a priest named Sigewulf asked his teacher Alcuin (d. 804) a series of 300 questions about the biblical book of Genesis. Among these was a question concerning the book's silence on the matter of the fall of the angels. Two centuries later, Ælfric of Eynsham translated Sigewulf's question: 'Hwi wæs þære engla syn forsuwod on þære bec Genesis, and þæs mannes swa gesæd?' (Why was the sin of the angels passed over in the book of Genesis, and that of mankind told?). Ælfric also rendered Alcuin's straightforward response: 'Forþan þe God gemynte þæt he wolde þæs mannes synne gehælan, na þæs deofles' (Because God determined that he would heal the sin of man, not the devil's).[1] Indeed, no traces of the overreaching pride of Lucifer, the war in heaven, or the fall of the rebel angels are to be found in Genesis, although certain verses in other biblical books were thought to allude to it.[2] On some level, Ælfric must have viewed Alcuin's response to his pupil as satisfactory. His Old English translation follows the Anglo-Latin text with general fidelity. However, the eleventh-century monk's writings also suggest that he viewed the story behind the sin as one of great complexity, dramatic tension, and vital importance for his contemporary moment. The fall of the angels – the rebellion's causes, consequences, and lessons – would become a topic Ælfric would return to in his writings again and again. In his homilies, epistolary correspondence, and his 'Preface to *Genesis*', Ælfric infuses the story of the angelic rebellion with narrative form as well as instructional substance. And he was not alone in doing so.

Over 600 years before John Milton's *Paradise Lost*, Anglo-Saxon authors told their own version of the fall of the angels. Retellings of this extra-biblical event are widely attested from the time of Bede all the way to the eve of the Norman Conquest and beyond, from the riddles of Aldhelm to early cosmographies such as those written by Aethicus Ister to late medieval Arthurian texts.[3] These stories, however, vary widely in both design and purpose throughout the Anglo-Saxon period. The Bible's relative silence on the matter, it would seem, only increased curiosity (and perhaps the narrative's adaptability) about the vexed heavenly relationship that first led creation to sin against its creator. The narrative can thus be traced through a wide range of genres: sermons, saints' lives, royal charters, riddles,[4] as well as devotional and biblical poetry[5] – each genre offering a distinct window into the myth's place within the Anglo-Saxon literary imagination. It is the aim of the present book to explore how the story of the angelic rebellion can illuminate other areas of the Anglo-Saxon imagination and social world: namely, perceptions of territory, dissent, power, and popular belief. The argument thus progresses through several of these genres (biblical poetry, royal charters, saints' lives, and homilies) in an attempt to reconstruct early medieval attitudes about the fall of the angels and how perceptions of that narrative changed from roughly the eighth to the eleventh centuries. Alcuin's (and later Ælfric's) deceptively simple answer to Sigewulf's question would not keep early medieval poets, theologians, political thinkers, and kings from persistently interrogating what went on in the wee hours of angelic creation. Nor would that deceptively simple answer prevent them from retelling and repurposing the story with a growing confidence that rested on the authority of their patristic inheritance.

At various turns, this book will consider how a narrative only vaguely alluded to in the Bible came to justify and explain religious and secular hierarchies in the Anglo-Saxon world. The following section will more thoroughly consider the role of the replacement doctrine, a teaching which, as I argue, assumed the status of a dominant mythos or social theory, a way of crafting meaning for the Anglo-Saxons as a Christian community. Under the terms of the replacement doctrine, humans were created expressly to repopulate the emptied spaces of the divine hierarchy. However, to Anglo-Saxons, the doctrine of replacement was not merely an arcane teaching or a page of sacred text. Indeed, the doctrine seems to have found some its most potent expressions in various corners of the spiritual, civil, and social realms.

In considering the various spheres in which iterations of the story of the angelic rebellion can be found, this book investigates how homilists and spiritual authorities such as Ælfric saw fit to use its precepts to warn every sinner that they could be like rebel angels, potentially forfeiting their eternal property rights and the good graces of their divine sovereign. Homilists mostly incorporate the motif of the fall of the angels in their renditions of catechetical *narratio*, or a short excursus upon 'Christian cosmology and Christian history',[6] which typically open with God's creation of heaven, earth, and humankind before turning to Christ's life and his undertakings up to the Last Judgement. Virginia Day has documented how the original *narratio* was Augustine's *De Catechizandis Rudibus* (*c.* 405). The genre was chiefly envisioned for priestly instruction, the spiritual edification of catechumenates, and even missionary endeavours. Day also charts the various branches of the *narratio* tradition through which other authors followed suit: from Martin of Bracara (*c.* 515–80) to Pirmin of Reichenau (d. 753), Hrabanus Maurus (*c.* 784–856), and Odo of Cluny (*c.* 879–942).[7] One wonders if the famed poet that Bede alludes to, Cædmon, learned his craft from the recitations and orations of *narratio* at Whitby, since Bede states that he possessed extraordinary skill in versifying the Bible. The influence of *narratio* is especially evident in the works of Ælfric, especially his *De Initio Creaturae* which inaugurates his colossal series of *Catholic Homilies*; his opening (which I discuss in Chapter 6) reveals the tremendous influence this salvific programme exercised upon vernacular literatures. For Ælfric and others such as Wulfstan, it would seem, *narratio* (and thus the fall of the angels) became the appropriate way of signalling a beginning. Many of his texts including his *Letter to Sigeweard*, *Letter to Wulfgeat*, and *Hexameron* commence thusly with a short reflection on the cosmic disruption of the fall of the angels and its earthly consequences. When it came to the instruction of monks, Ælfric imagines their mission to be much like the angels who reaffirmed their absolute loyalty to God following the rebellion of their sorry counterparts. In his *Letter to Sigeweard* (also discussed in Chapter 6), he describes those angels as always and forever meditating on the surrendering of their will to God, much like any worthy monk would be asked to do.

The fall of the angels narrative also finds its most distinctly political iteration at a critical moment of upheaval in the early English church: the Benedictine Reform. In this case, monastic reformers used the narrative as a weapon against their secular rivals by tethering replacement principles to their monastic ideals, claiming that their ecclesiastical adversaries were little more than rebel angels, rogue bodies in a corrupt ecclesiastical establishment, ultimately arguing that they themselves could better prepare flocks for heaven. Amid all this, we get just one glimpse of how sovereigns benefitted from the story of the angelic rebellion, their ruthless and formidable exercise of supreme authority allowing for a cleansing and (as my first chapter will demonstrate) a strengthening of lands. To put it another way, at a time when notions of sovereignty and sovereign authority were changing, we see how kings profit from the narrative by imagining their own powers as aligning with divine authorities.

Finally, we see poets craft this extra-biblical story into a complex epic filled with deceit, treachery, exile, tragedy, and triumph. In its poetic form, the narrative can tell us something significant about the dominant myths of the Anglo-Saxons. Of course, any discussion of the many myths that abided at the core of Anglo-Saxon cultural belief would be indebted to the work of Nicholas Howe, Andrew Scheil, and Samantha Zacher among others. Anglo-Saxons gathered a constellation of traditions that informed their sense of place in the world. Among them was the 'migration myth' as hypothesised by Howe. This mythos allowed Anglo-Saxons to recall the Germanic migrations from the Continent in a way that paralleled the Old Testament. That is, just as God guided the Israelites to the promised land, the Anglo-Saxons were so divinely directed to Britain. Authors such as Gildas, Bede, Alcuin, and Wulfstan all relied on this mythos to explore England's relationship to wider Christendom and cycles of decay and rebuilding in their own time.

The branches of Howe's thesis have been extended in provocative ways to encompass the *Populus Israhel* tradition, by which the Anglo-Saxons came to identify with the Jews, imagining themselves to be a present-day 'chosen people', as elaborated upon by Andrew Scheil and Samantha Zacher.[8] As Scheil puts it, '[t]he *Populus Israhel* [tradition was] a complex metaphor and political ideology ... The Jews were once the chosen people, but now the Anglo-Saxons represent a new covenant with God ... Jews provide a sense of history for Anglo-Saxon culture, an understanding of the relationship between the past and present'.[9] Although each of these ideologies are distinct, they manage to coexist in powerful and enmeshed ways. From the migration myth to their identification as 'New Israel' to their belief that they were to be the inheritors of heavenly spaces vacated in the angelic rebellion, early English men and women saw the history of the Old Testament as actively playing out in their own time. To be sure, the fall of the angels narrative was not simply a cautionary tale for the Anglo-Saxons, but a narrative that reveals the complex dialectical relationship between their legal, political, and theological literatures.

The fall of the angels in patristic theology

Anglo-Saxon authors eagerly adopted both apocryphal and patristic ideas surrounding the angelic rebellion. The earliest attempts to supply this noticeable lacuna appear in Jewish apocalyptic traditions such as *The Book of the Secrets of Enoch* (*c.* 70 CE),[10] and later in the exegetical commentaries of the Church Fathers. The two major patristic authorities on the subject were Augustine of Hippo and Pope Gregory the Great. Any author wishing to venture ideas about the angelic fall had to attend to the following pressing questions: when did angelic creation occur? When did the angels rebel? What (or who) were they rebelling against? What was their fate? How do these matters impact humankind? Augustine ponders these issues in his *Enchiridion ad Laurentium* 62 (CCSL 46.82), *De Genesi ad Litteram* 11.24 (CSEL 28.1), and *De Civitate Dei* 11.9, 22.1 (CCSL 48.807). The prevailing theory about the timing of the fall of the angels came from his *City of God*. Here he surmised that angelic creation came about with God's command of *fiat lux* ('let there be light', XI.9).[11] In conjunction with that command, Augustine argued that God's subsequent separation of light and dark simultaneously corresponds with the expulsion of the rebel angels. In other words, Augustinian logic would suggest that this rift in divine creation inaugurates time itself.

Augustine may have reconciled questions concerning the absence of angels from the book of Genesis, but it was Pope Gregory whose writings on the fall (in his *Homiliarum in Evangelia* 34 (CCSL 141A.6) and his *Moralia in Iob* (PL 76, especially 477ff)) came to dominate views about angelic unrest from antiquity through the Middle Ages. In his *Moralia in Iob*, Gregory elaborated upon the intricate hierarchies of angelic orders (citing as his evidence parables from the gospel of Luke). The sources of Gregory's ideas on the subject are difficult to trace, but he most probably derived some of his thinking from *The Celestial Hierarchy* by Pseudo-Dionysius.[12] Angelic society, according to Gregory, consisted of angels, archangels, virtues, powers, principalities, dominations, thrones, cherubim, and seraphim.

The second of Gregory's influential works on the subject of angels and how their fall would directly impact humanity derives from a sermon explicating Luke 15:1–10 (delivered in 591 CE).[13]

In this sermon, Gregory suggested that faithful Christians would inherit the heavenly territories forfeited by the rebellious order of angels. This idea came to be known as the 'doctrine of replacement'. Augustine broaches this same possibility in his *Enchiridion ad Laurentium* 62 and 29 (CCSL 46.82; CCSL 46.65) and *De Civitate Dei* 22.1 (CCSL 48.807), in which he describes how God intends to 'suppleat et instauret' (fill and repair) the blank spaces left by the rebel angels. Gregory's *Homiliae in Evangelia* 34 (CCSL 141A), however, gave the doctrine new vitality by reframing the issue around a salvific inheritance wherein humankind completes the orders. Several centuries later, the Frankish noblewoman, Dhuoda, in her *Handbook for William* (*c.* 841–4) (III.10 and IX.4), reveals that she knew the Gregorian metric quite well: 'The meaning, William my son, is that the high and omnipotent God saw fit to form man from the mud of the earth, to share in the splendor of angels and to restore their number ... Everything has to be reunited so that the tenth angelic order can be lawfully restored'.[14] Gregory's numerological theories were thus common within ninth-century Carolingian circles in texts devoted to the proffering of advice and counsel.

It is my contention that Anglo-Saxon Christians came to self-identify as among the rightful heirs to the territories forfeited by the rebel angels and were thus profoundly invested in envisioning their Christian community's inclusion in the spaces of heaven via replacement. The doctrine took on added potency for the British Isles when in 597 CE Gregory proposed missionary endeavours to convert the 'Angli' living in Britain after he allegedly saw Northumbrians for the first time. The anecdote famously goes that Gregory observed young Anglo-Saxon slaves or boys in Rome and, upon learning that they were pagans from 'Anglia', declared it fitting that they become coheirs of the 'angeli' and spend eternity among the angelic host. This story is attested (with some slight variations) in three different versions: an early *Life of Gregory the Great* written by an anonymous monk at Whitby,[15] Bede's *Historia ecclesiastica* 2.1,[16] and an Old English retelling of Bede which was translated during the reign of Alfred the Great.[17]

In the anonymous Whitby *Life*, Gregory asks the boys who they are and where they come from. They answer, 'Anguli dicuntur, ille de quibus sumus' (The people we belong to are called Angles), and Gregory exclaims, 'Angeli Dei' (Angels of God!). In Bede's account, Gregory sees the two boys for sale in the Roman marketplace. They are described as having 'candidi corporis ac uenusti uultus, capillorum quoque forma egregia' (fair complexions, handsome faces, and lovely hair). According to Stephen J. Harris, 'Bede's description of the boys as slaves or chattel implies ... that Gregory is delivering the Angles from bondage'.[18] He adds that, in their appearance, 'the Angles show they are already predisposed to receiving salvation'.[19] When Gregory asks about the race of the boys he learns that they are from the 'Brittania insula' (island of Britain), and he is told 'est quod Angli uocarentur' (that they were called Angli). 'Bene!' (Good!), Gregory responds, adding, 'angelicam habent faciem, et tales angelorum in caelis decet esse coheredes' (they have the faces of angels, and such men should be coheirs of the angels in heaven).

In the Old English version, the story similarly reads that the 'cneohtas' (youths) were 'hwites lichoman ⁊ færon ondwlitan men ⁊ æðellice gefeaxe' (men of fair complexion and handsome appearance and elegant hair). Gregory learns that they are 'Ongle nemde' (called Angles) and replies that 'heo ænlice onsyne habbað, ⁊ eac swylce gedafonað, þæt heo engla æfenerfeweardas in heofonum sy' (their form is peerless, and thus it is right, that they should be coheirs with the angels in heaven).

This sense that Anglo-Saxons were specially fit to become *coheredes* or *æfenerfeweardas* (from *efenyrfeweard*) or 'coheirs', fundamentally informs conceptions of early English Christian identity as numerous texts articulate an understanding of their role in the story of salvation history. In his commentary 'On Tobias' (CCSL 119B), Bede writes, 'Having been led to the heavenly homeland, humanity's [elect] will be welcomed by God ... and also by the angels whose number they will complete'.[20] This linking of the replacement doctrine to the conversion story of the Anglo-Saxons, initiated by Gregory and reasserted through Bede, is taken very much to heart by authors from Æthelwold to Cynewulf to Wulfstan. With this simple pun on 'Angles' and 'angels', the salvific destiny of the Anglo-Saxons is inscribed in the place they inhabit: the land of the *Angli*.

Augustine and Gregory's ideas achieved mainstream status, and later authors such as Martin of Braga and Haimo of Auxerre would make further deductions in their positions about the fall of the angels (interpretations I discuss in Chapters 2 and 3). But its solid exegetical credentials meant that the fall of the angels narrative was sufficiently poised to become the subject of popular study and elaboration in the medieval world. Taking their cues from Augustine, many authors wished to explore the nature of pride because, as

Richard Sowerby observes, 'this "first defect" among the angels must have been the sin of pride'.[21] For example, in Tatwine's *Enimga* XXV, 'pride' (the speaker of the riddle) describes its monstrous heavenly birth: 'a distinguished ancestor begot me long ago and lost his realm through me'.[22] Boniface's 'pride' riddle similarly describes its mothering by 'an angelic serpent [who] gave birth to me in the height of heaven, viperously and harmfully breathing sins into its heart'.[23] Bede also felt it necessary to elaborate upon the dangers of pride through the story of the fall of the angels. He discusses as much in Homily II, 3 (CCSL 122.205), *In Lucae Euangelium Expositio* (CCSL 120A.285ff), his Commentary on the Epistle of Jude 6 (CCSL 121A), as well as his commentaries on Ezra 6:14–15 (CCSL 119A), and Tobias (CCSL 119B) (already quoted); as I will discuss in Chapter 3, he also makes several allusions to the angelic rebellion in his correspondence. He closely follows Jerome in his *In principium Genesis* (CCSL 118A) in his commentary on Lucifer's fall:

> One of these morning stars indeed, in view of his scorn of the common praise of God, deserved to hear, How you are fallen from heaven, O Lucifer, who did rise in the morning! *How are you fallen to earth, who did wound the nations! And you said in your heart: I will ascend into heaven, I will exalt my throne above the stars of God* [Isa.14:12–13]. In his commentary on this passage St Jerome even mentions the higher heaven, writing as follows: *Either he said these things before he fell from heaven or after he fell from heaven. If he were still in heaven, how is that he says, 'I will ascend into heaven'? But since we read, 'the heaven of heaven is the Lord's',* [Ps. 113:16 (115:16)] *although he was in heaven, that is, in the sky, Lucifer wished to ascend into the heaven where the Lord's throne is, not out of humility but from pride. But if he speaks these haughty words after he fell from heaven, we ought to understand him to be one who, having been cast down, will not be quiet, but still promises great things for himself, not to be among the stars but above the stars of God.*[24]

While Bede relies heavily on Jerome's exegesis here, eventually he and others will begin to describe the rebellious pride of the angels as analogous to the catastrophic failures in pastoral and spiritual leadership that they witnessed in their own day.

One additional crux that Anglo-Saxons wrestled with had to do with the possibility of a heavenly rivalry (between either Satan and Adam or Satan and Christ). The idea that Satan engaged in a bitter feud with Christ originates within the patristic period, but is quite rare. According to Thomas D. Hill, one patristic text that suggests Satan's rebellion is aimed at Christ is the *Divine Institutes* of Lactantius (CPL 85).[25] Beyond this, Augustine once glossed John 8:44 with this suggestion, which was subsequently echoed by Alcuin in his own commentary, and then by Ælfric in his *Heptateuch*.[26] In a late seventh-century Ascension Day homily (PG 43, cols. 481–4) commonly attributed to Bishop Epiphanius of Salamis (d. 403), a fourth-century Greek author, Satan describes the 'Son of Mary' as his heavenly opponent, stating:

> I seek to catch him, and see, as with a lead weight I am dragged down. I seek to seize him and by a strange force I am held back. What in my misery can I do? He has driven me out from every place. From the heaven he threw me down to earth like a little whirling stone.[27]

Even though a majority of Anglo-Saxon retellings of the fall of the angels focus on Satan's contempt towards God and his overweening pride (as evinced in texts such as *Genesis A* and *Genesis B*), there are some exceptions (such as *Christ and Satan*) which recalibrate the story so as to include Satan's enmity towards Christ. One brief example appears in the penitential poem known as *Resignation*, found in the Exeter Book. It reads:

> ne læt þu mec næfre deofol seþeah
> þin lim lædan   on laðne sið,
> þy læs hi on þone foreþonc   gefeon motan
> þy þe hy him sylfum   sellan þuhten
> englas oferhydige   þonne ece Crist. (ll. 52b–6)

[let no devil lead me, your offspring, on a hateful journey, lest they might rejoice in that original fore-thought in which they, those arrogant angels, considered themselves better than eternal Christ.]

C. Abbetmeyer's 1903 work titled, *Old English Poetical Motives Derived from the Doctrine of Sin*, offered the first comprehensive overview of the Old English and Anglo-Latin texts that incorporated the theme of the fall of the angels alongside their relevant patristic backgrounds.[28] Following Abbetmeyer's work, there has been a consistent interest in exploring the poetic adaptations of the fall of the angels along with its patristic connections,[29] as well as those in prose writings (by both anonymous and known authors).[30] Source analysis has also yielded valuable insights into the transmission and appropriation of this narrative throughout Anglo-Saxon England.[31] No doubt, this is because extra-biblical narratives and their accompanying patristic traditions offered

Anglo-Saxon authors an important avenue through which to explore the connections (and tensions) between their inherited Christian beliefs and native Germanic worldview. Further critical interest in the fall of the angels narrative concentrates on how authors converted complex theological exegesis into dramatic narratives about betrayal and rebellion. As Malcom Godden observes, Anglo-Saxons found the Old Testament to be 'an ever-useful storehouse of information and inspiration ... [the] emphasis upon glory in war, fealty to one's lord, and the importance of a unified and strong nation was easily converted and translated into compelling heroic poetry'.[32] Anglo-Saxon authors thus recycle their inherited patristic teachings while characteristically imagining Satan as a powerful nobleman or veteran retainer who betrays his lord's munificence in a struggle for power and landed supremacy; he is subsequently banished from his homeland, doomed to wander in exile.[33] Magennis further observes that '[Satan's] treachery represents the reverse of the great Anglo-Saxon ideal of loyalty'.[34] The narrative's intrinsic connections to lordship and its subversion coupled with the precedent for forfeiture of inheritance would have thus had immediate socio-political and spiritual relevance for Anglo-Saxon readers. This book aims to bring together various cultural moments, genres, and relevant comparanda to recover the story that they tell, from the legal and social world to the world of popular spiritual ritual and belief.

Matters of space and sovereignty

Because Anglo-Saxon conceptions of legal and sovereign authority were, as this book will argue, directly inflected by the fall of the angels, the narrative's core repertoire of themes can illuminate broader literary representations of space, power, and identity. As we have seen, the fall of the angels in patristic traditions was thought to be associated with the beginning of time immediately following God's command of *fiat lux*. One reason why this narrative so captivated poets, homilists, political thinkers, and even kings, was because it also gave them a symbolic language through which to discuss when and how space and territory – heavenly, earthly, hellish – first came into being. For early medieval men and women, the fallen bodies of Satan and his rebellious cohort, in a certain sense, impacted the very arrangement of spiritual and earthly spaces: from the vastness of heaven, to the disorder of hell, and the impressionable earth.

Introduction

What does this story have to do with space? The narrative, of course, would have been crucial for Anglo-Saxons attempting to think about both divine time and space as ways to order their earthly experiences. Space as it shaped early medieval culture is thus a theme of this book. Because Satan's crime results in the first forfeiture of space (and the chance for humankind to inherit his former estates), in most cases, early medieval English narratives of the fall of the angels coalesce around disputes concerning lands and territories (a common theme in charters and lawsuits), especially those with occupants deemed idle, rebellious, or in desperate need of penitential cleansing.

Old English terms for 'space' recur throughout the narratives describing heavenly dominions, earthly lands, and even Satan's ruinous kingdom in hell. Terms such as *fæc* ('space, interval, distance, portion of time'), *gemet* ('a measure, space, distance' or 'bounds, limit, boundary'[35]) are frequent glosses for Latin *spatium* (which the *Dictionary of Medieval Latin from British Sources* defines as an 'area or expanse of land, ground, or space, region, area or expanse of sky or heavens' or 'space available or designated for a purpose, room'). The term *gerum* has both spatial and temporal force ('space of time'),[36] whereas *hwil* refers to 'a while, space of time' (sometimes an 'indefinite space of time').[37] It is in this indeterminate sense that *hwilum* features prominently in *Christ and Satan* when Satan fails to comprehend and order his physical and temporal surroundings, his fraught subjectivity defined by the immeasurable space he inhabits. The term *rum* appears to be the commonest way to describe earthly and heavenly spaces (as with the adjectival form *rume rodor* 'the spacious firmament on high'). The frequency with which authors employ these terms to represent both the acquisition of space as well as its loss suggests that texts – whether a charter, a boundary clause, a biblical poem from the Junius Book, or a saint's life – offered Anglo-Saxon authors one way to establish their sense of place and order in the world.

The works of Henri Lefebvre, Jacques Le Goff, and Anthony Smith all suggest that cultures imagine themselves according to distinct spatial structures and organisations, whether those spaces are in their possession or simply desired and hoped for.[38] As Fabienne Michelet puts it, 'Narrative also constitutes a powerful weapon in the struggle for control and appropriation of space ... narrative always grounds claims to a given land, justifies its possession, and defines the limits of the space thus occupied ... the making of poetry is always linked to the making of worlds'.[39]

Anglo-Saxons must have also imagined their narratives as fragile (if not fledgling) and subject to erasure (particularly during eras dominated by invasion). Similarly, their lands and spatial communities were occasionally seen as vulnerable and subject to change.

If poetry afforded Anglo-Saxons an opportunity to imagine ideal spaces, popular belief and practices (such as the feast of Rogationtide) would have only reinforced this notion of earthly space as a conduit towards the perfect spaces of heaven. According to Howe, Anglo-Saxons would have been distinctly aware of 'all things on earth [as] *læne*, that is, transitory ... Home is, finally, the place that lies beyond direct human experience or apprehension. It can be entered only by those ... who knew that insubstantial buildings are the appropriate dwelling for those awaiting salvation'.[40] Because the fall of the angels tells the story of how an ideal space – teeming with bliss, stability, and love – can become threatened and destabilised through simple acts of thinking and speaking, and then how such spaces can be one day restored if faithfully earned by humankind, it follows that this narrative touches on the themes of divine and earthly time and territory that would have been on the minds of authors such as Bede and Ælfric.

'Sovereignty', as Lefebvre reminds us, 'implies space'.[41] Just as Anglo-Saxon poets used this narrative to emphasise themes of disobedience and disinheritance, the administrators of the secular world were also formulating their actual legal cases of forfeiture in significantly analogous ways, particularly crimes of treachery, plotting, and oath-breaking. In King Alfred's England, for instance, the threat of total confiscation (both of titles and inheritances) ensured absolute loyalty. From Alfred on, we can see changing notions of kingship and power in early medieval England. Charters narrativise how all land comes from the king with the possession of such lands demanding obligations. Moreover, the law codes reveal that the bonds between a king and his thane can be forever undone through especially heinous crimes. In numerous places, we also read that sovereigns revoke privileges and transfer ownership to fortify their realm. All this would suggest that rulers would have seen in the fall of the angels a narrative precedent allowing for the assertion that all land belongs to and derives from the king.

Rebels are thus cast out as kings repopulate territories with loyal subjects, mirroring the politics of salvation as seen in poems like *Genesis B* and the politics of submission as in the land charters of the Benedictine Reform.[42] In the former, we read about how Adam and Eve must earn salvation through penance. In the latter, we find

Introduction

that to submission to the *Rule of St Benedict* becomes a requisite for authorised religious life and worship; any refusal of the *Rule* makes one a rebel. In Anglo-Saxon England, we also find varying expressions of sovereignty. Thomas Bisson explains that medieval '[l]ordship matters because the human realities of power – command, allegiance, accountability, coercion, and violence – were bound up with it'.[43] While Anglo-Saxon rulers and writers alike looked to biblical figures for their models of kingship, Katherine O'Brien O'Keeffe has argued that obedience to sovereign authority underwent a distinct process of internalisation during the Anglo-Saxon period as 'compensation for wrongdoing [shifted] from an external, and in some ways, communal, responsibility satisfiable by compurgation and fine ... to an internal guilt in the eleventh-century codes (in a mutilation which forever forces the body to confess to its guilt as a part of the process of salvation)'.[44] In other words, sovereign authority has both a regal level (as seen in the royal charters which license the banishment of individuals from communities) as well as an individual or self-imposed dimension (as established by documents such as the *Regularis Concordia* which monks swore to obey); such tensions are frequently revealed in the texts that comprise this book.

Unlike Irish and Old Norse versions of the fall of the angels where clear-cut laws and prohibitions are brokered in heaven even before the angelic rebellion, Anglo-Saxon authors take time to point out how, at the moment of angelic creation, there are no pre-existing legal orders in place, only systems of obligation and reciprocity owing to God's gifts of 'gleam and dream' (beauty and joy, *Genesis A*, l. 12b) and 'gewit' (intelligence, *Genesis B*, l. 250b); furthermore, authors typically explain that the angels 'Synna ne cuþon' (knew nothing of sin, l. 18b). The angelic rebellion thereby requires the production of laws and limits following Lucifer's attempt to surpass God's sovereignty. Crucially, for Anglo-Saxons, out of this rebellion emerges the ambit of earthly creation, formal commandments and laws, and also new subjects – humankind – created with the express purpose of repairing the loss of loyal subjects incurred at the beginning of time. Ultimately, the fall of the angels serves as the event that establishes precedents for the kind of relationship God desires from his human subjects.

The following six chapters begin by examining how the narrative of the angelic rebellion resonated within secular, military, and legal spheres, where lordly obligations were given pride of place. Chapter 1 considers the proems of land charters (extending from the reign of King Edgar to Æthelred and even Cnut), which evoke the angelic rebellion before establishing the transfer and re-granting of property. After providing an overview of the legal outlook surrounding treachery and rebellion from the age of Alfred – whose legal reforms sought to establish that landed entitlements and seisen were privileges descending from kings – onwards, I consider this social context alongside *Genesis A*, a vernacular poem that includes a striking episode detailing earthly creation alongside the doctrine of replacement using distinctly legal terminology. The poet of *Genesis A* imagines Satan's rebellion as a story of forfeiture and disinheritance followed by God's response as a legalistic compensation with the promise a future re-granting, aligning the poem with practices witnessed in Anglo-Saxon law codes and land charters. The connection between the charters and the biblical story thus allow us to see how notions of replacement may have had physical, earthly repercussions, and how new modes of sovereignty emerged through a growing reliance on biblical authority: the power of replacement (the re-granting of land) becoming a written legal instrument, a kingly action.

In Chapter 2, I argue that the poet of *Genesis B* imagines Satan's crime as a failure to accept sovereign checks on his power and limits upon his territorial ambitions. The latter stages of the poem reveal Satan's post-lapsarian pursuit of space and territory as he operates a rival kingdom in hell and laments the fact that Adam and Eve will one day claim and settle his former habitations in heaven. Themes of territorial competition, expansion, and inheritance manifest in various wider traditions concerning the fall of the angels, too. Irish vernacular adaptations in particular depict how Satan views humankind as rival-inheritors of lands to which he feels entitled. These accounts, found in texts such as *Saltair na Rann* and *Lebor Gabála*, derive from the apocryphal 'Life of Adam and Eve'. In these narratives, Lucifer upsets clearly defined spatial and social limits. In *Saltair na Rann* a conflict arises between Adam and Lucifer over the issue of seniority, a controversial matter in medieval Ireland. Lucifer believes he possesses greater *febas*, a subtle concoction of positive qualities frequently evoked in Irish succession disputes, denoting one's dignity, reputation, or overall nobility. *Lebor Gabála* similarly sets up Lucifer's revolt as a response to Adam's territorial inheritance of earth with terminology connected to landed jurisdiction. Lucifer's heavenly authority is revoked by God in this account because he fails in his duties as an *airchinnech* ('governor, nobleman'). We see Irish authors thus adapting apocryphal traditions for a powerful socio-political effect, imagining features of their own ecclesiastical and secular administrations as mimetic representations of divine structures.

My third chapter explores how Bede's epistolary exchanges suggest that he viewed spiritual corruption as an earthly reflex of the sins of the rebel angels. This idea re-emerges in the city of Winchester in the tenth century amid the Benedictine Reform movement. Here, monastic reformers reinstate Bede's idea that ecclesiastical treacheries find an analogue (and perhaps their origin) in angelic strife in order to advance their own agenda: namely, labelling their rivals (wayward secular clerics) as rebellious, prideful, and unfit to keep their ecclesiastical endowments. For Henri Lefebvre, space is not an a priori concept, but a cultural construct, something that is carefully fashioned especially during moments of change and turmoil.[45] We might compare Lefebvre's thesis to any space or structure that allows a given community to look inward and thus structure meaning. In Anglo-Saxon England, we might extend this to a variety of spaces both fixed and abstract: properties, ecclesiastical endowments, minsters, parish boundaries, the distinct kingdoms of Anglo-Saxon England, cities, and ultimately the island itself. The case of Winchester with its newly constructed minster and adjoining grounds (c. 963–75) offers us a unique vantage point from which to view the careful refashioning of physical and ideological space by individuals like King Edgar, his wife Queen Ælfthryth, and chief adviser, Æthelwold.

Proems evoking the fall of the angels reach an apex of expression in King Edgar's 'New Minster Charter', the prime textual forerunner to the Benedictine Reform. A defining document of late Anglo-Saxon history, the New Minster Charter served as the official royal and monastic response to the ecclesiastical conflicts of the 960s. The literary and theological content of this charter, which begins by rehearsing the fall of the rebel angels, had significant cultural and political consequences. The charter's author portrays the secular clerics at Winchester as a subversive threat to English ecclesiastical unity by aligning their alleged sinful behaviour with that of the 'superbentium angelorum' (pride-filled angels). As Sowerby puts it, in this era it happened that a 'myth about an expulsion of angels from heaven had become a matter of cardinal importance in early medieval England, central to the Anglo-Saxons' understanding of humanity and its origins'.[46] The charter thereby legitimates the exclusion of fallen and rebellious bodies in the nation and redefines the authority of King Edgar, a new theocratic sovereign. I build on the work of Sowerby and others by examining how the Winchester charters attest to the potency of biblical narrative in the lived experience of Anglo-Saxons through their depiction of adversaries to the English Christian community and in their aim to legally establish the secular canons as rebels. I also consider how these charters were not the first English documents to imagine disobedient and disorderly ecclesiastics as earthly replicas of the rebel angels, but represent part of a longer tradition of viewing the church as a reflection of the heavenly polity.

In all these cases, rebellion is figured as a lapse of loyalty, a furtive betrayal, a broken oath, or a lethal desire for possession, not necessarily a fully fledged martial opposition against a lord. Charters like the ones issued during the reign of Edgar, with their hybridising of biblical, doctrinal, and legal registers can help bring the interests of both Anglo-Saxon literature and sermons into clearer focus. As I discuss in Chapters 1 and 3, Vercelli Homily 10, for instance, directly responds to the brazen landed ambitions of the monastic reformers as expressed in their stately charters. Such regal documents, moreover, become earthly tools of replacement, inscribing the restoration of loyalties and lands into collective memory; what we see in them is the drama of expulsion and replacement playing out on an earthly, and altogether human, space and scale.

From here, I turn to the narrative's appearance in Old English saints' lives wherein holy men and women articulate the fall of the angels narrative as though it were a charm, a verbal defence mechanism offering spatial, geographical, and bodily protections. Chapter 4 examines accounts of the angelic rebellion in four hagiographical poems in which saints articulate the story of the angelic fall to protect themselves from marauding demons. Just as Anglo-Saxon charms master something threatening by defining and reciting its name, properties, and origins, so too in *Elene* and *Juliana*, do Cynewulf's saintly protagonists Judas Cyriacus and Juliana master their demonic tempters by identifying them and recounting their originary sin. While in these poems the origin narrative is itself apotropaic, in *Andreas* the fall of the angels narrative is linked to the protective power of the baptismal seal (or *sphragis*) that safeguards Christians against the devil. Similarly, *Guthlac A* relates how Guthlac disarms his demonic tormentors by recounting the story of their fall and by expressing his faithful expectation that he will be one of their replacements in heaven.

Just as the saints' lives I discuss in Chapter 4 deal with the retelling of the narrative by individual saints, Anglo-Saxon communities were also known to re-enact the purging of the rebel angels within the yearly liturgical cycle. Linking the fall of the angels with Judgement Day, Chapter 5 considers how the poet of *Christ and Satan* portrays Satan's attempts to disrupt Christ's authority in both heavenly and earthly territories. In the same way that the New Minster Charter legitimised the rescinding of clerical lands and the exclusion of canons from religious communities, Satan's fitting punishments in this poem include forfeiture of his territories, expulsion from heaven, and exile to the chaotic spaces of hell. I approach the poem through the liturgical traditions of the Rogationtide festival, when Anglo-Saxons participated in three days of 'perambulations' meant to demarcate communal boundaries. This feast symbolically re-enacted the original exclusion of the rebel angels from heaven and also foreshadowed the final inclusions and exclusions at the Last Judgement. The poem's eccentric chronology and bizarre conclusion – in which Christ forces Satan to measure the *ymbhwyrft* ('circuit') of hell with his hands – can be understood as an inversion of Rogation rituals, whereby Satan parodies his own condition of lordlessness as he circuits the spaces of hell. By situating his poem within the framework of liturgical and localised practice, the poet appeals to an audience readily familiar with the primary goals of Rogationtide, namely, the purification of earthly boundaries in the interest of making oneself a suitable heir to otherworldly geographies.

This book closes with eleventh-century renderings of the narrative in the homilies of Ælfric and Archbishop Wulfstan of York. Ælfric explores the complex relationship between sovereigns and disobedient subjects, imagining the angelic fall as a crisis of individual agency and an unfortunate consequence of the gift of *agen cyre* ('free choice'). Wulfstan adopts Ælfric's approach in the wake of the viking invasions. With Wulfstan, I work to overturn some predominant readings of his famous *Sermo Lupi ad Anglos* (namely, that he characterises the vikings as heralds of Antichrist). Instead, Wulfstan puts the force of the replacement doctrine behind his admonishment of the English. He chides the English for imagining themselves as the elect (or *praedestinati*), or souls with a clear path towards a heavenly inheritance. Armed with the doctrine as his rhetorical weapon, Wulfstan suggests that the English body politic has instead come to resemble the rebel order of angels, implying that the vikings could supplant them and take their place as 'replacements', inbound colonisers destined for heavenly seats. Just as the originally pagan Anglo-Saxons had been replacements for the sinful Christian Britons, Wulfstan urges Anglo-Saxon Christians not to cede to the vikings their providential role in salvation history.

This book ultimately aims to investigate how Anglo-Saxon authors reimagined the extra-biblical story of the fall of the angels to work through contemporary challenges and to serve as a foundational myth of origin. According to Nicholas Howe, any 'shift in a people's destiny – a migration or a revolution – can be set within [a] mythic pattern ... When an origin myth is deeply registered in a culture, it may become difficult to interpret the present except as it accords with the pattern of the past.'[47] For these early Christians, the events of angelic creation shaped prevailing attitudes about their status as an emergent Christian community and their understanding of earthly space and sovereign authority. Far from seeing the textual absence of the fall of the angels in Genesis as a constraint, Anglo-Saxons viewed it as an opportunity to write the beginning of their story as a converted Christian people eager to become heirs to the idle and unused thrones and territories the rebels left behind.

Notes

1 Alcuin, *Interrogationes et responsiones in Genesin*, ed. J.-P. Migne, PL 101 (Paris: Garnier Frères, 1851), cols. 613–66. See also, 'A Critical Edition of Ælfric's Translation of Alcuin's *Interrogationes Sigwulfi Presbiteri* and of the Related Texts *De creatore et creatura* and *De sex etatibus huius seculi*', ed. W. Stoneman, PhD dissertation, University of Toronto, 1983, p. 85 and 'Ælfric's Version of *Alcuini Interrogationes Sigeuulfi in Genesin*', ed. M. E. MacLean, *Anglia*, 6 (1883), 425–73; 7 (1884), 1–59. All translations are my own unless otherwise noted.
2 Old Testament references to the fall of the angels appear in Ezra 28:12–17 and Isaiah 14:13–15 and in the New Testament at Luke 10:18 and 15:9, the Epistle of Jude 6, John 8:44, and Revelation 12:9.
3 Aldhelm, *Aldhelm: The Poetic Works*, ed. and trans. Michael Lapidge and James L. Rosier (Suffolk: D. S. Brewer, 1985). In his riddle, *De Lucifero*, Aldhelm plays on Lucifer's identity as the 'morning star' or 'light-bearer' (p. 88); Aethicus Ister, *The Cosmography of Aethicus Ister: Edition, Translation, Commentary*, ed. and trans. Michael W. Herren, Publications of the Journal of Medieval Latin 6 (Turnhout: Brepols, 2011), p. 8ff. The fall of the angels is the subject of a riddling contest between Parzival and Trevrizent in Book IX of Wolfram von Eschenbach's *Parzival*; see Wolfram von Eschenbach, *Parzival*, ed. Wolfgang Spiewok, 2 vols (Stuttgart: Reclam, 1981).

Introduction

4 *The Old English Dialogues of Solomon and Saturn*, ed. and trans. Daniel Anlezark, Anglo-Saxon Texts 7 (Cambridge: D. S. Brewer, 2009), ll. 265–97. Anlezark argues that *Solomon and Saturn II* was influenced by various apocrypha including 2 Enoch in 'The Fall of the Angels in Solomon and Saturn II', in *Apocryphal Texts and Traditions in Anglo-Saxon England*, ed. Kathryn Powell and Donald G. Scragg (Cambridge: D. S. Brewer, 2003), pp. 121–33. In response to Saturn's question about 'the beginning of all torments' (ll. 265–8), Solomon describes how an 'ofermodan' (proud one) once boasted of his desire to 'completely ravage the kingdom of the heavens and to occupy half himself' (ll. 276–7a).
5 The fall of the angels also appears in the poem *Vainglory* (ll. 52–64). See *The Exeter Book*, ed. George Philip Krapp and Elliot Van Kirk Dobbie, ASPR III (New York: Columbia University Press, 1936).
6 For an overview, see Virginia Day, 'The Influence of the Catechetical *narratio* on Old English and Some Other Medieval Literature', *ASE*, 3 (1974), 51–61 (p. 51).
7 Ibid., pp. 53–4.
8 For Zacher's discussion of the *Populus Israhel* tradition, see *Rewriting the Old Testament in Anglo-Saxon Verse: Becoming the Chosen People* (London: Bloomsbury, 2014), pp. 24ff. See also Andrew P. Scheil's *The Footsteps of Israel: Understanding Jews in Anglo-Saxon England* (Ann Arbor: University of Michigan Press, 2004), pp. 143–91.
9 Scheil, *The Footsteps of Israel*, p. 19.
10 *The Book of the Secrets of Enoch* (or 2 Enoch) suggests that corruption is the work of fallen angels. See *The Book of Enoch or 1 Enoch: A New English Translation with Commentary and Textual Notes*, ed. and trans. Matthew Black (Leiden: Brill, 1985). For its conjectured circulation, see *SASLC: The Apocrypha*, ed. Frederick M. Biggs, Instrumenta Anglistica Mediaevalia 1 (Kalamazoo, MI: Medieval Institute Publications, 2007), p. 10.
11 Augustine, *De ciuitate Dei*, ed. Bernhard Dombart and Alfons Kalb, CCSL 47–8 (Turnhout: Brepols, 1955), ii. 329.
12 Pseudo-Dionysius, *The Celestial Hierarchy*, ed. Günter Heil and Adolf Martin Ritter, *Corpus Dionysiacum II* (Berlin: de Gruyter, 1991).
13 Gregory the Great, *Homeliae in Evangelia*, ed. Raymond Étaix, CCSL 141 (Turnhout: Brepols, 1999), pp. 299–319.
14 Dhuoda, *Liber Manualis*, ed. Marcelle Thiébaux, Cambridge Medieval Classics 8 (Cambridge: Cambridge University Press, 1998), p. 116 and p. 214. Translation from Carol Neel, *Handbook for William: A Carolingian Woman's Counsel for her Son by Dhuoda* (Washington, DC: Catholic University Press, 1991), p. 93.
15 *The Earliest Life of Gregory the Great*, ed. and trans. Bertram Colgrave (Cambridge: Cambridge University Press, 1968), pp. 90–1.

16 Bede, *Bede's Ecclesiastical History of the English People*, ed. and trans. Bertram Colgrave and R. A. B. Mynors (Oxford: Clarendon Press, 1969), pp. 132–5.
17 *The Old English Version of Bede's Ecclesiastical History of the English People*, ed. and trans. Thomas Miller, EETS os 95 (London: Oxford University Press, 1890; repr. 1997), pp. 96–7. See also Kathy Lavezzo, *Angels on the Edge of the World: The Geography of English Identity from Ælfric to Chaucer* (Santa Barbara: University of California, 1999).
18 Stephen J. Harris, 'Bede and Gregory's Allusive Angles', *Criticism*, 44 (2002), 271–89 (p. 273).
19 Ibid., p. 277.
20 Bede, *In Tobiam*, ed. David Hurst, *Bedae Venerabilis Opera*, CCSL 119B (Turnhout: Brepols, 1983).
21 Richard Sowerby, *Angels in Early Medieval England* (Oxford: Oxford University Press, 2016), p. 26; for Augustine on pride, see *De ciuitate Dei* (11.13 and 12.6–7), Dombart and Kalb, ii. 333–5 and 359–62) and Augustine, *De Genesi ad litteram* (11.14–26), ed. Joseph Zycha, *Sancti Aureli Augustini De Genesi ad litteram libri duodecim eiusdem libri capitula, De Genesi ad litteram imperfectus liber, Loctunionum in Heptateuchum libri septem*, CSEL 28.1 (Vienna: Tempsky, 1894), pp. 346–59.
22 Tatwine, *Enigma*, ed. and trans. Maria De Marco, *Collectiones aenigmatum merovingicae aetatis*, CCSL 133 (Turnhout: Brepols, 1968), pp. 192 and 325.
23 Boniface, *De uirtutibus et uittiis*, ed. and trans. Maria De Marco, *Collectiones aenigmatum merovingicae aetatis*, CCSL 133 (Turnhout: Brepols, 1968), ll. 251–2.
24 Bede, *In Genesin*, ed. C. W. Jones, *Bedae Venerabilis Opera*, CCSL 118A (Turnhout: Brepols, 1967). Translation by Calvin Kendall, *On Genesis* (Liverpool University Press, 2008), pp. 69–70. For pre-Gregorian ideas concerning the fall of the angels, see *St Augustine: The First Catechetical Instruction (De Catechizandis Rudibus)*, trans. Joseph P. Christopher (New York: Newman, 1946), p. 126 (n. 191); ed. I. B. Bauer, CCSL 46 (Turnhout: Brepols, 1969).
25 Thomas D. Hill, 'The Fall of Satan in the Old English *Christ and Satan*', *JEGP*, 76 (1977), 315–25 (p. 317). Anselm proposed that Satan refused to venerate Christ; see Stella Purce Revard, *The War in Heaven: Paradise Lost and the Tradition of Satan's Rebellion* (Ithaca, NY: Cornell University Press, 1980), p. 60.
26 T. D. Hill, 'The Fall of Satan', p. 319ff.
27 See *Christ and Satan: A Critical Edition*, ed. and trans. Robert Emmett Finnegan (Waterloo, Ontario: Wilfrid Laurier University Press, 1977), p. 40 (n. 18).
28 C. Abbetmeyer, *Old English Poetical Motives Derived from the Doctrine of Sin* (Minneapolis: H. W. Wilson Company, 1903).

29 See Bernard F. Huppé, *Doctrine and Poetry: Augustine's Influence on Old English Poetry* (New York: State University of New York Press, 1959).
30 See Michael Fox, 'Ælfric on the Creation and Fall of the Angels', *ASE*, 31 (2002), 175–200.
31 See, for instance, J. M. Evans, '*Genesis B* and Its Background', *RES*, 14 (1963), 1–16 and J. M. Evans, '*Genesis B* and Its Background', *RES*, 14 (1963), 113–23; Thomas D. Hill, 'The Fall of Angels and Man in the Old English *Genesis B*', in *Anglo-Saxon Poetry: Essays in Appreciation, For John C. McGalliard*, ed. Lewis E. Nicholson and Dolores Warwick Frese (Notre Dame, IN: University of Notre Dame Press, 1975), pp. 279–90.
32 Malcolm Godden, 'Literature and the Old Testament', in *The Cambridge Companion to Old English Literature* (Cambridge: Cambridge University Press, 1991), pp. 206–26 (p. 206).
33 See Michael Cherniss, 'Heroic Ideals and the Moral Climate of *Genesis B*', *Modern Language Quarterly*, 30 (1969), 479–97.
34 Hugh Magennis, *Images of Community in Old English Poetry*, CSASE 18 (Cambridge: Cambridge University Press, 1996), p. 15.
35 Bosworth-Toller, *fæc*, sense 1 and 4.
36 Bosworth-Toller, *gerum*, sense 2.
37 Bosworth-Toller, *hwil*, sense 1.
38 Henri Lefebvre, *The Production of Space*, trans. Donald Nicholson-Smith (Oxford: Blackwell, 1991), p. 280 and Jacques Le Goff, 'Discorso di chiusura', in *Popoli e paesi nella cultura alltomedievale*, 2 vols, Settimane di studio del Centro italiano di studi sull'alto medioevo 29 (Spoleto: Presso la sede del Centro, 1983), pp. 805–38. See also, Fabienne L. Michelet, *Creation, Migration, and Conquest: Imaginary Geography and Sense of Space in Old English Literature* (Oxford: Oxford University Press, 2006), p. 2.
39 Michelet, *Creation, Migration, and Conquest*, p. 11.
40 Nicholas Howe, *Writing the Map of Anglo-Saxon England: Essays in Cultural Geography* (New Haven, CT: Yale University Press, 2008), p. 46.
41 Lefebvre, *The Production of Space*, p. 280.
42 On Anglo-Saxon kingship, see Patrick Wormald, '*Lex scripta* and *verbum regis*: Legislation and Germanic Kingship from Euric to Cnut', in *Legal Culture in the Early Medieval West: Law as Text, Image, and Experience* (London: Bloomsbury, 1999), pp. 1–48 (p. 38).
43 Thomas N. Bisson, *The Crisis of the Twelfth Century: Power, Lordship, and the Origins of European Government* (Princeton: Princeton University Press, 2009), pp. 31–68 (p. 34).
44 Katherine O'Brien O'Keeffe, 'Body and Law in Late Anglo-Saxon England', *ASE*, 27 (1998), 209–32 (p. 217). On the role of penance within the Anglo-Saxon legal landscape, see Tom Lambert, *Law and*

Order in Anglo-Saxon England (Oxford: Oxford University Press, 2017), pp. 216–37.
45 Lefebvre, The Production of Space, p. 10.
46 Sowerby, Angels in Early Medieval England, p. 42.
47 Nicholas Howe, Migration and Mythmaking in Anglo-Saxon England (Notre Dame, IN: University of Notre Dame Press, 2001), pp. 4–5.

1
Lands idle and unused

Sometime in the 880s or early 890s, King Alfred commissioned Bishop Werferth of Worcester, one of the prominent members of his intellectual think-tank, to translate Gregory the Great's *Dialogues* into Old English. As part of Alfred's project for intellectual and cultural revitalisation, he called upon scholars and those in offices of authority to translate such texts into the vernacular in the hope that they would be widely disseminated, thus promoting a sense of common origin (and destiny) among Anglo-Saxon Christians. Asser tells us that, in this spirit, Werferth translated Gregory's work 'imperio regis' (at the king's command).

Alfred's programme of translation into the vernacular of those texts he viewed as 'nidbeðyrfesta sien eallum monnum to witanne' (most needful for all to know),[1] supported his wider political agenda of enhancing his authority as king of the West Saxons and overlord of the allied kingdoms of Mercia and Wales. One of Alfred's greatest concerns was to establish the sanctity of royal lordship and to condemn the breaking of oaths. The story of the fall of the angels as told by Gregory and the later vernacular biblical poem *Genesis A* touch directly upon these themes. Gregory's *Dialogi* (written in 593) constitutes just one of the places where the pope recorded his ideas about the cosmic significance of the fall of the angels. In this particular text, Gregory explains how the 'superna regio' (celestial region) of heaven was fortified in the aftermath of the angelic rebellion (III.14):

> Sed quid mirum quod hoc de homine dicimus, quando illa superna regio in ciuibus suis ex parte damna pertulit et ex parte fortiter stetit, ut electi angelorum spiritus, dum alios per superbiam cecidisse conspicerent, ipsi tanto robustius quanto humilius starent? Illi ergo regioni sua etiam detrimenta profecerunt, quae ad aeternitatis statum ex parte suae destructionis est solidius instructa.[2]

[But what wonder is it that we say this concerning man, when that celestial region in part suffered a loss in its citizens, and in part stood strongly, so that the elect spirits of the angels, when they were seeing others fall through pride, themselves stood so much the more firmly as they did the more humbly? Therefore they profited even by their loss in that region, which was more firmly prepared for the condition of eternity by the part of its destruction.]

The influence of Gregory's ideas concerning creation and salvation history looms large in Anglo-Saxon narratives recounting the fall of the rebel angels and their unhappy fate. Of particular note here is his suggestion that heavenly space, first compromised by insurrection and treachery, is 'solidius instructa' (more firmly prepared) for future inhabitants once the rebels have been expelled. Werferth rendered this as follows:

> Ac hwylc wundor is, þeah þe we þis be mannum secgan, nu seo uplice leodræden, þære ængellican <gecynde> of sumum dæle æfwerdlan & wonunge aræfnede of <hyra> efenceasterwarum & on sumum dæle fæstlice gestod & gewunode, swa þæte þa gecorenan engla gastas selfe swa myccle strenglicor & fæstlicor gestodon, swa myccle swa hi eadmodran wæron, þurh oferhigde þa oðre ofdune afeollon? Soðlice hi forð fremedon & þungon þurh þa wununge heore geferscipes, & of ðam dæle heora toworpnysse & gedales to ecnesse staðole þy staðolfæstlicor hi wæron getrymede.³

[But what wonder is it, though we speak this about men, since the celestial region of angelic nature in some part suffered loss and diminishment of their fellow citizens and in some part stood firmly and remained, so that the elect spirits of angels themselves stood so much more strongly and firmly, as they were the more humble, because the others fell downward through pride? Truly they advanced forth and prospered through their abiding fellowship, and because of the one part's destruction and separation they were strengthened the more steadfastly in that estate for eternity.]⁴

Overall, Werferth's translation follows Gregory with general fidelity. The 'efenceasterwarum' (fellow citizens) are, of course, former angels, and the heavenly space along with the remaining 'gecorenan engla gastas' (elect spirits of angels) who experience renewal following the dispossession of proud rebels whose crimes are only obliquely alluded to here. In other words, spaces and angels are shown to experience renewal in much the same way. The heavenly polity is described as a *staðol*, which Bosworth-Toller defines as 'a foundation' or 'the firmament, the heavens' and which frequently glosses *firmamentum*.[5] As a simplex, *staðol* can also mean an 'estate',[6] and when joined with the compound *eðel-* (as with the hapax legomenon 'eðelstaðolas' found in *Genesis A*, l. 94a), the idea presented is that of an 'established home, settlement' deriving from the verb *staðolian* ('to establish, found settle, fix').[7] With the image of the *staðol* made *staðolfæstlicor* – the heavenly 'firmament' becoming 'firmer' – Werferth echoes the Gregorian expression that heaven has been stabilised after the removal of the disloyal angels.[8]

The crimes of the rebel angels – lord-betrayal, oath-breaking,[9] and treason – as they are enumerated throughout the Old English corpus would have been all too familiar to men like Alfred, who oversaw a period of renewed and reconceived political ideals and loyalties, as well as a strengthening of the kingdom of Wessex, and the establishment of his lordship over western Mercia after he 'freed' it from Danish rule. Both Gregory and Werferth – the Church Father whose *Dialogues* Alfred selected for translation and the translator whom Alfred commissioned for the job – describe a sacral, originary restoration of lands and inhabitants based on theological doctrines (the confirmation of the angels and the doctrine of replacement) deriving from the fall of the angels narrative. Biblical and para-biblical narratives offered Anglo-Saxons an important site through which to explore the connections between their inherited Christian beliefs and Germanic worldview as well as a framework for understanding the conflicts and social pressures of their own day.

Although it is difficult to date the composition of *Genesis A* with any precision, the poem's treatment of the fall of the angels complements Werferth's translation of the *Dialogues* and fits in well with the political concerns expressed throughout the Alfredian corpus. In *Genesis A* and elsewhere, Satan is uniquely imagined as a powerful nobleman or veteran retainer who betrays his lord's munificence in a struggle for power and landed supremacy; he is subsequently banished from his homeland, doomed to wander in exile. The poet of *Genesis A*, the first poem in the illustrated codex known as the Junius Manuscript (Oxford, Bodleian Library, MS Junius 11), imagines heaven much like the *Dialogues*: a physical location that suffers the shocks of pride, rebellion, and treachery.[10] The poem's opening describes the bliss of the newly created angels followed by their failure to maintain harmony in heaven, which, in Scott T. Smith's words, is figured as both a 'spatial ... [and] political kingdom'.[11] Anglo-Saxon authors, in other words, embrace heaven as a site to explore complex political ideologies, spatial destabilisation, and the trauma of apostasy followed by regeration. In this way, the fall of the angels narrative represents the moment when idealised spaces become compromised, and when the need for new spaces abruptly arises. *Genesis A* depicts a rebellion that threatens the very landscape of the celestial region, followed by the creation of fledgling earthly realms. After recounting the treason and downfall of the rebels, the poet goes on to describe their punishments in uniquely Anglo-Saxon terms: forfeiture of rank, status, and hereditary rights.

One reason why creation narratives so captivated Anglo-Saxon poets, homilists, political thinkers, and even kings (as in the case of Alfred), was because they represented the moment when space and territory first came into being. Howe's fundamental insight serves as a useful starting point for the present study: Anglo-Saxons thought of their earthly lands as a conduit for salvation – the temporary space or *lænland* ('loanland') – where Christians might work to achieve a more permanent heavenly residence.[12] The opening of *Genesis A*, as I will demonstrate, suggests that the fallen bodies of Satan and his rebellious cohort structure the world: from the vastness of heaven, to the disorder of hell, and the impressionable earth. The *Genesis A* poet also alludes to a promised inheritance amid the vacant spaces of heaven, which await the elect as worthy tenants. For Anglo-Saxon Christians, this idea of a ready-and-waiting inheritance had the force of doctrine behind it.

The so-called 'replacement doctrine' formulated by Augustine and subsequently elaborated upon by Gregory the Great stipulated that humankind was created to repopulate (literally 'fill the blanks') left behind by the fallen angels. Explications of the doctrine of replacement can be found in Augustine's *Enchiridion ad Laurentium* 62 and 29 (CCSL 46.82; CCSL 46.65) and *De Civitate Dei* 22.1 (CCSL 48.807), which describes how God intends to 'suppleat et instauret' (fill and repair) the spaces left by the rebels angels. Gregory's *Homiliae in Evangelia* 34 (CCSL 141A), which explicates Luke 15:8–10, similarly suggests that the rebellion quite literally decimates the original order of angels by precisely one tenth. For Augustine and Gregory, humanity decidedly comes about after the fall of the angels. David F. Johnson has effectively shown that the *Genesis A* poet not only invokes the doctrine of replacement, but also crucially takes it one step further than the exegetes. For the *Genesis A* poet, as Johnson observes, 'it is not simply man who was created to fill the void occasioned by the primal lapse of the rebel angels, but the whole of physical creation which was called into being for this purpose'.[13] In other words, for our poet, both humanity and earthly space are represented as cosmic afterthoughts, whether or not the poet assumed that God had foreknown them. God creates humankind with the express purpose of settling unoccupied earthly lands and, eventually, inheriting the heavenly territories forfeited by rebels. Replacement, in this sense, becomes a vehicle of lordly compensation, a way to restore what was lost. As I will demonstrate, by framing replacement as a kind of legal transaction echoing the patterns of many contemporary law codes, the poet replicates the power structures of the Anglo-Saxon world in his literary representations of divine power.

Dorothy Haines's important work on the replacement doctrine similarly reveals telling nuances in the ways Anglo-Saxon poets and homilists adapted their narratives to accommodate the theme of 'resettlement'. While many narratives of the angelic rebellion quantify the depletion of varying numbers of angels, Haines rightfully observes that, for Anglo-Saxons, replacement is 'not simply about completing numbers, but moreover about resettling residences and stabilising the spaces'.[14] She concludes that replacement 'is perhaps to be thought of as equivalent to the granting of estates'.[15] Along the same lines, Howe argues that a guiding concern of the Junius MS is the desire of wandering souls to find a fixed place in the scheme of salvation.[16] It is not surprising, then, that Werferth, who mentions the 'æfwerdlan & wonunge' (loss and diminishment) of heaven, describes the process of making the firmament a 'firmer' place, thus signalling a concern over the stabilising of spaces left idle.

Just as Anglo-Saxons articulated the doctrine of replacement in ways that emphasised settlement and inheritance, they also formulated actual legal cases of forfeiture in significantly analogous ways. The case of the Ealdorman Wulfhere (defector of probably 877 or 878) offers an instructive perspective on the consequences of treason and disloyalty.[17] Sawyer 362 (a grant by King Edward the Elder to Æthelwulf) asserts that, during Alfred's reign, Wulfhere lost his office and inheritance because of desertion and oath-breaking:

> Ista vero praenominata tellus primitus fuit praepeditus a quodam duce, nomine Wulhere, et eius uxore, quando ille utrumque et suum dominum, regem Ælfredum, et patriam, ultra iusiurandum quam regi et suis omnibus optimatibus iuraverat, sine licentia dereliquit. Tunc etiam, cum omnium iuditio sapientium Gevisorum et Mercensium, potestatem et hereditatem dereliquit agrorum.

[Truly this aforementioned estate was originally forfeited by a certain ealdorman, Wulfhere by name, and his wife, when he deserted without permission both his lord King Alfred, and his country, in spite of the oath that he had sworn to the king and all his leading men. Then also by the judgement of all the councilors of the Gewisse (West Saxons) and of the Mercians, he lost the control and inheritance of his lands.][18]

What makes Wulfhere's loss of the 'potestatem et hereditatem' (control and inheritance) of his 'agrorum' (estates) so telling is that it reveals crucial differences between Anglo-Saxon and Continental practices concerning the treatment of rebels and their estates. As Janet Nelson observes, the Carolingian custom of punishing traitors typically involved stripping the guilty party of offices and benefices. Inherited lands, on the other hand, were viewed as separate from royal jurisdiction and would thus remain under the control of the guilty.[19] Not so in Alfred's England. Under Alfred and his successors, the threat of total confiscation (both of titles and inheritances) ensured absolute loyalty. Wulfhere's military service afforded him landed privilege, but also demanded *fyrd* obligations towards his king deriving from that possession.[20]

That difference between Anglo-Saxon and Continental legal models for the treatment of lord-betrayal is also echoed in the way Anglo-Saxon poets frequently chose to craft their narratives of the angelic rebellion. In *Genesis A*, for example, when the rebel angels no longer wish to obey their lord they lose their native lands as a consequence of having violated the very space they have been asked to safeguard. In a similar way, Alfred's treason law leaves no room for negotiation: a traitor 'sie he his feores scyldig ⁊ ealles þæs ðe he age' (forfeits his life and all that he owns).[21] Nelson continues: 'Alfred's treason law, like Charlemagne's prescription for oaths of fidelity, was a response to the ever-present threat of faithlessness on the part of those whom the king relied on most'.[22]

Following the account of Wulfhere's forfeiture in S 362, the bounds of his former estate are recorded in Old English before the final anathema: 'Si autem euenerit quod nonoptamus ut alicuius persone superuenerit, qui hoc infringer uel mutare uoluerit, sciat se esse epicarmae a consortio Dei, et sanctorum eius' (If, however, it shall happen – as we hope it will not – that anyone of any status wherever shall appear to wish to infringe or change this, let him know that he is cut off from the fellowship of God and his saints).[23] The severity of Alfred's policies may be better understood through his historical challenges as a ruler dealing with intermittent viking invasions. Lands held by would-be rebels, for Alfred, would have weakened all of England in the face of the Danish threat. Unlike his Carolingian counterparts who could expand territory only through the invasion of other kingdoms, Alfred could strengthen regions which had sustained loss (analogous to the kind Gregory and Werferth describe), and thereby 'create a new political solidarity in his composite realm'.[24] The only fitting solution for men like Wulfhere would be to deprive them of all privileges.

In a time when the stability of the kingdom was paramount, Alfred reveals himself to be judicious in the management of lands and loyalty, with Wulfhere's fate most likely serving as a 'deterrent to potential defectors'.[25] The author of S 362 also states that councillors from both the West Saxon and the Mercian sides agreed that the region would be strengthened through the purging of rebels. Crucially, in addition to having symbolic and literary value, the fall of the angels narrative had profound implications for the actual treatment of lands and properties that were deemed 'forfeit' or 'idle' in Anglo-Saxon England. It is not surprising, then, that allusions to the fall of the angels are often attested not just in biblical poetry and homilies, but also in Anglo-Latin and vernacular charters, investing the very landscape of Anglo-Saxon England with a sacral precedent. As hybrids of literary and legal diction, charters falling under both secular and ecclesiastical rubrics occasionally open with proems concerning the fall of angels; such *narratio* tell us something about the porous boundaries between this biblical narrative and the Anglo-Saxon legal world. My contention is that many charters invoke replacement as a worldly strategy, not simply a deferred spiritual ambition, but something that kings can accomplish in the here-and-now: they find new inheritors to fill up 'idle and unused' spaces thus strengthening their territories. Anglo-Saxons, who self-identified as 'replacements' or the rightful heirs to the lands forfeited by the rebel angels, conceived of physical space and territory through their reading of Augustine and Gregory; the doctrine became a mechanism to legitimate the removal of rebels as well as the resettlement of potentially prosperous spaces.

Henri Lefebvre and Jacques Le Goff tell us that space is explicitly linked with expressions of sovereignty.[26] Alfred's bold projections of power reveal his careful consideration of *anweald* ('power, sovereignty, sway').[27] Scott T. Smith and Jacqueline Stodnick have discussed the subsequent promotion of a West Saxon dynasty through the regulating of both *eðel* and *anweald* ('space' and 'sovereign authority') in texts such as the *ASC*.[28] Such expressions of power not only derived from access to secular property in Anglo-Saxon England, but also ecclesiastical lands (the subject of Chapter 3). These lessons of confiscation and expulsion, as well as the legal mechanisms by which better caretakers could take possession of idle lands, are crystallised in the narrative of the rebel angels. While the doctrine of replacement was ultimately focused on the deferred acquisition of a heavenly *eðel* ('homeland', 'inheritance', or 'territory'), we might also think of the twin narratives of rebellion and replacement as influencing Anglo-Saxon discourses surrounding vacant spaces, legal settlements, and obedient occupants. The charters that invoke the fall of the angels use that sacral narrative as a legal precedent to underwrite Anglo-Saxon sovereign power which was, in many ways, dependent upon the well-being and safeguarding of land, revered halls, and holy houses.

But what of the spaces left temporarily uninhabited? In addition to describing the expulsion of the rebel angels as a forfeiture, the *Genesis A* poet reveals an abiding interest in the proper stewardship of both earthly and heavenly spaces left *idel ond unnyt* ('idle and unused'), a common formulaic phrase used by Anglo-Saxon authors to refer to both mental spaces and landscapes. In her valuable work on what she describes as the 'Anglo-Saxon spatial *imaginaire*',[29] Michelet notes a fundamental overlap between how Anglo-Saxons imagined physical space and 'space as a mental structure'.[30] On the subject of uninhabited space, she argues that creation accounts 'betray an urge not to leave empty places vacant, but to people them with worthy occupants'.[31]

Of course, God must craft two new spaces in the aftermath of the angelic rebellion: earth and hell. If the *Genesis A* poet represents the primal moment when space first comes into being, the rest of the poem considers the ways in which idle space should be properly settled, maintained, and passed on to better caretakers. The *idel ond unnyt* earth must be peopled, although, as the poet states, humankind is eventually destined to 'eðel secean' (seek [another] homeland) amid the 'broad thrones' (setl ... wide) of heaven. Indeed, the *Genesis A* poet's formulation of space which has been savagely disordered echoes Beowulf's description of Heorot, which is similarly *idel ond unnyt* (l. 413a) after the attacks of Grendel; this phrase also appears at the conclusion of Vercelli Homily 10 as part of a litany of dire warnings about the transience of earthly prosperity. On the one hand, these representations of idle space reveal a major source of Anglo-Saxon antipathy: such lands do not fulfil their true potential. On the other hand, vacant space implies potential ownership, wealth, and prosperity. Unclaimed lands were sites of uncertainty as well as legal sticking-points in Roman law all the way down to the eighteenth century, when *terra nullius* ('nobody's land') denoted territory where sovereignty was nonexistent. According to Della Hooke, the transfer and granting of privileges '[followed] the established principles of Roman law ... [and] land documents'.[32] Anglo-Saxon charters similarly recognise *nanes monnes land* ('no man's land'), referring to territories that were unoccupied or unclaimed.[33] The *Genesis A* poet represents a legalistic settlement of 'idle and unused' space and alludes to the transference of heavenly properties from the rebels to humankind, the 'selran werode' (better troop, l. 95b). Viewing their 'idle' spaces as markers of vulnerability, fragile to threats from within and without, Anglo-Saxon authors thus demonstrate an eagerness to reassert sovereign order upon the wastes and the wilds.

Concerns over rebellious lands can also reveal more about how Anglo-Saxons conceived of 'idle' mental spaces and structures. Indeed, the Alfredian age, as well as subsequent periods in Anglo-Saxon England's history, saw a revived focus on the ordering of both the physical world and the world of the mind, seen especially throughout the late homiletic corpus where idleness is often figured as a principle vice.[34] *Genesis A*, then, serves as an important first look into how Anglo-Saxons imagined the forces that disrupt fragile boundaries, both physical and psychic.

The Anglo-Saxons' abiding interest in space – its procurement and management – was not purely materialistic. Patrick Geary has argued, for example, that property in early medieval Europe had a 'symbolic language through which people discussed, negotiated, affirmed, and delimited the boundaries'.[35] The status of lands (whether they be heavenly, earthly, or hellish) would have been a vital concern to medieval authors, readers, and auditors. Of course, such concerns were not limited to the age of Alfred.[36] The themes in *Genesis A* that I explore here are decidedly concomitant with practices throughout the Anglo-Saxon period, so issues surrounding land, lordship, crime, and punishment could assume a potent ideological force for an Anglo-Saxon audience within any likely date for the poem or for the Junius Manuscript.[37]

Lefebvre proposes that space is not an a priori concept, but a cultural construct, something that is carefully fashioned especially during moments of change and turmoil.[38] Anglo-Saxon Christians viewed the angelic rebellion as a primal territorial and legal dispute, making it foundational to their conceptions of both heavenly space and earthly space as well as sovereign authority as the narrative was told and retold throughout the Anglo-Saxon period, passing through the hands of kings, poets, political thinkers, and artists. What follows constitutes an initial step in considering how authors shaped their narratives of rebellion, and how that narrative, in turn, may have helped shape the Anglo-Saxon world.

Lands and laws in *Genesis A*

For Anglo-Saxon Christians, the fall of the angels represented the moment when space – heavenly, earthly, hellish – first came into being. *Genesis A* offers a favourable starting point to consider some of the dominant spatial metaphors and vocabularies used by Anglo-Saxon authors to describe lands that have been unsettled by rebellion, treason, and pride. Once misleadingly known as the 'Cædmon Manuscript', Junius 11 contains a diverse collection of Old English poems: *Genesis A*, *Genesis B*, *Exodus*, *Daniel*, and *Christ and Satan*. The poems recount major biblical events, beginning with God's creation of heaven and earth, the story of Adam and Eve, Cain and Abel, Noah and the flood, Abraham and the sacrifice of Isaac, Moses and the Red Sea, and the Babylonian Captivity, ending with several episodes from the New Testament, including Christ's Temptation in the wilderness. Three of the five poems in Junius 11 – *Genesis A*, *Genesis B*, and *Christ and Satan* – contain extended narratives devoted to the story of the fall of the rebel angels. These narratives represent the most comprehensive and dynamic treatments of the angelic rebellion in the Old English corpus.

The image of the fall of the angels found on Page 3 of the manuscript can tell us more about how Anglo-Saxons viewed this narrative in distinctly spatial terms.[39] The three-tiered register first shows Lucifer – outfitted as an Anglo-Saxon warrior and nobleman – gesturing towards his heavenly seat and what he perceives to be his possessions, possibly those in the 'norðdæle' (northern part) of the kingdom. How closely the illustrations relate to the text of *Genesis A* continues to be a matter of critical debate, as Barbara Raw has noted.[40] Despite occasional 'dislocations' from the text, Thomas Ohlgren and Catherine Karkov have both argued that the Junius illustrations constitute their own unique narrative cycle.[41] The fall of the angels illustration is no exception. Several details set Lucifer apart from the other angels. He holds a sceptre in his hand and either accepts symbols of authority from the other angels

Lands idle and unused

1 Oxford, Bodleian Library, MS Junius 11, fol. 3r

or distributes gifts to his loyal thanes. The subtle bruise on his knee signals to viewers that he has, until now, been reverent, the mark suggesting that he kneels before God.[42] He points towards a throne (most likely the *setl* referenced by the poet) under a two-storied structure consisting of intricate towers and roofs.

Asa Mittman and Susan Kim have recently discussed the spatial implications of this page. Following Ohlgren, who suggests that the second register depicts Lucifer's pride and influence over the other angels, they propose that the scene depicts 'incipient rebellion' followed by 'palm fronds of victory ... [and] powerful cross-nimbed Jesus wielding spears'.[43] Furthering this interpretation, the second register could represent the poet's description of the confirmation of loyal angels, recently discussed by Charles D. Wright, as they reaffirm heavenly peace with palms.[44] Our eyes track downwards, following the motion of the angels from the second to third registers which, as Karkov notes, '[repeats] the motion of the falling angels'.[45] Mittman and Kim address the role of the *her* ... ('here ...') formulae, stating that these 'textual notes locate the sequences of images both spatially and temporally within the narrative'.[46] Ultimately, their interest lies in the fragmentary nature of the inscription reading, *Her se* ... ('Here he ...'), which exists in the gutter between the second and third register. They propose that this fragment rests in 'the very space and moment between the representation of rebellion and ... the completed transformation of Lucifer into Satan [which] locates that transformation in the act of reading/viewing itself'.[47] In its entirety, the artist attempts to capture a moment of simultaneous creation and destruction, the originary instant wherein time, space, bodies, and abstract concepts such as good and evil, all are differentiated visually. Page 16 similarly shows discrete spaces separating the good angels from the bad, as well as a stellified barrier shielding heavenly creation.[48]

The fall of the angels illustration is one of the few images in the manuscript that contains colour symbolism (the fall from light to darkness is manifest on the page as the figures move from red to brown), mirroring Augustine's exegetical assertion that angelic creation corresponds to God's command of *fiat lux* ('let there be light'). According to Augustine, God's separation of light and dark (time itself) occurs at the precise moment of the fall of the angels.[49] It makes sense, then, that in the lowest register, as Mittman and Kim observe, '[Satan's] skin is now darkened and streaked', revealing himself to be 'stained with his sin, marked by his transgression'.[50] Here, Satan's body is inverted and contorted before it is

ealpa monðpa mægt. Spa deð monna gehpilc þe
pið hip paldoño pinnan ongynneð. mid mane pið
þone mæpan opæhtm. þa peapð pemihtiga ge-
bolgen. hehpta heopones paldoño. pth þp hine
op þan heán stole. hete hæpde he æt hip hlan-
nan gepunnen. hyldo hæpde hip pip lopene.
gnam peapð him se goda on hip mode. sopþon
he sceolde gpund gpecean. heapd hip helle picp.
þæt þe he pann pið heopnes paldoño. acpæð hine
þa spam hip hyldo. 7 hine on helle peapp. on
þa deopan dala. þæp he to deopla peapð. pe
seond mid hip gesiþum eallum. peollon þa upon
op heopnum. þupth longe spa þpeo niht 7 dagar
þa englar op heopnum on helle. 7 hig ealle
sop scop opæhtm to deoplum.

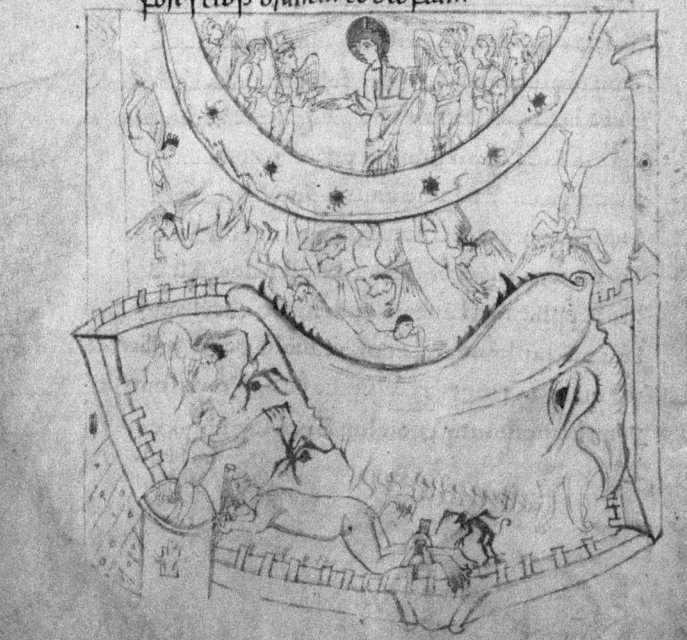

2 Oxford Bodleian Library, MS Junius 11, fol. 16r

shown to be fully bedeviled in the jaws of a hellmouth.[51] The rebel angels have forfeited splendid robes and symbols of authority for nakedness, and an esteemed throne for teeth and jowls. Although the figure of Satan in the third register is markedly separated from heaven, his attention is still fixed on heavenly space and all his disinheritance. Mittman and Kim suggest that he looks 'up mournfully at his former state, his former glory'.[52]

More can be said about this complex image.[53] Like the poet, the illustrator clearly works to show the reorientation of space, bodies, and time. Karkov helpfully connects the threat of damnation in this image to Augustine's conception of time itself, stating: 'If, as Augustine believed, eternity has no past or future, but only an "eternal present" (*totum esse praesens*), then these events are always taking place and the sequential repetition, or layering, of image and story may be one way of documenting this phenomenon.'[54] Amid the chaos of this image, one particular detail has received little critical attention from scholars: a chunk of matter hurtling alongside the demons as they fall towards the hellmouth. This could be the roof of heaven, which formerly sheltered the rebels in the first register, but is at last tumbling into the unknown alongside them.[55] With these ruins of heaven the illustrator signals architectural instability in the aftermath of the rebellion. In a strikingly different way, the following pages of Junius 11 (especially pages 6 and 7) depict protective orbs and circles, new possibilities coming into being with plants sprouting at God's command. Several pages later (page 10), a roof resembling the former one seems to reassert itself as God oversees Adam and Eve's settlement of the earthly paradise; the spaces of heaven and earth are reunited under one roof. Renée R. Trilling has argued that the opening of *Genesis A* is 'decidedly temporal ... Narrative thus enters into historical time with the act of Creation ... the joys and revelry, bliss and splendor, are things of the past rather than the present.'[56] These distinct temporalities extend to the visual presentation of creation in Junius 11. Compared to the overcrowded image depicting the fall of the angels, these later illustrations are altogether stark and empty. Page 10 also shows God pointing upwards towards heaven rather than downwards towards the human couple's earthly settlement. For Anglo-Saxon viewers, this gesture reinforces the connection between earthly and heavenly kingdoms, and may indeed signal replacement.

For Anglo-Saxon authors, the story of the fall of the angels anticipates the fall of Adam and Eve and determines humanity's place within salvation history. Unlike the rebel angels at

3 Oxford Bodleian Library, MS Junius 11, fol. 10r

the start of *Genesis A*, Adam and Eve are given a commandment – a legal landscape – in their earthly home. In what follows, I propose that *Genesis A* is concerned with exploring the creation of earthly legal orders and, by extension, commonplace Anglo-Saxon legal practices. I will argue that the poet's representation of the replacement doctrine – God's plan for rectifying the fallout of the angelic rebellion – dramatises the legal practice of compensation.[57] Moreover, by exploring how the themes of lordship and scuttled rebellions find their expression in vernacular poetry, I suggest that the originary revolution in heaven also has broader implications for our understanding of how the fall of the angels shaped and was shaped by socio-political structures in the early medieval world.

Insular narratives devoted to the extra-biblical story of the fall of the angels afford us a way to gauge how Anglo-Saxon authors refashioned an inherited tradition. A variety of liturgical, exegetical, and even versified angelic fall narratives might have been accessible to the *Genesis A* poet.[58] Aspects of the *Genesis A* poet's portrayal of creation have been traced back to hexameral commentaries, accounts of the creation of the world organised into six-day schemes.[59] According to Michael J. Allen and Daniel Calder, the conceivable hexameral influences on *Genesis A* include the writings of Ambrose, Basil of Caesarea, Isidore of Seville, Bede, Alcuin, and Rabanus Maurus.[60] Despite some similarities with these sources, they rightly caution that 'while the *Genesis A* poet may well have been aware of and even utilised materials from the hexameral tradition, there [are] neither formal nor material analogues for the poem as a whole'.[61]

An immediate problem facing any Anglo-Saxon poet who paraphrased Genesis is that both the creation and fall of the angels are absent from the biblical narrative. A. N. Doane, the most recent editor of *Genesis A*, notes that the creation of the angels derives from a long tradition of 'Jewish attempts to reconcile various Old Testament mentions of angels', observing that the most conventional 'traditions tended to treat the Fall as part of the angelic creation itself'.[62] A survey of scriptural commentaries available in the British Isles, ranging from Bede to Alcuin,[63] reveals major discrepancies among the varying explanations surrounding this conspicuous absence. For example, differing authors would have had varying responses to the following questions: Did God or Christ drive the rebel angels out of heaven? Did God have a plan for humanity before (or only after) the angelic rebellion? Who (or what) carried out the temptation of Adam and Eve? Despite some of the varied responses Anglo-Saxon authors might call upon for their answers to such questions, the sheer range of sources in some cases (and lack of reliable sources in others) might mean that, at times, *Genesis A* offers a uniquely Anglo-Saxon treatment of the rebel angels.

Scholars such as Bennett A. Brockman, Nina Boyd, Thomas D. Hill, J. R. Hall, A. N Doane, and Charles D. Wright have all considered whether *Genesis A* is first and foremost a poem that operates on a level highly invested in exegetical interpretations or whether the poet places greater emphasis on relating the events of scripture as history.[64] While approaches that stress allegorical, figural, and typological readings have no doubt enlarged our understanding of the theological interests of the poet, Hill argues that the Old English *Genesis* is 'before all else a historical poem'.[65] Hall similarly situates the Junius collection, when he describes it as an 'Epic of Redemption',[66] thereby privileging a more catechetical understanding of the poem and finding its contents more in line with texts such as Augustine's *De Catechizandis Rudibus* and Wulfstan's *Sermo* 6. Wright argues that *Genesis A* lends itself more readily to the 'Universal History' or 'World Chronicle' genre.[67] He draws attention to 'the poet's fundamentally historical approach to the biblical narrative [which] rendered both allegory and typology peripheral to his concerns' and 'as a rule, [he does not] prompt meditation on extra-literal meanings'.[68] In representing God's desire to see earth (and eventually heaven) populated, the poet eschews certain doctrinal expectations pertaining to replacement.

As discussed earlier, this particular account of the angelic rebellion antedates God's intention to create humankind and earth itself. The poem opens with the angels dwelling in peace and contentment (ll. 1–20a). Predictably, this serenity is short-lived. The rebellion begins at line 20a, followed by God's construction of hell (ll. 34b–46b), the exile of the rebels (ll. 47–77b), the return of peace (ll. 78–91b), and ending with God's desires for humanity (ll. 95b–101). As I have observed, no source text follows this organisation exactly. As Doane puts it, 'the arrangement and narrative movement are the poet's'.[69] In this opening sequence, we see how one of God's angels creates disorder where there is none:

    elles ne ongunnon
ræran on roderum nymþe riht and soþ
ær ðon engla weard for oferhygde
dæl on gedwilde. noldan dreogan leng
heora selfra ræd ac hie of siblufan
godes ahwurfon. hæfdon gielp micel

> þæt hie wið drihtne   dælan meahton
> wuldorfæstan wic   werodes þrymme,
> sid and swegltorht.   him þær sar gelamp,
> æfst and oferhygd   and þæs engles mod
> þe þone unræd   ongan ærest fremman,
> wefan and weccean.   þa he worde cwæð,
> niþes ofþyrsted,   þæt he on norðdæle
> ham and heahsetl   heofena rices
> agan wolde. (ll. 20b–34a)

[They strove to exalt nothing else in heaven except for right and truth until a part of the angels was in error through arrogance. They no longer desired to live for their own good, but they turned away from God's intimacy. They made a great boast that they might partition with the Lord the wondrous dwelling the glory of the host, wide and shiny. Sorrow occurred to them there, envy and pride and the mind of the angel who first began to frame folly, weave and work the treachery. Then he spoke words, thirsted for enmity, that he would possess a home and a throne in the northern part of the kingdom of heaven.]

The poet depicts the angels as a collective unit, referring to them with third-person plural pronouns (*heora, hie, him*) until the whole 'werod' (troop) acts out of 'oferhygd' (arrogance). The syntax highlights an immediate transformation: there was unchanging joy and bliss in heaven 'ær ðon' (until) a portion of angels chose to pursue their own desires. Here, *ær ðon* functions much like *oþþæt* ('until') elsewhere in the Old English corpus – the most famous example of course being the *Beowulf* poet's introduction of Grendel – by indicating a narrative break, effectively signalling disorder.[70] The flawless heavenly territories are initially described as 'sid and swegletohrt' (wide and heavenly bright).[71] Such wholeness is disrupted and the kingdom threatened with fragmentation as soon as the angels hope to 'dælon' (partition) the land and turn from God's 'siblufan' (intimacy). At the end of the passage, the poet locates the source of this turmoil in the 'mod' (mind) of a singular angel who 'niþes ofþyrsted' (thirsted for enmity) and a 'heahsetl' (throne) for himself.

Throughout *Genesis A*, a cluster of terms invoking heaven as a homeland appear: *eðel* occurs some 35 times; *eard* ('dwelling place') 10 times; *ham* ('home') 8 times; *yrfe* ('inheritance') 13 times. Heaven's physicality is reinforced with terms such as *norðdæle* ('northern part') along with Satan's desire to *agan* ('to possess'),

Lands idle and unused

which denotes 'ownership of land',[72] as well as 'control of, rule over (a country, territory)'.[73] Variants of the verb *agan* also recur in legal contexts, meaning 'to have jurisdiction (*dom* or *socn*) over' and 'power' more generally.[74]

That a narrative concerned with rebellion in an Anglo-Saxon text is heavily inflected with heroic ideas surrounding a retainer's duty to obey his lord is hardly surprising. Authors frequently textured their retellings of Old Testament poetry with English cultural ideologies, social structures, and idealised visions of a homeland. As Milton McCormick Gatch explains: 'Society – whether in the world or in Christ's kingdom – is a matter of corporate relationships; and the individual defines, understands, identifies himself in terms of his obligations to a lord.'[75] The rhetoric used to express the angel's will for domination traverses both heroic and religious discourses, and one can detect traces of the traditional Germanic concept of the *comitatus* as well as the 'heroic substratum which transforms the poetry at every level'.[76] Yet for all this episode's heroic and martial potential, the poet opts for a representation of rebellion that is highly personal, a rejection of intimate kinship with God. The change in angelic priorities from their desire to exalt 'riht and soþ' (right and truth) to their desire to 'ahwurfon' (turn away) from God is represented as almost instantaneous as they mentally 'dwæl' (strayed) from the desire to seek 'heora selfra ræd' (their own good).[77]

Learning about their conduct, God builds hell as a punishment for the 'werloga' (pledge-breaker), which implies that some form of mutual *wær* ('compact') or heavenly oath of lordship was betrayed (*-loga*). In becoming rebels against God's authority by violating the reciprocal bonds of fealty, they commit 'unræd' (folly),[78] diminishing their capacity for prudent 'ræd' (counsel):

> Hæfdon hie wrohtgeteme
> grimme wið god gesomnod.   him þæs grim lean becom!
> Cwædon þæt heo rice,   reðemode,
> agan woldan   and swa eaðe meahtan.
> Him seo wen geleah   siððan waldend his,
> heofona heahcining,   honda arærde
> hehste wið þam herge.   Ne mihton hygelease,
> mæne wið metode,   mægyn bryttigan
> ac him se mæra   mod getwæfde,
> bælc forbigde.   Þa he gebolgen wearð,
> besloh synsceaþan   sigore and gewealde,
> dome and dugeþe,   and dream benam
> his feond, frið   and gefean ealle,

> torhte tire, and his torn gewræc
> on gesacum swiðe selfes mihtum
> strengum stiepe. Hæfde styrne mod
> gegremed grymme, grap on wraðe
> faum folmum and him on fæðm gebræc
> yrre on mode. æðele bescyrede
> his wiðerbrecan wuldorgestealdum. (ll. 45b–64)

[They had grimly gathered a crime-troop against God; a grim reckoning befell them for that! The hostile-minded ones said that they would possess a kingdom, and might do so easily. Their expectation deceived them, after the ruler, the high-king of heaven, raised His hands, the most high against that army. The thoughtless ones might not share power with the measurer, but the mighty one took away their courage, suppressed their arrogance. When He became angry, He struck down the evil ones of triumph and rule, glory and nobility, and took joy from his enemy, peace and all delight, splendid honour, and in His anger wrought vengeance on His adversaries with a violent downward motion in His own might. He had a stern mind, grimly aggrieved, gripped them in rage with hostile hands and broke them in His embrace, angry in mind; He deprived his foes of the native land with wondrous dwellings.]

Once again, the desire to 'rice ... agan' (possess a kingdom) is featured as the core criminal motive of the rebel 'herge' (army) whose 'Him seo wen geleah' (expectation deceived them).[79] In addition to being stripped of joys, splendour, and honour, they are also 'æðele bescyrede ... wuldorgestealdum' (deprived ... of the native land with wondrous dwellings, ll. 63b, 64b), an image of their home in the heavenly kingdom and a particularly tangible deprivation that recalls Alfred's law: a traitor loses 'ealles þæs ðe he age' (all that he owns).

To these elements, the *Genesis A* poet describes permanent exclusion from heaven as 'on langne sið' (a long journey) 'on wrace' (in exile, line 71b):

> Sceop þa and scyrede scyppend ure
> oferhidig cyn engla of heofnum,
> wærleas werod. waldend sende
> laðwendne here on langne sið,
> geomre gastas. wæs him gylp forod,
> beot forborsten and forbiged þrym,
> wlite gewemmed. (ll. 65–71a)

Lands idle and unused

[Our creator then adjudged and separated that arrogant race of angels from heaven, faithless troop. The ruler sent the hostile army on a long journey, more sad spirits. Their speeches were useless, their boasts broken and majesty brought low, beauty defiled.]

All the qualities which characterised their former ambitions such as 'beot' (boasts), the desire for 'þrym' (majesty), and their 'wlite' (beauty) have been undone in their condition of exile. The details of this opening sequence provide a narrative structure for *Genesis A* by introducing the guiding theme of obedience.[80] Heaven now holds the good angels who remained loyal and the seats permanently vacated by the rebels; it is to the reunification and strengthening of heaven that the poet turns next. After the fall of the angels, the poet offers an arresting image of God's private contemplation of the beginning of the replacement process. In a manner reminiscent of Werferth's depiction of the firmament after all 'orlegnið' (hostility) has ceased, the poet describes how heavenly lands convalesce:

Wæron þa gesome   þa þe swegl buan,
wuldres eðel.   Wroht wæs asprungen,
oht mid englum   and orlegnið
siððan herewosan   heofon ofgæfon,
leohte belorene.   Him on laste setl
wuldorspedum welig   wide stodan
gifum growende   on godes rice,
beorht and geblædfæst,   buendra leas,
siððan wræcstowe   werige gastas
under hearmlocan   heane geforan.
Þa þeahtode   þeoden ure
modgeþonce   hu he þa mæran gesceaft,
eðelstaðolas,   eft gesette,
swegltorhtan seld   selran werode
þa hie gielpsceaþan   ofgifen hæfdon
heah on heofenum.   Forþam halig god
under roderas feng   ricum mihtum
wolde þæt him eorðe   and uproder
and sidwæter   gesete*d* wurde,
woruldgesceafte   on wraðra gield
þara þe, forhealdene,   of hleo sende.
Ne wæs her þa giet   nymþe heolstersceado
wiht geworden   ac þes wida grund
stod deop and dim,   drihtne fremde,
idel and unnyt. (ll. 82b–106a)

[They became united, those who inhabit the sky, the homeland of glory. Wrath was fallen out, fear among the angels and hostility after the warlike ones abandoned heaven, deprived of light. In their absence stood widely broad thrones rich in glorious wealth, growing with gifts in God's kingdom, bright and teeming, deprived of inhabitants, after the accursed, humbled spirits went forth in confinement to the place of exile. Then our prince considered in His thought how He might settle the mighty creation of the native-seats afterwards, the radiant thrones with a better troop that the boasting adversaries had lost high in the heavens. Therefore, holy God took control under the firmament of the heavens with mighty powers desired that the earth and sky and wide water become settled, as a created world in compensation for the more hateful ones those whom, failed in purity, He sent from His protection. There was nothing yet except for dark shadows, nothing at all dwelling but the wide ground that stood deep and dim, foreign to the Lord, idle and unused.]

Once the 'eðel' (homeland) is purged of the warlike band that threatened its security, the poet describes how the 'setl ... wide' (broad thrones) of heaven have been left 'buendra leas' (uninhabited). The poet also alludes to unsettled earthly estates, describing newly created spaces as 'idel ond unnyt' or (idle and unused), a complex phrase I will return to at the conclusion of this chapter. Desiring to refill the 'eðelstaðolas' (native seats) and 'swegltorhtan seld' (radiant thrones) the poet characterises God's hopes for resettlement as a 'gield' (compensation), a term that would have had concrete legal associations for an Anglo-Saxon audience.[81] The term *gield* (like Old English *bot*) has a wide range of meanings, but in prose and in legal contexts it generally has the force of 'a payment exacted by law as compensation, payment for loss or injury' and can be found in the law codes of Ine, Alfred, and II Æthelstan.[82] The *gield* formula typically follows the pattern: *Gif he* ... [commits the following crime] ... *gielde* [the following compensation can be made]. An example can be found in Alfred's code: 'Gif beforen eagum asnase, gielde þone wer' (If one is stabbed before his eyes, he [the offender] will compensate that man).[83] Elsewhere, in perhaps its most well-known form in the compound *wergild*, it means 'the compensation paid for the death of a person'.[84] In religious contexts, the term can also refer to 'what is offered' or 'sacrificed'.[85] The *gield* as a compensation (or replacement) thus serves a very suitable Germanic image for the Christian doctrine it signifies.

Of course, cases of treachery against an earthly lord were often considered far too grievous for compensation (as in the account of Wulfhere's betrayal of Alfred found in S 362). As Hugh Magennis observes, 'King Alfred leads the way for later legislators in declaring that treachery to one's lord is the only crime which cannot be compensated for'.[86] Within the context of the poem, God cannot allow Satan to recover his former place in the heavenly homeland. The forfeiture remains final. As John M. Hill notes, when compensation cannot be made by the guilty party, 'the payment burden falls ... upon the perpetrator's ... paternal kindred in greater proportion'.[87] Through compensation, God can repair the loss by reassigning possession of the seats vacated by the rebel angels. The poet thus establishes the promise of salvation through a familiar, though deferred, legal practice. The *gield* implies that the law has begun to assert itself upon the land. Just as the poem signals the arrival of creation, the poet similarly cues the arrival of a new legal dimension in salvation history, the final compensation to be exacted at Judgement Day with the ultimate beneficiary to be the restored heavenly polity through the participation of humanity.

Although the *Genesis A* poet was likely familiar with alternative narratives of the fall of the angels which situate the event within created time (traditions I will discuss in Chapter 2), he has chosen instead to explain the origin of the law and the doctrine of replacement through the principle of compensation. Since Satan's crime is represented as a violation committed not only against God but also against the heavenly community at large, the compensation becomes a way to restore value to heaven. Through humanity, heavenly space becomes redeemable.

That God's response to the crisis in heaven results in a *gield*, a notion that for Anglo-Saxons would have been understood as the most basic theory of legal behaviour, suggests that the rebellion, in fact, brings about binding principles of order in the universe. As earthly space and the chronology of human history comes into focus, the poet chooses to cast God's first action following the rebellion as something that Anglo-Saxons would have seen as a rational, legal deed. By rendering complex doctrine as a familiar legal procedure, the poet appeals to an audience invested in understanding the fall and replacement as having consequence for their own social order and earthly practices. In illustrating how God secures and renews territories through customs of compensation, the poet communicates humanity's potential to become the 'selran werode' (better troop) who will be active participants in the restoration of the heavenly realm. Referring to *Guthlac A*, Smith observes that 'through dispute contested land is made new again'.[88] The settlement of earthly space in *Genesis A* is thus manifold: it is at once legal in its dramatisation of newly occupied spaces and literal in the sense that humankind will inhabit the earth until they become heirs to the heavenly kingdom on the Day of Judgement.

'Replacement' diplomas

Thus far, I have been discussing the representation of kingdoms, inheritance, and power in *Genesis A*. The poet explores the connection between regal authority and territorial possession through God, who safeguards the heavenly realm from treachery much like an Anglo-Saxon king. At the same time, the angelic rebellion opens up space, delimiting new realms such as earth and hell and revealing an axis of obedience for humankind. As demonstrated throughout the pages of Junius 11, the event fixes a kind of border between those loyal to God and those who are forever deprived of divine privileges.[89] Of course, earth eventually becomes a fallen place, cut off from heaven. After their fall, God's command to Adam reads:

> 'þu scealt oðerne   eðel secean,
> wynleasran wic,   and on wræc hweorfan
> nacod niedwædla   neorxnawanges ...' (ll. 927–9).

['you shall seek another homeland, a more joyless dwelling place, and go in exile from Paradise, a naked wretch'.]

Adam and Eve become spiritual refugees in search of an unearthly inheritance. The meaning of 'eðel secean' (seek [another] homeland) is twofold here.[90] On the one hand, it refers to the unknown ways the human couple must tread in search of a new home outside of paradise, while, on the other, it recalls the heavenly *eðel* that awaits new residents. The idea of a lasting homeland resonated strongly with Anglo-Saxons. As Nicholas Howe observes:

> Old English poets loved these polysemous terms as a means of aligning the two realms, of articulating their similarities while also suggesting their differences. This verbal technique manifests the Christian belief that the conditions of life in the earthly home are but a shadowy version of the life that the saved will know in the heavenly home.[91]

Since they viewed their earthly dominions as reflections of the heavenly, might Anglo-Saxon kings have viewed their sovereign duties as analogous to God's defence of his realm? A number of charters attest to the same pattern of casting out and resettlement that we witness in *Genesis A*. Kings could likewise restore land as a compensatory act (or *gield*) modelling replacement practices. I have already discussed how total confiscation practices were unique to Anglo-Saxon kings, who exercised this right in much the same way that God does in *Genesis A*.[92] Turning to charter evidence can help illuminate how the narrative of the angelic rebellion relates to Anglo-Saxon land customs. Drawing upon Henri Lefebvre's *Production de l'espace*, Michelet suggests that 'the production of space process goes both ways. A given society inherits from tradition a mere image of space that will be operative in shaping this group's perception of its surroundings ... this perception influences [the] way a community represents and thinks about itself'.[93] A distinctly biblical language of resettlement reverberates through Anglo-Saxon charters designed to supplant individuals, families, and groups seen as rebels and threats. As I will show, kingly grants designed to stabilise empty lands align neatly with the goals of the replacement doctrine.

A variety of crimes could result in the deprivation of land in Anglo-Saxon England, many of which echo the sins of Satan and his rebels.[94] Crimes such as oath-breaking, plotting, and other major offences against the sovereign or the realm were just a few of the indiscretions that likely resulted in the loss of land and title.[95] I am indebted to the work of both Smith and Johnson here, who have paved the way for comparing the fall of the angels with the surviving charter evidence from the Anglo-Saxon period – what Smith aptly calls the 'confluence of the legal and biblical'.[96] In his assessment of grants and forfeiture practices around the year 1000, the likely time of the compiling of the Junius Manuscript, Smith observes that kings would often, '[reward] loyal subjects with grants of property and [punish] the disloyal through the forfeiture of estates'.[97] Such sovereign activities, of course, were of central importance to the story our poet tells in *Genesis A*, where the banishment of rebels requires new earthly grants and investitures.

No fewer than eight Anglo-Latin royal charters invoke the creation and fall of the angels in their opening proems: S 745, S 821, S 853 (also known as the 'Peniarth' Diploma), as well as the so-called Orthodoxorum diplomas S 953 and S 954 (d. 1019) (modelled on S 880 (d. 994) – a diploma ostensibly written by Archbishop Sigeric of Canterbury – and paralleled in S 906).[98] A late diploma S 1021 (d. 1050) also has similar themes: the creation and orders of angels, Lucifer's fall through pride, the sin of Adam, and requests that God increase prosperity. C. R. Hart suggests that these numerous '[references to] Lucifer [form] part of the elaboration, so it seems likely that it was a contemporary theme'.[99] A common link among each of these charters is the granting of unclaimed or uninhabited lands.

I have already mentioned Johnson's important observation concerning the unique causality of replacement employed by the poet of *Genesis A* and several other charter authors (wherein God creates humankind and earth only after the angels have been expelled). One such charter that follows this pattern is National Library of Wales, Aberystwyth, Peniarth MS 390 (the 'Peniarth' Cartulary) (d. 984), a grant by Æthelred II to his scriptor, Ælfwine. The relevant portion of the proem reads as follows:

> Regnante domino nostro Ihesu Christo imperpetuum. Qui ante mundi constitucionem decem angelorum agmina mirifice collacauit. decemaque post per superbiam cum suo lucifero in barathrum boraginis elapsis.[100] nouem in sua stabilitate misericorditer conseruauit. quique decimam adimplere cupiens postquam celum terramque conderet. hominem ex limo terre formauit. formatmque prothoplastum serpentinus liuor ad mortem usque perduxit.[101]

[By our Lord Jesus Christ, perpetually ruling. He before the creation of the world wondrously established ten multitudes of angels and when the tenth had afterwards fallen through pride into the depths of the abyss with Lucifer, He mercifully conserved nine in their stability. And desiring to replenish the tenth order, He afterwards created heaven and earth, (and) he formed man from the slime of the earth. And serpentine envy brought the first created man unto death, and the entire human race after him.][102]

The charter author suggests that Lucifer falls through 'superbiam' (pride) along with a tenth of the order of angels 'in barathrum boraginis' (into the depths of the abyss). Here *boraginis* is a variant spelling of *voraginis*; the phrase *barathrum voraginis* enjoyed formulaic status in the works of Aldhelm. In his prose *De virginitate*, Aldhelm describes the travails of a 'spiritual' mariner who must sail between 'Scyllam Siciliae et barathrum voraginis' (Sicilian Scylla and the depths of the abyss) towards the safe harbour of Christian monastic life. The timing represented in this grant is indeed unique and accords with *Genesis A* (as Johnson suggests), as are God's subsequent desires to form 'celum terramque' (heaven and earth), both nascent spaces taking shape only after the rebellion, after room has been made in the heavens and on earth. These latter spaces stand in

Lands idle and unused

stark contrast to the turbulent spaces of Lucifer's hell (and the seas that Aldhelm's Christian mariner must overcome).[103]

A similar charter S 954 (d. 1019), drawn up to replace landbooks destroyed by Danes, confirms privileges from King Cnut to Abbot Æthelwold. Unlike the Peniarth Diploma, the confirmation opens with God's creation of heaven and earth as well as 'candida ... angelica agmina' (white bands of angels) whom God sets 'super firmamento' (above the firmament). The preamble illustrates how 'que et Lucifer cum decimo ordine per superbiam de celo ruit' (through pride Lucifer from heaven along with a tenth of the order fell). The author supplies a final reflection on the damnation of 'quo ipse miser et satellites illius de celo projecti sunt' (those wretches cast out of heaven along with his retinue) before turning to replacement. The author next links the restoration of the tenth order with the confirmation of earthly privileges:

> et antiquum inimicum superavit, et fortis fortem alligavit, et in imo baratho retrusit: juste periit quie injuste decepit, atque omnes antiquas sanctas turmas a fauce pessimi leonis eripuit, et ovem perditam in humeris posuit, et ad antiquam patriam reduxit, et decimum ordinem implevit. Unde ego Cnuth, rex Anglorum ceterumque gentium persistentium in circuitu patefacio omnibus hanc cartulam legentibus et auscultantibus, diruto monasterio a paganis et crematis priuilegiis quae antique reges concesserant supradicto coenobio.[104]

[(Christ) overcame the old enemy, bound brave and strong, and fastened in the hellish pit: the just man perished who was unjustly deceived, and all the saints of old in the jaws of the lion, and he (Christ) laid on his shoulders the lost sheep, and returned them to their own country, and replenished the tenth order. Thus, I Cnut, king of the English and other peoples present in this bounded space, open to all readers and listeners of this charter, grant the privileges burned by pagans inside the monastery, which were granted by the ancient kings to the aforementioned house.]

The text of Cnut's charter restores the rightful possessions of the 'patriam' (country). He evokes the bounded space of his legal and jural domain; by doing so, he ties his sovereignty to the land itself, not just those who identify as English. Just as Christ harrows the saints from hell and replenishes the tenth order of heaven, so Cnut returns written privileges once lost to the fires of 'paganis' (pagans). The connection is striking, not only because it reveals a close association between replacement ideology and the royal charters, but also because the power of replacement becomes a written legal instrument, a kingly custom.

Although they do not explicitly invoke the fall of the angels, Smith also considers S 927 and 934 (both Æthelred II charters) as documents that can better inform our understanding of *Genesis A*.[105] These charters also follow the same basic outline of banishment and replacement. The charter authors describe the removal of individuals perceived to be dangers to the political realm before describing the re-establishing of political order. Smith's examination of these charters reveals how families and kin were often implicated in forfeitures. An example can be seen in S 926, which recounts the treachery of ealdorman Leofsige who forfeited lands because of his 'superbie ... et audacie' (pride and rashness). The document recalls that Leofsige's sister, Æthelflæd, was also ousted 'et hac de causa aliarumque quam plurimarum exheredem se fecit omnibus' ([causing] herself to be disinherited from everything).[106] In *Genesis A*, the entire 'werode' (troop) of angels that chooses to turn away from intimacy with their Lord suffers a fall. Smith provocatively states that many 'charters inscribe their own "doctrine of replacement" as they replace old apostates with more fit landholders'.[107] Similarly, charters incriminate sisters and wives (S 362 likewise implicates Wulfhere's 'uxore' (wife) in his treacherous oath-breaking) when a king chooses to dissolve privileges. In this way, the crime of rebellion and treason is shown to be genderless in the eyes of Anglo-Saxon kings and lawmakers.

Nor did kings discriminate between the different types of Anglo-Saxon lands when it came to treasonous tenants. II Cnut 13.1 directly states that a traitor, 'gyf he bocland habbe, sy þæt forworht ðam cynge to hande' (if he has bookland, let that be forfeit into the king's possession).[108] The traditional classifications for lands in early medieval England include *bocland* ('bookland'), *folcland* ('folkland'), and *lænland* ('loanland'). According to Simon Keynes, an 'estate of bookland was held according to the privileges stated or implied in a "book", or diploma – that is, with immunity from all secular burdens ... with full power to bequeath the land to any heir of the owner's choosing'.[109] Unlike *bocland*, possessions of *folcland* centred around the family and kin-group and 'could not be alienated outside the owner's kindred'.[110] *Lænland*, on the other hand, derived from either bookland or folkland, but was subject to the passing of time as it 'might be leased to others'.[111]

One final example of rebellion reveals connections to the narrative of the angelic rebellion. S 918 (d. 1008) recalls the seizure of lands once owned by Wulfgeat. The later chronicler, Florence of Worcester,[112] remarks that Wulfgeat was beloved of the king, but guilty of 'propter injusta judicia' (unjust legal authority) and, tellingly, 'superbia ... opera' (arrogant ... deeds),[113] recalling the 'oferhygd' (pride) of Satan in *Genesis A* as well as the angel's former favour with God. A letter written by Ælfric addressed to *Wulfget æt Ylmandune*, which survives in MS Oxford, Bodleian Library, Laud Misc. 509,[114] admonishes the thane for his crimes against his lord. Appropriately, it opens in the same way as the charter proems I have examined here, with a catechetical *narratio* recalling the fall of the angels and their 'modignysse' (pridefulness). Ælfric states that the rebel angels lost their inheritances 'Forþam ðe hi forletan his hlafordscipe' (because they forsook [God's] lordship). They were thus 'asyndrode' (set apart, sundered, separated, removed from union) from heaven and the presence of their lord.[115] In this case, both charters and the letter perform the same function through the narrative of the fall of the angels by justifying the consequences of treachery and the transference of ownership.

Diplomas served a critical function in Anglo-Saxon England through the documentation and management of worldly privileges.[116] They affirm that the possession of land carries certain privileges and obligations; certain crimes sever the bonds between a king and his landholding thanes; kings can revoke privileges and transfer ownership of lands to fortify his realm. Rebels are thus cast out as kings repopulate territories with loyal subjects, mirroring the politics of salvation as seen in *Genesis A*. In all these cases, rebellion is figured as a lapse of loyalty, a furtive betrayal, a broken oath, or a lethal desire for possession, not necessarily a fully fledged martial opposition against a lord. If we can think of Anglo-Saxon charters as tools of replacement, inscribing the restoration of loyalties and lands, then what we see in them is the drama of expulsion and replacement playing out again and again on an earthly, and altogether human, scale.

Anglo-Saxon *horror vacui*

The foundational crisis in *Genesis A* results in a territorial ousting, a new settlement, and the legitimation of the change in possession from the rebels to the 'better troop'. The *Genesis A* poet describes the wee hours of earthly creation in ways that mirror the recently emptied spaces of heaven. Before the arrival of the human couple, the poet describes the earth as a 'rume land' (spacious land), newly 'gestaþelode' (established) by God's might. Nevertheless, the earthly landscape is 'wonn and weste' (dark and empty, l. 110a) and 'idel ond unnyt' (idle and unused). The description of earth as uninhabited and unsettled is reflective of cultural concerns over how to deal with 'idle and empty' territories and spaces. Far from celebrating and expanding open and empty spaces, seeing them as pure and worth preserving, Anglo-Saxons viewed their wide open and 'idle' spaces as visible markers of vulnerability, fragile to external and internal threats. Anglo-Saxon authors, as I will show, demonstrate an eagerness to refashion space by reasserting humanity and order upon such places.

The formulaic description of earthly lands as *idel ond unnyt* deserves special comment.[117] The poet most likely draws upon Genesis 1.2 here (*terra autem erat inanis et vacua*). The Old English *Heptateuch* closely resembles this formulation with, 'se eorðe soðlice wæs idel & æmti, & þeostra wæron ofer ðære nywelnysse bradnysse' (truly the earth was idle and empty, and darkness stretched over the surface of the abyss).[118] Bosworth-Toller suggests that *idel* in fact means 'empty' and 'not possessing, destitute, void, devoid'. The term can also refer to that which is 'vain, useless, idle, to no purpose', or even 'unoccupied, without inhabitants'.[119] The second component of this formula, *unnyt*, is similarly defined as 'useless, vain, idle, unprofitable'.[120] The phrase recurs throughout the Old English corpus (over thirty times). Interestingly, in most cases these terms refer to indolent speech or thought in Anglo-Saxon religious writing – as in the Blickling and Vercelli homily collections. Vercelli Homilies 9 and 20 warn against 'idele spræca', 'idele geþancas', and 'unnyttan geþohtas, idelne gylp'. Though breaking with the formulaic pattern, Wulfstan frequently evokes these terms in reference to mental weaknesses and failings. In the Old English translation of Bede's *Historia Ecclesiastica*, a bishop describes childish activities like horse-racing with this phrase, and in Ælfric's *Grammar* and various psalters the terms gloss either *superuacue* and *vanum*. By the eleventh century, a later valence of the phrase emerges in the so-called *Feudal Book* of Abbot Baldwin concerning the continuity of property tenure at Bury St Edmund's. Finally, the phrase appears several times throughout Alfred's West Saxon *Pastoral Care* and in Werferth's translation of Gregory's *Dialogues* to refer to a host of undesirable human behaviours.

Why would a phrase that so predominantly refers to mental states also signal the status of lands and territories? From mental spaces, to lands, to halls, and religious houses, idle and unused areas were seen as fragile and in need of a new foundation. Just as scholars of the visual arts detect *horror vacui* (the 'fear of empty space') among medieval artists and illustrators, I think it possible to locate a similar concern surrounding lands and properties that lay vacant, barren, or unsettled, what Michelet fittingly refers to as 'wasted space'.[121] Exploring lands, estates, and properties destabilised or made fallow through human or otherworldly action, reveals that Anglo-Saxons were invested in reclaiming those spaces viewed as idle and ailing in Anglo-Saxon England.

Both the *Beowulf* poet and the *Genesis A* poet employ the same terminology in their descriptions of idealised locations that are vulnerable to disorder and uselessness.[122] The *Beowulf* poet uses the phrase *idel and unnyt* in reference to the space of the hall. In the wake of Grendel's rampages, Beowulf tells Hrothgar what he has heard about Heorot's dwindling status:

'Mē wearð Grendles þing
on mīnre ēþeltyrf undyrne cūð;
secgað sæliðend þæt þæs sele stande,
reced sēlesta rinca gehwylcum
īdel ond unnyt, siððan æfenlēoht
under heofenes haðor beholen weorþeð.'[123] (ll. 409a–14)

['This matter of Grendel was made known to me in my native land; sailors say that this building, most excellent of halls, stands idle and unused, for every man, after evening light is hidden under the roof of heaven.']

Jennifer Neville notes that 'an *idel ond unnyt* natural world can become valuable only by divine or human effort; it is meaningless, even horrible, without reference to or contact with humanity'.[124] While earth in *Genesis A* has yet to achieve its usefulness, Hrothgar's hall needs to recover its own. Just as *Genesis A* requires a world inhabited by humanity to restore heavenly value, so Heorot is described as not fulfilling its true purpose as a place of joy and abundance, and must be reclaimed for human inhabitants.

In *Beowulf*, the building of Heorot is described as a foundational act which is reinforced by the scop's song of creation and the poet's description of Hrothgar's dominions. Alvin Lee and others have read the building of Heorot as the creation of a paradise on earth that comes to be savagely disordered.[125] Edward Condren suggests that Beowulf's use of the phrase *idel ond unnyt*, while literally referring to Heorot, also metonymically refers to Hrothgar and the

Danes.[126] Beowulf remakes Heorot into a place of prosperity, but not before suggesting that spaces can be emptied of their potential through the dwindling fortitude of their inhabitants.

Elsewhere in *Genesis A*, during the episode recounting the destruction of Sodom and Gomorrah, the poet offers a depiction of spaces rendered permanently *unnyt*:

> lig eall fornam
> þæt he grenes fond   goldburgum in
> swylce þær ymbutan   unlytel dæl
> sidre foldan   geondsended wæs
> bryne and brogan.   bearwas wurdon
> to axan and to yslan,   eorðan wæstma,
> efne swa wide   swa ða witelac
> reðe geræhton   rum land wera. (ll. 2550b–7)

[fire seized everything green it found in that gold-city, just as no small part of the wider earth was surrounded with burning and trembling. The cruel punishment spread through ashes and embers, so widely and so cruelly, across the spacious land of men, over the woods and fruit of the earth.]

Here, the land becomes entirely consumed and the poet finds no restorative potential. Lot's wife gazes back at the now infertile 'rum land wera' (spacious land of men) before turning into a salt-stone.

This idea of reclaiming 'idle' space and territory can also be seen in one of the foundational documents of the tenth-century Benedictine Reform. The *Regularis Concordia* provided a universalised liturgy for all the monasteries in England. The preface to the *Rule* recalls King Edgar's decision to drive out the secular canons whose behaviour was incompatible with the new order:

> Comperto etenim quod sacra cenobia diuersis sui regiminis locis diruta ac paene Domini nostri Ihesu Christi seruito destitute neglegenter tabescerent, Domini compunctus gratia, cum magna animi alacritate festinando ubicumque locorum decentissime restaurauit; eiectisque neglegentium clericorum spurcitiis non solum monachos uerum etiam sanctimoniales, patribus matribusque constitutes, ad Dei famulatum ubique per tantam sui regni amplitudinem deuotissime constituit, bonisque omnibus locupletans gratulabundus ditauit.

[When therefore he learned that the holy houses in all quarters of his kingdom, brought low, and almost wholly lacking in service of our Lord Jesus Christ, destitute diminished by neglect, moved by the grace of the Lord he most gladly set himself to restore them everywhere to their former good estate. Wherefore he drove out the negligent clerks with their abominations, placing in their stead for the service of God, throughout the length and breadth of his dominations, not only monks but also nuns, under abbots and abbesses; and these, out of gratitude to God, he enriched with all good things.][127]

These opening lines describe the neglect of the monasteries, Edgar's decision to restore them by driving out the 'negligent clerks with their abominations', and his resolution to restore their properties by investing lands with new tenants, 'monachos' (monks) and 'sanctimoniales' (nuns). The *Rule* echoes the repertoire of 'uselessness' with 'sacra cenobia' (holy houses) described as 'neglegenter tabescerent' (diminished by neglect). Moreover, the document links space with expressions of sovereignty in delineating the vastness of Edgar's dominions. The preface not only reminds us that the Benedictine Reform ushered in serious changes for the English ecclesiastical hierarchy, but also that it initiated a prolonged struggle between the clergy and the monastic reformers who envisioned themselves as new caretakers for Anglo-Saxon England.[128]

The most striking case justifying the seizure of idle property occurred in the city of Winchester and, crucially, used the angelic expulsion as its legal precedent. The New Minster Charter portrays the secular clerics at Winchester as a subversive threat to English ecclesiastical unity by tendentiously aligning their allegedly sinful behaviour with that of proud rebel angels. As I explore further in Chapter 3, what makes the connection between the secular clerics and their laxity so interesting is not just how their apparent sinfulness parallels that of the rebel angels, but how the author implies that the compromise of their earthly properties seems to alter the destiny of the English. New earthly custodians are needed if the English are to become heavenly inheritors. In a similar way, landed privileges must be revoked for the safeguarding of eternal estates.

Perhaps most relevant for our purposes here is an occurrence of the phrase *idel ond unnyt* found in Vercelli Homily 10, a Rogation homily which lacks a clear source.[129] Throughout this homily, one can detect the author's interest in contrasting things and places that are transitory with those that are permanent. Whereas in *Genesis A*, the poet uses the phrase *idel ond unnyt* to signal the potential richness of earthly space, the homilist of Vercelli 10 inverts this idea, suggesting that God can make prosperous lands infertile if human tenants mistakenly view earthly territories as more important than eternal inheritances.

The basic outline of Vercelli 10 is as follows: exhortation on the power of the gospel (ll. 1–8); Christ's Incarnation and ways to avoid damnation (ll. 9–54); scenes of the Last Judgement (ll. 55–110); exhortation to do good works (ll. 111–99); a plea for charity and reference to Christ's parable of the rich man (Luke 12:16–21); contemplation of the transience of earthly prosperity (expressed through the *ubi sunt* motif, ll. 210–11);[130] obligations of the rich (ll. 245–6); and a plea to turn away from worldly things and look towards salvation (ll. 246–75). This homily must have enjoyed some popularity, since roughly nine copies exist. In fact, Samantha Zacher asserts that it was 'one of the most widely circulating homiletic compositions to survive from Anglo-Saxon England'.[131] A central message is the ephemeral nature of earthly pleasures and the transience of landed possession itself. Evoking a good deal of eschatological and legal terminology as it recounts Luke 12:16–21 (the parable of the rich man who asks Christ to settle an inheritance dispute), the voice of Christ rebukes the vain man for believing that *bocland* – lands vested by royal diplomas which were, theoretically, inalienable – can be a permanent possession.[132] In the following section, our homilist expands greatly upon his probable source, Pseudo-Augustine, *De remedia peccatorum* (PL 39.2340–2). The idea that lands can be made *idel ond unnyt* serves as a cautionary reminder to audiences that the possession of earthly lands is, ultimately, something of a fiction, an imperfect copy of lands that await the faithful in heaven:

> Gif ðu wene þæt hit þin bocland sie ⁊ on agene æht gesaeld, hit þonne wæron mine wæter þa ðe on heofonum wæron, þanon ic mine gife dæle eorðwærum. Gif ðu mihta hæbbe, dæl regnas ofer þine eorðan. Gif ðu strang sy, syle wæstm þinre eorðan. Ic ahyrde mine sunnan ⁊ hie gebyrhte; þonne forbærneð hio ealle þine æceras. Þonne bist ðu dælleas mines renes, ⁊ þe þin eorðe bið idel ⁊ unnyt goda gehwylces.[133]

[If you think that (earth) is your bookland and given for your own possession, then it was my waters that were in the heavens, from where I share my gift with earth-dwellers. If you have the power, dispense rains over your earth. If you are strong, supply fruit to your earth. I will harden my sun and it will intensify; then it will burn all your fields. Then you will be with a share of my rain, and your earth will become idle and unused for any good.]

Significantly, the homilist renders the phrase *terra tua* from his source into *bocland*.[134] The vain man learns that even earthly lands of the most stable order are only made prosperous and usable through gifts and blessings from God. More importantly, the homily stresses that prosperity can be easily undone; earthly lands (like the wastes of Sodom and Gomorrah in *Genesis A*) can be made infertile. Through a series of challenges set up with conditional statements, Christ reminds the man of his all-powerful might and sway over earthly creation. According to Smith, the homily, 'underscores ... the idea that landholding brings with it a set of obligations to a superior authority who has the power both to issue and remove certain privileges of possession'.[135] In this context, Christ is the sovereign figure who can shower lands with gifts of rain and fruit, and just as easily return them to a state of waste.

The transitory nature of the world is echoed in the subsequent *ubi sunt* passage (ll. 238–43), recalling Satan's personal *ubi sunt* lament after his fall in the poem *Christ and Satan* where he cries out in distress, 'Hwær com engla ðrym' (Where is the glory of angels?, l. 36b). Owing to the homily's engagement with concerns over kingship and political power, it is fitting that Christ offers salvation through a *frumgewrit* (original charter). Smith observes that '[i]n this legalistic vision of the Last Judgment, the damned forfeit their place in paradise ... The offended Ruler/Judge revokes the privilege he had once restored in the *frumgewrit*'.[136] By setting up a contrast between the written earthly instruments that guarantee perpetuity and Christ's own written documents, the homilist suggests that prosperous *bocland* only thrives through divine favour. Surprisingly, the homilist imagines *bocland* as an imperfect earthly invention, or worse, a deceptive cipher that can lead one to vainglory and greed.

Sawyer 817 (also known as 'The Old Minster Charter') evokes some of the central principles of *bocland*. This particular charter narrates the turnover of ecclesiastical estates seized from secular canons and transferred into the possession of Benedictine monks under the authority of King Edgar. According to the charter author, in the lands formerly 'gesette' (settled) by 'modigan priests' (proud priests) there are now monks forever 'gelogode' (lodged) in perpetual service to another written document: the *Regularis Concordia*. Relying on the legitimacy of *bocland*, S 817 establishes the Benedictine monks as timeless tenants of ecclesiastical lands. The document purports that idle land is renewed by the written words and shaping hands of monks and kings, and I think it possible that such bold assertions of rights of *bocland* may have prompted the homilist of Vercelli 10 to denounce such capacious and seemingly incontrovertible grabs at landed property.¹³⁷

In some ways, the rich man's idle beliefs mirror the possible fate of the landscape he stubbornly sees as enduring. A rare vernacular charter, S 342, a grant of land by King Æthelred I to Earl Ælfstan, contains a hellish anathema that warns of the pursuit of 'idle þinge' (idle things) in the world:

> If þat ilimpe þat oniman þurch deules lore and for þeses middelerdes idle þinge on onni idale ilitel oþer michel þis ibreke oþer iwanie wite he hine fram alle leaffulle inne þese iworlde asceaden and he des sel in domes deghe beforen Criste rich agieldende bute he it are her on worlde mid richte ibete.¹³⁸

[If it happen that anyone, through the devil's teaching and for the sake of the idle things of this world, break or diminish this in any particular way, small or great, he shall find himself cut off from all believers in this world, and he shall render just account of it in the presence of Christ on the Day of Judgement, unless he has duly made amends for it in this world.]

Underlying this anathema is the call to 'agieldende' ([make] amends) for desiring impermanent things. Another charter, S 141 (also known as 'Hemming's Cartulary'), similarly warns against the 'vana ac caduca' (vain and fallen) temptations of the world in a proem.¹³⁹ Just as these documents fill vacant lands so, too, do they warn of the mental laxity, greed, and desire for transitory excesses that could spell its destruction.

For Anglo-Saxon Christians, the fall of the angels represented the moment when, for the briefest instant, heavenly space became vulnerable, in need of a deferred resettlement. As Michelet notes, 'the status of the land and the transformation of a wasted space are controversial issues' for Anglo-Saxons.¹⁴⁰ As a primal dispute that creates space, legal order, ideas of inheritance, and sovereign power, Anglo-Saxons looked to the fall of the angels to make sense of their homeland on earth. Social theorist Anthony Smith suggests that 'a group's sense of self and its destiny [is often linked] with the possession and control of a given territory'.¹⁴¹ Smith explains how a community's perceived site of territorial possession need not be physical – the very idea of an imagined heavenly homeland could suffice. Although creation narratives take place for their readers outside of space and time, as Michelet asserts, 'they clearly also say something about the contemporary world'.¹⁴² Although Anglo-

Saxon conceptions of homeland and nation shift in important ways over the course of a very long period (a subject I take up in both Chapters 3 and 6), the narrative of the fall (both of Satan and of Adam and Eve) reveals these authors' interest in the ordering of their physical realm as well as persistent concerns over idle minds and lapses in judgement.

The *Genesis A* poet initially represents Satan's crime as a mental lapse followed by 'gielp micel' (great boasts) revealing his desire to seize territories for himself, suggesting that Anglo-Saxon Christians saw a close connection between breaches of intellect and breaches of physical spaces.[143] Kathleen Davis observes that Ælfric, for this reason, championed the spiritually active mind. In his *Letter to Sigeweard*, Ælfric suggests that salvation rests upon good deeds and excessive contemplation, whereas eternal punishments await those who pass their lives in 'idelnisse' (emptiness) of thought.[144] Aggressively working against *idelnisse*, according to Ælfric, is crucial. An emptiness of mind leaves one vulnerable and prone to sin. Ælfric's remedy was, of course, the contemplative life, the continuous intellectual resistance of *idelnisse*.

Of course, not all idle spaces were thought to be useless. Ananya Jahanara Kabir has surveyed Anglo-Saxon perceptions of the 'interim paradise', which is both a physical region – a celestial waiting-room – and a condition of purification for the soul.[145] The *Liber Vitae* (British Library, Stowe 944) offers a striking visual contrast between the Last Judgement and the emptier spaces of the interim paradise, where we see patiently waiting souls eager to fulfil the Augustinian directive to 'suppleat et instauret' (fill and repair) the spaces of heaven.

The inverse of what authors such as Ælfric viewed as *idelnisse* is, of course, 'nytwyrðe' (usefulness) in both body and mind, the ultimate conduit towards salvation. Perhaps nowhere else is the connection between usefulness and salvific inheritance articulated so poignantly as it is in Alfred's Preface to Augustine's *Soliloquies*:

> ælcne man lyst, siððan he ænig cotlyf on his hlafordes læne myd his fultume getrimbred hæfð, þæt he hine mote hwilum þar-on gerestan ... and his on gehwilce wisan to þere lænan tilian, ægþer ge on se ge on lande, oð þone fyrst þe he bocland and æce yrfe þurh his hlafordes miltse geearnige. Swa gedo se weliga gifola, se ðe egðer wilt ge þissa lænena stoclife ge þara ecena hama. Se ðe ægþer gescop and ægðeres wilt, forgife me þæt me to ægðrum onhagige: ge her nytwyrðe to beonne, ge huru þider to cumane.[146]

[every man, when he has built a hamlet on land leased to him by his lord and with his lord's help, likes to stay there some time ... and to employ himself in every way on that leased land, both on sea and land, until the time when he shall deserve bookland and a perpetual inheritance through his lord's kindness. May the great benefactor, who rules both these temporary habitations as well as those eternal homes, so grant. May He who created both and rules over both grant that I be fit for both: both to be useful here and likewise to arrive there.]

The idea of space – both earthly and eternal – blends here. The Preface requests suitability 'to ægðrum' (for both) the 'lænena stoclife' (temporary habitations) that are by their very nature transitory and those 'ecena hama' (eternal homes) made firmer for human beings through the fall of the angels. Here, the wish to be *nytwyrde* signals a fitness for earthly *bocland* and divine 'yrfe' (inheritance).[147] As we have seen, the sin of the rebel angels was frequently understood as a psychological lapse with spatial consequences. Just how close the connection between mental and physical space was for Anglo-Saxons will become more evident through a survey of *Genesis B* and various apocryphal elaborations of Satan's fall found in Irish traditions, where we witness a marked interest in the combative rivalries for territory and inheritance that led to the angelic rebellion and compelled Satan's feud with humankind.

Notes

1. Alfred, *King Alfred's West-Saxon Version of Gregory's Pastoral Care*, ed. Henry Sweet (London: N. Trübner, 1871).
2. Gregory, *Dialogues*, ed. Adalbert de Vogüé, Sources Chrétiennes 260 (Paris: Editions de Cerf, 1979), p. 314. On Gregory's doctrine concerning the 'confirmation of the good angels', see Charles D. Wright '"fægere þurh forðgesceaft": The Confirmation of the Angels in Old English Literature', *MÆ*, 86 (2017), 22–37, whose translation of this excerpt I have included here.
3. Werferth, *Bischofs Wærferth von Worcester Übersetzung der Dialoge Gregors des Grossen*, ed. Hans Hecht, Bibliothek der angelsächsischen Prosa 5 (Leipzig, 1900–7; repr. Darmstadt, 1965), pp. 204–5.
4. I have drawn on Wright's translation (from 'The Confirmation of the Angels') though with some modifications.
5. Bosworth-Toller, *staþol*, sense 4. For an overview of *staþol*, see Eric Stanley, '*Staþol*: A Firm Foundation for Imagery', in *Text, Image,*

    Interpretation: Studies in Anglo-Saxon Literature and its Insular Context in Honour of Éamonn Ó Carragáin, ed. Alastair Minnis and Jane Roberts (Turnhout: Brepols, 2007), pp. 319–32.
6   Bosworth-Toller, *staþol*, sense 3a.
7   *DOE*, *eþelstaþol*, sense 1; Bosworth-Toller, *staþolian*, sense 1.
8   Wright explains how authors associate the 'confirmation' (confirmare) with God's creation of the 'firmament' ('The Confirmation of the Angels', pp. 25–7).
9   Richard Abels, *Alfred the Great: War, Kinship and Culture in Anglo-Saxon England* (London: Routledge, 1998), pp. 249–55 and 275–82. See Patrick Wormald's entry on 'oaths' in *The Blackwell Encyclopedia of Anglo-Saxon England*, ed. Michael Lapidge, John Blair, Simon Keynes, and Donald Scragg (Malden, MA: Blackwell, 1999), pp. 338–9.
10 The first edition of Oxford, Bodleian Library, MS Junius 11 was completed by the Dutch scholar Franciscus Junius (1591–1677), *Caedmonis monachi paraphrasis poetica Genesios ac praecipuarum sacrae pagina historiarum* (Amsterdam, 1655); repr. Peter J. Lucas (Amsterdam: Rodopi, 2000). A subsequent edition was completed by Sir Israel Gollancz, *The Cædmon Manuscript of Anglo-Saxon Biblical Poetry, Junius XI in the Bodleian Library* (London: Oxford University Press, 1927). Eventually, the manuscript was affixed with the name 'Junius' after its first owner and editor. It is edited in its entirety in *The Junius Manuscript*, ed. George Philip Krapp, ASPR I (New York: Columbia University Press, 1931).
11 The best reading of the tenurial discourses in *Genesis A* is by Scott T. Smith, 'Faith and Forfeiture in the Old English *Genesis A*', *MP*, 111 (2014), 593–615 (pp. 600–1).
12 See Howe, *Writing the Map*; Scott T. Smith, *Land and Book: Literature and Land Tenure in Anglo-Saxon England* (Toronto: University of Toronto Press, 2012); Michelet, *Creation, Migration, and Conquest*.
13 Johnson convincingly argues that the *Genesis A* poet's rendition of the doctrine is more radical than Augustine's. See David F. Johnson, 'Studies in the Literary Career of the Fallen Angels: The Devil and his Body in Old English Literature', PhD dissertation, Cornell University, 1993 and David F. Johnson, 'The Fall of Lucifer in *Genesis A* and Two Anglo-Latin Royal Charters', *JEGP*, 97 (1998), 500–21 (p. 517). I also thank him for sharing a forthcoming piece, 'Winchester Revisited: Æthelwold, Lucifer, and the Place of Origin of MS Junius 11'.
14 For Anglo-Saxon references to the replacement doctrine, see Dorothy Haines, 'The Vacancies in Heaven: The Doctrine of Replacement and *Genesis A*', *N&Q*, 44 (1997), 150–4 (p. 153).
15 Ibid.

16 On the theme of exile in the Junius Manuscript, see Nicholas Howe, 'Falling into Place: Dislocation in the Junius Book', in *Unlocking the Wordhord: Anglo-Saxon Studies in Memory of Edward B. Irving, Jr.*, ed. Mark C. Amodio and Katherine O'Brien O'Keeffe (Toronto: University of Toronto Press, 2003), pp. 14–37 (p. 32).

17 Abels hypothesises that Wulfhere's oath-breaking came at a particularly difficult time for landowners who hoped to retain their properties by siding with the Danes. See Richard P. Abels, *Lordship and Military Obligation in Anglo-Saxon England* (Berkeley: University of California, 1988), p. 152.

18 For text and translation, see Dorothy Whitelock, *English Historical Documents, 500–1042*, vol. 1 (2nd ed., Oxford: Oxford University Press, 1979), pp. 541–2. See also *The Early Charters of Northern England and the North Midlands*, ed. C. R. Hart, SEEH 6 (Leicester: Leicester University Press, 1975), p. 21 and p. 34 (n. 155) and Janet L. Nelson, 'A King Across the Sea: Alfred in Continental Perspective', *Transactions of the Royal Historical Society*, 36 (1986), 46–68 (pp. 53–9).

19 Nelson, 'A King Across the Sea', p. 54.

20 See Richard Abels, 'Bookland and *Fyrd* Service in Late Anglo-Saxon England', in *The Battle of Hastings: Sources and Interpretations*, ed. Stephen Morillo (Woodbridge: Boydell, 1996); repr. *Anglo-Norman Studies*, 7 (1984), 1–25.

21 Felix Liebermann, *Die Gesetze der Angelsachsen*, 3 vols. (Halle: Niemeyer, 1903–16), 4 (quotations are by clause and relevant line numbers) and Whitelock, *English Historical Documents*, p. 374.

22 Nelson, 'A King Across the Sea', p. 54.

23 *English Historical Documents*, ed. and trans. Whitelock, p. 500.

24 Nelson, 'A King Across the Sea', p. 67.

25 Ibid., p. 58.

26 Lefebvre, *The Production of Space*, p. 280 and Le Goff, 'Discorso di chiusura', pp. 805–38.

27 *DOE*, *anweald*, sense 1a, 'power, sovereignty, sway'.

28 Smith, *Land and Book*, pp. 153–89; Jaqueline Stodnick, 'What (and Where) is the *Anglo-Saxon Chronicle* About: Spatial History', *John Rylands University Library Manchester*, 86 (2004), 87–104 (p. 90).

29 Michelet, *Creation, Migration, and Conquest*, p. 23.

30 Ibid., p. 8.

31 Ibid., p. 62.

32 Della Hooke, *The Landscape of Anglo-Saxon England* (Leicester: Leicester University Press, 1998), p. 85.

33 Many tenth-century charters similarly recognise territories that lie unoccupied or vacated, also known as *nanes monnes land* ('no man's land') including S 80, S 141 ('Hemming's Cartulary'), and S 360 ('The Micheldever Forgery'), S 789, and an extract from S 1622. According to Hooke, 'Sometimes, a patch of land, usually heathland,

remained unclaimed or its ownership contested long enough for it to become known as "No Man's Land"' (p. 78).

34 See, for instance, Nicole Guenther Discenza, 'The Old English Boethius', in *A Companion to Alfred the Great*, ed. Nicole Guenther Discenza and Paul E. Szarmach (Leiden: Brill, 2014), pp. 200–34.

35 Patrick J. Geary, 'Land, Language, and Memory in Europe 700–1100', *Transactions of the Royal Historical Society*, 9 (1999), 169–84 (p. 171).

36 Smith makes a compelling case for poem's place in the age of Æthelred ('Faith and Forfeiture', pp. 593–615).

37 Recent reassessments of the manuscript favour *c*. 1000; see Leslie Lockett, 'An Integrated Re-examination of the Dating of Oxford, Bodleian Library, Junius 11', *ASE*, 31 (2002): 141–73.

38 Lefebvre, *The Production of Space*, p. 10.

39 Two illuminations – Page 3 and Page 16 – contain images of the fall of the rebel angels. A digitised version of the manuscript can be viewed in colour online at the Bodleian Library's website, http://image.ox.ac.uk.

40 Barbara Raw, 'The Probable Derivation of Most of the Illustrations in Junius 11 from an Old Saxon Genesis', *ASE*, 54 (1976), 133–48.

41 For studies on the illustrations of Junius 11, see Thomas Ohlgren, 'The Illustrations of the *Cædmonian Genesis*: Literary Criticism Through Art', *Mediaevalia et Humanistica*, 3 (1972), 199–212; Catherine E. Karkov, *Text and Picture in Anglo-Saxon England: Narrative Strategies in the Junius Manuscript*, CSASE 31 (Cambridge: Cambridge University Press, 2001); Herbert R. Broderick III, 'The Iconographic and Compositional Sources of the Drawings in Oxford Bodleian Library, MS Junius 11', PhD dissertation, Columbia University, 1978 and 'Observations on the Method of Illustration in MS Junius 11 and the Relationship of the Drawings to the Text', *Scriptorium*, 37 (1983), 161–77.

42 On bended or bruised knees as a symbol of humility, see Adam S. Cohen, 'King Edgar Leaping and Dancing Before the Lord', in *Imagining the Jew in Anglo-Saxon Literature and Culture*, ed. Samantha Zacher (Toronto: University of Toronto Press, 2016), pp. 219–36.

43 Asa Simon Mittman and Susan M. Kim, 'Locating the Devil "Her" in MS Junius 11', *Gesta*, 54 (2015), 3–25 (p. 3).

44 Wright, 'The Confirmation of the Angels', pp. 22–7.

45 Karkov, *Text and Picture*, pp. 38–9.

46 Mittman and Kim, 'Locating the Devil', p. 5.

47 Ibid., p. 7.

48 On representations of Satan's fallen state, see Benjamin C. Withers, 'Satan's Mandorla: Translation, Transformation, and Interpretation

in Late Anglo-Saxon England', *Insular and Anglo-Saxon Art and Thought in the Early Medieval Period* (2011), 247–70.

49 On Augustine's interpretation of *fiat lux*, see *De Civitate Dei* (11.9), ed. Dombart and Kalb, I, 329–30. See also Renée R. Trilling, *The Aesthetics of Nostalgia: Historical Representation in Old English Verse* (Toronto: University of Toronto Press, 2009), pp. 82–3 and Charles D. Wright, 'An Old English Formulaic System and its Contexts in Cynewulf's Poetry', *ASE*, 40 (2011), 151–74 (pp. 54–5).

50 Mittman and Kim, 'Locating the Devil', p. 9.

51 Karkov, *Text and Picture*, p. 40.

52 Mittman and Kim, 'Locating the Devil', p. 14.

53 Peter Dendle discusses the spatial incongruities associated with the Devil, namely 'that he is simultaneously chained in hell and roaming about the earth' (pp. 66–7). See *Satan Unbound: The Devil in Old English Narrative Literature* (Toronto: University of Toronto Press, 2001).

54 Karkov, *Text and Picture*, p. 67; Augustine, *Sancti Aureli Augustini Confessiones* (11.13), ed. P. Knöll, CSEL 33 (Vienna, 1896), p. 289.

55 Ohlgren guessed that this object might be the throne ('The Illustrations of the *Cædmonian Genesis*', pp. 199–212).

56 Trilling, *The Aesthetics of Nostalgia*, pp. 82–3.

57 For lordship in early medieval Europe, see Bisson, *The Crisis of the Twelfth Century*, p. 43. Bisson notes that medieval forms of 'power ... drew on a cluster of familiar ideas, a field of moral discourses derived from the biblical-patristic inheritance' (p. 10).

58 For the influence of the *Vetus Latina* (Old Latin bible) on *Genesis A*, see Paul G. Remley, *Old English Biblical Verse: Studies in Genesis, Exodus and Daniel*, CSASE 16 (Cambridge: Cambridge University Press, 1996).

59 Augustine's *De Genesi ad Litteram* was important for hexameral interpretation; see Frank Egleston Robbins, *Hexaemeral Literature: A Study of the Greek and Latin Commentaries on Genesis* (Chicago: University of Chicago Press, 1912) Huppé (*Doctrine and Poetry*, pp. 132–4). Johnson has explored the influence of hexameral traditions on *Genesis A* alongside the 'Origenist tradition' ('The Fall of Lucifer in *Genesis A*', pp. 500–21 at p. 512).

60 Michael J. B. Allen and Daniel Calder, *Sources and Analogues of Old English Poetry: The Major Latin Texts in Translation* (Cambridge: D. S. Brewer, 1976), p. 2.

61 Ibid., p. 3.

62 A. N. Doane, *Genesis A: A New Edition, Revised*, Medieval and Renaissance Texts and Studies 435 (Tempe: ACMRS, 2013), p. 227.

63 Evans, '*Genesis B* and Its Background', p. 1.

64 Bennett A. Brockman, '"Heroic" and "Christian" in *Genesis A*: The Evidence of the Cain and Abel Episode', *Modern Language Quarterly*,

35 (1974), 115–28; Nina Boyd, 'Doctrine and Criticism: A Revaluation of "Genesis A"', *NM*, 83 (1982), 230–8.
65 Thomas D. Hill, 'The "Variegated Obit" as an Historiographic Motif in Old English Poetry and Anglo-Latin Historical Literature', *Traditio*, 44 (1988), 101–24 (p. 101).
66 J. R. Hall, 'The Old English Epic of Redemption: The Theological Unity of MS Junius 11', *Traditio*, 32 (1976), 185–208; reprinted in *MS Junius 11: Basic Readings*, ed. R. M. Liuzza (New York and London: Routledge, 2002), pp. 20–52; See also J. R. Hall, '"The Old English Epic of Redemption": Twenty-Five-Year Retrospective', in *MS Junius 11: Basic Readings*, ed. R. M. Liuzza, Basic Readings in Anglo-Saxon England 8 (New York and London: Routledge, 2002), pp. 53–68.
67 Charles D. Wright, '*Genesis A* ad Litteram', in *Old English Literature and the Old Testament*, ed. Michael Fox and Manish Sharma (Toronto: University of Toronto Press, 2012), pp. 121–71 (p. 127).
68 Ibid., p. 123.
69 Doane, *Genesis A, Revised*, p. 227.
70 The relevant *oð ðæt* passage reads 'until one began to do evil, a fiend from hell' (ll. 100b–1). The *Beowulf* poet also incorporates an *oðþæt* transition during Hrothgar's sermon (ll. 1735–41a), which describes how the thoughts of man are focused on the joys in life 'until within him an enormous pride grows thrives and flourishes' (ll. 1740–1a). On this patterning, see Edward B. Irving Jr., *A Reading of Beowulf* (New Haven: Yale University Press, 1968), pp. 31–42.
71 Wright notes that poets emphasise earth's 'broadness' and heaven's 'brightness' ('An Old English Formulaic System', pp. 171–2).
72 *DOE, agan*, sense 1a and 2a.
73 *DOE, agan*, sense 1a and 3a.
74 *DOE, agan*, sense 1a, 5e, and 5f.
75 Milton McCormick Gatch, *Loyalties and Traditions: Man and his World in Old English Literature* (New York: Pegasus, 1971), p. 144.
76 Doane, *Genesis A, Revised*, p. 40. Concerning loyalty derived from the Germanic *comitatus* code, see Peter J. Lucas, 'Loyalty and Obedience in the Old English *Genesis* and the Interpolation of *Genesis B* into *Genesis A*', *Neophil*, 76 (1992), 121–35 especially at pp. 121–2. The concept of *comitatus* derives from the writings of Tacitus, who describes a thane's obligation 'to defend and protect [the chief]'. Text from Tacitus, *Germania* (ch. 14, § I), from *Germania*, trans. M. Hutton, Loeb Library 35 (London: Loeb Classical Library, 1970).
77 The Old Norse cognates *sjálf-ráð* ('self-counsel' or 'one's own accord') and *sjalf-ræði* ('self-rule') denote the capacity for independent action and free will; see *An Icelandic-English Dictionary*, ed. Richard Cleasby and Gudbrand Vigfusson (Oxford: Clarendon Press, 1975).

78 Smith notes that *unræd* occasionally takes on the added valence of 'treachery' when associated with the take-over of space ('Faith and Forfeiture', p. 601).
79 This phrase also occurs in *Genesis A* (l. 1446). On the 'reversal of expectations' formula in Old English, see Charles D. Wright, 'More Old English Poetry in Vercelli Homily XXI', in *Early Medieval English Texts and Interpretations: Studies Presented to Donald G. Scragg*, ed. Elaine Treharne and Susan Rosser (Tempe: ACMRS, 2002), pp. 245–62.
80 See Constance B. Hieatt, 'Divisions: Theme and Structure of *Genesis A*', *NM*, 81 (1980), 243–51 especially at p. 243.
81 *DOE, gyld*, sense 1b, 'recompense, return reward'; sense 2b, 'replacement, exchange'; sense C.1a, 'sacrifice, offering'. The term is used six times in *Genesis A* in reference to Abel's favoured 'offering' (l. 977), the birth of Seth as 'compensation' to Adam and Eve (ll. 1109a and 1104b), Noah's 'offering' to God (ll. 1501a and 1506a), and Abraham's 'offering' following the covenant (l. 2843b).
82 *DOE, gyld*, sense 3a.
83 Liebermann, *Gesetze*, 36.1.
84 *DOE, gyld*, sense 3a.
85 *DOE, gyld*, sense C.1a.
86 Magennis, *Images of Community*, pp. 15–16. The law reads, 'that secular lords might with their permission receive without sin compensation in money for almost every misdeed at the first offence, which compensation they then fixed; only for treachery to a lord they dared not declare any mercy, because Almighty God adjudged none for those who scorned him' (Liebermann, *Gesetze*, 49.7; translation from Whitelock, *English Historical Documents*, p. 408).
87 John M. Hill, *The Cultural World in Beowulf* (Toronto: University of Toronto Press, 1995), p. 17.
88 Smith, *Land and Book*, p. 213.
89 On this theme, see Lucas, 'Loyalty and Obedience', pp. 121–35.
90 The migration myth has also been examined by Paul Battles, '*Genesis A* and the Anglo-Saxon Migration Myth', *ASE*, 29 (2000), 43–66.
91 Howe, *Writing the Map*, p. 59.
92 Early editions of charters were prepared by J. M. Kemble, *Codex Diplomaticus Aevi Saxonici* (London: Sumptibus Societatis, 1839–48) and *Cartularium Saxonicum: A Collection of Charters Relating to Anglo-Saxon History*, ed. Walter de Gray Birch (London: Whiting & Company, 1885–99). All charters are sited by number as they appear in P. H. Sawyer, *Anglo-Saxon Charters: An Annotated List and Bibliography*, Royal Historical Guides and Handbooks 8 (London: Roman and Littlefield Publishers, 1968). An electronic version of Sawyer is available at http://www.esawyer.org.uk. On 'forfeiture' more specifically, see Andrew Reynolds, *Later Anglo-Saxon England:*

Life and Landscape (Stroud: Tempus, 1999), pp. 123–34 and Ann Williams on 'land tenure', *The Blackwell Encyclopedia of Anglo-Saxon England*, pp. 277–8.
93 Michelet, *Creation, Migration, and Conquest*, p. 5.
94 Relevant forfeiture laws include: Alfred 4 and 4.2, V Æthelred 28, and II Cnut 13.1 and 77 (Liebermann, *Gesetze*, 50, 244, 316, and 364). See also II Edmund 1.3 and 6 and Hundred Ordinance 3.1 (Liebermann, *Gesetze*, 118 and 192). See also Simon Keynes, *The Diplomas of King Æthelred 'The Unready' 978–1016: A study in Their Use as Historical Evidence*, Cambridge Studies in Medieval Life & Thought 13 (Cambridge: Cambridge University Press, 1980; repr. 2005). In addition to S 362, Keynes notes the prevalence of 'forfeiture' transactions from 995–1015 in S 883, S 886, S 877, S 896, S 926, S 927, S 934; further forfeitures from Æthelred's reign include S 842, S 892, S 901, S 923, S 869, S 893, S 911, S 916, S 918, S 937 (p. 97); for after Æthelred, see II Cnut 13 and 77 (Liebermann, *Gesetze*, 316 and 364).
95 Smith, 'Faith and Forfeiture', p. 596.
96 Ibid., p. 606.
97 Ibid., p. 594.
98 These charters open with a catechetical *narratio* (Keynes, *Diplomas of Æthelred*, p. 100); he describes those modelled on S 880 as forgeries (p. 32 n. 53, p. 100 n. 51).
99 Hart, *The Early Charters of Northern England*, p. 191. See also Eric John, 'The Sources of the English Monastic Reformation: A Comment', *Revue Bénédictine*, 70 (1960), 197– 203.
100 *Voraginis* commonly glosses *swelgend* ('a very deep place, an abyss, a gulf, whirlpool'). See Bosworth-Toller, *swelgend*, sense 1.
101 Hart, *The Early Charters of Northern England*, p. 187.
102 The most compelling study of this diploma has been made by Johnson, 'Winchester Revisited', forthcoming; I have drawn on his translation of this passage.
103 *De uirginitate*, ed. Scott Gwara, *Aldhelmi Malmesbiriensis prosa de uirginitate cum glosa Latina atque anglosaxonixa*, CCSL 124A (Turnhout: Brepols, 2001). Translation from *Aldhelm: The Prose Works*, ed. and trans. Michael Lapidge and Michael Herren (Suffolk: D. S. Brewer, 1979), p. 67.
104 For more on the king's titles, see Smith, *Land and Book*, n. 103 and Keynes, *Diplomas of Æthelred*, p. 69 (n. 135) and p. 66 (n. 124).
105 Smith, 'Faith and Forfeiture', pp. 606–8.
106 F. M. Stenton, *The Latin Charters of the Anglo-Saxon Period* (Oxford: Clarendon Press, 1955), pp. 79–80.
107 Smith, 'Faith and Forfeiture', p. 606.
108 Smith notes that *ar* typically signifies 'favour, honour, grace', but he also proposes, 'landed property' ('Faith and Forfeiture', p. 595).

109 Eric John, *Land Tenure in Early England* (Leicester: Leicester University Press, 1964), 51–3; see also Smith, *Land and Book*, p. 8ff.
110 Keynes, *The Diplomas of King Æthelred*, p. 31.
111 Ibid., p. 31. For bookland in military contexts, see Abels, *Lordship and Military Obligation*, pp. 43–57.
112 Florence of Worcester, *Chronicon: Florentii Wigorniensis monahi Chronicon ex Chronicis*, ed. Benjamin Thorpe (London: Kraus 1848–9), p. 158
113 Keynes, *The Diplomas of King Æthelred*, p. 211.
114 Ælfric, *Angelsächsische Homilien und Heiligenleben*, ed. Bruno Assmann, Bibliothek der Angelsächsischen Prosa 3 (Kassel: Wigand, 1889); repr. Peter Clemoes (Darmstadt: Wissenschaftliche Buchgesellschaft, 1964), 2.31ff.
115 *DOE, asyndrian*, sense 1a.
116 Keynes, *The Diplomas of King Æthelred*, p. 39.
117 Doane notes that *idel* and *unnyt* frequently glosses *inanis et vacua* (*Genesis A, Revised*, p. 367). The formula also appears in Cotton Faustina A.IX for the Fifth Sunday after Epiphany (l. 80), Napier Homily 40 for Tuesday in Rogationtide (l. 207), Vercelli Homily 10 (l. 175), and Vercelli Homily 18 (l. 185), *King Alfred's West-Saxon Version of Gregory's Pastoral Care*, Gregory the Great's *Dialogues*, the Old English Version of Bede's *Historia ecclesiastica* (6.400.3), a feudal document (*c.* 1081) describing fallow land, and in the Psalms from the Lambeth Psalter (30.7, glossing *supervacue*) and (126.2, glossing *vanum*).
118 *The Old English Version of the Heptateuch, Ælfric's Treatise on the Old and New Testament and his Preface to Genesis*, ed. Samuel J. Crawford, EETS os 160 (London: Millford, 1922; repr. Oxford: Oxford University Press, 1969).
119 Bosworth-Toller, *idel*, sense 1.
120 Bosworth-Toller, *unnyt*, sense 1.
121 Michelet, *Creation, Migration, and Conquest*, p. 47.
122 Magennis suggests 'uselessness' indicates 'divine antipathy' to such a condition (*Images of Community*, p. 150).
123 *Klaeber's Beowulf and the Fight at Finnsburg*, eds. R. D. Fulk, Robert E. Bjork, John D. Niles (4th ed. Toronto: University of Toronto Press, 2008).
124 Jennifer Neville, *Representations of the Natural World in Old English Poetry*, CSASE 27 (Cambridge: Cambridge University Press, 1999), p. 30.
125 See Alvin A. Lee, *The Guest-Hall of Eden: Four Essays on the Design of Old English Poetry* (New Haven: Yale University Press, 1972).
126 Edward Condren, '"Unnyt" Gold in "Beowulf" 3168', *PQ*, 52 (1973), 296–9.
127 *Regularis Concordia: The Monastic Agreement of the Monks and Nuns*

of the English Nation, ed. and trans. Dom Thomas Symons (London: Thomas Nelson and Sons, 1953), pp. 1–2.
128 Initially, Guthlac's *beorg* is described as *idel one æmen* (l. 216).
129 Donald Scragg asserts single authorship. See *The Vercelli Homilies and Related Texts*, EETS os 300, ed. D. G. Scragg (Oxford: Oxford University Press, 1992), pp. 191–5. For more on this homily's rhetorical embellishments, see Samantha Zacher, *Preaching the Converted: The Style and Rhetoric of the Vercelli Book Homilies* (Toronto: University of Toronto Press, 2009) pp. 106–39.
130 This includes material from Book II of Isidore of Seville's *Synonyma* (PL 83, 865); see Claudia Di Sciacca, *Finding the Right Words: Isidore's Synonyma in Anglo-Saxon England* (Toronto: University of Toronto Press, 2008).
131 Zacher, *Preaching the Converted*, pp. 112–13.
132 Smith revealed the important theme of *bocland* and its connection to the 'frumgewrit' (glorious charter) of Judgement Day (*Land and Book*, p. 137).
133 *The Vercelli Homilies*, ed. Scragg, 206.170–6. References to Vercelli homilies are by page number and line numbers.
134 Smith, *Land and Book*, p. 144; *The Vercelli Homilies*, ed. Scragg, 206.
135 Ibid., p. 135.
136 Ibid., p. 141.
137 Wright has argued that Vercelli Homilies 11–13 constitute a 'bitter complaint about the Benedictine Reform from the perspective of a secular cleric' (p. 224). See Wright, 'Vercelli Homilies XI–XIII and the Anglo-Saxon Benedictine Reform: Tailored Sources and Implied Audiences', in *Preacher, Sermon and Audience in the Middle Ages*, ed. Carolyn Muessig (Leiden: Brill, 2002), pp. 203–27.
138 *Anglo-Saxon Charters*, ed. Robertson, pp. 22–3.
139 See Petra Hofmann's study, 'Infernal Imagery in Anglo-Saxon Charters', PhD dissertation, University of St Andrews, 2008 (p. 17).
140 Michelet, *Creation, Migration, and Conquest*, p. 47.
141 Anthony D. Smith, *The Ethnic Origins of Nations* (Oxford: Blackwell, 1986), pp. 28–9; Michelet, *Creation, Migration, and Conquest*, p. 2.
142 Michelet, *Creation, Migration, and Conquest*, p. 38.
143 Ibid., p. 21.
144 Kathleen Davis, 'Boredom, Brevity and Last Things: Ælfric's Style and the Politics of Time', in *A Companion to Ælfric*, ed. Hugh Magennis and Mary Swan (Leiden: Brill, 2009), pp. 321–44. See also, *The Old English Heptateuch and Ælfric's Libellus de Vetri Testamento Novo*, ed. Richard Marsden, EETS os 330 (Oxford: Oxford University Press, 2008), p. 201.
145 For more on the 'interim paradise', see Ananya Jahanara Kabir, *Paradise, Death, and Doomsday in Anglo-Saxon Literature*, CSASE 32 (Cambridge: Cambridge University Press, 2001).

146 *King Alfred's Version of St. Augustine's Soliloquies*, ed. Thomas A. Carnicelli (Cambridge, MA: Harvard University Press, 1969), p. 48. Translation draws upon *Asser's Life of King Alfred and Other Contemporary Sources*, trans. Simon Keynes and Michael Lapidge (London: Penguin, 1983) with some modifications, p. 139.

147 Alfred's 'overwhelming concern with becoming *inutilis* (useless)' has been recently discussed by Stephanie Clark, *Compelling God: Theories of Prayer in Anglo-Saxon England* (Toronto: University of Toronto Press, 2018), p. 205.

2
The anxiety of inheritance

While the close of Alfred's Preface to the *Soliloquies* champions usefulness and action amid the 'lænena stoclife' (temporary habitations) of earth, its opening offers a concrete image of how one can structure a life surrounded by the wisdom found in books such as Augustine's *Soliloquiae*. The first-person narrator likens the quest for wisdom to the careful construction of a dwelling place, built up with wood gathered from a forest replete with knowledge:

> Gaderode me þonne kigclas and stuþansceaftas, and lohsceaftas and hylfas to ælcum þara tola þe ic mid wircan cuðe, and bohtimbru and bolttimbru, and, to ælcum þara weorca þe ic wyrcan cuðe, þa wlitegostan treowo be þam dele ðe ic aberan meihte. ne com ic naþer mid anre byrðene ham þe me ne lyste ealne þane wude ham brengan, gif ic hyne ealne aberan meihte; on ælcum treowa ic geseah hwæthwugu þæs þe ic æt ham beþorfte. Forþam ic lære ælcne ðara þe maga si and manigne wæne hæbbe, þæt he menige to þam ilcan wuda þar ic ðas stuðansceaftas cearf, fetige hym þar ma, and gefeðrige hys wænas mid fegrum gerdum, þat he mage windan manigne smicerne wah, and manig ænlic hus settan, and fegerne tun timbrian, and þær murge and softe mid mæge on-eardian ægðer ge wintras ge sumeras, swa swa ic nu ne gyt ne dyde.[1]

[I then gathered for myself posts and props, and tie-shafts and handles for each of the tools with which I knew how to work, and curved timber and straight timber, and, for each of the structures which I knew how to build, the finest timbers I could carry; I never came away with a single bundle without wishing to bring home the whole of the forest, if I could have carried it all; in every tree I saw something for which I had a need at home. Therefore, I would advise everyone who is strong and has many wagons, that he might direct his steps to that same forest where I cut props, and to fetch more for himself, and to load his wagons with fair branches, so that he may weave many elegant walls, and set up many splendid houses, and so construct a fine dwelling, and there may live pleasantly and quietly both in winter and summer, just as I have not yet done!]²

The speaker describes a judicious selection of timbers – *bohtimbru, bolttimbru, byrðene, wlitegostan treowo* – and expresses his wish to bring home the whole forest. The posts, props, and beams of our speaker's home are none other than the words of Augustine, Gregory, and Jerome, words that he believes will help him attain an eternal home. With their inherited wisdom, he can 'fegerne tun timbrian' (construct a fine dwelling). Recent work by Nicole Guenther Discenza speaks to the Anglo-Saxon impulse to create meaning through their habitations. She observes that 'Anglo-Saxons did not simply exist in ready-made spaces and places but constructed the places around them mentally and often materially. To make places is to make sense of the world around one and take ownership of it'.³

While on one level, the wood-gathering metaphor captures the speaker's desire to collect texts and extract their data for meaning, on another level it may also reference Alfred's strategic recruitment of a scholarly circle of *luminaria* to help in revitalising learning in England (a process Asser famously describes in the *Vita Alfredi*).⁴ The fine dwelling place, in this sense, parallels the restructuring of Alfred's court with men from various Anglo-Saxon regions such as Werferth (Worcester), Plegmund (Canterbury), Æthelstan and Werwulf (both from Mercia). Alfred's 'laudabilis' (praiseworthy) thirst for knowledge – which Asser characterises as 'regalis avaritia' (royal greed) – also led him to summon Continental scholars such as Grimbald and John the Saxon before calling up Asser himself from 'ultimis Britanniae finibus' (the furthest bounds of Britain). This community of scholars would help transform England from a place that was once *idel ond unnyt* into a dynamic hub for learning.

No definitive source has been located for this passage from the Preface.⁵ Indeed, its influence on the Old English corpus may be more far reaching than scholars have hitherto acknowledged. Alfred's building metaphor speaks to the wider Anglo-Saxon political and social theme, suggesting that Christians should attend to edifying both lands and the self in anticipation of a spiritual inheritance. As I argued in Chapter 1, Anglo-Saxons were distinctly aware of their earthly spaces – lands, hamlets, holy houses, and halls – as metaphors for the heavenly spaces they sought to inhabit. Nicholas Howe observes that the 'dwellings of Anglo-Saxons may have been built of impermanent materials, but they were marked by a historical sense of place that reached beyond the immediate and familiar experience of home'.[6] The imagery in the Preface also raises some vital questions: how can one distinguish between the finest of timbers and the faulty ones? Can one fashion a dangerous edifice around oneself, or edify the self in destructive ways? If the metaphor partially refers to Alfred's rejuvenated court defined by its elegant and learned counsel, might another king (a tyrant perhaps) construct an echo chamber of evil and become housed in by *unræd* ('ill-counsel') and treachery? *Genesis B* opens with Satan's desire to construct such a home, not with the power and wisdom of others, but with his 'anes cræft' (own craft).[7] Furthermore, as David Pratt has remarked upon, a prominent theme in both the *Soliloquies* and the *Boethius* is the relationship between a lord and his nobles, who are expected to share reciprocal obligations and loyalty towards one another.[8] Satan's aspirations to build a rival kingdom directly violate the bonds of loyalty he should share with God:

> þuhte him sylfum
> þæt he mægyn and cræft   maran hæfde
> þonne se halga god   habban mihte
> folcgestælna.   feala worda gespæc
> se engel ofermodes.   þohte þurh his anes cræft
> hu he him strenglicran   stol geworhte,
> heahran on heofonum.   cwæð þæt hine his hige speonne
> þæt he west and norð   wyrcean ongunne,
> trymede getimbro.   cwæð him tweo þuhte
> þæt he gode wolde   geongra weorðan. (ll. 268b–77)

[It seemed to him that he himself had greater strength and skill, might have more soldiers than holy God. The angel of arrogance spoke many words. He conceived of how through his own power he might create a stronger throne for himself, higher in the heavens. He said that his heart urged him to begin to build west and north, build up a foundation. He said that it seemed doubtful to him that he would continue to be a subject for God.]

The poet tells us that Satan wished that he 'trymede getimbro' (build up a foundation) in the northwest region of heaven.[9] Unlike the metaphorical *tun* constructed by the speaker in the Preface, Satan's desired home is to be buttressed with malice, enmity, and the desire to supersede his lord. Terms for construction (*geworhte, wyrcean,* and *trymede*) abound. The verb *trymman* can refer to both material objects ('to construct strongly') as well as mental or moral strength ('to confirm, establish, give strength to').[10] Just as the speaker in the Preface seeks to craft something that is both material and mental, Satan desires to construct an adversarial throne through his own mental and material means, which he views as superior to God's. Moreover, Satan claims that he can recruit legions of 'folcgestælna' (soldiers) far outnumbering God's loyal angels, a direct challenge to the heavenly court of his sovereign.[11]

Satan's desire to build a home rivalling God's inverts the imagery of edifying wood-gathering seen in the Preface's opening metaphor. His wish to build is a breach of his social, spatial, and spiritual limits as he seeks to surpass divine jurisdiction. His inverse gathering lacks knowledge and wisdom, especially considering the powerful intellect he inherited from God; it is wholly antithetical to the insight the speaker hopes to surround himself with in the Preface. He yearns to establish a *getimbro* (from *getimbru*, 'edifice, building, structure').[12] As Howe notes, 'the usual verb ... for "to construct" or "to erect" was *getimbrian*, literally, "to timber"',[13] which was often used with reference to building transcendent holy sites such as churches, minsters, and temples as well as heavenly or infernal dwellings. In contrast to the spiritual 'timbering' of the Preface, rebellious 'timbering' can also be seen in Vercelli Homily 19 as Lucifer similarly begins to *getimbrian* his kingdom in the *norðdæle* of heaven (ll. 19–20). With these ideas, both the *Genesis B* poet and Vercelli homilist echo and invert the timber terms found in the *Soliloquies*. That Satan desires to timber a stronghold in heaven is telling, as is a moment towards the end of *Genesis B* when the demonic messenger announces in a fit of glee that he will inherit the 'heofonrice heahgetimbro' (high-timbers of the heavenly kingdom, l. 739) after Adam eats the fruit.

Although the sin of pride is, of course, a fixture in narratives about the angelic rebellion (and while the *Genesis B* poet identifies Satan's deficiency as *ofermod*, a word both much discussed and infamous in the Old English poetic corpus),[14] Satan's violation in *Genesis B* is not adequately explained simply as a reflex of the patristic 'doctrine of sin',[15] or even as 'a drama driven by psychological realism'.[16] Insular authors invite audiences to see more at work in their dramatic retellings of angelic treachery. This chapter will argue that *Genesis B* as well as other Anglo-Saxon and Irish retellings of Satan's fall have important political implications, encoding cultural anxieties about power, socio-political status, inheritance, and disinheritance. Amplifying Isaiah 14:12–15, the poet of *Genesis B* reveals these tensions by affording Satan approximately 132 lines of direct speech, inviting his audience to hear the voice of the rebellious subject. The poet of *Genesis B* imagines Satan's crime as a failure to accept sovereign checks on his power and limits upon his territorial ambitions. Fuelled by the idea that he should be entitled to a 'strenglicran stol' (stronger throne), the poet imagines Satan's revolt as a grab for regional hegemony. The latter stages of the poem likewise reveal Satan's continued pursuit of space and territory as he operates a rival kingdom in hell and laments the fact that Adam and Eve will claim and settle his forfeited habitations in heaven – their own 'rice mid rihte' (kingdom through right, l. 424a) – with *rihte* denoting a clear legal and tenurial privilege. The poet also patterns Eve's fall after Satan's when her tempter invites her to see beyond the limits of 'monnes geþeaht' (human intellect) into the territory of heaven, making *Genesis B* a powerful comment upon the boundaries of proper Anglo-Saxon Christian subjectivity.[17]

Themes of territorial competition, expansion, and inheritance manifest themselves in various Insular traditions concerning the fall of the angels. Irish vernacular adaptations make for an instructive comparison with those in Old English, because the Irish interpreted the narrative in relation to culturally specific social and legal customs, and also because the Irish drew directly on a particular apocryphal source, the *Vita Adae et Evae* ('The Life of Adam and Eve'), which seems to have had limited influence at best in Anglo-Saxon England. In Irish accounts such as *Saltair na Rann* ('Psalter of the Quatrains') and *Lebor Gabála Érenn* ('Book of the Taking of Ireland'), Satan views humankind as rival-inheritors of lands to which he feels entitled. Neither of these accounts has received much scholarly attention. In these narratives Lucifer upsets clearly defined spatial and social limits. He rebels not simply in opposition to the exaltation of Adam, but in response to the division of wealth and the parcelling out of authority and property. In *Saltair na Rann* a conflict arises between Adam and Lucifer over the issue of seniority, a controversial social and political topic in medieval Ireland, as Patrick Wormald, Bart Jaski, and Katherine Simms have all shown.[18] Lucifer maintains that since he is *siniu* ('older') it would be insulting for him to submit to his *sósur* ('junior'), Adam. As I will demonstrate, Lucifer believes he possesses greater *febas*, that subtle concoction of positive qualities frequently evoked in Irish succession disputes, denoting one's 'splendour, glory, fame'.[19]

Lebor Gabála similarly sets up Lucifer's revolt as a response to Adam's territorial inheritance of earth using terminology associated with landed jurisdiction. The author stresses the idea of 'governance' by referencing the title of *airchindeacht* (a variant of *airchinnech*), a term widely attested from the seventh to the twelfth centuries which referred to a 'head, leader, superior', often connected to both ecclesiastical leadership and the supervision of land in medieval Ireland, especially for an 'administrator (of ecclesiastical land, monastic estates').[20] God's divine judgement in *Lebor Gabála* is thus a repeal of Lucifer's governance of his formerly gifted territories. In this way, Irish authors adapt apocryphal traditions to underwrite socio-political ideology, dramatising rivalries over inheritance and claims to lordship that would have been all too common in medieval Ireland. These traditions reveal Lucifer's misapprehension of divine sovereignty by underscoring his deficient *febas*. Ultimately, in adapting the *Vita Adae* to accommodate vernacular concepts related to power and succession, medieval Irish authors constructed an apocryphal narrative framework for contemporary cultural practices while also supplying a Christian origin story for their customary political disputes.

According to J. M. Evans, the fact that the bible only obliquely alludes to the story of the fall of the angels may account for the 'problems and peculiarities of *Genesis B*'.[21] He suggests that the poem may owe more to esoteric and apocryphal texts such as 2 Enoch and *The Gospel of Nicodemus*, as well as to less widely circulated works such as Bede's Commentary on the Epistle of Jude 6.[22] In this chapter I will trace some of these varying traditions. Whereas *Genesis A* connects the story of the angelic rebellion to the precarious status of unpopulated land, the texts I consider now reveal the narrative's inherent connection to territorial ambitions and the threat of disinheritance. *Genesis B* and the Irish comparanda under consideration here instructively reveal cultural assumptions about sovereignty and its manifestations as well as the wide variety of source traditions that circulated in the medieval Insular world.[23] In structuring their narratives about the fall of the angels, we see an amalgam of scriptural, apocryphal, and patristic inheritance at work, as authors carefully assembled their stories from various sources and traditions. In the case of *Genesis B*, we see a poet who gathers widely from a wood of disparate materials in order to assemble a complex and innovative narrative, one that builds a good deal of ambiguity into the heavenly dispute at the centre of this originary myth.

Sibling rivalries in early Irish apocryphal traditions

Various apocryphal elaborations purported to supply the story of the fall of the rebel angels so conspicuously missing from the Bible; the most influential of these was the widely disseminated *Vita Adae et Evae* (a text that was of interest to authors well into the fourteenth century, as evidenced by the Auchinleck MS).[24] In this account, Lucifer rebels only after the creation of Adam, when God commands that all heavenly creation worship the new being made in his own image. When the two meet during Adam's penitence in the Tigris river, Satan describes how he was cast out of heaven on the day Adam was made. He recalls how the archangel Michael called together all the orders of angels to worship Adam. Michael tells Lucifer to 'Adora imaginem dei' (Worship the image of the Lord). Lucifer curtly responds: 'Ego non adorabo Adam' (I will not worship Adam).[25] He then makes his complaint: 'Prior enim omnium factus sum. Antequam ipse fieret ego iam eram: ille me debet adorare, non ego illum' (For I was made first of all. Before he [Adam] was made, I already existed: he should worship me, not I him).[26] Two Middle Irish texts, the *Saltair na Rann* ('The Psalter of the Quatrains') and *Lebor Gabála Érenn* ('The Book of the Taking of Ireland' or 'The Book of Invasions'), contain versions of the fall of the rebel angels that draw on the *Vita Adae*.[27] In these Irish narratives, the creation of Adam precipitates the rebellion of Lucifer. Following a detailed angelology, the *Saltair na Rann* opens with God informing his head angel, Lucifer, that his first order of business as commander of archangels is to ensure the worship of Adam:

> Mo rí rígda ōs cach thur
> ro rāide fri Luciphur;
>   'bíait fót, feib do changen ngel,
>   airbri imdai archangel.
> Tabair úait airmitiu iar sreith
> do Ādom, dom chomdelbaid;
>   na noí ngrād coibli gléir glain
>   bíait foimti frit airitein. (ll. 833–40)

[My royal king above every host said to Lucifer: 'There shall be many bands of archangels under you by virtue of your bright claims. Give reverence accordingly to Adam, to the one shaped like me; the nine modest excellent pure orders will be in readiness to receive you'.]

It is possible that an Irish audience might understand this command via cultural assumptions surrounding *feb*. While seniority was viewed as important in Irish laws and literature, claims to *feb* or *febas* could override one's senior status. *Feb* typically carries the force of 'excellence, distinction, used of external condition, prosperity, appearance, and also to denote a high degree of a quality or state'.[28] According to Jaski, the legal term *feb* (or the rule of *febta la flaith*) 'can be translated as "dignity", "excellence", or "worth" in the immaterial sense, or as "wealth" or "property" in the material ... [a] person without sufficient *febas* [lacks] the qualification ... to fulfil his obligations towards those under his authority [making] him unsuitable for the lordship'.[29] In *Saltair na Rann*, God identifies Lucifer as superior to the other nine angelic orders and grants him special privileges owing to his noble qualities. Because of Lucifer's inherent *feb*, God gives him a higher rank while still wishing for him to view Adam as even more exceptional.

The phrase 'feib ... changen' is somewhat challenging to translate in this context. While the term *feib* is used adverbially by the poet here to mean 'in like manner' or 'according to',[30] which Greene and Kelly render as 'by virtue of your bright tasks', this translation does not adequately account for the noun 'changen' (claim, covenant, pact).[31] A more precise rendering of this sequence might read 'by the virtue of your bright claims', suggesting that Lucifer has been singled out for his exceptional qualities among the rest of angelic creation.[32] The poet earlier directly invokes this special form of *feb* in its primary nonadverbial sense amid a lengthy enumeration of angelic qualities:

> Dia febsai aidchi uimle,
> dia cennsai, dia ngnāthchuibdi,
> > dia caīndūthracht cen chaire,
> > dia ndeeirc, dia trōcaire. (ll. 721–4)

[Of their (the angelic host's) excellence, of their state of humility, of their mildness, of their customary propriety, of their fair diligence without fault, of their charity, of their mercy.]

Here, the phrase 'febsai' clearly refers to the 'excellence of the angelic hosts'. The subsequent phrase, however, is somewhat marred. Greene's unfinished typescript of the manuscript elides the phrase 'aidchi uimle' (obedient night) altogether because it makes little sense in this context. Alternatively, 'aidchi', could be emended to 'aicde', a reference to the perfect 'state of humility' performed by the angelic hosts.[33] Regardless of the contextual challenges, Irish readers would probably intuit the idea of *febas* in connection with the subsequent heavenly drama that plays out in this opening sequence. Lucifer, believing that he possesses greater dignity and status, refuses the command to worship Adam, proclaiming that he will not bow to anyone created after him. Instead, he expresses his desire for domination, boasting that he will become a *rí* ('king') served by angels and people alike:

'Airmitiu d'Ādam, nī chél,
ar im siniu, nī thibēr,
    ar bad airnel fiad cach thur
    dianam thairber fon sósur'.
Ro rāidi fris rí na rind,
a Fíadu fīrēn fīrfind:
    'nocot bía airmitiu glan
    úar nā tabrai rēir d'Ādam'.
Ro rāidi Lucifur lēir
a aithesc ndīumosach ndrochcēil:
    'bam rī rēil ōs cach caingin,
    fom-gnīfet ind ilaingil.
Betit ind angeil fom thrāig,
do-gén féin mo chomthocbāil,
    biam tigerna ōs cech drung,
    ni bía rí aile húasum'.
Lucifer co līn a grāid
ro tascair a chomthocbāil,
    ro tairinn a dīummus tind,
    do-rimmart dochum n-Iffirn. (ll. 841–60)

['I will not give reverence to Adam, I will not conceal it, since I am older, for it would be a snare, in the presence of every host, if I should submit myself to the junior.' The king of the heavenly bodies, his righteous truly pure Lord, said to him: 'you shall not have pure reverence, since you do not submit to Adam'. Earnest Lucifer said a vain speech with evil intent: 'I will be a bright king above every dispute, the many angels will serve me. The angels will be subdued by me, I will myself make my opposition, I will be a king over every people, there will be no other king above me.' His opposition overthrew Lucifer with all his order, it subdued his sore pride.]

The conflict arises from the issue of birthright. Lucifer maintains that since he is *siniu* it would be insulting for him to bow to his *sósur*. He asserts that Adam is both younger and inferior. Lucifer's perception that his seniority has been bypassed by God in favour of Adam might suggest that he expected to be recognised as next in line to rule the kingdom of heaven or some portion of it. In Ireland, competition among kinsmen over inheritance was common, with bitter disputes between brothers often turning on the relative claims of merit and seniority. This derived, in part, from the somewhat unusual practice wherein a king appointed a *tánaise* ('expected one' or 'heir designate', literally 'second in rank or dignity') who need not be eldest born.[34]

The early fifteenth-century Irish manuscript *Leabhar Breac* ('Speckled Book') also contains an account of the fall of Lucifer, which follows a similar trajectory to *Saltair na Rann*, wherein Lucifer will not pay homage to Adam. The text recalls Lucifer's announcement after learning that he must show deference to Adam with: 'I will be a king myself ... over many troops of angels and they will make submission to me and build my dwelling in the north-east of heaven, in a deep place and there shall not be another king over me'.[35] Bart Jaski observes that, in succession disputes, dignity and worth (*febas*) typically won out over seniority. Nevertheless, a status-tract in the legal compilation known as the *Senchas Már* upholds the value of seniority: 'Age is rewarded in Irish law, save that age is not disgraced ... it is he who is older who takes precedence'.[36] Lucifer may be appealing to such promulgations when he makes his opposition in heaven. By contrast, some legal maxims, such as the following from *Bretha Nemed*, tell a different tale: 'excellence is more venerable than age, and youth takes precedence over the dotage of old age'.[37] Lucifer's expectation that there would be an order of succession in heaven is ultimately at the heart of the problem, since it signals his fundamental misunderstanding of divine authority within the heavenly polity. Such conflicts of seniority are largely absent from Anglo-Saxon narratives, which adopt a different chronology wherein the creation of humankind takes places after the fall of the angels (to accommodate the doctrine of replacement).[38]

God's pronouncement does not go over well with the angel, who views his seniority as supreme. Despite his professed pre-eminence in this pseudo-sibling rivalry, the poem subtly reinforces the idea that Adam, while junior, enjoys a more blessed status within the socio-political structures of heaven. According to Irish custom, the junior party might vie for seniority and rights to succession by proving that they are of exemplary *febas*.[39] Occasionally, kingdoms could be managed cooperatively by *leth-rí* ('joint kings'),[40] which

The anxiety of inheritance

is perhaps the kind of scenario the poet imagines here. However, Lucifer reveals his deficient *febas* through his desire for overlordship. As Jaski puts it: 'When the unity within a dynasty broke down and internal rivalries flared up, an overkingdom could lose its cohesion and dissolve'.[41] God works to stave off this fragmentation and collapse in the narrative by deposing and banishing Lucifer.

Irish laws and customs ultimately reveal entitlements as flexible based upon both *febas* and one's *rígdamna* ('fitness to be king'), an idea that has affinities with *tánaise*. Jaski observes that '*rígdamna* [receive] a certain territory to rule as part of his position'.[42] The popular eleventh-century *Lebor Gabála Érenn* frames its fall of the angels narrative around a heavenly rivalry similar to the one seen in *Saltair na Rann* while also imagining the conflict as a property dispute over territorial claims. The second recension presents Lucifer and Adam as competitors owing to the division of realms for them to govern.

The text opens with a discussion of angelic and earthly creation followed by the struggle that breaks out in heaven. In *Lebor Gabála* §3 (17–9 and 26–7), Lucifer's revolt is stimulated by his 'pride and haughtiness' and is a response to the juridical boundaries of his kingdom and Adam's governance of earth:

> Dobert Día airc(h)indeacht Níme do Luicifiur, con nǽ ngrádaib aingel imbe. Dobert íarsain aircindecht talman do Adam ⁊ do Eua, cona chlainn. Ro immarbsaigestar Lucifuir for Nim ar úail ⁊ díumus fri Día, co ro hindarbadh i cinaigh in díumsa sin do Neimi, co triun slúaig aingeal laiss, in nIffrinn. Conid andsin asbert Día fri muintir Níme: 'Ro-díumsaich intí Lucsifiur:' *et dixit, 'uenite ut uideamus ⁊ confundamus consilium eius,* .i. táit co ro fégum ⁊ co ro melachtnaigium comairle indí Lucifiur'. Issí cét breath rucad ríam sin.

[God gave the leadership of Heaven to Lucifer, with nine orders of Angels about him. Thereafter He gave the leadership of Earth to Adam and to Eve with his progeny. Lucifer then made an assault upon Heaven, by reason of pride and haughtiness against God, so that he was expelled for that crime, out from Heaven, with a third of the host of angels in his company, into Hell. So that then God said unto the Folk of Heaven: 'Over-haughty is this Lucifer: come and let us see and put to shame the counsel of this Lucifer'. That is the first judgement which was ever pronounced.][43]

The author imagines the division of land between co-heirs, a common practice among nobility in medieval Ireland.[44] It makes sense that Irish versions of the fall would be more congenial to a story about apportioning wealth and governance owing to the system of partible inheritance that was commonly practised there. Lucifer upsets clearly defined limits set by God regarding his status or *airchindeacht* ('governance').[45] This term, which frequently glosses Latin *princeps* (a 'governor', 'nobleman', or even the 'head' of a religious house), has received a fair amount of critical attention.[46] Some scholars think of it in relation to the authority held by abbots who enjoyed the 'same status as a tribal king and similar duties'.[47] Jean-Michel Picard notes that a *princeps* would have 'the highest social responsibilities, with the charge of supervising the administration of the land, [and] legal and diplomatic functions'.[48] Early attitudes towards *principes* suggest that they were often seen as local noblemen. As Colmán Etchingham observes, in addition to being charged with the care and maintenance of land, in an ecclesiastical context an *airchinnech* would have had a role in enforcing judgements.[49] Furthermore, he notes that 'failure on the part of the *airchinnech* to provide for pastoral ministry invites loss of entitlement to compensation and authority'.[50]

The question of how individuals acquired this title (whether through merit or filiation) is a difficult one, but it is believed that they 'saw their powers in much the same light as secular powers'.[51] A popular seventh-century Hiberno-Latin text cataloging 'the twelve abuses' of wicked kings can perhaps tell us more. The sixth abuse, which later became a popular way of elaborating upon *unrædlic* ('ill-advised') counsel and leadership in Anglo-Saxon England, states that the unworthy *princeps* who does not fulfil his duties brings about 'social and economic ruin and, eventually, the loss of sovereignty'.[52] Mary Clayton observes that despite their powers of punishment and involvement in 'the administration of justice' the *principes* 'had to regard themselves and their power as entirely dependent on God'.[53] Read in this way, Lucifer's offence in *Lebor Gabála* is presumption and pride but, more pointedly, a failure to govern properly and see his authority as connected to God. God's divine judgement, then, is a repeal of Lucifer's authority to administer his own justice.

In addition to these literary examples of Irish narratives of the fall of the angels imagined as inheritance disputes, the precedent of the fall of both Lucifer and humankind permeated Irish contract law, as Damien Bracken has shown.[54] This is evidenced by the text of an Old Irish law from an eighth-century collection known as *Di Astud Chor* ('On the Securing of Contracts'). Item §13 states:

> The contract of a competent person is not released on account of reflecting with belated wisdom, if it be a competent person who acts. There has been fastened around Lucifer his ill-advised base disadvantageous contract for which he cannot discharge payment.[55]

Bracken's study suggests that scriptural exegesis was routinely consulted by Irish lawyers and clerics to resolve disputes pertaining to contractual exchanges. Much like the charters I discussed in Chapter 1, these practices bring the angelic fall down to earth, so to speak, directly linking the events with human action in the present. According to Bracken, in adopting this 'legalistic approach' to understanding the fall, the Irish viewed Lucifer's fall as 'irreversible'. His crime was accordingly cited 'in defence of the principle that contracts are indissoluble',[56] whereas the crime of Adam and Eve came to be characterised as one of *étged* ('negligence').[57] Since theirs was not the direct result of malicious intent, the fall of humankind was considered 'redeemable'. Janet Ericksen has convincingly argued that we see traces of Irish contractual discourse in *Genesis B* in the exchange between Adam and the devilish *boda* ('messenger'), with the fruit serving as a *tacen* ('token') or the sign of the contract.[58] Anglo-Saxons similarly code the fall of the angels as a legal clash (an act of lord-betrayal and oath-breaking) for which no compensation can be made, while also focusing on his actions as *unræd* ('ill-advised'). In Irish traditions, Adam also becomes heir-apparent when Satan loses his stature within the heavenly polity. A similar drama plays out in the Old English *Genesis B*.

Since medieval authors were undoubtedly scrupulous in their attention to the motivations, sequence of events, and consequences surrounding the fall, we should consider how Anglo-Saxon poets chose to structure and stylise their fall narratives.[59] Rather than depicting Satan's reaction against limits or prohibitions (as in the Irish examples explored here), Anglo-Saxon authors represent heaven as a place of unspecified limits and indeterminate boundaries before the fall (and paradise as a place with a single limitation). The poet of *Genesis B*, moreover, imagines Satan's assault on humankind as an attempt to cut off Adam and Eve from both their home in paradise and their promised heavenly inheritance. Furthermore, their sin is the direct result of the tempter's 'ill-counsel'. What Eve then perceives as appropriate and accurate wifely *ræd* ('counsel'), and a faithful discharge of obligations to her lord, is in fact a cruel recitation of the tempter's fictitious claims. The poet's rendering of the Genesis story in this way defines the human couple's crime as unpremeditated (*étged*) in the Irish legal variety.

In the section that follows, after providing a brief account of the interpolation of *Genesis B*, I will consider the poet's 'flashback' recounting of the fall of the rebel angels, which occurs at the precise moment when God utters his prohibition to Adam and Eve. At the point where the relationship between sovereign and human subject is defined, the narrative's abrupt return to the fall of the angels directly links them with human history and offers a space for understanding the mental operations of rebellion.

Territories and entitlements in *Genesis B*

Apocryphal texts circulated widely during the Middle Ages throughout both Ireland and England. The line between authoritative and apocryphal texts was often a blurry one. Joyce Hill notes that the distinction between apocryphal and canonical texts would have been 'fundamentally fluid', and that, to a certain extent, 'it did not matter at all'.[60] It is, in part, because of this fundamental fluidity that *Genesis B* presents a set of challenges for scholars interested in tracing the poet's sources. The works of Juvencus, Cyprianus Gallus, Caelius Sedulius, Arator, and Prudentius have all been put forward as likely influences for the fall of the angels in *Genesis B*. Daniel Calder and Michael Allen's *Sources and Analogues* postulates that Avitus of Vienne was the most plausible source, while cautioning that his work only contained nine lines devoted to the angelic rebellion, hardly accounting for the lengthy and vivid stylisation of events in *Genesis B*.[61] On the fall of Satan, Avitus's *Poematum De Mosaicae Historiae Gestis Libri Quinque* ('Five Books of Poetry on the Events in Moses' History') (PL 59, col. 331A–B) reads as follows:

> The enemy was once an angel, but then he became inflamed with his own evil and burned to attempt arrogant deed. Thinking he had made himself and was his own creator, as it were, he went mad in his fierce heart, denied his creator and said, 'I will acquire God's name and build an eternal throne above the sky like the most high, with my vast power I shall be a match for him'. While he thus boasted, the supreme power hurled him from heaven, and as he fell stripped him of his former honor.[62]

How and (perhaps more crucially) why did the *Genesis B* poet transform these compressed versions of the fall of the angels into over two hundred lines of Old English poetry when, one could argue, the story had already been sufficiently told in *Genesis A*? Further puzzling through sources which loosely relate to *Genesis B*, J. M. Evans and Rosemary Woolf both observe several conspicuous later episodes – the devil's subordinate and his angelic disguise, the failed temptation of Adam, his demand for a 'token', the tempter's encounter with Eve, her unusual vision (which I discuss further on), the final temptation, and the poet's ostensible exoneration of the couple – that have no close antecedents.[63]

Although coexisting in a single manuscript, *Genesis A* (ll. 1–234; 852–2936) and *Genesis B* (ll. 235–851) derive from disparate traditions.[64] In the late nineteenth century, Eduard Sievers first reported that the Old English *Genesis* contained a metrically and lexically unique section resembling the Old Saxon *Heliand*.[65] As Andrew Cole observes, 'Sievers named this material *Genesis B* as a means to distinguish it from the surrounding poetry, which he termed *Genesis A*'.[66] On philological grounds alone, Sievers concluded that *Genesis B* was derived from an Old Saxon original.[67] Remarkably, Sievers's hypothesis was later confirmed when Karl Zangemeister discovered several fragments of that postulated Old Saxon biblical *Genesis* at the Vatican Library.[68] Biblioteca Apostolica Vaticana, MS Palatinus Latinus 1447 contains 337 lines of verse, twenty-six lines of which are virtually identical to the Old English *Genesis B*.[69] This Old Saxon *Genesis* was probably composed on the Continent in about 850. The text then circulated within Carolingian scriptoria (extracts were eventually copied at Mainz in around 875) before finding its way to England in the second half of the ninth century, where it was to be transcribed into the West Saxon dialect sometime later.

The unconventional arrangement of Junius 11 raises some important questions about textual transmission in the early medieval world. Why was an Old Saxon text brought to England? Why was it translated into Old English, and who was it that merged the two rather different Old English Genesis narratives? Finally, why did an Anglo-Saxon compiler feel it necessary to include the story of the fall of the rebel angels once in *Genesis A* and then once more in *Genesis B*? Arguments addressing these questions were first put forth by Alois Brandl in 1908.[70] Both Robert Priebsch and C. L. Wrenn have suggested that the interpolation was made to aesthetically 'enhance' the *Genesis A* narrative, but the view that *Genesis B* was interpolated because it was of 'a much better quality than *Genesis A*' has been generally dismissed, particularly since Barbara

Raw's discovery that *Genesis B* had already been interpolated in the Junius 11 scribe's exemplar.[71] The joining of the two texts, as Renée R. Trilling points out '[is] quite likely due to the vicissitudes of textual transmission rather than to the plan of a knowing author'.[72] Any aesthetic motivations aside, questions remain concerning the circumstances of this interpolative repair, which was likely meant to make up for the loss of some of *Genesis A*'s pages.

And yet there remains the curious fact that the story of the fall of the angels is a twice-told tale and that, in its second telling, it is the product of a narrative digression or flashback. While the dates of composition of both *Genesis A* and *Genesis B* remain unknown, Leslie Lockett's recent comprehensive redating of Junius 11 to the period around 960–90 means that the production of the manuscript probably coincided with the early days of the Benedictine Reform (*c.* 964–84), a historical moment that saw a revived interest in the narrative of the fall of the rebel angels as well as a reimagination of the idea of kingship in Anglo-Saxon England under the aegis of King Edgar.[73] As I will discuss in the next chapter, appealing to God's expulsion of the angels as his precedent, Edgar revoked lands and privileges of clerics who were themselves cast as 'rebels' driven only by desires and appetites that opposed the will of God.[74] In a period that saw a revitalised commitment to conforming to rules in priestly, monastic, and lay circles, Anglo-Saxon authors would have found the story of the angelic fall a compelling precedent for the sanctioning of the disobedient and rebellious.

While Lockett's redating helpfully reveals information about the extant manuscript, it is still difficult to date the composition of the individual poems with much precision. Even though *Genesis B* was likely influenced by miscellaneous sources, its mysterious inclusion serves as an important reminder that the manuscript as we know it was part of a series of various iterations. At some point in its mysterious history, *Genesis B* was deliberately integrated with the narrative of *Genesis A*. This fusion probably happened at some point in the ninth century, quite possibly during the reign of Alfred, whose genealogical interest in the Old Testament is well documented.[75] Was *Genesis B* embedded simply to patch up the missing portion of *Genesis A*? In what other ways might this unconventional narrative have appealed to the translators, poets, or copyists who found themselves with an incomplete version of the Genesis story? Biblical stories and apocryphal extra-biblical material like the story of the fall of the angels – whether they originated in Hebrew, Greek, or Slavonic – presented just one way for broader ideas to find a residence in England. Not content with being cut off, Anglo-Saxon authors sought to incorporate information from a wider global network of ideas. The embeddedness of *Genesis B* gives us evidence of a moment in the evolution of a manuscript, when something from the wider world was deliberately stitched into a now lost codex, in part, to amplify the story of the angelic rebellion.

The curious qualities of *Genesis B* and the possibility that the poem could have been influenced by Irish texts have caught the attention of scholars such as Doane and Ericksen, who note that it was perhaps better poised than *Genesis A* to intercept these lines of transmission. According to Michael Fox and Manish Sharma, it is no longer controversial to argue that *Genesis B* bears 'some relationship to exotic apocryphal and exegetical works on the fall, perhaps associated with a Continental centre that was a destination for Anglo-Saxon and Irish missionary activity'.[76] But who was it that merged the two rather different Old English Genesis narratives together? I suspect that the poet of *Genesis B* as well as the compiler who joined the two texts together were concerned with the social questions of loyalty, obligation, and (dis)inheritance that both Genesis poems share. Moreover, both Old English Genesis poems reveal a sustained interest in the question of material and mental spaces and the shaping of the human intellect, one's *mod* or *hige* 'mind, heart, spirit'.

In addition to the shared thematic interests, the two biblical poems are similar in terms of generic conventions and style. Biblical stories offered an account of origins, peoples, and the territories they inhabited. Charles D. Wright sees affinities between texts like *Genesis A* and *Lebor Gabála*, which both blend 'biblical narrative with pseudo-historical information drawn both from patristic and apocryphal sources'.[77] Máire Ní Mhaonaigh similarly observes that 'the bible [was] a major source of inspiration ... [providing] a framework for [a people's] own recorded history'.[78] Drawing upon the work of Paul Battles, Wright suggests that the writing of biblical poetry was a historiographical enterprise because adaptations allowed authors to view their own story as part of a 'historic continuum'.[79] Wright's study focuses on *Genesis A*, but the author of *Genesis B* probably pursued many of these same goals.

The retrospective account of the fall of the angels in *Genesis B* only adds to the list of items that scholars find bewildering. Thomas D. Hill trenchantly flags *Genesis B* as one of the 'most puzzling poems in the corpus of Old English poetry'.[80] While the poet's adaptation of the fall of angels has been overshadowed by critical interest in his vivid representation of the temptation and fall of Adam and Eve, attempts to understand the drastic analepsis recalling the angelic insurrection in this opening sequence have resulted in several perceptive re-evaluations of this unusual narrative juncture. In considering the role of authority and aesthetic mediation in biblical poetry, Trilling concedes that the poet's recapitulation of the creation of the angels is 'disruptive', as it introduces a 'simultaneity of narrative'.[81] Trilling's argument that the fall of the angels and humankind share a 'narrative space' is convincing, as are her observations regarding the relationships between this passage and Augustine's exegetical commentary on angelic creation.[82] She proposes that the fall of the angels 'establishes temporality in the poem; it is the foundation not only of the narrative, but of time itself'.[83] Just as Anglo-Saxon authors understood the fall of the angels as the event that inaugurates time and sets the narrative of salvation history in motion, they also saw it as the moment in which physical space and territory were first created and then struggled over.

Unlike *Genesis A*, *Genesis B* offers a very immediate portrait of Satan. The *Genesis B* poet imagines the process of rebellion against God as a psychological drama that opens directly after God's spoken prohibition to Adam and Eve and the command to 'wariað inc wið þone wæstm' (guard yourselves both against that fruit, ll. 236a). God's prohibition and promise to the human couple, phrased in highly formulaic language that can be found in *Beowulf*,[84] states that if they obey this rule 'ne wyrð inc wilna gæd' (there will be no unsatisfied desire for you two, l. 2365b). The poet's reflection upon this command is to the point, stating that 'heo wæron leof gode ðenden heo his halige word healdan woldon' (they were loved by God while they desired to keep his holy word, ll. 244b–5). Following this, God surveys his creation one last time and affirms his wish for Adam and Eve to dwell in happiness.

The subsequent flashback closely resembles chronological 'interruptions' that occur elsewhere in the Junius Manuscript with the so-called 'Patriarchal digressions' in *Exodus* recounting Noah (ll. 362–76) and Abraham (ll. 377–446).[85] The purpose of the sudden retrospection in *Genesis B* is to reveal how consequences of a past event are about to resurface in the present.[86] The poem then traces the creation of the angels (ll. 246–60), Satan's thoughts and behaviour (ll. 261–77), the expulsion of the proud angels

The anxiety of inheritance

(ll. 292–306a), the fall to hell (ll. 306b–20a), the confirmation of the good angels (ll. 320a–1), the first lament of Satan (ll. 322–89), and his second lament (ll. 390–441).[87] As in *Genesis A*, Lucifer is not explicitly named by the poet, but here referred to simply as 'ænne' (one). In concretising his physical and intellectual qualities, the poet transitions to hypermetric lines, a method used by Old English poets for 'signaling an important point'.[88] The poet evokes the primal lapse of the rebel angels in line 246:

> Hæfde se alwalda   engelcynna
> þurh handmægen,   halig drihten,
> tene getrimede   þæm he getruwode wel
> þæt hie his giongorscipe   fyligan wolden,
> wyrcean his willan   forþon he him gewit forgeaf
> and mid his handum gesceop,   halig drihten.
> gesett hæfde he hie swa gesæliglice,   ænne hæfde he swa swiðe geworhtne
> swa mihtigne on his modgeþohte,   he let hine swa micles wealdan,
> hehstne to him on heofona rice,   hæfde he hine swa hwitne geworhtne,
> swa wynlice wæs his wæstm on heofonum: þæt him com from weroda drihtne,
> gelic wæs he þam leohtum steorrum. (ll. 246–56a)

[The ruler of all, the holy Lord, had arranged ten orders of angels, through the might of His hands, whom He confidently trusted that they would follow in His obedience, work His will, because He gave them intelligence and the holy Lord shaped them with His hands. He had established them so blessedly, one He had made so strong, so mighty in his intellect, He let him rule so much, next to Him in the kingdom of heaven, He had made him so radiant, so splendid was his stature in heaven: that came to him from the Lord of hosts, he was like the shining stars.]

The poet underscores the superlativeness of God's higher-ranking retainer who is 'swa swiðe' (so strong), 'swa mihtigne on his modgeþohte' (so mighty in his intellect), 'swa hwite geworhtne' (so radiant), and 'swa wynlice' (so splendid) in his 'wæstm' (stature), with 'wæstm' here referring to his bodily form but also anticipating the *wæstm* ('fruit') that Adam and Eve will later consume in Paradise.[89] Amid this enumeration of qualities, the poet observes that God does not define limits for him, but 'let hine swa micles wealdan' (lets him rule so much). His impulse to build suggests that Satan perceives his powers and territories as limitless.

The passage also describes how God, like a craftsman, 'getrimede' (arranges) the orders of angels before Satan wishes to try his own hand and 'trymede getimbro' (build up a foundation). On the one hand, God is the architect of the angels, and Satan wishes to be the master builder of his own kingdom or 'getimbro' (foundation) as well as the sole ruler of his rational world. Satan's desired construction can be read as both physical (as it affects the very landscape of heaven) and mental (in that he wishes to throw off his subservient status in relation to God). Æthelwold's rendering of the term *aedificatione* ('building, establishment') in his Old English version of the *Rule of St Benedict* states that the programme is intended 'to hyra gastlican getimbrunge' (for the spiritual construction) of its practitioners.[90] As Ruth Wehlau puts it, Æthelwold's translation of *aedificatione* reveals that 'construction is mental, a building of the mind'.[91] Not only was the idea of spiritual *aedificare* ('edification') an integral part of the *lectio divina* (the Divine Office) but it also reminds us of Alfred's metaphorical concern with the process of both material and spiritual edification in his Preface to the *Soliloquies*. Spatial construction for Anglo-Saxon authors is at once metaphorically mapped onto the plane of the spiritual. *Genesis B* traces the adversarial *aedificare* of Satan's rival kingdom as well as his spiritual state.

Even though God has not articulated restrictions or laid out laws for the angels to follow, the poet still stresses the need for obedience within this heavenly economy. Doane notes that 'obedience is expected' because the angels have been endowed with 'gewit' (knowledge) by God, 'a gift which not only confers an obligation but gives the power of understanding what is owed'.[92] Ideally, the gifts given by God, if properly used and reciprocated, should maintain a perfect order. As Doane explains, 'Unlike Adam and Eve in the Prohibition section, bound to God by an oath like lay persons having a sworn duty to an unseen world, [the angels] are not bound by oath but by immediate intuition and understanding'.[93] In other words, the angels are indebted to God's sovereignty by the conferral of gifts, rather than the clear expression of laws and commands as seen in the Irish traditions. As for the 'one' God chooses to exalt, Doane notes that as 'his rank is greater, so are the gifts, and the sanctity of the obligation'.[94] Satan's rebellion is therefore represented as a rejection of the gifts and glorified status bestowed on him by God:

The anxiety of inheritance

ac he wende hit him to wyrsan þinge,[95]   ongan him winn up
    hebban
wið þone hehstan, heofnes waldend   þe siteð on þam halgan stole.
deore wæs he drihtne urum,   ne mihte him bedyrned weorðan
þæt his engyl ongan   ofermod wesan,
ahof hine wið his herran,   sohte hetespræce,
gylpword ongean,   nolde gode þeowian.
cwæð þæt his lic wære   leoht and scene,
hwit and hiowbeohrt.   ne meahte he æt his hige findan
þæt he gode wolde   geongerdome,
þeodne þeowian. (ll. 259–68a)

[But he overturned it for a worse thing for himself, began to raise up discord against the highest ruler of heaven, who sits on the holy throne. He was dear to our Lord, but it might not be concealed from Him that his angel began to become proud, lifted himself up against his Lord, sought hateful speech, defiant words against Him, would not serve God. He said that his body was bright and shiny, beautiful and radiant. He might not find it in his heart that he desired discipleship towards God, to serve the prince.]

Rebellion is represented as an interior conflict.[96] The poet describes Lucifer's turning away from God with the verb *wende* (from *awendan*), which has both physical and psychological connotations ('to alter, turn, move, translate, create a reversal of direction or fortune, convert, overturn, or overthrow').[97] In the angel's first speech, we see the poet's portrayal of his self-absorption:

'hwæt sceal ic winnan?' cwæð he.   'nis me wihtæ þearf
hearran to habbanne.   ic mæg mid handum swa fela
wundra gewyrcean.   ic hæbbe geweald micel
to gyrwanne   godlecran stol,
hearran on heofne.   hwy sceal ic æfter his hyldo ðeowian,
bugan him swilces geongordomes?   ic mæg wesan god swa he.
bigstandað me strange geneatas   þa ne willað me æt þam striðe
    geswican,
hæleþas heardmode.   hie habbað me to hearran gecorene,
rofe rincas.   mid swilcum mæg man ræd geþencean,
fon mid swilcum folcgesteallan.   frynd synd hie mine georne,
holdeon hyra hygesceaftum.   ic mæg hyra hearra wesan,
rædan on þis rice.   swa me þæt riht ne þinceð,
þæt ic oleccan   awiht þurfe
gode æfter gode ænegum   ne wille ic leng his geongra wurþan'. (ll.
    278–91)

['Why should I toil?' he said. 'It is not at all necessary for me to have a master. I may work as many wonders with my own hands. I have great authority to make ready a more goodly throne, higher in heaven. Why should I slave after His grace, bow to Him with such servitude? I might be a god as He is. Beside me stand strong comrades, headstrong heroes who do not desire to abandon me in battle. They have chosen me as their master, brave soldiers; with such men one can devise counsel, and undertake it with such warriors. These are my eager friends, loyal in their hearts. I may become their lord, rule in this kingdom. So it does not seem right to me, that I need to embrace God at all for any good thing. I will no longer be His disciple'.]

The angel fixates upon his outward beauty and strength, and also his potential as a builder, someone who can 'gewrycean' and 'gyrwanne' (make) 'wundra' (wonders) and a 'stol' (throne). Wishing to renounce his position as subject or 'geongra' (disciple), he evokes structures of fealty and obligation among his companions, a mere copy of the originary structure of the lord-retainer system – his relationship to God. He hopes to rise 'hearran' (higher) in heaven (echoed by his stated longing to become a 'hearra' (lord) above the other angels), possibly meaning that Satan wishes to rise to a position of *subreguli*. The term *hearra* (from Old Saxon *hêrro*), meaning 'lord, master, or superior',[98] recurs with a surprising frequency (twelve times) in *Genesis B*. The repetition of this term, which is mostly uttered by Satan with reference to his desired status, reveals his inability to grasp God's own sovereign stature.

In narratives recounting the fall of the angels, medieval authors often introduce an impetus of desire, that is, how Satan conceives of himself in relation to God. This requires a glossing of the term *similis* from Isaiah.[99] Anglo-Saxon authors typically suggest that Satan's sin is grounded in his ambition to be *gelic* ('like') God.[100] Occasionally, authors will depart from this practice and offer their own personal spin on this desire. The *Genesis B* poet intensifies the angel's conventional motive. He wishes not simply to be 'like' God, but 'wesan god swa he' (to be a god as He, l. 283b).[101] In modifying the common scriptural expression, the poet produces a more radical expression of the angel's self-construction. Satan's desire unfolds more clearly in the context of his speeches in *Genesis B* but, at this point in the narrative, the poet firmly affixes his proper 'likeness' as part of God's circuit of creation. The angel's resolve to assume the stature of sovereignty reminds readers of the

The anxiety of inheritance 93

poet's earlier expression of what the angel is truly *gelic*: 'gelic wæs he þam leohtum steorrum' (he was like the shining stars).[102] The poet thus creates a tension between the angel's longing to disrupt his fixed heavenly course around God. The illumination on page 16 of MS Junius 11 reinforces this idea by depicting heaven and hell at the moment of the fall of the angels (see Figure 2). Here, the remaining cohort of loyal angels look on from heaven as Satan and his companions are banished to hell. Interestingly, the illustration calls up specific imagery from the text with a ring of stars, acting as a barrier, separating heaven from fallen spaces.

The rebellion in *Genesis B* thus arises from a desire for self-glorification, originating in the 'hige' (heart) or (mind). The poet draws attention to the individualistic nature of sin while also locating its impetus in Satan's awareness of his own body, concentrating on his realisation that 'lic wære leoht and scene, hwit and hiowbeohrt' (his body was bright and shiny, beautiful and radiant, ll. 265–6a). God responds to the heavenly crisis, this lapse of loyalty, in the following manner:

þa hit se allwalda   eall gehyrde
þæt his engyl ongan   ofermede micel
ahebban wið his hearran   and spræc healic word
dollice wið drihten sinne,   sceolde he þa dæd ongyldan,
worc þæs gewinnes gedælan   and sceolde his wite habban,
ealra morðra mæst.   swa deð monna gehwilc
þe wið his waldend   winnan ongynneð
mid mane wið þone mæran drihten.   þa wearð se mihtiga
    gebolgen,
hehsta heofones waldend,   wearp hine of þan hean stole.
hete hæfde he æt his hearran gewunnan,   hyldo hæfde his
    ferlorene,
gram wearð him se goda on his mode.   forþon he sceolde grund
    gesecean
heardes hellewites   þæs þe he wann wið heofnes waldend.
acwæð hine þa fram his hyldo   and hine on helle wearp,
on þa deopan dala,   þær he to deofle wearð,
se feond mid his geferum eallum   feollon þa ufon of heofnum
þurlonge swa,   þreo niht and dagas[103]
þa englas of heofnum on helle,   and heo ealle forsceop
drihten to deoflum   forþon heo his dæd and word
noldon weorðian.   forþon he heo on wyrse leoht
under eorðan neoðan,   ællmihtig god,
sette sigelease   on þa sweartan helle.
þær hæbbað heo on æfyn   ungemet lange,

ealra feonda gehwilc,   fyr edneowe,
þonne cymð on uhtan   easterne wind,¹⁰⁴
forst fyrnum cald.   symble fyr oððe gar,
sum heard geswinc   habban sceoldon,
worhte man hit him to wite,   – hyra woruld wæs gehwyrfed –
forman siðe   fylde helle
mid þam andsacum. (ll. 292–320a)

[When the ruler of all heard all this, that His angel began to raise great strife against his Lord and spoke haughty words foolishly against his Lord, then he had to pay for the deed, share the pain in this struggle, and should have his punishment, the greatest of all woes. Just as any person does when he begins to strive against his ruler with sin against the great lord. Then the mighty one, the highest ruler of heaven, became angry, and threw him off the high throne. He had earned hate from his master, he had forsaken favour, the good one had become angry with him in His mind. Therefore, he had to seek the abyss of hard hell-torments, because he fought against the ruler of heaven. He banished them from His favour and thrust them into hell, into the deep chasm, where he became a devil, the fiend with all his companions. They fell out of heaven nonstop for three nights and days, the angels out of heaven into hell, and they were all reshaped by the Lord into devils. Because they would not abide by His word and deed, therefore the almighty God set them in a worse light underneath the earth, placed victory-less in that dark hell. There they had an immeasurably long evening, each and every enemy, and an ever-new fire, when at dawn comes an east wind, a wickedly cold frost. Whether fire or cold, they must have a certain hard torture. It was made to torment them – their world was overturned – for the first time hell was filled with those adversaries.]

God's swift response to the angel's haughtiness, insolent words, and desire to establish a rival kingdom, ends with Satan being thrown from 'of þan hean stole' (the high throne). Here, the poet reflects on how falls from lordly favour in the heavenly kingdom operate much like those upon earth. That is, Satan is punished 'swa deð monna gehwilc þe wið his waldend winnan ongynneð mid mane wið þone mæran drihten' (Just as when any person begins to strive against his ruler with sin against the great lord, ll. 297b–9a). The Old English terms *waldend* ('ruler') or *drihten* ('lord') can be used interchangeably to refer to a secular lord or God, meaning that the idea of lordship bridges the earthly and the divine, suggesting that an earthly, secular ruler might have the authority to respond to crises just as God did in this case. Satan's desire for his own measure of lordship results in a kingdom he can call his own. Whereas before he was described as an 'engel ofermodes' (angel of pride, l. 272a), he is now described as a 'ofermoda cyning' (proud king, l. 348a). As Doane points out, his new title of king is one of 'reproach' and 'an inverted kingship, as his world is inverted'.[105] He has, however, inherited an undesirable kingdom. With the understatement 'hyra woruld wæs gehwyrfed' (their world was overturned, l. 3318b), the poet stresses the fact that their desire to reverse the hierarchy in heaven reverses everything, right down to the identity of the former angels. Theirs is an utterly failed revolution. Instead of fomenting change, they have been subject to it.[106]

Sight and spatial limits

After Satan's expulsion from heaven, his desires for expansion shift as he sets his sights on enlarging his territories to encompass earth. Satan's surroundings in hell are described with decidedly spatial imagery. Words for hell as a physical landscape recur with *styde, oþer land, laðran landscape* and *grimman grundas*. Satan contrasts his new 'ham' (home) against his former one:

'is þæs ænga styde   ungelic swiðe
þam oðrum ham   þe we ær cuðon,
hean on heofonrice,   þe me min hearra onlag.
þeah we hine for þam alwaldan   agan ne moston,
romigan ures rices'. (ll. 356–60a)

['This narrow place is very unlike that other home we knew before, high in the kingdom of heaven, which my lord had granted to me, although because of that ruler we might not possess it, strive for our realm'.]

Satan recalls that his former estate in heaven was 'onlag' (granted).[107] Those lands have been forfeited on account of his rebellious plans for expansion, here signalled with the hapax legomenon *romigan* (from Old Saxon *rómon* meaning 'to aim at, strive after'), which offers a clear image of his former landed ambitions.[108] He now wishes to incite rebellion from below and interfere with Adam and Eve's inheritances:

'Ac ðoliaþ we nu þrea on helle,   þæt syndon þystro and hæto,
grimme, grundlease.   hafað us god sylfa
forswapen on þas sweartan mistas.   swa he us ne mæg ænige synne gestælan
þæt we him on þam lande lað gefremedon   he hæfð us þeah þæs leohtes
                                                     [bescryrede,
beworpen on ealra wita mæste   ne magon we þæs wrace gefremman,
geleanian him mid laðes wihte   þæt he us hafað þæs leohtes bescyrede.
he hæfð nu gemearcod anne middangeard   þær he hæfð mon geworhtne
æfter his onlicnesse.   mid þam he wile eft gesettan
heofona rice mid hluttrum saulum'. (ll. 389–97a)

['But we now suffer hardship in hell, there is darkness and heat, grim, bottomless. God Himself has swept us into these dark mists. Although He could not accuse us of any sin, that we committed in anger against Him in that land, He has deprived us of light, cast us down into the greatest of all punishments, nor may we carry out revenge for this, repay Him with any kind of harm that He has deprived us of light. He has now fixed the boundaries of a middle place, where He has created humanity after His likeness. He desires afterwards to settle with them the heavenly kingdom with pure souls'.]

With scorn and derision, Satan expresses his contempt over the fact that earthly space has been allotted for humanity by God. He states that God has 'gemearcod' (fixed by marks, fixed the boundaries of earth),[109] and that humankind is destined to 'gesettan' (settle) his former heavenly estates. The idea that earth has been surveyed by God denotes a clear territorial register, since *mearc* frequently appears in Anglo-Saxon charters with reference to a 'limit or bound'. In this way, the poet legitimises Adam and Eve's rights over lands which have been granted to them by their lord, just as any charter would.

The poet emphasises Satan's astonishment at how different hell is from his former home in heaven.[110] Hell's terrain, at times, defies logic. Although earlier he described hell as 'ænga' (narrow), Satan here characterises his new realm as 'grundlease' (bottomless, unbounded, endless).[111] Are the spaces of hell unstable or is this merely further evidence of Satan's clouded intellect? Satan's logbook of complaints over his fate has puzzled critics. The most unusual feature is his allegation that God's actions against him were pre-emptive. The poet's subtle inclusion of Satan's self-delusion and failure to recognise his ontological state of damnation here are telling.[112] It is troublesome that Satan maintains his own innocence, as Thomas D. Hill has observed.[113] Satan appeals to the lack of formally demarcated rules in heaven, thereby revealing that God operated above and beyond any prescribed laws or commandments. Readers are invited to consider whether 'sin' existed at all prior to the angelic rebellion, as this passage recalls Paul's Epistle to the Romans 3:20 which reads 'per legem enim cognito peccati' (by the law is the knowledge of sin). The point, then, is to stress the fact that God's sovereignty rests above ordinances and extends beyond fathomable limits, even while it is able to impose parameters.

The suggestion of Satan's envy and malice towards humankind and his 'successors' may derive from some subtle narrative links proposed by a sixth-century bishop, Martin of Braga. Perhaps extending Augustine's theory of replacement, Martin suggested that 'When the Devil saw that the reason man had been created was so that he could succeed to the place in the kingdom of God from which he himself had fallen, he was moved by envy and persuaded the man to transgress against God's commands'.[114] But what may have appeared to medieval authors as a negligible subtlety, would have been a stretch for Augustine. Although Martin of Braga's statement may seem like a mere logical outgrowth of what Augustine says on the subject, his change had clear and prominent ripple effects on how authors (such as the poet of *Genesis B*) imagine humankind as created for the 'reason' of inheriting formerly forfeited lands, a theological claim that Augustine – wanting to view the whole of early creation history as a kind of simultaneity – was never so bold as to make.[115]

Owing to his restraints, Satan must appeal to his demonic comrades for assistance in the ruin of Adam and Eve. Whereas the *Genesis A* poet elucidates the replacement doctrine through the viewpoint of God substantiating 'compensation' for the rebellion and loss in heaven, in *Genesis B* our clearest representation of newly created humanity is filtered through Satan's unreliable narration and logic:

'nu hie drihtne synt
wurðan micle   and moton him þone welan agan

þe we on heofonrice   habban sceoldon,
rice mid rihte.   is se ræd gescryred
monna cynne.   þæt me is on minum mod swa sar,
on minum hyge hreoweð,   þæt hie heofonrice
agan to aldre'. (ll. 421b–7a)

['Now they are more honoured by the Lord, and might possess for themselves what we should have in the heavenly kingdom, the kingdom through right. The advantage is given to humankind. That to me is the greatest sorrow in my heart, grieves my mind, that they might possess the kingdom of heaven forever'.]

Satan's frustrations mirror some of the conflicts seen in the Irish versions of the fall of the angels: he derides his loss of inheritance, possession, and lost sense of superiority or *febas*. Surveying his losses, Satan expresses contempt for Adam and Eve as both rivals and inheritors destined to 'hie heofonrice agan' (possess the heavenly kingdom). Doane observes that replacement here 'is seen not as doctrine but as an imperfectly grasped set of circumstances. Instead of an explanation of grace and predestination, the doctrine is expressed as an act of divine vengeance'.[116] Doane rightly suggests that by incorporating the 'teleology of replacement', the audience is called upon to 'recognize the gap between true doctrine and what Satan says'.[117] Worse still, Satan laments that Adam is poised to earn 'minne stronglican stol' ([his] godly throne, l. 365) – recalling the *stol* Satan wished to make before his fall (l. 280b) – 'mid rihte' (through right), *rihte* being a term that confirms tenurial entitlement.

As with historical poems such as *The Battle of Maldon*, where audiences already know that things will turn out badly in the end, the poet's recapitulation of the story of the fall of the angels in *Genesis B*, narrated at the precise moment of God's prohibition to Adam and Eve, heightens the tragedy. By situating the *Genesis B* flashback accordingly, the poet underscores that the absence of prohibitions and limits leads to the fraught construction of spiritual identity.

Far from a mere digression, the fall of the angels in *Genesis B* serves as the focal point for the poet's elucidation of the unregulated self. In accepting Lockett's redating of Junius 11, I would suggest that the central tensions such as the rebellious desire for rival territory, the stripping of lands, and the failed edification of the spiritual self in these narratives would have been especially timely and relevant for readers – monastic, clerical, or lay – during the Benedictine Reform, a period characterised by a heightened awareness about the place of rules and obligation in the structuring of individual Christian identity and communal religious life. This awareness was, by and large, the institutionalised response to a population of allegedly lax clerics who were seen as predisposed to rebellious behaviour because they were not bound to obey rules such as those of Chrodegang or Benedict. Recently, Katherine O'Brien O'Keeffe has suggested that in texts of the period 'the pride that accompanied [Satan's] disobedience was understood as a reflex of self-will'.[118] In the authorised rules and customaries of this era, according to O'Brien O'Keeffe, one can detect an 'explicit form of self-fashioning' which is 'self-conscious yet denying the self; using the will to deny the will'.[119] If the copy of Junius 11 that we have extant today did indeed have a place within this milieu, *Genesis B* would have resonated with audiences who saw obedience to one's lord and the regulation of the self as paramount.

Much has been written on the temptation and fall of Adam and Eve in *Genesis B*. While it is not my intent here to delve deeply into their story or the long-standing questions surrounding the poet's presentation of their fall, I would like to consider how the poet connects the fall of Eve with the fall of the angels. Critics often divide into two camps when exploring the *Genesis B* poet's purpose in linking the two falls. On the one hand, the poet appears to forge close connections between the two events in order to establish them as equally egregious sins and, additionally, to demonstrate the recursive cycle of sinfulness in creation. Focusing on the theme of loyalty in the poem, Michael Cherniss argues that 'the description of the angels' failure to obey God, when seen in light of God's instructions to Adam and Eve, serves … to illuminate the parallel between the situations of the angels and Man before their respective falls'.[120] Similarly suggesting that the first fall prefigures the fall of humankind, Doane asserts that the two are 'causally and typologically linked. [They] are not merely contiguous but typologically woven'.[121] Thomas D. Hill finds there to be latent typological associations between the two falls but cautions against a strict typological reading. He instead argues for a more nuanced view, suggesting that the aesthetic technique of 'interlace', or the maintenance of a 'dialectical tension', is at work in the poem.[122] Hill ultimately proposes that the poet works to establish an uneasy tension between the falls by developing Eve's role in the poem. 'Far from rebelling against the commands of God', Hill contends,

'Eve believes she is fulfilling the will of God and saving Adam from God's wrath'.[123] Following Hill, I think that the poets of *Genesis A* and *B* portray a discernible gap between 'rebels' and 'replacements', wherein humankind possesses the ability (and desire) to conform to God's rules in a uniquely new way. With God's simple command to Adam and Eve, the poet stresses the importance not just of expectations derived from obligation, but of the internalisation of rules so that one does not fall prey to deceit and *unræd* ('ill-counsel').

The tempter tells Eve that if she eats the fruit, she will be protecting her husband who has offended God. But fraught spatial perception seems to be at the heart of Eve's temptation.[124] As proof, the angelic tempter explains that with one bite her 'eagan swa leoht' (eyes will be illuminated, l. 564) and she will be able to see more 'wide ofer woruld' (widely over the world, l. 565). In short, the tempter entices Eve with the promise of enlarging her ability to 'geseon' (see) God's creative works and broadening her intellect. Falling prey to the temper's stratagem, Eve tastes it in the hopes that her conformity will safeguard Adam. She then receives a 'siene' (vision):

> þe meahte heo wide geseon
> þurh þæs laðan læn þe hie mid ligenum beswac,
> dearnenga bedrog þe hire for his dædum com
> þæt hire þuhte hwitre heofon and eorðe
> and eall þeos woruld wlitigre and geweorc godes
> micel and mihtig, þeah heo hit þurh monnes geþeaht
> ne sceawode ac se sceaða georne
> swicode ymb þa sawle þe hire ær þa siene onlah
> þæt heo swa wide wlitan meahte
> ofer heofonrice. (ll. 600b–9a)

[then by the loan of the hateful one who deceived her with lies, secretly misled, he who had come to her for these deeds, she was able to see widely so that heaven and earth seemed more bright to her, and the entire world more stunning, and the work of God great and powerful, although she did not see it through human intellect, but the enemy, he who had loaned her the vision, eagerly disordered her soul, so that she might see widely across the heavenly kingdom.]

Eve is given a vision of land. The poet uses an important verb of seeing with the term *sceawian* ('to see') here, that is, the kind of seeing that engages the intellect, though what she sees is tragically false. Strikingly, the poet characterises Eve's apparition as a *læn* ('loan'), something *onlah* ('granted, loaned'). Whereas translators typically render this as a 'gift', the term also has potential territorial valences in that it can mean a 'loan, grant, gift, land that may be recalled'.[125] Land that was classified as *lænland*, as I discussed in Chapter 1, is fleeting, subject to the passing of time and the whims of its issuer. Given the transitory nature of *lænland*, and the fact that it is subject to seizure, this brief episode resonates with the lesson that Satan learned at the start of *Genesis B* when his heavenly lands were revoked. Eve's vision of land is similarly fleeting, impermanent, and wholly deceptive. The term reminds the poet's audience that such lands are temporary, imperfect versions of more permanent lands such as *bocland*. The tempter succeeds through this promise of expansion as Eve momentarily enjoys more capacious sight and a clarity in viewing her earthly habitations. All the while, she believes that she is enlarging her mind, just as the tempter had formerly promised Adam that the fruit would allow him a 'breostum rum' (spaciousness of intellect, l. 519b). Eve's vision is in effect a false grant of land. She views these roomier spaces as within her grasp, but her ability to discern permanence from impermanence is compromised.[126] Her momentary longing for spatial expansion mirrors Satan's mistaken views in the opening of the poem, his same transgressive desire. In both cases, falls originate in spatial desire and a lapse in perception. Adam and Eve go on to build a home for themselves on earth, but only after Adam says that an evil 'gemearcod uncer / sylfra sið' (journey has now been marked for us, ll. 791b–2a). Together they must charter new boundaries in lands unknown to them.

The Old Saxon remnants of the Vatican *Genesis* end with Adam and Eve noticing that they are 'naked ... unclothed' ('bara ... unuuerid', l. 21) as they begin their search for 'covering' or 'protection' ('scura') (roughly corresponding to line 813a of *Genesis B*) before moving on to the story of Cain and Abel.[127] *Genesis B*, however, continues. Before the poem rejoins with *Genesis A*, the poet offers an arresting image of Adam and Eve exiting paradise and entering a forest, hoping to clothe themselves and having much to learn. Adam says,

'uton gan on þysne weald innan
on þisses holtes hleo'. hwurfon hie ba twa,
togengdon gnorngende on þone grenan weald.
sæton onsundran bidan selfes gesceapu

heofoncyninges.   þa hie þa habban ne moston
þe him ær forgeaf   ælmihtig god.
þa hie heora lichoman   leafum beþeahton. (ll. 839b–45)

['let us go into this forest, into the protection of the wood'. The two of them turned, went separately grieving into that green woodland. They sat apart from one another awaiting the judgement of the heavenly king himself. Then they might no longer have what Almighty God had granted them before. Then they covered their bodies, protected themselves with the wood.]

The *Genesis B* poet extends the Old Saxon account of their progress and prolonged wait for God within the woods, emphasising their need for bodily cover. It is significant that the human couple mourn separately; their fallen condition has pushed them apart to a certain extent. They undergo acts of daily penance as they wait for God to find them and instruct them on 'hu hie on þam leohte forð / libban sceoldon' (how they henceforth should go forth into that light, l. 851–2b). Amid this extended woodland stay, the poet reflects upon the human couple's desperate need for renewed spiritual edification. Removed from their home in paradise, the only space they know is the wood, their only source of cover being its leaves which they use to 'beþeahton', from 'beþeccan' (cover, clothe, protect), their bodies. While the speaker of Alfred's Preface searches for metaphoric textual leaves (*folium*) amid a wood of spiritual knowledge, for Adam and Eve, the process of spiritual edification must begin with penance. Scott DeGregorio has shown that Alfred was greatly influenced by Gregory's idea that 'reading or hearing a text (*lectio*) [was] only the first stage of a process whose end is the internalization of the text into one's memory, language and behaviour'.[128] The Preface gives us an instance of this close association between how the Anglo-Saxon self might be uniquely constructed through the metaphor of woods, leaves, and by extension, texts. This final gathering of leaf and wood is where *Genesis B* reunites with *Genesis A*. Just as the builder-speaker of the Preface to the *Soliloquies* must go into woodland to learn and to begin the construction of a dwelling place, so too must Adam and Eve. They must learn to reorder their intellects towards God as they labour in the construction of their new earthly home.

There is evidence to suggest that Insular authors chose to foreground aspects of the Genesis narrative that spoke to contemporary cultural and societal concerns both in Ireland and Anglo-Saxon

The anxiety of inheritance

England. In both traditions we see biblical history employed by authors as a way to understand contemporary issues and challenges and to establish common myths of origin. As an extra-scriptural event, the fall of the angels stands outside of God's laws as encoded in the biblical narrative. By identifying Anglo-Saxon Christians as 'replacements' for a rebellion, these authors associate their early English Christian community with the heavenly community in a unique way and fashion a distinct Christian identity for a converted people. Since the fall of the angels was, according to David F. Johnson, an example of 'the kind of subject for which no canonical or otherwise authoritative narrative account existed, no single text could be regarded by the Church Fathers – or Christian poets – as authoritative'.[129] Far from seeing this as a theological problem, Anglo-Saxon poets viewed this as an opportunity to write the beginning of their story as a Christian people.

These first two chapters have looked at the Old English poetic Genesis material found in the Junius 11 codex. I will return to MS Junius 11 in Chapter 5 to discuss *Christ and Satan*, the fourth and final poem in that manuscript dedicated to biblical stories surrounding the angelic rebellion. Up to this point, my focus has mainly centred on how the fall of the angels story may have resonated within secular, military, and legal spheres, where lordly obligations were given pride of place. From here, I turn to the ways in which this narrative came into contact with timely questions concerning ecclesiastical and spiritual obligations during a period of sustained religious upheaval, where pastoral leadership was heavily scrutinised and beliefs about the proper stewardship of church lands were at the core of prolonged disputes between the Anglo-Saxon ruling class, the religious intelligentsia, and clerics who came to be seen as rebellious, possessive of their properties, and dismissive of rules. Here, the story of the fall of the angels will undergo a discernable leap: what was a popular tale with a rich literary tradition will come to shape the historical realities of the Anglo-Saxon world as monastic reformers attempt to redraw the boundaries of early medieval spiritual identity and the physical borders of one of England's most important secular and spiritual capitals: Winchester.

Notes

1 Carnicelli, *King Alfred's Version of St. Augustine's Soliloquies*, ll. 1–12. Although it does not impact my argument, King Alfred's purported authorship of the *Soliloquies* and the *Boethius* has been

questioned by Malcolm Godden, 'Did King Alfred Write Anything?', *MÆ*, 76 (2007), 1–23. For responses, see Janet M. Bately, 'Did King Alfred Actually Translate Anything? The Integrity of the Alfredian Canon Revisited', *MÆ*, 78 (2009), 189–215 and 'Alfred as Author and Translator', in *A Companion to Alfred the Great*, ed. Nicole Guenther Discenza and Paul E. Szarmach (Leiden: Brill, 2015), pp. 113–42. See also Richard Abels, *Alfred the Great*, 'Appendix on the Authenticity of Asser's *Life of King Alfred* and Alfred's Translations', forthcoming.

2   My translation draws upon *Asser's Life of King Alfred and Other Contemporary Sources*, trans. Keynes and Lapidge, p. 138.

3   Nicole Guenther Discenza, *Inhabited Spaces: Anglo-Saxon Constructions of Place* (Toronto: University of Toronto Press, 2017), p. 7.

4   Asser, *Asser's Life of King Alfred Together with the Annals of Saint Neots Erroneously Ascribed to Asser*, ed. W. H. Stevenson (Oxford: Clarendon Press, 1904; repr. 1959), §77 (pp. 62–3).

5   See M. R. Godden, 'The Sources of Alfred's Augustine Soliloquies (Cameron C.B.9.4)', *Fontes Anglo-Saxonici: World Wide Web Register*, http://fontes.english.ox.ac.uk/, accessed July 2017. Valerie Heuchan, 'God's Co-Workers and Powerful Tools: The Sources of Alfred's Building Metaphor in his Old English Translation of Augustine's *Soliloquies*', *N&Q*, 54.1 (2007), 1–11, suggests a connection to 1 Corinthians, where Paul describes himself as a 'sapiens architectus' (wise architect).

6   Howe, *Writing the Map*, p. 50.

7   Peter Clemoes proposes that *cræft* is 'the operative word in the creative relationship between each soul and God' in 'King Alfred's Debt to Vernacular Poetry: The Evidence of *ellen* and *cræft*', in *Words, Texts, and Manuscripts: Studies in Anglo-Saxon Culture Presented to Helmut Gneuss*, ed. Michael Korhammer (Woodbridge: D. S. Brewer, 1992), pp. 213–38 (pp. 232–3).

8   David Pratt, 'Problems of Authorship and Audience in the Writings of King Alfred the Great', in *Lay Intellectuals in the Carolingian World*, ed. Patrick Wormald and Janet L. Nelson (Cambridge: Cambridge University Press, 2007), pp. 162–91 (pp. 182–90).

9   Whereas the location of Lucifer's rival throne is typically in the 'north' (due to Is. 14:14), *Genesis B* suggests that Lucifer builds *west and norð*, which echoes the *Visio Pauli*. See Thomas D. Hill, 'Some Remarks on "The Site of Lucifer's Throne"', *Anglia*, 87 (1969), 303–11 (p. 305); Antonette DiPaolo Healey, *The Old English Vision of St. Paul*, Speculum Anniversary Monographs 2 (Cambridge, MA: The Medieval Academy of America, 1978), pp. 55–6.

10 Bosworth-Toller, *trymman*, senses 1 and 3.

11 Imagery of edification appears in the story of St. Paul from *King*

Alfred's West Saxon Version of Gregory's Pastoral Care, ed. H. Sweet, EETS os 45, 50 (London: Oxford University Press, 1871–2; repr. 1978), pp. 442–4: 'And soon after the fall of that pride, he began to construct humility ... for we cut down trees in the wood to erect them afterwards in the dwelling which we desire to build'.
12 Bosworth-Toller, *getimbru*, sense 1.
13 Howe, *Writing the Map*, 49.
14 For a recent study, see George Clark, 'The Anglo-Saxons and *Superbia*: Finding a Word for It', in *Old English Philology: Studies in Honour of R. D. Fulk*, ed. Leonard Neidorf, Rafael J. Pascual, and Tom Shippey (Cambridge: D. S. Brewer, 2016), pp. 172–89. For the most complete analysis of *ofermod*, see Helmut Gneuss, '*The Battle of Maldon* 89: Byrtnoð's *ofermod* Once Again', *SP*, 73 (1976), 117–37. See also Hans Schabram, *Superbia: Studien zur altenglischen Wortschatz*, vol. 1, *Die dialektale und zeitliche Verbreitung des Wortguts* (Munich: Wilhelm Fink, 1965). On the sin of pride, see also Rosemary Woolf, 'The Devil in Old English Poetry', *RES*, 4 (1953), 1–12.
15 Abbetmeyer, *Old English Poetical Motives*.
16 Richard Marsden, *Cambridge Old English Reader* (Cambridge: Cambridge University Press, 2004), p. 166.
17 On Anglo-Saxon subjectivity, see Katherine O'Brien O'Keeffe, *Stealing Obedience: Narratives of Agency and Identity in Later Anglo-Saxon England* (Toronto: University of Toronto Press, 2012).
18 Patrick Wormald, 'Celtic and Anglo-Saxon Kingship: Some Further Thoughts', in *Sources of Anglo-Saxon Culture*, ed. Paul Szarmach (Kalamazoo, MI: Medieval Institute Publications, 1986), pp. 151–83; Bart Jaski, *Early Irish Kingship and Succession* (Dublin: Four Courts Press, 2000); Katherine Simms, *From Kings to Warlords: The Changing Political Structure of Gaelic Ireland in the Later Middle Ages* (Woodbridge: Boydell, 1987).
19 *eDIL*, s.v. *febas*. See Jaski's overview of *febas*, which he describes as 'worth, dignity, stature, seniority, suitability, reputation, wealth and power' (*Early Irish Kingship*, p. 276).
20 *eDIL*, s.v. *airchinnchecht*; *eDIL*, s.v. *airchinnech*.
21 Evans, '*Genesis B* and Its Background', p. 4. For more on the source tradition of Genesis see J. M. Evans, *Paradise Lost and the Genesis Tradition* (Oxford: Clarendon Press, 1968), p. 4ff.
22 Frederick M. Biggs, *SASLC: The Apocrypha*, p. 10; Evans, '*Genesis B* and Its Background', pp. 6–8; *SASLC: Bede*, Part 2, Fascicles 1–4, ed. George Hardin Brown and Frederick M. Biggs (Amsterdam: Amsterdam University Press, 2018), pp. 136–40.
23 Accounts of biblical offshoots and expansions can be found in Brian Murdoch, *The Medieval Popular Bible: Expansions of Genesis in the Middle Ages* (Cambridge: D. S. Brewer, 2003).

24 *Vita Latina Adae et Evae*, ed. Jean Pierre Pettorelli, Jean-Daniel Kaestli, et al., 2 vols, CCSA 18–19 (Turnhout: Brepols, 2012), 1:304–14. Evidence for the knowledge of the *Vita Adae* in Anglo-Saxon England is circumstantial; see Frederick M. Biggs, 'Life of Adam and Eve' (*SASLC: The Apocrypha*, pp. 3–4). Its influence in Ireland is summarised by Martin McNamara, *The Apocrypha in the Early Irish Church* (Dublin: Dublin Institute for Advanced Studies, 1975; repr. 1984); Martin McNamara, *The Bible and the Apocrypha in the Early Irish Church (A.D. 600–1200)*, Instrumenta Patristica et Mediaevalia 66 (Turnhout: Brepols, 2015); see also Charles D. Wright, *The Irish Tradition in Old English Literature*, CSASE 6 (Cambridge: Cambridge University Press, 1993), pp. 130–3; St. J. D. Seymour, 'The Book of Adam and Eve in Ireland', *Proceedings of the Royal Irish Academy*, 36 (1921–4), 121–33 and Seymour, 'Notes on Apocrypha in Ireland', in *Proceedings of the Royal Irish Academy*, 37 (1926), 107–17; Murdoch, *The Irish Adam and Eve Story*, p. 44. A similar chronology can be found in the Hiberno-Latin Genesis commentary in St. Gall Stiftsbibliothek 908; see Charles D. Wright, 'Apocryphal Lore and Insular Tradition in St. Gall Stiftsbibliothek 908', in *Irland und Christenheit: Bibelstudien und Mission*, ed. Próinsías Ní Chatháin and Michael Richter (Stuttgart: Klett-Cotta, 1987), pp. 124–45 (p. 130). For biblical apocrypha in early Ireland, see David N. Dumville, 'Biblical Apocrypha and the Early Irish: A Preliminary Investigation', in *Proceedings of the Royal Irish Academy* 73C (1973), 299–338.

25 *Vita Latina Adae et Evae*, p. 309.

26 Ibid., p. 311.

27 For a partial edition and translation, see *The Irish Adam and Eve Story from Saltair na Rann*, ed. and trans. David Greene and Fergus Kelly, 2 vols (Dublin: Dublin Institute for Advanced Studies, 1976). Greene's unfinished typescript edition and translation is available online at the Dublin Institute for Advanced Studies: www.dias.ie/celt/celt-publications-2celt-saltair-na-rann/. I have included translations from these editions throughout, but have noted several modifications were relevant. An older edition is *Saltair na Rann: A Collection of Early Irish Poems*, ed. Whitley Stokes, *Anecdota Oxoniensa*, Mediaeval and Modern Series 1 (Oxford: Clarendon Press, 1883), which can be accessed online from Dublin Institute for Advanced Studies: http://dias.ie/images/stories/celitics/pubs/saltairnarann/canto001–010.pdf. On the dating of *Saltair na Rann*, see Martin McNamara, *The Apocrypha*, pp. 14–16 who proposes *c*. 988; this has been questioned by G. Mac Eoin, 'The Date and Authorship of *Saltair na Rann*', *Zeitschrift für celtische Philologie*, 28 (1960), 51–67 and 'Observations on *Saltair na Rann*', *Zeitschrift für celtische Philologie*, 39 (1982), 1–27. See also James Carney, 'The Dating of Early Irish Verse Texts,

500–1100', *Éigse*, 19 (1983), 177–216 (pp. 178; 207–6), who suggests *c*. 870; *Leabhar Gabhála Érenn: The Book of the Taking of Ireland*, Part I, ed. and trans. R. A. S. Macalister, Early Irish Texts Society 34 (Dublin: Educational Company of Ireland, 1938), pp. 26–7. While there are three redactions, only two discuss the fall of the angels (*The Book of Leinster* (T.C.D. Library, H.2.18) and the Stowe Collection (R.I.A. Library)). While Macalister suggests the material is eleventh century, there is compelling evidence suggesting that the material dates from as far back as the ninth (p. 3). For a comprehensive account of the manuscripts, dates, and redactions, see R. Mark Scowcroft, '*Leabhar Gabhála* Part I: The Growth of the Text', *Ériu*, 38 (1987), 79–140; R. Mark Scowcroft, '*Leabhar Gabhála* Part II: The Growth of the Tradition', *Ériu*, 39 (1988), 1–66; see also John Carey, *A New Introduction to Lebor Gabála Érenn*, Subsidiary Publication Series No. 1 (Dublin, Irish Texts Society, 1993).

28 *eDIL*, s.v. *feb*, sense I.
29 Jaski, *Early Irish Kingship*, p. 124. See also Immo Wartnjes, 'Regnal Succession in Early Medieval Ireland', *Journal of Medieval History*, 30 (2004), 277–410; T. M. Charles-Edwards, *Early Christian Ireland* (Cambridge: Cambridge University Press, 2004), pp. 90–2. Charles-Edwards notes that a king could endow subordinates with *febas*: 'All dynasties were governed by the dominant ambition to stay at the top by demonstrating febas, political standing' (p. 480).
30 *eDIL*, s.v. *feb*, sense II1 and II3a.
31 *eDIL*, s.v. *caingen*, sense a and d.
32 I wish to thank John Carey for his helpful correspondence regarding the adverbial use of *feib* in this passage.
33 I owe this suggestion to Charles D. Wright.
34 See 'Tánaiste', *Medieval Ireland: An Encyclopedia*, ed. Seán Duffy (New York: Routledge, 2005); *eDIL*, s.v. *tánaise, tánaiste*, sense III.
35 *Leabhar Breac*, ed. and trans. Bartholomew Mac Carthy, *The Codex Palatino-Vaticanus, No. 830*, Todd Lecture Series 3 (Dublin: Royal Irish Academy, 1892), pp. 45–7.
36 Jaski, *Early Irish Kingship*, p. 125.
37 Fergus Kelly, *A Guide to Early Irish Law*, Early Irish Law Series 3 (Dublin: Dublin Institute for Advanced Studies, 1988), 268–9. See also Jaski, *Early Irish Kingship*, p. 124ff.
38 One possible exception is *Christ and Satan*, which obliquely suggests that Satan and Adam may have coexisted in heaven (ll. 19–20). For more on the doctrinal implications, see James K. Morey, 'Adam and Judas in the Old English *Christ and Satan*', *SP*, 87 (1990), 397–409; see also Jill M. Fitzgerald, 'Measuring Hell by Hand: Rogation Rituals in *Christ and Satan*', *RES* (2017), 1–22 (pp. 10–11).
39 Ibid., p. 134.
40 Ibid., p. 212.

41 Ibid., p. 211.
42 Ibid., p. 240.
43 *Leabhar Gabhála*, ed. and trans. MacAlister, pp. 26–7.
44 *Lebar Gabála* features other episodes in which co-heirs (usually brothers) vie for territorial supremacy. One story recounts Donn (oldest son of Míl), whose younger brothers (Éremón and Éber) battle over titles and inheritance until Ireland is eventually split in two.
45 For more on inheritance, see D. A. Binchy, 'Some Celtic Legal Terms', *Celtica*, 3 (1956), 221–31 and Kelly, *A Guide to Early Irish Law*, 102–4. For a concise account of *airchinnech*, see Colmán Etchingham, *Church Organisation in Ireland, A.D. 650–1000* (Maynooth: Laigin Publications, 1999), p. 63ff.
46 Ibid., p. 26.
47 Jean-Michel Picard, '*Princeps* and *principatus* in the Early Irish Church', in *Seanchas: Studies in Early Irish Archaeology, History and Literature in Honour of Francis J. Byrne*, ed. Alfred P. Smyth (Dublin: Four Courts, 2000), pp. 146–60 (p. 155).
48 Ibid., p. 153.
49 Etchingham, *Church Organisation*, p. 82.
50 Ibid., p. 72.
51 Wendy Davies, 'Clerics as Rulers: Some Implications of the Terminology of Ecclesiastical Authority in Early Medieval Ireland', in *Latin and the Vernacular in Early Medieval Britain*, ed. Nicholas Brooks (Leicester: University of Leicester Press, 1982), pp. 81–97 (p. 85).
52 Donnchadh Ó Corráin, 'Nationality and Kingship in Pre-Norman Ireland', in *Historical Studies XI: Nationality and the Pursuit of National Independence (Papers Read before the Conference Held at Trinity College, Dublin, 26–31 May 1975)*, ed. T. W. Moody (Belfast: Appletree Press, 1978), pp. 1–35 (p. 16).
53 Mary Clayton, '*De Duodecim Abusiuis*, Lordship and Kingship in Anglo-Saxon England', in *Saints and Scholars: New Perspectives on Anglo-Saxon Literature and Culture*, ed. Stuart McWilliams (Cambridge: D. S. Brewer, 2012), pp. 141–63 (p. 159). See also *Two Ælfric Texts: The Twelve Abuses and the Vices and Virtues*, ed. and trans. Mary Clayton (Suffolk: Boydell and Brewer, 2013). For the treatise, see Pseudo-Cyprianus, *De XII abusivis saeculi*, ed. Siegmund Hellmann, Texte und Untersuchungen zur Geschichte der altchristlichen Literatur 34 (Leipzig: J. C. Hinrichs, 1909).
54 Damien Bracken, 'The Fall and the Law in Early Ireland', in *Ireland and Europe in the Early Middle Ages: Texts and Transmission*, ed. Próinséas Ní Chatháin and Michael Richter (Dublin: Four Courts, 2002), pp. 146–69 (pp. 165–8).
55 Neil McLeod, *Early Irish Contract Law*, Sydney Series in Celtic

Studies I (Sydney: University of Sydney, 1992), pp. 138–9; translation from Bracken, 'The Fall and the Law', p. 151.
56 Bracken, 'The Fall and the Law', p. 147.
57 Ibid., p. 157.
58 Janet Schrunk Ericksen, 'Legalizing the Fall of Man', *MÆ*, 74 (2005), 205–20 (p. 209).
59 A. N. Doane, *The Saxon Genesis: An Edition of the West Saxon Genesis B and the Old Saxon Vatican Genesis* (Madison, WI: The University of Wisconsin Press, 1991). Doane observes that similarities between *Genesis B* and the *Book of the Secrets of Enoch* may have 'come through Irish sources' (p. 98) and Ericksen notes that such a connection 'rests on the presence of Irish material on the Continent' ('Legalizing the Fall of Man', p. 206).
60 Joyce Hill, 'The Apocrypha in Anglo-Saxon England: The Challenge of Changing Distinctions', in *Apocryphal Texts and Traditions in Anglo-Saxon England*, ed. Kathryn Powell and D. G. Scragg (Cambridge: D. S. Brewer, 2003), pp. 165–8 (p. 165).
61 Allen and Calder, *Sources and Analogues*, pp. 3–5.
62 Text can be found in *MGH*, *Auctores Antiquissimi*, 6, 2 (Berlin, Weidmann, 1883), 212–19; translation from Allen and Calder, *Sources and Analogues*, p. 6.
63 On the tempter's disguise, see Rosemary Woolf, 'The Fall of Man in *Genesis B* and *The Mystère d'Adam*', in *Studies in Old English Literature in Honor of Arthur G. Brodeur*, ed. Stanley B. Greenfield (New York: Russell and Russell, 1973), pp. 187–99; on the tempter, see Eric Jager, 'Tempter as Rhetoric Teacher: The Fall of Language in the Old English *Genesis B*', *Neophil*, 72 (1988), 434–48; John Vickrey, 'Adam, Eve, and the *tacen* in *Genesis B*', *PQ*, 72 (1993), 1–14; John Vickrey, 'Some Further Remarks on *selfsceaft*', *Zeitschrift für deutsches Altertum und deutsche Literatur*, 110 (1981), 1–14; on the function of the *tacen*, see Ericksen, 'Legalizing the Fall', pp. 205–20; See Jager, 'Tempter as Rhetoric Teacher', pp. 442–3; see also Gillian R. Overing, 'On Reading Eve: *Genesis B* and the Readers' Desire', in *Speaking Two Languages: Traditional Disciplines and Contemporary Theory in Medieval Studies*, ed. Allen J. Frantzen (Albany: State University of New York Press, 1991), pp. 35–63 and Andrew Cole, 'Jewish Apocrypha and Christian Epistemologies of the Fall: The *Dialogi* of Gregory the Great and the Old Saxon *Genesis*', in *Rome and the North: The Early Reception of Gregory the Great in Germanic Europe*, ed. Rolf H. Bremmer, Kees Dekker, and David F. Johnson (Paris: Peeters, 2001), pp. 157–88. Woolf proposes a lost apocryphal source ('*Genesis B* and *The Mystere D'Adam*', pp. 187–99).
64 John Josias Conybeare initially postulated that there was interpolated material in the poem; *Illustrations of Anglo-Saxon Poetry*, ed. William Daniel Conybeare (London: Hardin and Lepard, 1826), pp. 190–7.

65 Eduard Sievers, *Der Heliand und die angelsächsiche Genesis* (Halle: M. Niemeyer, 1875).
66 Cole, 'Jewish Apocrypha and Christian Epistemologies', p. 155.
67 On the relationship between *Genesis B* and the Old Saxon *Genesis*, see Doane, *The Saxon Genesis*, pp. 43–55; R. Derolez, '*Genesis*: Old Saxon and Old English', *ES*, 76 (1995), 409–23; Bernhard Bischoff, 'Paläographische Fragen deutscher Denkmäler der Karolingerzeit', *Frühmittelalterliche Studien*, 5 (1971), 101–34 at p. 105 who dates the fragments to the third quarter of the ninth century. Also printed in *Mittelalterliche Studien: Ausgewählte zur Schriftkunde und Literaturgeschichte* (Stuttgart: A. Hiersemann, 1981), pp. 73–111.
68 Karl Zangemeister and Wilhelm Braune, 'Bruchstücke der altsächsichen Bibeldichtung aus der Bibliotheca Palatina', *Neue Heidelberger Jahrbücher*, 4 (1894), 205–94. The fragments had been in the Vatican Library since 1623 and were discovered by Zangemeister in 1894.
69 This overlap occurs at the beginning of Palatinus Latinus 1447 (ll. 1–26a) and the final episode of *Genesis B* as Adam blames Eve for their fall (ll. 790–817a).
70 Alois Brandl, *Die Angelsächsische Literatur*, in *Grundriss der Germanischen Philologie*, ed. Hermann Paul, 3 vols (Strassburg: Trübner, 1901–9).
71 See Robert Priebsch, *The Heliand Manuscript Cotton Caligula A VII in the British Museum: A Study* (Oxford: Clarendon Press, 1925); C. L. Wrenn, *A Study of Old English Literature* (London: Harrap, 1967); Lucas, 'Loyalty and Obedience', p. 123; Barbara Raw, 'The Construction of Oxford, Bodleian Junius 11', *ASE*, 13 (1984), 133–48; see also Doane, *The Saxon Genesis*, pp. 30–4.
72 Trilling, *The Aesthetics of Nostalgia*, p. 70.
73 Lockett, 'An Integrated Re-examination', pp. 141–73.
74 The Benedictine reformers who combated negligence and abuse were drawn to the Carolingian concept of *norma rectitudinis* or the 'rule of uprightness' as an ideal for clerics.
75 See Marsden, *The Cambridge Old English Reader*, p. 167. Alfred's purported biblical lineage and the West Saxon kingship has been discussed by Kenneth Sisam, 'Anglo-Saxon Royal Genealogies', *Publications of the British Academy*, 39 (1953), 287–348; David N. Dumville, 'The West Saxon Genealogical Regnal List and the Chronology of Early Wessex', *Peritia*, 4 (1985), 21–66 and 'The West Saxon Genealogical Regnal List: Manuscripts and Texts', *Anglia*, 104 (1986), 1–32.
76 Fox and Sharma, *Old English Literature*, p. 12; Kathleen E. Dubs, '*Genesis B*: a Study in Grace', *American Benedictine Review*, 33 (1982), 47–64; Doane, *The Saxon Genesis*, pp. 98–107; Remley, *Old English Biblical Verse*, pp. 165–7.
77 Wright, '*Genesis A* ad litteram', p. 165.

78 Máire Ní Mhaonaigh, 'The Learning of Ireland in the Early Medieval Period', in *Books Most Needful to Know: Contexts for the Study of Anglo-Saxon England*, ed. Paul Szarmach, Old English Newsletter Subsidia 36 (Kalamazoo, MI: Medieval Institute Publications, 2016), p. 97.
79 Wright, '*Genesis A* ad litteram', 168–9; Battles, 'The Anglo-Saxon Migration Myth', p. 65. Wright also points out that moments of *Genesis A* resemble *ASC* entries with their use of the '*her* convention [that] is both temporal and spatial' (p. 171).
80 T. D. Hill, 'The Fall of Angels and Man in the Old English *Genesis B*', p. 279.
81 Trilling, *The Aesthetics of Nostalgia*, p. 91 and p. 92.
82 Ibid., p. 95.
83 Ibid., p. 86; Doane states that Satan falls 'into the realm of time' (*The Saxon Genesis*, p. 127).
84 Cherniss, 'Heroic Ideals', pp. 479–97, observes the similarities between God's promise and Hrothgar's promise to Beowulf (p. 484).
85 The so-called 'Patriarchal Digressions' have been explored by Stanley R. Hauer, 'The Patriarchal Digression in the Old English *Exodus*, Lines 362–446', in *Eight Anglo-Saxon Studies*, ed. Joseph Wittig (Chapel Hill, NC: University of North Carolina Press, 1981), pp. 77–90; Phyllis Portnoy, 'Ring Composition and the Digressions of *Exodus*: The "Legacy" of the "Remnant"', *ES*, 82 (2001), 289–307; Daniel Anlezark, 'Connecting the Patriarchs: Noah and Abraham in the Old English *Exodus*', *JEGP*, 104 (2005), 171–88; Remley, *Old English Biblical Verse*, pp. 168–230.
86 For a conspectus on the digressions in *Beowulf*, see Robert E. Bjork, 'Digressions and Episodes', in *A Beowulf Handbook*, ed. Robert E. Bjork and John D. Niles (Lincoln: University of Nebraska Press, 1997), pp. 193–212. On the aesthetic effect of such flashbacks, see Roberta Frank, 'The *Beowulf* Poet's Sense of History', in *The Wisdom of Poetry: Essays in Early English Literature in Honor of Morton W. Bloomfield*, ed. Larry D. Benson and Siegfried Wenzel (Kalamazoo, MI: Western Michigan University, 1982), pp. 53–85.
87 Doane, *The Saxon Genesis*, pp. 116–17.
88 Hieatt, 'Divisions', p. 245. Regarding Old English hypermetric verse, see Thomas A. Bredehoft, *Early English Meter* (Toronto: University of Toronto Press, 2005), p. 57ff.
89 Places where *wæstm* refers to 'fruit' include ll. 466, 470, 462, 236, 594, 643.
90 *Councils and Synods*, ed. and trans. Whitelock, Brett, Brook, p. 143.
91 Ruth Wehlau notes the prominence of architectural metaphors and references to God as an architect in *The Riddle of Creation: Metaphor Structures in Old English Poetry* (New York: Peter Lang, 1997), pp. 15–54 (quote at p. 24).

92 Doane, *The Saxon Genesis*, p. 117.
93 Ibid.
94 Ibid., p. 118.
95 See Doane's discussion of this phrase (*The Saxon Genesis*, p. 119).
96 Leslie Lockett suggests that the heart was viewed as the seat of thought, with its constriction as a sign of distress in *Anglo-Saxon Psychologies: The Vernacular and Latin Traditions* (Toronto: University of Toronto Press, 2011), with specific reference to *Genesis B* at pp. 70–2.
97 *DOE, awendan*, sense 1.
98 *DOE, hearra*, sense 1.
99 For a helpful overview of patristic treatments, see Revard, *The War in Heaven*, pp. 44–6.
100 Ericksen states that 'when characters are disobedient to God, they are in the land of unlikeness and see and recognize ungodly things'. See Ericksen, 'Lands of Unlikeness in *Genesis B*', *SP* (1996), 1–20 (p. 2).
101 The closest approximation to this desire can be found in Ælfric's *Letter to Sigeweard*, which reads that '[Satan] desired to win a kingdom for himself by force and through pride make himself into a god' (l. 66). Similarly, Ælfric's *Letter to Wulfgeat* reads 'he desired … to be a god himself' (*Angelsächsische Homilien und Heiligenleben*, l. 38).
102 Doane suggests that this is an allusion 'to the prefallen angelic name Lucifer' derived from *luci-ferens* or 'light-bearing' (*The Saxon Genesis*, pp. 258–9, n. 456a).
103 On the unusual detail about the three-day fall from heaven, see Stephen Pelle, '*Ræd, Unræd*, and Raining Angels: Alterations to a Late Copy of Ælfric's *De Initio Creaturae*', *N&Q*, 53 (2010), 295–301, who notes a similar motif in a twelfth-century homily in MS Vespasian D xiv. See *Early English Homilies from the Twelfth Century MS. Vesp. D. XIV*, ed. Rubie D-N. Warner, EETS os 152 (London: Trübner and Oxford University Press, 1917), p. 2.
104 To my knowledge, no critic has called attention to the direction the winds blow in hell. This could derive from the symbolic significance of the east (see my comments in Chapter 3 on the east's traditional association with the location of heaven and God's throne).
105 Doane, *The Saxon Genesis*, p. 130.
106 Ibid., p. 119.
107 Bosworth-Toller, *onleon*, sense 2, 'to grant, bestow'.
108 See Doane's note on *romigan*, *The Saxon Genesis*, p. 270 (n. 360a).
109 Bosworth-Toller, *gemearcian*, sense 1.
110 For a compelling reading of this portion of the poem, see Ericksen's discussion of Augustine's notion of 'regions of dissimilarity' ('Lands of Unlikeness', p. 3).
111 Bosworth-Toller, *grundlease*, sense 1.
112 On the issue of exilic lands, see Cherniss ('Heroic Ideals', p. 487).

113 T. D. Hill, 'Satan's Injured Innocence in *Genesis B*', p. 289. Hill suggests Gregorian source for this tirade (p. 290).
114 Martin of Braga, *De correctione rusticorum*, ed. C. W. Barlow, *Martini episcopi Bracarensis opera Omnia* (New Haven, CT: Yale University Press, 1950), p. 185.
115 For more on this subtle theological change, see Sowerby, *Angels in Early Medieval England*, pp. 29–30.
116 Doane, *The Saxon Genesis*, p. 132.
117 Ibid.
118 O'Brien O'Keeffe, *Stealing Obedience*, p. 27.
119 Ibid., p. 14.
120 Cherniss, 'Heroic Ideals', p. 484. Doane argues that the 'psychological mechanisms by which Satan fell are relevant because ... [a]ll men since the Fall are the historical residue of Satan's fall' (*The Saxon Genesis*, p. 129).
121 Doane, *The Saxon Genesis*, p. 116.
122 See John Vickrey, 'The Vision of Eve in *Genesis B*', *Speculum*, 44 (1969), 86–102 who interprets Eve as 'sense' and Adam as representative of 'reason'; for T. D. Hill's response, see 'The Fall of Angels and Man', p. 289.
123 Ibid., p. 280.
124 On the possible sources of Eve's vision, see Thomas D. Hill, 'Pilate's Visionary Wife and the Innocence of Eve: An Old Saxon Source for the Old English Poem *Genesis B*', *JEGP*, 101 (2002), 170–84.
125 Bosworth-Toller, *læn*, sense 1.
126 Lockett examines this moment from the perspective of the demon tempter whose 'mind-in-breast' is made 'roomy ... the deputy devil expresses his joy as an alleviation of constriction' (p. 70) with 'hyge ymb heortan gerume' (my mind is spacious around my heart, l. 759a), much like Eve's (*Anglo-Saxon Psychologies*, pp. 70–1).
127 For the state of the manuscript, see Doane, *The Saxon Genesis*, pp. 17–19.
128 Scott DeGregorio, 'Texts, *Topoi* and the Self: A Reading of Alfredian Spirituality', *Early Medieval Europe*, 13 (2005), 79–96 (p. 81)
129 Johnson, 'The Fall of Lucifer in *Genesis A*', p. 500.

3
Rebel clerics, monastic replacements

The West-Saxon translation of Pope Gregory's *Pastoral Care* summarises the lessons to be gained from the story of the fall of the angels. In particular, the treatise cautions that men are susceptible to the same 'wiðerweardan' (rebellious) impulses that led to the heavenly insurrection:

> Se wilnode synderlices ealdordomes, & forsieh ða geferræddene oðerra engla & hira lif, ða he cuæð: Ic wille wyrcean min setl on norðdæle, & wielle bion gelic ðæm hiehstan, ond ða wunderlice dome gewearð ðæt he geearnode mid his agne inngeðonce ðone pytt þe he on aworpen wearð, ða he hine his agnes ðonces upahof on swæ healicne onwald. Buton tweon ðonne se mon oferhygð ðæt he bio gelic oðrum monnum, ðonne bið he gelic ðæm wiðerweardan & ðæm aworpnan deofle.[1]

[He desired a separate sovereignty, and despised the fellowship of the other angels and their way of life, when he said: 'I will build my seat in the north, and be like the highest.' And then by a wondrous judgement he merited through his own inner thought the abyss into which he was cast, when he exalted himself in his own thought to such a height of power. Without doubt when a man is scornful of being like other men he becomes like the rebellious and cast out devil.]

While containing all the familiar tropes of the angelic fall, this allusion also suggests that ordinary men can be *gelic* ('like') rebel angels through the corruption of their intellect and the desire for 'synderlices ealdordomes' (separate sovereignty). The prose thus narrates a shift in likeness, with the state of being '*gelic* oðrum monnum' (like other men) giving way to the state of being '*gelic* ðæm wiðerweardan' (like the rebellious one). Even though this passage speaks to the potential for any person to fall prey to vainglory, it was probably intended for special reflection by clergymen to encourage them to remain faithful to their pastoral commitments and to acknowledge their own temptations as custodians of power, knowledge, and ecclesiastical wealth.

The connection between the corruption of clergy and the fall of the angels tradition was a very old one. Just as Old English poets developed the tradition's implications for lords and thanes, Anglo-Latin writers such as Bede, Alcuin, and Aldhelm did so for priests, monks, and even nuns. Alcuin also underscored the connection between prideful men and angels not only in his dialogue with Sigewulf (referenced in my Introduction), but also in his correspondence with a priest named Monn:[2] 'What manner of place is reserved for the prideful man, if infernal punishments were prepared for the prideful angel?'[3] Alcuin assuredly had male priests in mind when he wrote this letter, but others viewed the lessons of the angelic rebellion as equally applicable to nuns. In his *Carmen de Virginitate*, Aldhelm, writing for his audience of nuns at Barking Abbey, emphasises the perils of jewellry and gemstones in his depiction of how vanity led to the angelic fall:

> that Monster, of which my page is now speaking, took his beginnings on the high summits of heaven, when the angelic leader and the first shining light of heaven eagerly desired to promote his own greatness from the north and in his wickedness vowed to be like the Lord. Then bedecked with the lovely shape of nine gem-stones he began, in vain, to swell up against the Creator, as he pondered a horrendous crime in his dark breast, namely that in his boldness he might be equal to the Lord with his own powers.[4]

Aldhelm crafts a more feminised version of the fall reflecting his concerns over bodily adornments worn by religious women.[5] In sum, early Anglo-Saxon authors thought that the fall of the angels could appeal to and instruct diverse communities and they tailored different aspects of the story to suit their purposes.

A more graphic instructional adaptation of the fall of the angels aimed at priests and bishops can be found in Blickling 4, rubricated for the Third Sunday in Lent.[6] Blickling Homily 4 opens with a discussion about the importance of tithing and almsgiving before turning to directives for administering confession and the punishments befalling priests who fail in their duties to their earthly flock. After its reflection upon pastoral care, the homily ends with an explanation of how people ought to bless themselves seven times daily (ll. 119–21) and a final reflection on the goodness of charity. Throughout the midsection of the homily, the author draws upon material from the *Visio Pauli*, specifically an episode where Saint Paul witnesses bishops and priests suffering torments in hell. The homilist first describes how those who were proud and neglected their ecclesiastical duties hang from trees before the gates of paradise.[7] Paul then witnesses a particularly gruesome spectacle involving a sinful bishop:

> [St Paul] said that he saw ... an old man being drawn by the iron hook led by four accursed angels with great cruelty into the dark river. They plunged him into the boiling water up to his knees, and bound him with fiery chains so that he could not say, 'God have mercy upon me!' The great teacher [St Paul] at that moment said to the angel that led him, 'Who is that old man?' The angel replied, 'He is a bishop who performed more evil than good. Before the world he had a great name, but disregarded it all as well as his Maker who had given him that name'.[8]

At first glance, Paul does not recognise the sinner as a bishop, only an 'ealdne man' (old man) tormented by 'awyrgde englas' (accursed angels). His guide explains that the derelict bishop once had a 'mycelne noman' (great name), implying that his identity is now utterly lost, cancelled out by sinfulness.

Immediately following this portion of the vision, the homily compares the sins of mass-priests to those of the rebel angels and cautions against failures to properly serve God's Church:

> Gif se Godes þeow nelle þære cyrican on riht þeowian, þæt he þonne mid læwedum mannum onfó þæs heardestan þeowdomes. Ond þis sceal se mæssepreost nede bebeodan, oþþe þæs Godes þeowes synna onfón. Ond he biþ þonne seoþþan þæm englum gelíc, þe geó Gode wiþsocan, ond þa wurdon on helle besencte.

> [But if anyone will not listen to him, the priest must punish him as it is here decreed. If the servant of God will not serve the Church correctly, let him receive together with the laity the severest punishment. The mass-priest must do this out of necessity, or else take upon himself the sins of God's servant. He will then be like the angels of old who contended against God and were thrown into hell.][9]

The homilist rebukes failed Church leaders but, more to the point, compares their negligence to the crimes of rebel angels who 'geó Gode wiþsocan' (formerly strove against God); priestly sinners, the homilist suggests, will become *englum gelic* ('like the angels') who reside in hell. This valuation carries a bit of sardonic irony.

Frederick Biggs has pointed out that the formulaic phrase *englum gelic* (derived from the phrase *aequales enim angelis* in Luke 20:36) typically evokes positive associations for human nature, specifically in the poem *Genesis A* (l. 185), where the poet likens Adam and Eve's pre-lapsarian state to angelic purity.[10] In Cynewulf's *Elene* (l. 1320), this phrase similarly references purified souls on Judgement Day. The Blickling homilist, however, inverts the meaning altogether, turning the phrase's positive associations on their head, and reminding readers that angelic nature exists in both good and bad forms.

In addition to the *Visio Pauli*, the other known source for Blickling 4 is Caesarius of Arles's Sermon 33, *De reddendis decimis* (CCSL 103A).[11] However, *Fontes Anglo-Saxonici* lists no known source for the passage quoted above, which suggests that the homilist has departed from both sources here to elaborate upon the punishments befalling sinful priests.[12] Who might have been the intended recipients for such a message? Milton McCormick Gatch suggests that the Blickling collection may have been written for a clerical audience, since the homilies typically encourage proper pastoral care and the reformation of abuses.[13] The question of fallen priests, their lands, and pastoral obligations, as this chapter will show, clearly weighed heavily on the minds of Anglo-Saxon writers from Bede to the anonymous Blickling homilist to the Benedictine Reformers of the tenth century.

Moving from rebellion to reform, this chapter turns to a high-profile case of property seizure justified by the precedent of the angelic expulsion. My focus will be on the period known to scholars as the Benedictine Reform, when rival ecclesiastical groups – the secular clerics and monastic reformers – contended over claims to property, piety, and conceptions of sovereign authority. The fall of the angels narrative became a prism through which to view and later filter the turbulent events of this era. The reformers who documented their righteous efforts sought to characterise secular clerics just as the homilist of Blickling 4 did: wicked angels who strive against God.

In the city of Winchester, secular canons who refused to take monastic vows were systematically expelled under King Edgar beginning in 964. The charters from this era recall Edgar's expulsion of the canons as the event that cleared the way for the redefinition of rules for religious communities and the relationship between the tenth-century Anglo-Saxon Church and State. The charters, British Library, Cotton MS Vesp. A. viii, fols. 2^v–33^v known as the 'Refoundation of the New Minster, 966' (or, as it is sometimes referred to, 'Edgar's Privilege to New Minster') and British Library, Add. MS 15350, fols. 9ʳ–13ᵛ called the 'Confirmation of Endowment of the Old Minster (*c.* 964–75) are classified by Peter Sawyer as S 745 and S 821 respectively. For ease of reference, I will refer to S 745 as the 'New Minster Charter' and S 821 (and the accompanying Old English translation, S 817) as the 'Old Minster Charter'. Both the Old and New Minster Charters contain extended accounts of the extra-biblical story of the fall of the angels and explicitly link angelic transgressions to the secular canons of Winchester. Along with the *Regularis Concordia*, these defining documents of tenth-century Anglo-Saxon royal and monastic history portray the clerics at Winchester as a subversive threat to English ecclesiastical unity by aligning their alleged sinful behaviour with that of the *superbentium angelorum* ('pride-filled angels').[14] In the New Minster Charter, King Edgar (941–75) revokes ecclesiastical residences and lands formerly entrusted to the clerics because they have been neglected. The charter thereby legitimates the expulsion of fallen and rebellious bodies from sacred lands and properties, and redefines the authority of King Edgar as a theocratic sovereign.

'The Old Minster Charter' (S 817) similarly reveals a far-reaching concern over the status of ecclesiastical estates, pronouncing that these same lands may never again be 'gesette' (settled) by 'modigan preostas' (proud priests). The monks, S 817 states, are to be forever 'gelogode' (lodged) within minsters and lands in perpetual service to the *Rule*. I will demonstrate how these charters and customaries achieve their ideological ends through Augustinian notions of reform and replacement as they purport to usher out a rebellious order and install a new order of pious monks better equipped to discharge pastoral care to English Christians.

This chapter will also trace the longer tradition of labelling wayward religious figures as 'rebel angels'. Rebecca Stephenson has explored how tenth-century authors frequently cast the secular clerics as slothful and uneducated.[15] In his *Enchiridion*, the late tenth-century monk Byrhtferth of Ramsey notes that secular clerics were mostly *dignissimi* ('of high birth'), but lacking in education and self-control.[16] While hailing the superior learning of monks, Byrhtferth frequently characterises priests as *indocti* ('unlearned'), *imperiti* ('unskilled'), *desides* ('lazy'), and *suburbani* ('rustic').[17] Stephenson suggests that these unfavourable qualities formed a predominant 'caricature' of the secular clerics.[18] It is possible that there are additional layers to this trope since many texts of this era portray the secular canons as not simply uneducated, but also as prideful, overreaching, and damned. In major ecclesiastical communities such as Winchester, the story of disobedient angels was used as part of the play of power to legitimise the consolidation of monastic and secular authority.

The authors of the reform-era charters – with their hybridising of biblical, doctrinal, and legal registers – were likely employing familiar tropes to justify the expulsions at Winchester. That a comparison of a sinful bishop to the rebel angels can be found in the Blickling Homily collection squares nicely with Charles Insley's assertion that charters were 'to some extent, quasi-liturgical documents ... the whole tone of many charters gives them almost a homiletic aspect'.[19] While I do not claim direct connections between Blickling 4 and Winchester, the trope of the rebel cleric clearly had potent ideological and rhetorical resonance in tenth-century England. As the next section will demonstrate, this trope most likely derives (and retrospectively invokes) earlier moments in English ecclesiastical history.

Beginning with Bede

While the caricature of the rebel cleric was certainly active during the tenth century, the genealogy of the rebellious, corrupt religious figure who shuns God and hoards earthly lands and treasures stretches back to Bede. Surprisingly, Bede says next to nothing about the fall of the angels throughout his surviving works, which makes his brief remarks on the subject – in his Commentary on the Epistle of Jude 6 (CCSL 121A) and his *Epistola ad Ecgbertum* (PL 94.657– 68) – all the more striking.[20] In his Commentary on Jude 6, Bede condemns both heresy and false teachings, noting that Church leaders are charged with the crucial task of repopulating the seats of heaven. Bede forecasts God's judgement as all the more severe for those who fail in their pastoral obligations:

> Deinde inferendum quod qui angelis peccantibus non pepercit, nec hominibus parcit superbientibus sed hos quoque, cum suum principatum non seruauerint illum uidelicet quo per gratiam adoptionis filii Dei effecti sunt, sed dereliquerunt suum domicilium, id est ecclesiae unitatem in qua Deo renati sunt uel certe sedes regni caelestis quas accepturi erant si fidem seruarent.

[Then, there must be brought in the fact that he who did not spare the angels when they sinned does not spare proud human beings, but will condemn them also both severely before the judgement and more severely in the universal judgement when they have not served their place of leadership, namely, that by which they were made the sons of God through the grace of adoption, but have abandoned their dwelling place, that is, the unity of the Church in which they were reborn to God, or at least their seats in the heavenly kingdom which they would have received if they kept their faith.][21]

There are several significant points of contact to be found here between Bede and the imagery in the Winchester charters. Bede draws a parallel between proud angels and 'superbientes' (proud) human beings who betray or abandon their sacred 'domicilium' (dwelling place). In addressing the relationship between the particular and the universal, he correlates the unity of the Church with the unity of the heavenly kingdom. By evoking the integrity of the unified Church on earth, Bede maintains that individuals who compromise this unity abandon the 'sedes' (seats) in heaven which would have been theirs through faith.

Bede admonishes failures in ecclesiastical leadership at length in his *Epistola ad Ecgbertum* (written 5 November 734), a letter to his former pupil, Archbishop Ecgbert of York (d. 766).[22] Lamenting the general decay in religious values, he cites concerns over the disorderly conduct of religious houses in the north of England. In some ways, his letter serves as a manifesto for pastoral responsibilities as Bede urges the newly minted archbishop to advise King Ceowulf, to 'ad rectam uitae normam reuocare contendas' (correct standards of conduct as far as is in your power).[23] With a 'humble and fervent plea',[24] he beseeches Ecgbert to improve the current conditions of the Church and keep its lands and properties from falling into unlawful hands and disrepair. Topically, the problems and fears expressed in Bede's letter and the Winchester charters I will examine next are framed similarly, especially the issue of ecclesiastical possessions:

> At si opus esse uisum fuerit ut tali monasterio causa episcopatus suscipiendi ampliusaliquid locorum ac possessionem augeri debeat, sunt loca innumera stilo stultissimo, ut nouimus mones, in monasteriorum ascripta uocabulum, sed nichil prorsus monasticae conuersationis habentia ... Et quia huiusmodi maxima et plurima sunt loca quae, ut uulgo dici solet, neque Deo neque hominibus ultilia sunt quia uidelicet neque regularis secundum Deum ibidem uita seruatur.

Rebel clerics, monastic replacements

[if it were to appear necessary that such a monastery were to need enlarging with any greater possession of land in order to establish a bishopric, there are numerous places, as we are all well aware, described by the title monastery by a most foolish pen, but which have absolutely no trace of monastic life ... (they ought) to be acquired as the bulwark of an episcopal see which ought by then to be established. And because there are very many extensive sites of this kind, which are, as is commonly said, neither of use to God nor men because quite clearly no regular monastic life as God desires it is followed there.][25]

Bede alludes to the sorry condition of many monasteries, specifically their greatly enlarged 'amplius' landholdings which are administered by false abbots and legitimised by fake charters. Although no Northumbrian charters survive from this era, the scenario Bede describes suggests that charlatan monks have been acquiring *folcland* (lands typically granted to those who performed military services for the king) and converting those lands to *bocland* (perpetual lands granted through writing) for their 'sham' monasteries.[26] He states that any charters affording the nomenclature of 'monastery' to such places must have been written by a 'stilo stultissimo' (most foolish pen). These glutted church lands and holy houses, according to Bede, have grown 'neque Deo neque hominibus utilia' (useless to God and man), a suggestive verbal link and Latin parallel to the Old English phrase *idle ond unnyt* discussed in Chapter 1. Bede's alarm over this unsanctioned gorging of lands that should, by right, go to military veterans or revert to the control of the king, continues:

> Sicque usurpatis sibi agellulis siue uicis liberi exinde a diuino simul et humano seruitio suis tantum inibi desideriis, laici monachis imperantes, deseruiunt; immo non monachos ibi congregant sed quoscumque ob culpam inoboedientiae ueris expulsos monasteriis alicubi forte oberrantes inuenerint aut euocare monasteriis ipsi ualuerint ... horum distoris cohortibus suas quas instruxere cellas implent – multumque informi atque inaudito spectaculo!

[And having thus seized either fields or villages for themselves they are free from divine or human services and serve only their own desires there as laymen giving orders to monks, yet they do not gather monks there but whatever men they come across wandering from place to place, who have been expelled from true monasteries, being guilty of disobedience ... They fill the cells they have built with crooked cohorts of these men – an absolutely vile and unheard of spectacle!]²⁷

Bede expresses outrage that monks who have been expelled from other monasteries roam freely, seeking refuge within Ecgbert's jurisdiction despite their sins of disobedience. Not particularly forgiving here, Bede fumes over these 'crooked cohorts' of men who occasionally bring wives and children with them. He implores Ecgbert to be vigilant and to do his duty:

> Tui, inquam, est officii procurare ne in locis Deo consecratis diabolus sibi regnum usurpet, ne pro pace discordia, pro pietate iurgia.

[So I must insist that it is part of your duty to see that the devil does not seize hold of a kingdom for himself in places consecrated by God, and that strife does not lay claim to the proper place of peace for itself, nor boasting that of humble devotion.]²⁸

Bede infuses much of this passage with imagery commonly associated with the fall of the angels: rebelliousness, devilish kingdoms, discord, boasting, and the seizing of thrones. A direct allusion to the angelic fall appears at the close of his letter, where Bede implies that ecclesiastical treacheries find their analogue (and perhaps their origin) in angelic strife:

> ut ad superiora ueniamus, haec angelos a caelo deiecit et protoplastos a paradiso perpetuae uolupatatis expulit.

[to turn to higher things, it was this that threw the angels out of heaven, and expelled the first-formed humans from the garden of perpetual pleasure.]²⁹

For Bede, failures among religious individuals are an earthly reflection of the sins of the rebel angels. The situation in Edgar's time will offer clear and striking parallels, especially the crisis of landholding, and it is possible that reformers looked to Bede as they sought guidance for the troubles of their own days.³⁰

Bede does not always differentiate between different Church orders, namely monks or priests, but often speaks of a broader category of ecclesiastical *principatum* ('leadership') as in his Commentary on Jude 6. Precedents in patristic writings for comparing the lives of priests and monks to the ministry of angels would have certainly been available to him. He may have known of John Chrysostom's dialogue concerning the duties of priests, *De sacerdotio* ('On the Priesthood') (CPG 4316).[31] Gerhart B. Ladner suggests that, in Chrysostom's view, 'the priest's soul, just because he lives and works in the midst of the world's storms and dangers, must be stronger and purer even than the monk's, who stays as it were in a safe port'.[32] In this way, a 'priest's throne is set up in heaven and stands on a higher place than all human rulership'.[33]

Monks were thought to face dire worldly trials as well. As Jean Leclercq observes, 'It is for monks to go out of this sinful world, to be strangers to it, as it were outside it, *extra mundum fieri*, and to become, as far as is possible to human frailty ... they must live as the angels, joining with them in the eternal praise of God'.[34] Given the fact that Bede so vehemently laments problems within monastic settings in his Letter to Ecgbert, it is also likely that he derives many of his ideas from Augustine's *De Genesi ad Litteram* 11.24 (CSEL 28.1). Here, Augustine addresses the connection between the angelic rebellion and the integrity of the Church:

> Lucifer, then, who rose at dawn and fell, can be understood as the brood of apostates from Christ and the Church, a race that turned towards darkness on losing the light which it bore, just as those who turn towards God pass from darkness to light, that is, those who were darkness become light.[35]

Bede appears to have shared this notion that fallen Church leadership resembles the first fall from heaven. Through the devastating logic of Bede's analogy, if men like Ecgbert fail, they will be of the same ilk as the angels who first sinned against God, destined to receive the same punishment.

The fall of the angels thus served as an important vehicle for narrating different categories of ecclesiastical authority in Anglo-Saxon England and as a way to clearly demarcate holy and unholy houses, lands, and individuals from eighth-century York down to tenth-century Winchester. Sarah Foot has argued that Æthelwold may have looked to Bede for his own rhetorical polemics, observing that his writing, at times, resembles 'the letter that Bede wrote to Bishop Ecgbert of York in 734, in which he complained about declining religious standards in his own day'.[36] The questions and analogies posed by Bede, Alcuin, and Aldhelm suggest that the story of the fall of the angels was on the minds of Anglo-Saxon writers as they sought to reform ecclesiastical spaces and the souls of their religious inhabitants. Their writings reveal an inquisitiveness about the subject and an interest in the social mores of the narrative.

Æthelwold, the purported author of the New Minster Charter, as we will see, cleverly updates Bede's analogy comparing fallen leadership within the Church to rebel angels by applying their sins to the secular clergy of his own time. Barbara Yorke rightly observes that the Benedictine Reform movement was, above all, attempting to 'recover the high standards of monasticism which could be found in Bedan England'.[37] Yet, for Æthelwold, abuses within the Church became decidedly clerical. By identifying fallen canons with fallen angels, Æthelwold typologically frames the programme of reform not as something radically new but as the renewal of a venerable monastic tradition harkening back to the age of Bede.

After examining the similarities between Æthelwold's use of the fall of the angels motif in the New Minster Charter and the wider tradition of rebel clerics, I will demonstrate how the practical aims of the Winchester charters – the expulsion of the canons, the installation of the monks at Winchester, and the transfer of endowments throughout the heart of Wessex – were rhetorically legitimised through the doctrine of replacement. In Chapter 1, I argued that, in many cases, diplomas use the rhetoric of replacement to marshal their claims for granting and repurposing land. This chapter affords an opportunity to extend that argument. By encoding the legal framework of the Benedictine Reform within the terminology of the angelic fall and Christian fulfillment, Edgar and the reformers situate the refoundation of the minsters and estates of Winchester within the narrative context of salvation history.

Pride and privileges in Winchester

'Sovereignty', as Henri Lefebvre reminds us, 'implies space'. Tenth-century Winchester offers scholars an important vantage point from which to view the exercise of sovereignty and refashioning of space. This section will consider the background and symbolic status of the city of Winchester, the roles of Edgar and Æthelwold during the Benedictine Reform movement, and the unusual genre and content of the charters issued during this period of change.

In the late seventh and early eighth centuries, monasteries were the most powerful intellectual and cultural centres in the British Isles. When Edgar came of age in the mid-tenth century, monasticism was waning in England and the days of Aldhelm and Bede were remembered with nostalgia as the 'golden age' of Anglo-Saxon monastic life.[38] The original aim of the reformers

Dunstan, Æthelwold, and Oswald was, in part, to rekindle this former age by regulating belief and practice for monks and nuns in England, reprogramming their daily life and behaviour to a specific interpretation of the monastic *Rule of St Benedict*.[39] For Edgar, monasticism offered a means of unifying the realm, and an opportunity to counteract the growing power and influence held by the tenth-century nobility.[40]

By the time the reform came to fruition, reformist ideology penetrated not only Christian belief and tradition, but also wider secular culture from politics and customs to lands and laws. Through the study of charters and rules, the central documents of the Benedictine Reform, we can date, with reasonable precision, the beginnings of the reform movement in England. The *Regularis Concordia* was 'drawn up as the standard reform consuetudinary in a council held at Winchester' under the supervision of King Edgar sometime between 970 and 973.[41] Afterwards, the reforming trio of Dunstan, Oswald, and Æthelwold were firmly established in key positions throughout England. Dunstan went to the metropolitan see in Canterbury, Æthelwold to the royal city of Winchester, and Oswald to the wealthy see in Worcester.

In many ways, the Benedictine Reform movement coalesced around the issue of property and ecclesiastical lands. Reformers looked to the *Rule of St Benedict* for insights into tenurial practice and standards for communal properties. Chapter 33 of the *Rule* examines the following sticking-point: *Si Quid Debeant Monachi Proprium Habere* ('Whether Monks should have anything of their own'):

> Praecipuae hoc vitium radicitus amputandum est de monasterio: ne quis praesumat aliquid dare aut accipere sine iussione abbatis, neque aliquid habere proprium, nullam omnino rem, neque codicem, neque tabulas, neque graphium, sed nihil omnino: quippe quibus nec corpora sua nec voluntates licet habere in propria voluntate.

[This vice in particular should be torn out at the roots in the monastery: no one should presume to give or receive anything without the abbot's permission, or have any private property, nothing at all, no book or tablets or stylus, but absolutely nothing, since the brothers may not have either their bodies or their wills under their own control.][42]

The rule leaves little room for interpretation on the matter of monastic property. Even the bodies and wills of monks, according to this edict, ultimately belong to God. Chapter 32 extends the discussion concerning the mistreatment and abuse of communal property and presumably lands:

> Si quis autem sordide aut neglegenter res monasterii tractaverit, corripiatur; si non emendaverit, disciplinae regulari subiaceat.

[If someone fails to keep monastery property clean or is careless with it, he should be rebuked; if he does not mend his ways, he should undergo the discipline of the Rule.]⁴³

The behaviour of the canons, many of whom came from powerful families who passed down lands through inheritance, was seen to be incompatible with these edicts. The *Regularis Concordia* similarly provided a universalised code of conduct for all the monasteries in England, stipulating that men and women who refused to follow its precepts would be considered sinful. The preface recalls Edgar's decision to drive out the canons because of their neglect of communal property and *locis* ('places') (quoted in Chapter 1).⁴⁴ Within the opening lines we learn about the clerics' disregard for the monasteries and Edgar's decision to restore such spaces by driving out the 'negligent clerks with their abominations', fully revoking their entitlements. Just as Anglo-Saxon poets frequently describe revered locations which suffer depravities as *idel ond unnyt* ('idle and unused'),⁴⁵ the *Rule* characterises the monasteries as 'sacra cenobia' (holy houses) which have been 'neglegenter tabescerent' (diminished by neglect). This passage also delineates the reach of Edgar's sovereign authority by stressing the 'length and breadth of [his] dominations'.

The preface to the *Regularis Concordia* not only reminds readers that the reform brought about profound changes for the English establishment, both lay and clerical, but also that it initiated a prolonged struggle between the clergy and the monastic reformers who envisioned a new kind of Church for Anglo-Saxon England. By citing biblical and exegetical precedents, the New and Old Minster Charters optimise their use of the fall of the angels by framing the narrative as a quasi-legal sanction justifying the seizure of land and the expulsion of apostates.

To the house of the West Saxon kings, says T. A. Shippey, 'Winchester remained for one reason or another, somewhere special'.⁴⁶ By the tenth century, Winchester was a very old ecclesiastical centre, which Eric John characterised as a city with a 'reforming conscience'.⁴⁷ Throughout the Anglo-Saxon period, the city of Winchester underwent various renewal projects, the most robust of which occurred in the late ninth and early tenth centuries during the reign of Alfred and later his son Edward the Elder (r. 899–924). Alfred's renewal was motivated, in part, out of necessity. At the time, Winchester was not only a centre of royal power but a site of strategic importance as part of the Alfredian network of *burh* fortifications meant to protect against viking incursions.

The mother church at Old Minster played an important symbolic role within the city. Documentary evidence suggests that there was a growing connection between the ancient Minster and the spiritual well-being of the English royal house, especially after Alfred's interment there following his death in 899. Although Alfred had conceived plans for a New Minster, he died before work could begin. Its eventual groundbreaking probably took place under the direction of Grimbald, who encouraged the new king, Edward, to proceed with the foundation project sometime between 899 and 901.[48] Edward not only inherited his father's construction plans for New Minster, but also went about elevating the political stature and influence of the West Saxon dynasty through his maintenance of the site, firstly by relocating his father's body to the newly renovated Minster.[49] The idea of ensuring the legacy of the West Saxon kings began to drive construction efforts at New Minster in later decades, especially between 963 and 975.[50]

The imposing structure of New Minster (nearly double the size of Old Minster) and the clout of the West Saxons only grew during the time of Edgar. Amid a shifting political landscape, the king ordered further renovations of the physical grounds at both Old Minster and New Minster.[51] Additionally, groundbreaking for three new monastic precincts took place in the southeast quarter. This renovation would have held clear symbolic significance for Anglo-Saxon Christians. Anglo-Saxon authors routinely locate hell in the northwest because of Lucifer's desire to build a rival heavenly kingdom there (in the *Visio Pauli*, Paul is led to the 'northwest').[52] The southeast, conversely, was thought to be the location of heaven, God's throne, and the direction from whence Christ would come on Judgement Day. Through this remapping of physical space, the new monastic inhabitants could, in a sense, enjoy cardinal validity. The expulsion of the secular clerics and the rise of a newly fortified monastic order, in many ways, restructures Winchester in terms of divine spatiality.

Edgar's career was both expansive and impressive, though we know little about his childhood. Byrhtferth says that when

Edgar came to the throne there were no monks in England, only 'dignissimi clerici' (high-born clerics). This is obviously a slight exaggeration because Edgar managed to garner the favour of a few monks, such as Æthelwold, during his youth. Meanwhile, his brother, Eadwig, only seems to have succeeded in alienating monastic communities. The relationship between Edgar and Eadwig is equally difficult to trace. For a time, the two seemed to have amicably divided and ruled their own portions of England, with Edgar stylising himself as 'King of the Mercians' and assuming rule over Mercia, Northumbria, and the Danelaw, and with Eadwig brokering the auspicious title of 'King of the English' and controlling Wessex and Kent. Sex scandals and property controversies followed Eadwig. Charter records indicate that he seized extensive landholdings from Dunstan (one of the chief architects of the Benedictine Reform) and even revoked lands from his own grandmother, Eadgifu (S 1211). Her lands would be later restored by Edgar in none other than S 745 alongside the confirmation of privileges to New Minster. As Smith notes, *King Edgar's Establishment of the Monasteries* 'memorably blames Eadwig for the division of the kingdom and the despoliation of church lands' only to portray Edgar as a unifier.[53]

By the time he was sixteen, Edgar was *rex Merciorum*, a title he held from 957 to 959 before he became *rex Anglorum* from 959 to 975. At his consecration in 973, he had been king of Mercia for seventeen years and of Wessex for fourteen. In his charters, Æthelwold makes ample use of imperial titles such as *imago Christi* to establish and enrich Edgar's stature as sovereign.[54] With Edgar, we also see the first application of the terms that indicate divinely sanctioned kingship in the British Isles such as *Vicarius Dei* and *Vicarius Christi*. Smith observes that other titles frequently emphasise Edgar's 'territorial' governance with *Edgar totius Brittanniae gubernator* (S 687, S 690, S 703) and *Edgar rex totius Albionis insulæ* (S 697).[55] These expressions of kingship directly relate to the New Minster Charter and its later iconographic representation of Edgar. Catherine Karkov suggests that under Alfred the 'Christological dimensions of Anglo-Saxon kingship were first established ... and that Æthelwold's portrayal of Edgar as a Christ-like ruler was in many ways a simple development of an association already firmly in place'.[56]

One important feature of Edgar's early life was his upbringing in a monastic setting, Æthelwold being his former tutor. Æthelwold possessed an indefatigable energy for the Church. After his return to Winchester in 963, he wasted no time in placing the Minsters under new management. A few short months after his consecration as bishop, he oversaw the expulsion of the clerics from Old Minster and from New Minster in that same year.[57] Nunnaminster was also converted into a Benedictine house according to Æthelwold's wishes.[58] Foot observes that Æthelwold probably felt that 'there were only a few monks in a few places in so large a kingdom who lived by the right rule'.[59] In all, he oversaw a complete overhaul of the religious population of Winchester, orchestrating a near total *décapité* of the established ecclesiastical hierarchy. Wormald suggests that Æthelwold was less forgiving in his 'severity towards the clerks of Old Minster' owing to 'the strength of his local connections ... at least one of the clerks was apparently related to him'.[60] Afterwards, according to John, Æthelwold's influence spread even more widely from Abingdon to Peterborough, and then outwards to Crowland (966), St Albans (969), Ely (970), Thorney (972), and St Neot's (974) as reformed monasticism began to take root throughout Edgar's kingdom.

Ostensibly penned by Æthelwold in 966, the New Minster Charter has received a fair amount of critical attention. The case for Æthelwold's authorship of the New Minster Charter has been asserted by F. M. Stenton, Dorothy Whitelock, Francis Wormald, Mechthild Gretsch, and Alexander Rumble. Lapidge and Gretsch have made the case on stylistic grounds, finding Æthelwold's work as imitative of Aldhelm.[61] Whitelock has also convincingly argued for Æthelwold's authorship of the tract in British Library, Cotton Faustina A.x, fols. 148^r–51^v, which is appended to his Old English translation of the *Rule*, by tracing the verbal links between 'Edgar's Reestablishment of Monasteries' and several passages found in the New Minster Charter.[62] Gretsch carried things further, observing that the 'Reestablishment of the Monasteries' praises Edgar's expulsion of the debauched canons throughout the 'haliga stowa' (holy places) in England and offers 'a glowing account of the early stages of the Benedictine reform and a long panegyric on the pivotal role played by King Edgar'.[63] Gretsch ultimately finds that works by Æthelwold repeatedly claim that the newly installed monks and nuns share the special duty of ensuring the protection and salvation of Edgar and his queen, Ælfthryth, who herself may have been a fierce promoter of the reform movement. Her approval of the expulsion is recorded in the witness list of S 745, where she is described as the 'legitima ... coniuncx' (legitimate wife) of the king; she also became a staunch advocate for the nuns at Nunnaminster.

Scholars have frequently explored the New Minster Charter's iconography, its use of hermeneutic Latin, its legality, and its theological claims. The key to understanding this document within the context of the nascent stages of the Benedictine Reform, when conspicuous lines were drawn between political and religious spheres of authority, lies in the interpretive framework offered by the extended narrative of the fall of the rebel angels. In other words, the Winchester charters can be productively interpreted in a literary context. The proem recounts the fall of the angels within the hexameral tradition. It reads:

> Male pro dolor libero utens arbitrio . contumaci arrogans fastu . creatori uniuersitatis famulari dedignans . semetipsum creatori equiperans . aeternis baratri incendiis cum suis complicibus demersus . iugi merito cruciatur miseria . Hoc itaque themate totius sceleris peccatum exorsum est.

[Alas, making bad use of its free will, assuming with stubborn arrogance, disdaining to serve the Creator of the Universe, placing itself equal to the Creator, it plunged into the eternal fires of the Abyss with its confederates, and is deservedly tormented with perpetual misery. At this theme all sin sprang up.][64]

Here, we get an enumeration of the sins that led to the angelic rebellion. The charter characterises the wickedness of the rebel angels as fourfold: bad use of free will, stubborn arrogance, failure to properly serve, and a misguided sense of equality with the Creator. By chapter seven, the charter fully discloses the actions of the rebel angels as parallel to those of the secular canons. The implication running throughout this opening sequence is that the secular canons were behaving badly and, moreover, neglecting their sacred duty towards the authority of their sovereign in the form of both God and king.

Because the text so fluently wields legal, biblical, patristic, and kingly authority, the New Minster Charter and other Edgarian documents have also presented special problems for critics. Eric John once observed that Edgar's charters are among 'the most enigmatic in Anglo-Saxon history'.[65] Francis Wormald rightly asked why such a high-profile document like the New Minster Charter would be 'concocted in this strange form?'.[66] Dorothy Whitelock nearly put the matter to rest when she asserted that the New Minster Charter was 'not really a charter' at all.[67] The critical questions only accumulate when one considers Anglo-Saxon charters more

Rebel clerics, monastic replacements

broadly. Simon Keynes defines a charter as the 'recording [of] a grant of land or privileges by the king to a particular person or to a religious house, drawn up in accordance with prevailing (but changing) conventions and invested with all the force and formality of a legal instrument'.[68]

Keynes's definition is tidy and straightforward, yet scholars continue to debate whether charters can be best understood as ecclesiastical instruments. Because the trespassing of sanctions is threatened with punishments of a religious nature, Pierre Chaplais once characterised both the form and function of Anglo-Saxon charters as 'purely religious'.[69] Yet Keynes finds this delineation somewhat restrictive, arguing that while 'the penalties imposed on those who contravened [sanctions] were ecclesiastical', we ought to remember that 'the diploma, though written by the Church, was nevertheless presented as an act of the king' and they must therefore be understood first and foremost as secular documents.[70]

Charles Insley carries this valuation further and observes that charters, like the law codes, 'had a very real role in the development and dissemination of English royal political and ideological agendas'.[71] Insley poses the question: 'are the elaborate and often baroque proems of charters from the period c. 930–90 simply the academic exercises of clever monastic scribes or did they have a more important function?'.[72] He stresses a deeper ideological dimension: the charters, with their lengthy accounts of the fall of the angels, seem to represent an ongoing dialectic between 'the king and his elite negotiating the limits of royal power'.[73] What we see during the late tenth century, then, is the Anglo-Saxon sovereign figurehead, Edgar, and his reformers identifying 'monastic irregularities' and seizing control of lands and properties unlawfully controlled by canons.[74] The Winchester charters construct a distinct understanding of medieval power structures through their depiction of adversaries to the English Christian community. In a sense, they legally inscribe the secular canons as rebels to the reformist cause. To discover how, we must look below the surface narrative describing reformers and their hated rivals, at the level of Christian doctrine and salvation history, to understand the full significance of this dispute.

Cuneus canonicorum

Before turning to the charters more fully, an assessment of what is known about the canons of this era and a brief conspectus of the sources attesting to their expulsion will be useful. A short treatise in

Old English appended to the Old English version of the *Regularis Concordia* was likely drafted (initially in Latin) by Æthelwold. Known as 'King Edgar's Establishment of Monasteries', this preface recounts Edgar's decision to expel the secular clergy from holy 'stowa' (places) in England:

> He þearle swiþe wearþ gegladod þurh þæt gastlice munyca angin ... Halige stowa he geclænsode fram ealra manna fulnessum, no þæt an on Wesseaxna rice, ac eacswylce on Myrcena lande. Witodlice he adref canonicas þe on þæm foresædum gyltum oferflede genihtsumedon, ⁊ on þam fyrmestum stowum ealles his andwealdes munecas gestaþelode to weorþfulre þenuge Hælendes Cristes.

[Edgar was greatly gladdened by that spiritual beginning with the monks ... He cleansed holy places from all men's foulness, not only in the kingdom of the West Saxons, but in the land of the Mercians also. Assuredly he drove out canons who abounded beyond measure in the aforesaid sins, and he established monks in the foremost places of all his dominion for the glorious service of the Saviour Christ.][75]

In place of the canons, Edgar has 'gestaþelode' (established, settled, fixed) monks in their place. From the West Saxon Kingdom to Mercia, the picture that emerges is that one of the key motivations behind the reform was the revoking of the landed privileges of the *canonicas* ('canons'), whose reported licentiousness and ability to hand down estates were cause for concern.

But who exactly fell into the category of *canonicus* during this era? And what of the more generic 'cleric', sometimes used synonymously with 'canon'? Winchester was a cathedral, meaning that the clergy evicted from its grounds would have fallen into the more technical category of *canonicus*.[76] But before the reform the line between monks, clerics, and canons was not so clearly defined. Part of the confusion may stem from terminology, with Latin *monasterium* and Old English *minster* referring to the dwelling spaces inhabited by both groups.[77] They each laid claim to pastoral care, but in the tenth century allegiance to the standardised version of monasticism put forward by the *Rule of St Benedict* strictly divided the groups. Stephenson has argued that the reform brought about new ideals for spiritual identity and that language played a major role in monastic 'self-definition' in particular.[78] Byrhtferth, it would seem, reinforced this divide with his habit of referring to clerics as lazy and 'minus indocti' (less educated), whereas the monks had 'abisgod on cræftigum bocum ... childhad' (busied themselves with learned books ... [since] childhood).[79] The New Minster Charter specifically states that 'regulares ... monachi' (regular monks) and 'non seculares' (not seculars) would be permitted to dwell in the Minster because of their fealty towards Christ and conformity to the rules.[80]

Following the model set forth in both the *Rule of St Benedict* and the *Regularis Concordia*, texts of the era sometimes subtly and sometimes not so subtly construct monastic identity and clerical identity as fundamentally different, even diametrically opposed. Stephenson locates a major source of this division in the writing of hermeneutic Latin, emphasising 'the importance of Latinity in monastic identification'.[81] Cryptic by design, hermeneutic Latin was made to challenge and alienate casual readers, to separate the intellectually weak from the strong as it were. This 'difficulty' as Stephenson puts it, '[encodes] in linguistic terms the division between monks and clerics'.[82] In his discussion of the brilliance of hermeneutic Latin, Byrhtferth is swift to point out that such writings might flummox 'clericum and uplendiscea preostum' (clerics and rustic priests),[83] *uplendisca* ('rustic') being a somewhat derogatory term denoting one who is backward, ignorant, or cut off. The New Minster Charter follows this highly stylised, esoteric form suitable for an audience of monastic elites, not an *uplendisc preost*.

There is some evidence suggesting that a few decades prior to the expulsion of the canons and the drafting of the *Regularis Concordia*, another document may have been used to achieve some of the goals of the reform. Joyce Hill proposes that well before it took hold there was a tradition of distinguishing between monks and seculars through their rules: monks, of course, followed the *Rule of St Benedict* and the secular clergy who, 'if they lived a communal and regulated life, did so according to other regimes, such as the Rule of Chrodegang'.[84] Both Dunstan and Æthelwold may have overseen the compilation of *The Enlarged Rule of Chrodegang*, which was intended for the explicit use of priests. Whatever part *The Enlarged Rule of Chrodegang* may have played in the Benedictine Reform, Hill observes, 'there has rarely been such a conspicuous blending of royal and religious interests' as we see in the *Regularis Concordia*.[85]

For Eric John, however, the 'origin' of the reform was not the drafting of the *Regularis Concordia* at all. He locates the beginning of the reform with Edgar's resolution to expel the canons and his quest for legal means to secure this expulsion.[86] According to Nicholas Brooks, in this case 'the political needs of the kingdom seem to have overridden the traditions of the provincial organization of the English church'.[87] The A-text of the *ASC* (sometimes called the 'Parker Chronicle' or the 'Winchester Manuscript') only offers a brief snippet concerning the expulsion.[88] The entry for 963 describes Abbot Æthelwold's succession as the bishop of Winchester. The entry for the following year (964) reads that 'Her dræfde Eadgar cyng þa preostas on Ceastre of Ealdanmynstre' (Here King Edgar drove out the priests in the city from the Old Minster) as well as the priests from Chertsey and Milton. It goes on to say that he replaced them with monks, including Abbot Æthelgar for New Minster, Ordberht for Chertsey, and Cyneweard for Milton.[89] This record, written with very little flourish, stands in stark contrast to the dramatic narratives in the *Vitae* of the major reformers. Accounts of the clerical expulsion feature prominently in two out of three *Vitae*. Byrhtferth of Ramsey's *Vita S. Oswaldi* suggests that the clerics were, by and large, well-born married men, and that the treasures of the Church went straight to their wives and families.[90] The expulsion also receives discussion over the course of Chapters 26–28 in Wulfstan of Winchester's *Vita S. Æthelwoldi*. Wulfstan paints an especially vivid picture of priestly depravity and this opening salvo of the Benedictine Reform (Chapter 26):

> Erant autem tunc in Veteri Monasterio, ubi cathedra pontificalis habetur, canonici nefandis scelerum moribus implicati, elatione et insolentia atque luxuria praeuenti, adeo ut nonnulli illorum dedignarentur missas suo ordine celebrare, repudiantes uxores quas inlicite duxerant et alias accipientes, gulae et ebrietati iugiter dediti.

[Now at that time there were in the Old Minster, where the bishop's throne is situated, cathedral canons involved in wicked and scandalous behaviour, victims of pride, insolence, and riotous living to such a degree that some of them did not think fit to celebrate mass in due order. They married wives illicitly, divorced them, and took others; they were constantly given to gourmandising and drunkenness.][91]

The *Vita* goes on to describe how the monks became counted among the king's *witan*, and how the royal reeve Wulfstan of Dalham was invested with 'regia auctoritate' (royal authority) to strong-arm the clergy out of Winchester. According to Wulfstan, the monks hardly needed to use force because the canons would instantaneously flee from their presence (Chapter 28): 'At illi, nimio pauore conterriti et uitam execrantes monasticam, intrantibus monachis ilico exierunt' (Stricken with terror, and detesting the monastic life, they left as soon as the monks entered).[92] An even more cinematic version of events can be found in Ælfric's *Vita S. Æthelwoldi*. This describes how, upon his election as bishop, Æthelwold burst into the Minster with monks and royal officials during mass, declaring that submission to the monastic life was the only means to clerical immunity; either those 'evil-living clerics, possessed by pride' acquiesce to the rule or disperse. Several of the clerics decide to convert, but others harbour enough bitter resentment that they later attempt to poison Æthelwold. After he survives, he carries out more expulsions at New Minster.[93]

These characterisations of the canons, like the portraits we see in other surviving documents of the era were, of course, fashioned by their rivals. While these *Vitae* provide the most detailed accounts of the expulsion, both Michael Lapidge and Simon Coates have called attention to its noticeable absence from the *Vita S. Dunstani*, written by the author known simply as 'B'. Lapidge has compellingly suggested that B may have been among the ranks of the dispossessed class of canons, considering his reluctance to talk about these events.[94]

There is also papal correspondence that attests to the expulsion. Sometime around 963, a young Pope John XII (955–64) appears to have written to an equally young Edgar authorising him to unseat the secular canons. Pope John's letter suggests that the continued residence of the canons would mean extreme peril for the city of Winchester and the whole of England:

> decreeing with apostolic authority that the canons, with their prior, the vessel of the Devil indeed, should be thrown out from the monastery in the city of Winchester built in honor of the Holy Trinity and of the most blessed apostles Peter and Paul, which is called the Old Minster in contrast to the New one which is adjacent, [each of them] being hateful to the Lord and His bishop and to all cultivators of the true faith because of the open foulness of their crimes and persisting shamelessly in the same according to his impenitent heart.[95]

Pope John invokes the history of the Old Minster, which was first dedicated to Saints Peter and Paul by Cenwalh of Wessex in 648, implying that the new and the old structures stand at odds.[96] The language used by Pope John here echoes the characterisation of the canons found in the Winchester charters. They possess the same 'impoenitens cor' (impenitent heart) as the devil.

Pope John goes on to authorise Edgar with 'authoritate apostolica' (apostolic authority), encouraging him to decree that clerks should be barred from positions of ecclesiastical authority. Rather, he states, 'sed potius ex alia qualibet congregatione qui dignus inuentus fuerit monachus assumatur et ... præficiatur' (a monk who is worthy should be found from some other monastery, adopted, and put in charge).[97] While these texts present us with differing interpretations regarding the expulsion, what they do tell us is that the characterisation of the canons – whether it be connected to their debauchery, their enlarged estates, their feeble intellect, or their seditiousness – was crucial to the forward momentum of the reform. The language used to describe the canons, in each of these texts, attests to the construction of their identity as more than simply rustic or uneducated; they were perceived as a threat to the realm.

We are relatively sure that the removal of the canons took place in 964 with the approval of the king's *witan*, first in Winchester and then elsewhere, and that a Synod was held at Easter enacting a general policy of rescinding the ecclesiastical endowments held by the canons.[98] At this Synod, it was announced that only those who professed allegiance to the *Rule of St Benedict* would be eligible for titles to endowments.[99] Two years later, the reformers appropriated a literary and theological dimension for these events with the help of the narrative of the fall of the angels. John suggests that the 'reformers promoted a "political theology" of an extreme kind'.[100] The fusion of royal and monastic power was deemed necessary to eradicate the deeply rooted tradition of hereditary lands controlled by the secular clerics. Linguistically, Æthelwold may have followed the Latin stylisations of Aldhelm but, topically, his subject matter most closely resembles the themes found in Bede's *Letter to Ecgbert*, making the New Minster Charter an impassioned polemic concerning pastoral duties and the administrative prerogatives for bishops serving in episcopates in dire need of reform.

Cuneus monachorum

In his preface to the Old English *Rule*, Æthelwold evokes the intimate relationship shared between England and Rome by referencing Bede's account of the Gregorian mission to convert the 'iglond' (island):

⁊ se mæra Wyrhta þe rihsigende wylt ⁊ gemetegaþ eal þæt he geworhte, no be þem anum lætan wolde, ac eornostlice ofer þone garsecg þone ylecan leoman þæs fullan geleafan aspringan let, ⁊ fornean þæt ytemeste iglond ealles middangeardes, mid Ongolcynne genihtsumlice gefylled, wundorfullice anlyhte ⁊ mærsode. Soðlice þæt ylece iglond, on ærum tydum mid [h]æþengilde afylled, þearle swiþe beswicyn, deofolgilde þeowede; þeahhwæþere þurh fultum þære þancweorþan Cristes gyfe ⁊ þurh sanctum Gregorium, þæs Romanisces setles bisceop, fram þæm þystrum heora geleafleaste wearþ genered.

[And the glorious Creator who reigning controls and moderates all that he made, was not willing to stop at that alone, but earnestly allowed the same light of the full faith to spring up over the ocean, and about the outermost island of the whole world, abundantly filled with the English race, wondrously illuminated and glorified. Truly that same island, filled in former times with idolatry, very grievously deceived, served demonic idols; nevertheless, by the help of the thankworthy grace of Christ and by St Gregory, the bishop of the Roman seat, it was saved from the darkness of their unbelief.][101]

According to Gretsch, Æthelwold 'took great care to point out that Pope Gregory, having been prevented from coming to England himself, remained, nevertheless, closely involved in the progress of the English mission'.[102] Æthelwold's evocation of Gregory once again situates the reform within the context of the replacement doctrine. If Gregory's conversion first gave Anglo-Saxon Christians the potential to repopulate the seats of heaven, then the reformers, by reiterating the fall of the rebel angels in their own time, reaffirm the Christian community's ability to maintain their role as replacements in the future heavenly kingdom.

The text of the New Minster Charter was written as if spoken by the king himself, although that voice of kingship was likely crafted by Æthelwold. As noted by Dorothy Whitelock, the text of the charter is 'preceded by a full-page picture showing Edgar, flanked by the Virgin and St. Peter, holding up the charter towards Christ seated in glory, surrounded by angels … Nothing has been spared to make it a magnificent object for display, presumably on the altar'.[103] In addition to those names of the men and women inscribed on its lengthy witness list, we can be sure that this document had some kind of public presence. It may have even been read to the community throughout the year so that its contents would be familiar to all the monks of New Minster.[104]

4 London, British Library, Cotton, MS Vespasian A. VIII, fol. 2v

Although there are a number of charter preambles that reference the motif of the fall of the angels, New Minster stands out as unique in terms of its sheer length and sustained focus on crafting a succinct mythos of rebellion and replacement. Æthelwold's mimetic comparison implies that Winchester has been subject to the same Old Testament cycle of expulsion and renewed lordly munificence. The main text of the charter consists of twenty-two short chapters culminating with Edgar's desire to do Christ's bidding on earth. Any investigation of the New Minster Charter's use of the fall of the angels must begin with David Johnson's important work on the subject.[105] Johnson has twice made convincing cases for the similarities between the New Minster Charter's presentation of the fall of the angels and the opening of *Genesis A* (ll. 1–101).[106] Both depict a synchronised (and somewhat radical) view of the earliest moments of creation. Johnson's interest in the New Minster Charter revolves, in particular, around the causality of the replacement doctrine. He observes that both the New Minster Charter and *Genesis A* are 'implicitly [accounts] of the human condition ... God created the world so that men might live there who could eventually become worthy to inherit the places in heaven vacated by the fallen angels'.[107] The fall of the angels, in these contexts, results in the creation of humankind and, somewhat unusually, physical earthly creation as well – both are created to restore things from the chaos caused by the angelic rebellion. Æthelwold's choice to use an unconventional model for replacement suggests that this 'version of the Creation myth ... had particularly apt resonances for the political context in which the document was composed'.[108] This seemingly subtle change highlights the role of earthly space and humankind's role as stewards of the lands that God has granted to them.

In his proem, Æthelwold also draws upon a homiletic genre known as 'catechetical *narratio*', intended to provide 'an outline of Christian cosmology and Christian history'.[109] Virginia Day suggests that the fall of the angels was an important component of *narratio* in Anglo-Saxon homilies because it offered a 'framework for the unlettered, placing each particular point of Christian doctrine in relation to the pattern of the whole'.[110] Æthelwold was hardly writing for the unlettered, but his *narratio* in the charter's proem announces a foundational mythology for the Benedictine Reform, connecting the spaces of Winchester with heavenly politics.

Charters frequently operate within a distinct theological dimension through the citing of such biblical motifs in proems and anathemas. As Smith notes, 'documentary provisions consequently all [become] figuratively charged as matters of salvation and damnation'.[111] New Minster greatly amplifies these stakes. Charters that evoke heavenly inheritance and disinheritance become, in Smith's words, 'talismanic' in the sense that they 'signify both the idea of eternal possession and the promise of salvation'.[112] From the New Minster Charter's opening, we see that politics, even in heaven, are less than perfect. The rhetorical posturing done in the proem is the fullest presentation of syncretism between biblical legend and the historical act of state meant to repair Winchester's crisis.

Early on, the charter describes the emptying of heavenly thrones, the 'eliminata tumidi fastus spurcitia' (filth of torrid arrogance being eliminated). Tellingly, Æthelwold also observes that 'summus totius bonitatis arbiter lucidas cęlorum sedes non sine cultore passus torpere' (the Supreme Judge of All Goodness did not allow the bright dwellings of Heaven to remain idle without a user),[113] with *cultor* being an agrarian term referring to a 'cultivator, inhabitant, worshiper', and *torpere* a descriptor for the condition of uninhabited territories. The act of replacement accordingly follows:

> Cui uniuersa totius cosmi superficie condita subiciens . seipsum suosque posteros sibi subiecit . quatenus eius exsecutura posteritas angelorum suppleret numerum celorum sedibus superbia turgente detrusum.

[Subjecting all created things on the surface of the whole universe to Man, He subjected Man and his progeny to Himself, in order that his posterity, which was to follow, should complete the number of the heavenly angels driven out, by swelling pride, from the thrones of heaven.][114]

Here, we get a clear picture of God's desire to replace the fallen angels and refill the empty seats of heaven.[115] As previously noted, the doctrine of replacement was derived from Augustine's *Enchiridion ad Laurentium* 62 and 29 (CCSL 46.82; CCSL 46.65) and *De Civitate Dei* 22.1 (CCSL 48.807), which states that God created the human race 'ut inde suppleat et instauret partem, quae lapsa est angelorum' (so that he might fill the place of the fallen angels and restore their number). Augustine's notion of the doctrine of replacement is inextricably linked with his conception of reform in *De Civitate Dei*.[116] According to Ladner, everything about reform, for Augustine, is expressed in terms of rectifying

Rebel clerics, monastic replacements

the loss of angels through continually perfecting the Church on earth. In his *Enchiridion*, Augustine suggests that the Church must be filled with 'men capable of reform' who will ultimately restore the kingdom of heaven, 'in the sense that they will replenish the angelic host whose number was depleted by the fall of the rebel angels'.[117] Such a message would have assuredly appealed to both Æthelwold and Edgar, who viewed the Church as emerging from a similar period of turmoil.

Gregory the Great's *Homiliae in Evangelium* 34 (CCSL 141A.6) offers an exegesis of Luke 15:8 (the parable of the ten drachmas) which further enumerates the doctrine of replacement.[118] Here, Gregory characterises the angelic parties in heaven as 'orders', explaining how the nine orders will one day be accompanied by a tenth:

> Angelorum quippe et hominum naturam ad cognoscendum se Dominus condidit, quam dum consistere ad aeternitatem uoluit, eam procul dubio ad suam similitudinem creauit. Decem uero drachmas habuit mulier, quia nouem sund ordines angelorum. Sed ut compleretur electorum numerous, homo decimus est creatus, qui a conditore suo nec post culpam periit, quia hunc aeterna sapientia per carnem miraculis coruscans ex lumine testae reparauit.

[The Lord created the essential nature of angels and humans so that they might come to know Himself. Since He intended it to last forever, beyond any doubt He created it in His own likeness. The woman had ten silver coins since there are nine ranks of angels, but that the number of the elect might be complete humanity was created as a tenth. Humanity was not lost by its Creator after its sin, because eternal Wisdom, shining by his physical miracles with the light of the clay vessel, restored it.][119]

The popularity of Gregory's metric in early medieval England cannot be overstated. It is, in fact, the version that Bede opts for in his *In Lucae Euangelium Expositio* (CCSL 120A.285ff).[120] But it was the Carolingian homilist, Haimo of Auxerre (d. 875), who extended Gregory's reading, aligning the tenth order more explicitly with the angelic rebellion. For Haimo, the rebel angels are the lost tenth order which humankind will replace, thus completing the divine numerology.[121] This conception of replacement signals an awesome spiritual potentiality within humanity, a capacity to fill the ancient voids of heavenly space.[122] Immediately following the proem, the New Minster Charter moves further into this familiar territory, explaining that God will 'make good the number of angels driven out, full of pride, from the dwellings of Heaven'.[123]

Further on, Æthelwold links conceptions of replacement and reform through his use of the term *cuneus*. Chapter 7 turns to Edgar's design for salvation, and specifies the king's desire for efficacious prayers, suggesting that those of the *cunei canonicorum* were worthless on his behalf: 'uitiosorum cuneos canonicorum . e diuersis nostri regiminis coenobiis Christi uicarius eliminaui' (I, the vicar of Christ, have expelled the depraved troop of canons from the various monasteries of our kingdom).[124] Commonly found in the early medieval poetry and prose of authors such as Aldhelm, Alcuin, Fortunatus, and Prudentius, the term *cuneus* – here used to refer to the expelled canons – is often used as a metaphor for Christian souls engaged in spiritual combat for Christ. For instance, Prudentius uses *cuneus* to refer to 'legions' fighting a spiritual combat in *Peristephanon* (CCSL 126A). The charter thus evokes these martial associations and places the conflict with the canons on both a spiritual and militaristic plane.

Originally a military term, *cuneus* denoted a group of warriors or a military subdivision. According to the *Dictionary of Medieval Latin from British Sources*, *cuneus* referred to the shape of a military formation, a 'wedge' (1). Elsewhere, it denotes a 'compact body of men, troop' or 'throng, band' (2). Aldhelm's use of *cuneos* is glossed with *wereda* and *were*, meaning that the language harmonises closely with *Genesis A* where the rebel angels, described as a 'wærleas werod' (faithless troop, l. 67a), are subsequently replaced by the 'selran werode' (better troop, l. 95b) that God crafts in humankind. Other texts gloss *cuneus* with the phrase 'getrymmed feþa' (troops arranged) such as the Latin–Old English Glossaries in Plantin-Moretus MS 32 and British Museum MS Additional 32246. The Harley Latin Old English Glossary similarly glosses *cuneus* with 'getrymed feþa' (band, host, company).[125] The Hymn for Vespers of the Feast of All Saints includes the following lines in Latin and Old English:

> Caetus omnes angelici,
> patriarchum cunei
> & prophetarum merita
> nobis pręcentur veniam.
> werodu ealle ængellice
> heahfædera heapas
> ꝼ witegena geearnunga
> us biddan forgifenyssa.[126]

Rebel clerics, monastic replacements

[May the entire host of angels and the troops of the patriarchs and the prophets through their merits plead forgiveness for us.]

In addition to its martial contexts, then, the idea of *cunei ... werodu* ('troops') was clearly connected with the desire for heavenly salvation and the efforts of men and women who pray for earthly souls.

Æthelwold judiciously uses the term *cuneus* twice in the New Minster Charter. The new abbot and the monks are a defensive *cuneus* meant to protect the king from the temptations of devils (Chapter 15):

> Abbas autem armis succinctus . spiritalibus . monachorum cuneo hinc inde uallatus . carismatum celestium rore perfusus . aerias demonum expugnans uersutias . regem omnemque sui regiminis clerum . Christo cuius uirtute dimicant iuuante . a rabida hostium persecutione inuisibilium . sollerter spiritus gladio defendens . fidei scuto subtili protegens tutamine . robusto prelians triumpho miles eripiat inperterritus.

[Moreover, let the abbot, girded with spiritual arms, defended on all sides by a troop of monks, drenched with the dew of celestial gifts, conquering the phantom-like tricks of devils, skilfully defending with a sword of the spirit, protecting with the subtle shield of faith as a defence, fighting in hardy triumph as an undaunted soldier, snatch the king and all the clergy of his kingdom from the rabid persecution of invisible enemies, with the help of Christ, through whose power they contend.][127]

The language of this passage is overtly militaristic; the rise of monasticism is likened to a military conquest, a retaking of the kingdom. Stephenson has gone so far as to suggest that the reform movement ideologically 'colonized' pastoral spaces once held by the secular clerics.[128] We are presented with a clear portrait of the *Abbas* as *miles Christi* girded 'spiritus gladio' (with the sword of the spirit). By employing the precise terminology he used to refer to the now dispossessed 'troop of canons', Æthelwold effectively translates and transforms its signification from the old 'order' to the new, compelling readers to consider how these concepts are tied together, and how the act of replacement is now complete, seamless, and also essential for the divine protection of the realm.[129] This conspicuous blending of the martial and the spiritual suggests that the New Minster Charter, despite its extravagant appearance and ostentatious literary flair, commemorates displays of power that were undoubtedly violent and unforgiving.

When Edgar says he has restored the 'Uuintaniensis ecclesiae Noui Monasterii' (New Minster of the church of Winchester), he puts English Christians on the path towards once again becoming replacements for the fallen order (chapter eight):

> rebelliones omnipotentis uoluntati obuiantes possessionem Domini usurpare non sustinens clericos lasciuientes repuli . ac ueros Dei cultores monachico gradu fungentes . qui pro nostris nostrorumque inibi quiescentium excessibus sedulo intercederent seruitio . quo eorum intercessionibus nostri regminis status uigeret munitus . abbatem Christo cooperante eligens altithrono subiectus illic deuote ordinaui.

[not supporting rebels who oppose the will of the Almighty in usurping the Lord's property, I have driven away the wayward clerks, and I, subject to the High-throned One, choosing an abbot with Christ's help, have faithfully appointed thither true worshippers of God, observing the monkish degree (of humility), who might intercede for our sins, and for those of our people lying at rest there, by zealous service, (so that), fortified by their intercessions, the condition of our kingdom might thrive.][130]

This rendition of the doctrine of replacement imagines the city of Winchester – a city that was once fortified against the viking menace and recently besieged by 'rebelliones' (rebels) – now 'reminis ... munitus' (fortified anew). The rhetoric is also highly tenurial. Edgar wrests the 'possessionem Domini' (Lord's property) from wicked tenants so that it might thrive anew. His policies reallocate the boundaries for a new Christian community at Winchester, establishing a newly ordained physical space for the monks ready to recuperate the kingdom. As Johnson so aptly puts it, the re-establishment of the monastery is 'not thus a random act of generosity but the fulfillment of Christian history in England in Edgar's reign'.[131] Edgar's coronation verse from 973 evokes his special part to play in salvation history, where he is described as 'Engla waldend' (ruler of the English, l. 1b) or alternatively 'ruler of Angels'. In a similar way, Æthelwold's discursive manoeuvres in the New Minster Charter, which are frequently suggestive of Gregory's *Angli/Angeli* pun, imply that only through the Benedictines and Edgar can Anglo-Saxons become the replacements for the fallen angels.[132]

I have already suggested that Æthelwold was evoking and updating the literary topos of the rebellious and prideful cleric.

Both the New Minster Charter and the Old Minster Charter advance arguments for suspending the rights and lands of the rebel clergy by outlining their follies and fates as coterminous with those of the rebel angels. The Old Minster Charter, unlike the lavish New Minster Charter, only exists as a twelfth-century cartulary copy within the *Codex Wintoniensis* and has, consequently, received less critical attention. According to Rumble, it contains provisions about the Benedictine Reform and the ancient estate of Chilcomb.[133] This provision seems to have been significant because it is accompanied by an Old English vernacular translation.[134]

The prime concern of the Old Minster Charter is not justification for the sovereign action or the reform movement but, as Rumble puts it, an 'attempt to appeal to a sense of continuity'.[135] The text employs a familiar casting of the likely suspects who behaved like the 'angelo praeuaricatore superbissimo' (very proud transgressor angel), guilty 'in rashly seeking to gain the heavenly splendors of the universe itself and in losing the benefits of the celestial dwelling-place'.[136] The charter appeals to the future of numerous West Saxon estates, stating that 'no bishop ... should dare to transfer that land ... nor presume to give it to any secular person for any type of reward' (chapter two). The author acknowledges Edgar's royal genealogy, citing his wishes to carry out 'the decrees of former kings', whom he identifies as Cynegisl, Cenwealh, Ecbeorht, Æthelwulf, Alfred, and Edward. The charter frequently reiterates that all secular claims to West Saxon lands are null and void. The *Freolsboc to Ciltancvmbe* (S 817), the Old English vernacular version, conveys roughly the same idea as the Latin account (chapters three to five):

> ꜹ he bead þurh Godes ælmichtiges myclan mægenþrymm þæt nan his bearna ne nan heora æftergengcana þæt menster æfre leng mid preostan gesette . ac þæt hit efre mid munecan stode . swa swa he hit mid Godes ælmihtiges fultume gesette . þa þa he hit þa modigan preostas for heora mandædon þanan ut adrefde . ꜹ þerinne munecas gelogode þæt hi Godes þeowedom æfter sancte Benedictes tæcinge . ꜹ dæghwamlice to Gode cleopodon for ealles Cristenes folces alidsednesse.

[And he commanded through the great power of Almighty God that none of his sons nor any of their successors should ever settle that minster with priests, but that it should stand ever afterwards with monks, just as he established it with the help of Almighty

God, when he drove the proud priests out because of their sins, and lodged therein the monks so that they might do God's service according to the teaching of Saint Benedict, and daily call upon God for the salvation of all Christian people.]¹³⁷

Not only does this provision forbid the resettlement of the minster with secular priests, it establishes the lands for the monks in perpetuity, transforming a once unstable landscape into something resembling inalienable *bocland*. The Old Minster Charter goes out of its way, almost to the point of absurd predictability, to remind readers that lands belong to monks, not 'proud clerics'. Such places, it states, 'locus idem semper monachis ... deputetur' (should always be allotted to monks), in keeping with their 'iure ... perpetuo' (perpetual rights).¹³⁸ A further provision about the office of bishop hardly surprises when it states that the seat should be filled with a 'monachus' (monk) and 'non autem canonicus' (not a canon).¹³⁹ In these charters, we see a highly controlled continuation of biblical legend to support and commemorate Edgar's historical act of state.

The charter's insistence on perpetuity may tell us something about the era directly following Edgar's death. *The Life of Oswald* ominously recounts that Edgar died on 8 July 975:

> Cuius obitu turbatus est status totius regni: commoti sunt episcopi, irati sunt principes, timore concussi sunt monachi, pauefacti populi, clerici leti effecti sunt, quoniam tempus eorum aduenit.

[at his death the commonwealth of the entire realm was shaken: bishops were perplexed, ealdormen were angry, monks were struck with fear, the people were terrified, and the secular clerics were made happy, because their time had come.]¹⁴⁰

Rumble speculates that many of the charters drafted during this period are the products of 'fear' of an uprising against the monks.¹⁴¹ After the death of Edgar, there was a sense that monastic landholdings were not at all safe and that the secular clerics could retake their territories. Sometimes referred to as the 'Anti-Monastic' reaction,¹⁴² texts such as *The Death of Edgar* allude to instability throughout the realm, particularly when it comes to the lands and boundaries that had been reapportioned during the reform.¹⁴³

By exchanging the 'modigan preostas' (arrogant priests) with the monks,¹⁴⁴ the Old Minster Charter somewhat desperately affirms the provisions in the New Minster Charter recalling that Edgar 'as a diligent ploughman has inserted seeds of virtues'.[145] Punishments for criminal priests or 'weofodðegen' (altar thanes) would later find a legal basis in the Laws of Cnut (I.II Cnut 41), which states that criminal priests must forfeit 'ægþer ge hades ge eðles' (both rank and lands), with *eþel* ('homeland') being the common poetic term used to describe the 'heavenly homeland' forfeited by Satan after his rebellion.

What do we stand to gain by examining the expulsion of the secular canons alongside the narrative of the fall of the angels? Although they are charters by form, the Winchester charters contain rich literary and homiletic discursive registers. They provide us with a striking image of the way kingship in the tenth century was strengthened, in part, by the Benedictine Reform movement. Written in a period when, as Hugh Magennis notes, the 'links between the church and secular authority had introduced new ideological dimensions to the exercise of power in England, as models of Christian kingship and legitimizations of secular rule were developed',[146] the fall of the angels represents an ongoing dialectic between Christian sovereigns and subjects in a changing Anglo-Saxon world. Ideas of kingship morphed as power became concentrated in locations such as Winchester and once competing kingdoms became tied to theocratic authority.[147] By removing the rebellious canons from the ecclesiastical hierarchy and appropriating the doctrine of replacement, the early monastic reformers promoted the idea that they alone could reactivate English replacement – that the way to heaven would be reopened by way of King Edgar and the spiritual protection of a reformed monasticism. What we see in tenth-century England is a Christian community clearly invested in the theology of the fall of the angels tied to the perception of a prodigious threat to the salvation narrative of a people. Gregory had situated the English people in a theological paradigm whereby they might become the *cuneus* to replace the fallen ranks of angels; the reformers now laid claim to this narrative of replacement and to authority for its safe-keeping and perpetuation.

Julia Barrow has recently asked if 'reform' is the correct term to apply to the efforts undertaken by the Benedictines during this era, arguing that what 'Æthelwold and his colleagues were doing might be better summed up in their own words as "cleansing" or "exorcising", or more neutrally, as "monasticizing" or "regularizing"'.[148] Æthelwold's stylistic and ideological manoeuvres in the New Minster Charter, as I have shown, do not concern themselves with reimagining Christianity in England, but fall very much in line with Augustine's and Bede's thinking about reform in the Church: that it is always tied to the idea of repairing the loss in heaven. Edgar's career opens with his 'gastlice munyca angin' (spiritual beginning with the monks) and ends with the expulsion of a rebel *cuneus* and the installation of a new order.[149] What these reform period pieces demonstrate, through their dynamic use of this narrative, is that rebel angels were also foundational to the tenth-century narrative of English Christian identity. The Winchester charters reveal the power of written narrative in the shaping of human events.

Even though numerous official documents of this period affirm the divisions between monks and clerics and uphold monastic claims to lands, some isolated but distinct voices react against this dominant narrative which endorses the monks as everlasting tenants of the lands throughout Winchester and beyond. As discussed in Chapter 1, Vercelli Homily 10 offers an account of the transience of earthly possessions through its use of *ubi sunt* catalogues and an account of Luke 12:16–21, the parable of the rich man who asks Christ to settle a dispute. Evoking a good deal of legal terminology, the homilist chastises those who believe that *bocland* ('bookland') can be a permanent possession. This admonition could indeed be a reactionary note against the early Benedictine reformers and their 'timeless' repossession of ecclesiastical territory. While the narrative of the angelic rebellion became a useful tool for kings and reformers hoping to reaffirm the boundaries of their ecclesiastical lands and polities, some authors also viewed it as a powerful reminder that spiritual inheritances cannot simply be secured by earthly charters, no matter how authoritative they may look and sound. Texts such as Vercelli 10 remind Anglo-Saxon Christians that inheritance is earned through the habitual practice and articulation of lordly devotion. The narrative of the fall of the angels, as the next chapter will show, was even thought to possess a powerful, almost talismanic quality, when uttered by saints.

Notes

1 *King Alfred's West Saxon Version of Gregory's Pastoral Care*, pp. 111–12.
2 This is most likely a nickname. See Mary Garrison, 'The Social World of Alcuin: Nicknames at York and at the Carolingian Court', in *Alcuin of York: Scholar at the Carolingian Court, Proceedings of the Third Germania Latina Conference held at the University of Groningen*

May 1995, ed. L. A. J. R. Houwen and A. A. MacDonald, Germania Latina III (Groningen: Forsten, 1995), 59–79.
3 *Alcuini Epistolae*, ed. Ernst Dümmler, MGH Epistolae Karolini aevi 4 (Berlin: Weidmann, 1895), Epp. IV.2 (p. 211).
4 *Carmen de uirginitate*, ed. Rudolf Ehwald, *Aldhelmi Opera Omnia*, MGH Auctores antiquissimi 15 (Berlin: Weidmann, 1919), p. 246. Translation from Lapidge and Rosier, *Aldhelm: The Poetic Works*, p. 163.
5 Ibid., p. 73.
6 *The Blickling Homilies*, ed. R. Morris, EETS ss 58, 63, 73 (London: Oxford University Press, 1874–80; repr. 1967). I cite Richard J. Kelley's edition and translation by page number, *The Blickling Homilies* (London and New York: Continuum, 2003).
7 On the transmission of the *Visio Pauli*, see Wright, *The Irish Tradition*, pp. 115–37.
8 *The Blickling Homilies*, ed. and trans. Kelley, pp. 28–9.
9 Ibid., pp. 32–3.
10 Frederick M. Biggs, '*Englum gelice*: *Elene* line 1320 and *Genesis A* line 185', *NM*, 86 (1985), 447–52.
11 For the homilist's use of Caesarius, see Marcia A. Dalbey, 'Hortatory Tone in the Blickling Homilies: Two Adaptations of Caesarius', *NM*, 70 (1969), 641–58.
12 See M. Atherton, 'The Sources of Blickling Homily 4 (Cameron C.B.3.2.14)', *Fontes Anglo-Saxonici: World Wide Web Register*, http://fontes.english.ox.ac.uk/, accessed August 2017.
13 Milton McCormick Gatch, 'The Unknowable Audience of the Blickling Homilies', *ASE*, 18 (1989), 99–115 (pp. 100–4). Rudolph Willard, 'The Blickling-Junius Tithing Homily and Caesarius of Arles', *Philologica: The Malone Anniversary Studies* (1949), 65–78 notes that another version appears in Oxford Bodleian MS Junius 85–6.
14 *Property and Piety in Early Medieval Winchester: Documents Relating to the Topography of the Anglo-Saxon and Norman City and its Minsters*, trans. and ed. Alexander Rumble, Winchester Studies 4, Part 3 (Oxford: Clarendon Press, 2002), p. 77.
15 Rebecca Stephenson, 'Scapegoating the Secular Clergy: The Hermeneutic Style as a Form of Monastic Self-Definition', *ASE*, 38 (2009), 101–35; see also her chapter of the same title in *The Politics of Language: Byrhtferth, Ælfric, and the Multilingual Identity of the Benedictine Reform* (Toronto: University of Toronto Press, 2015).
16 Stephenson, 'Scapegoating the Secular Clergy', p. 104.
17 Ibid., p. 124.
18 Ibid., p. 105ff.
19 Charles Insley, 'Where Did All the Charters Go? Anglo-Saxon Charters and the New Politics of the Eleventh Century', *Anglo-Norman Studies*, 24 (2002), 109–27 (p. 119).

20 Bede does not always follow Augustine's allegorical readings of angelic creation in his *Homelarium euangelii* (2.11), ed. David Hurst, *Bedae Venerabilis Opera. Pars IV: opera rhythmica*, CCSL 122 (Turnhout: Brepols, 1960), p. 256; *Commentarius in epistolas VII catholicas* (3.2.4), ed. David Hurst, *Bedae Venerabilis Opera*, CCSL 121 (4 ed. Turnhout: Brepols, 1983), p. 270; *In Lucae euangelium exposition* (3.10.18), ed. David Hurst, *Bedae Venerabilis Opera*, CCSL 120 (Turnhout: Brepols, 1960), p. 218; and his *Epiostola ad Ecgberhtum episcopum*, ed. and trans. Christopher Grocock and I. N. Wood, *Abbots of Wearmouth and Jarrow* (Oxford: Clarendon Press, 2013), pp. 158–60.

21 Text and translation from, David Hurst, *The Commentary on the Seven Catholic Epistles of Bede the Venerable*, Cistercian Studies Series 82 (Kalamazoo, MI: Cistercian Publications, 1985), p. 244.

22 *SASLC: Bede*, Part 2, ed. Brown and Biggs, pp. 256–9. Brown and Biggs characterise the major themes of the letter as 'pastoral care, bogus monasteries, a crisis in landholding, and a crisis in the military' (p. 258).

23 *Epistola Bede ad Ecgbertum Episcopum*, ed. and trans. Grocock and Wood, pp. 138–9.

24 Ibid., pp. 124–5.

25 Ibid., pp. 142–3.

26 See Grocock and Wood's introduction to the letter (*Abbots of Wearmouth and Jarrow*, l–lviv).

27 *Epistola Bede ad Ecgbertum Episcopum*, ed. and trans. Grocock and Wood, pp. 146–7.

28 Ibid., pp. 152–3.

29 Ibid., pp. 160–1.

30 Patrick Wormald thinks it likely that Bede's letter was known to the monastic reformers. See Patrick Wormald, 'Æthelwold and his Continental Counterparts: Contact, Comparison, Contrast', in *Bishop Æthelwold: His Career and Influence*, ed. Barbara Yorke (Woodbridge: Boydell, 1988), pp. 13–42.

31 According to Michael Lapidge, a Latin translation circulated in the Anglo-Saxon period, although it postdated Bede. See Lapidge, *The Anglo-Saxon Library* (Oxford: Oxford University Press, 2006), pp. 144–5; 317.

32 Gerhart B. Ladner, *The Idea of Reform: Its Impact on Christian Thought and Action in the Age of the Fathers* (Cambridge, MA: Harvard University Press, 1959), p. 126.

33 Ibid.

34 Jean Leclercq, et al., *The Spirituality of the Middle Ages* (New York: Burnes & Oates, 1986), p. 107.

35 Translation from *The Literal Meaning of Genesis*, trans. John Hammond Taylor S. J., vol. 2, Ancient Christian Writers: The Works

of the Fathers in Translation (New York: Newman Press, 1982), p. 156.
36 Sarah Foot, *Monastic Life in Anglo-Saxon England, c. 600–900* (Cambridge: Cambridge University Press, 2006), p. 17.
37 Barbara Yorke, 'Introduction', in *Bishop Æthelwold: His Career and Influence*, ed. Barbara Yorke (Woodbridge: Boydell, 1988), pp. 1–12 (p. 5).
38 Simon Coates suggests that reformers sought to recover a 'golden age in ecclesiastical life ... the *Rule of St Benedict* [was not seen] as innovatory but rather as an act of restoration' (p. 62). See 'Perceptions of the Anglo-Saxon Past in the Tenth-Century Monastic Reform Movement', in *The Church Retrospective: Papers Read at the 1995 Summer Meeting and the 1996 Winter Meeting of the Ecclesiastical History Society*, Published for The Ecclesiastical History Society, ed. R. N. Swanson (Woodbridge: Boydell, 1997).
39 For a comprehensive account, see Dom David Knowles, *The Monastic Order in England: A History of Its Development from the Times of St. Dunstan to the Fourth Lateran Council 943–1216* (Cambridge: Cambridge University Press, 1950).
40 On Edgar's charters, see Simon Keynes, 'A Conspectus of the Charters of King Edgar, 957–75', in *Edgar, King of the English 959–75: New Interpretations*, ed. Donald Scragg (Woodbridge: Boydell, 2008), pp. 60–82; see also Eric John, *Orbis Brittaniae and Other Studies* (Leicester: Leicester University Press, 1966), pp. 158–80.
41 Joyce Hill, 'The Benedictine Reform and Beyond', in *A Companion to Anglo-Saxon Literature*, ed. Phillip Pulsiano and Elaine Treharne (Malden, MA: Blackwell, 2008), pp. 151–68 (p. 153).
42 *The Rule of Saint Benedict*, ed. and trans. Bruce L. Venarde (Cambridge, MA: Harvard University Press, 2011), pp. 122–3.
43 *The Rule of Saint Benedict*, ed. and trans. Venarde, pp. 120–1.
44 *Regularis Concordia*, ed. and trans. Dom Thomas Symons, pp. 1–2.
45 See my discussion of *idel ond unnyt* in Chapter 1.
46 T. A. Shippey, 'Winchester in the Anglo-Saxon Period and After', in *Winchester: History and Literature: The Proceedings of a Conference in Celebration of the 150th Anniversary of the Founding of King Alfred's College Held on 16th March 1991*, ed. Simon Barker and Colin Haydon (York: King Alfred's College, 1992), pp. 1–21 (p. 1).
47 Eric John, 'The Church of Winchester and the Tenth-Century Reformation', *Bulletin of the John Rylands University Library of Manchester*, 47 (1965), 404–29 (p. 416).
48 Mechthild Gretsch, *The Intellectual Foundations of the Benedictine Reform*, CSASE 25 (Cambridge: Cambridge University Press, 1999), p. 76; Biddle, '*Felix Urbs Winthonia*', p. 128.
49 Nicole Marafioti suggests that the tomb was a site of political sanctuary. See Nicole Marafioti, 'Seeking Alfred's Body: Royal Tomb as

Political Object in the Reign of Edward the Elder', *Early Medieval Europe*, 23 (2015), 202–28.
50 Ibid., p. 139. *Charters of the New Minster, Winchester*, ed. Sean Miller, Anglo-Saxon Charters 9 (Oxford: Oxford University Press, 2001), p. xxvi.
51 On the changing topography of Winchester, see Alexander Rumble, 'The Laity and the Monastic Reform', in *Edgar, King of the English 959–75: New Interpretations*, ed. Donald Scragg (Woodbridge: Boydell, 2008), pp. 242–51.
52 T. D. Hill, '"The Site of Lucifer's Throne"', p. 305.
53 Scott T. Smith, 'The Edgar Poems and the Poetics of Failure in the Anglo-Saxon Chronicle', *ASE*, 39 (2010), 105–37 (p. 109). Edgar and Eadwig's relationship has been considered by Frederick M. Biggs, 'Edgar's Path to the Throne', in *Edgar, King of the English 959–75: New Interpretations*, ed. Donald Scragg (Woodbridge: Boydell, 2008), pp. 124–39.
54 Gretsch, *Intellectual Foundations*, p. 310.
55 For an account of Edgar's royal titles, see Smith, 'The Edgar Poems', pp. 108–12.
56 See Catherine E. Karkov, *The Ruler Portraits of Anglo-Saxon England* (Suffolk: Boydell, 2004). Karkov suggests that the charter's frontispiece attempts to represent the purification of the Minster (p. 88).
57 See both Wulfstan of Winchester (*Vita S. Æthelwoldi*, pp. 32–3) and the A-text of the *The Anglo-Saxon Chronicle: A Collaborative Edition, Volume 3: MS A*, ed. Janet Bately (Cambridge: D. S. Brewer, 2004), p. 75.
58 Wulfstan of Winchester (Chapter 22), *The Life of St Æthelwold*, ed. and trans. Michael Lapidge and Michael Winterbottom (Oxford: Clarendon Press, 1991), p. 35. Thomas N. Hall has proposed that Oxford, Bodleian Library, Bodley 451 ('De natale Domini') was intended for a twelfth-century female audience. It reads: 'Truly the devil is ever envious of us like a roaring lion, lest we should occupy those ancient seats from which he fell through pride along with his band of retainers' (pp. 214–15). See Thomas N. Hall, 'Preaching at Winchester in the Early Twelfth Century', *JEGP*, 104 (2005), 189–218.
59 Foot, *Monastic Life*, p. 13.
60 Wormald, 'Æthelwold and his Continental Counterparts', p. 87.
61 On the authorship debate, see Lapidge, 'Æthelwold as Scholar and Teacher', in *Anglo-Latin Literature 900–1066*, part 2 (London: Hambledon Press, 1993), pp. 189–211 and an overview of the hermeneutic style, see Lapidge, 'The Hermeneutic Style', in *Anglo-Latin Literature 900–1066*, part 2 (London: Hambledon Press, 1993), pp. 123–8. Lapidge proposes that Æthelwold may have been familiar with Odo of Cluny's *Occupatio* (c. 925), which contains a brief account of Satan's rebellion ('The Hermeneutic Style', p. 110).

62 Dorothy Whitelock, 'The Authorship of the Account of King Edgar's Establishment of the Monasteries', in *Philological Essays: Studies in Old and Middle English Literature in Honour of Herbert Dean Meritt*, ed. J. L. Rosier (The Hague: Mouton, 1970), pp. 125–36 (p. 131).
63 Gretsch, *Intellectual Foundations*, pp. 122 and 230–3.
64 *Property and Piety*, ed. and trans. Rumble, pp. 74–5.
65 John, *Orbis Britanniae*, p. 175.
66 Francis Wormald, 'Late Anglo-Saxon Art: Some Questions and Suggestions', in *Studies in Western Art: Acts of the Twentieth International Congress of the History of Art*, ed. M. Meiss and I. E. Rubin, 4 vols (Princeton: Princeton University Press, 1963), pp. 190–26; repr. *Francis Wormald: Collected Writings*, II, Studies in English and Continental Art of the Later Middle Ages, ed. J. J. G. Alexander, T. J. Brown, and J. Gibbs, 2 vols (London: Harvey Miller, 1984), pp. 19–26 (p. 24).
67 *Councils and Synods with Other Documents Relating to the English Church Volume I A.D. 871–1204*, part 1, *871–1066*, ed. Dorothy Whitelock, Martin Brett, Christopher N. L. Brook (Oxford: Clarendon Press, 1981), p. 131.
68 Simon Keynes, 'Charters and Writs', *The Blackwell Encyclopedia of Anglo-Saxon England*, p. 99.
69 Pierre Chaplais, 'The Origin and Authenticity of the Royal Anglo-Saxon Diploma', *Journal of the Society of Archivists*, 3 (1965), 48–61 (p. 36).
70 Keynes, *The Diplomas of King Æthelred*, p. 29 and p. 30.
71 Insley, 'Where Did All the Charters Go?', p. 112.
72 Ibid., p. 109.
73 Ibid., p. 114.
74 Foot, *Monastic Life*, p. 346.
75 *Councils and Synods*, ed. and trans. Whitelock, Brett, Brook, pp. 149–50.
76 Stephenson, 'Scapegoating the Secular Clerics', p. 102 (n. 2). See Stephenson's helpful account of varying priest terms (pp. 114–6). See also, Julia Barrow, *The Clergy in the Medieval World: Secular Clerics, Their Families and Careers in North-Western Europe, c. 800–c. 1200* (Cambridge: Cambridge University Press, 2015), pp. 89ff.
77 This has been argued by Sarah Foot, 'Anglo-Saxon Minsters: A Review of Terminology', in *Pastoral Care before the Parish*, ed. J. Blair and R. Sharpe (Leicester: Leicester University Press, 1992), pp. 212–25 (pp. 222–4).
78 Stephenson, 'Scapegoating the Secular Clerics', pp. 105–6.
79 *Byrhtferth's Enchiridion*, ed. Peter S. Baker and Michael Lapidge, EETS ss 15 (Oxford: Oxford University Press, 1995), p. 120.
80 *Property and Piety*, ed. and trans. Rumble, p. 85.

81 Stephenson, 'Scapegoating the Secular Clergy', p. 134.
82 Ibid., p. 107.
83 Ibid., p. 116.
84 J. Hill, 'The Benedictine Reform and Beyond', p. 152.
85 Ibid., p. 154.
86 John conjectures that the expulsion of the canons was the aim from the start (*Orbis Britanniae*, p. 250).
87 Nicholas Brooks, *Anglo-Saxon Myths: State and Church 400–1066* (London: Hambledon Press, 1998; repr. London: Hambledon Continuum, 2003), p. 131.
88 Trilling notes that the A-text of the *ASC* is especially concerned with abuses of power among ecclesiastical authorities (*The Aesthetics of Nostalgia*, pp. 177–9).
89 *ASC MS A*, ed. Bately.
90 *The Life of St Æthelwold*, ed. and trans. Lapidge and Winterbottom, p. 35. On the controversy over clerical marriage, see Cubitt, C., 'Images of St. Peter: the Clergy and the Religious Life in Anglo-Saxon England', in *The Christian Traditions in Anglo-Saxon England: Approaches to Current Scholarship and Teaching*, ed. P. Cavill, Christianity and Culture: Issues in Teaching and Research (Cambridge: D. S. Brewer, 2004), pp. 41–54 (pp. 50–4).
91 *The Life of St Æthelwold*, ed. and trans. Lapidge and Winterbottom, pp. 30–1.
92 Ibid., pp. 32–3.
93 *Three Lives of English Saints*, ed. Michael Winterbottom (Toronto: PIMS, 1973), pp. 17–29; *English Historical Documents*, p. 835.
94 See Michael Lapidge, 'B. and the *Vita Dunstani*', in *Anglo-Latin Literature 900–1066*, part 2 (London: Hambledon Press, 1993), pp. 279–91 and *The Early Lives of St Dunstan*, ed. and trans. Michael Winterbottom and Michael Lapidge, Oxford Medieval Texts (Oxford: Clarendon Press, 2012).
95 *Property and Piety*, ed. and trans. Rumble, p. 236.
96 Martin Biddle, '*Felix Urbs Winthonia*: Winchester in the Age of Monastic Reform', in *Tenth-Century Studies: Essays in Commemoration of the Millennium of the Council of Winchester and Regularis Concordia*, ed. David Parsons (London: Phillimore, 1975), p. 125.
97 *Property and Piety*, ed. and trans. Rumble, p. 237. Julia Barrow argues that this document is spurious; see 'English Cathedral Communities and Reform in the Late Tenth and Eleventh Centuries', in *Anglo-Norman Durham, 1093–1193*, ed. David Rollason, Margaret Harvey, and Michael Prestwich (Woodbridge: Boydell, 1994), pp. 25–39. For an alternative reading, see Charles D. Wright, 'Vercelli Homily XV and *The Apocalypse of Thomas*', in *New Readings in the Vercelli Book*, ed. Samantha Zacher and Andy Orchard (Toronto: University

of Toronto Press, 2009), pp. 150–84. Wright suggests that the letter is a 'post-facto confirmation (represented as prior approval)' (p. 183).
98 John, *Orbis Britanniae*, p. 163.
99 Ibid., p. 264.
100 Ibid., p. 177.
101 *Councils and Synods*, ed. and trans. Whitelock, Brett, Brook, pp. 143–4.
102 Gretsch, *Intellectual Foundations*, p. 291.
103 *Councils and Synods*, ed. and trans. Whitelock, Brett, Brook, p. 199.
104 Gretsch, *Intellectual Foundations*, p. 92.
105 Patrick Wormald, *The Making of English Law: King Alfred to the Twelfth Century. Vol. 1 Legislation and Its Limits* (Oxford: Blackwell, 1999), pp. 416–76.
106 Johnson, 'The Fall of Lucifer', and Johnson's forthcoming work ('Winchester Revisited').
107 Johnson, 'The Fall of Lucifer', p. 516.
108 Johnson, 'Studies in the Literary Career', p. 77.
109 Day, 'Catechetical *narratio*', p. 51.
110 Ibid., p. 59.
111 Smith, *Land and Book*, p. 27.
112 Ibid., p. 232.
113 *Property and Piety*, ed. and trans. Rumble, p. 75.
114 Ibid.
115 Miller observes, 'It seems very likely that some of the reformers would have made the parallel between those empty thrones in the heavens and the choir stalls vacated by the secular clerics of the Old Minster' (*Charters of the New Minster*, p. 108).
116 Ladner, *The Idea of Reform*, pp. 240–1.
117 Ibid., p. 277.
118 For a recent overview of the differing patristic takes on replacement, see Sowerby, *Angels in Early Medieval England*, pp. 30–2.
119 *Forty Gospel Homilies: Gregory the Great*, trans. David Hurst, Cistercian Studies Series 123 (Kalamazoo, MI: Cistercian Publications, 1990), p. 285.
120 Haines, 'The Vacancies in Heaven', p. 152.
121 Haimo of Auxerre, *Homiliae de tempore CXIV*, ed. J.-P. Migne, PL 188 (Paris, Garnier Frères, 1851), col. 613.
122 Johnson, 'The Fall of Lucifer', p. 516.
123 *Property and Piety*, ed. and trans. Rumble, pp. 75; 77.
124 Ibid., p. 81.
125 *DOE*, *feþa*, sense 3a and *getrymmed feþa* as 'troops drawn up', sense 3biii.
126 Inge B. Milfull, *The Hymns of the Anglo-Saxon Church: A Study and Edition of the 'Durham Hymnal'*, CSASE 17 (Cambridge: Cambridge

University Press, 1996), 358–60. Another version can be found in *Hymnar und Hymnem im Englischen Mittelalter*, ed. Helmut Gneuss, *Studien zur Überlieferung, Glossierung und Übersetzung lateinischer Hymnem in England*, Buchreihe der Anglia 12 (Tübingen: Niemeyer, 1969), p. 382.

127 *Property and Piety*, ed. and trans. Rumble, pp. 88–9.
128 Stephenson, *The Politics of Language*, p. 145.
129 Karkov remarks that 'Angels are replaced by Angles ... It was God who oversaw the former event, and Edgar who oversaw the latter' (*Ruler Portraits*, p. 90).
130 *Property and Piety*, ed. and trans. Rumble, p. 82.
131 Johnson, 'The Fall of Lucifer', p. 520.
132 The remainder of the charter contains an anathema against the 'deiecti canonici' and those who would interfere with monastic property.
133 Keynes proposes a date of *c.* 1150 ('A Conspectus of the Charters of King Edgar', pp. 75–9).
134 *Property and Piety*, ed. and trans. Rumble, p. 99.
135 Ibid., p. 104.
136 Ibid., p. 105.
137 Ibid., p. 113.
138 Ibid., p. 111.
139 Ibid., p. 133.
140 Byrhtferth of Ramsey, *Byrhtferth of Ramsey: The Lives of St Oswald and St Ecgwine*, ed. and trans. Michael Lapidge (Oxford: Clarendon Press, 2009), pp. 122–3.
141 *Property and Piety*, ed. and trans. Rumble, p. 65.
142 D. J. V. Fisher, 'The Anti-Monastic Reaction in the Reign of Edward the Martyr', *Cambridge Historical Journal*, 10 (1952), 254–70 (p. 264).
143 *Liber Eliensis: A History of the Isle of Ely from the Seventh Century to the Twelfth*, trans. J. Fairweather (Woodbridge: Boydell, 2005), pp. 133–4; Smith, 'The Edgar Poems', pp. 131–3.
144 Gretsch notes that the adjective for 'pride' (*modig*) was the favoured translation of *superbia* in the Winchester vocabulary (*Ideological Foundations*, p. 95).
145 *Property and Piety*, ed. and trans. Rumble, p. 80.
146 Magennis, *Images of Community*, p. 14.
147 For an assessment of kingship in Anglo-Saxon England, see William A. Chaney, *The Cult of Kingship in Anglo-Saxon England: The Transition from Paganism to Christianity* (Manchester: Manchester University Press, 1970).
148 Julia Barrow, 'The Ideology of the Tenth-Century English Benedictine "Reform"', in *Challenging the Boundaries of Medieval History: The Legacy of Timothy Reuter*, ed. Patricia Skinner, SEMA (Turnhout: Brepols, 2009), pp. 141–54 (p. 153).
149 *Councils and Synods*, ed. and trans. Whitelock, Brett, Brook, p. 149.

4
The angels' share

Moving from the role of the fall of the angels narrative within specific Anglo-Saxon historical and cultural moments, this chapter focuses on the uses of the narrative in the context of hagiographical poetry in relation to issues of martyrdom, conversion, apostleship, and salvation. As discussed previously, the connection between corrupt religious houses and heavenly discord was probably a very old one, part of a longer tradition extending all the way back to Bede's eighth-century *Epistola ad Ecgbertum*. Nevertheless, at least one Anglo-Saxon author rejected the analogy between rebel clerics and rebel angels. We begin with the story of St Guthlac. In Vercelli 23,[1] the last homily in the Vercelli collection, a throng of demons 'slidan' (slide) out of the sky to capture Guthlac:

> hie hine læddon in þam andrysenlicum fiðerum betuh ða caldan facu þære lyfte. Þa he ða wæs on þære heannesse þære lyfte up gelæded, þa geseah he ealne norðdæl heofones swylce he wære þam sweartestum wolcnum afylled swiðra genipa.[2]

[they carried him on terrible wings among the cold divisions of the air. When he was then carried up into the highness of the air, then he saw all the northern part of heaven as if it were filled with the darkest clouds of utter darkness.]

While in flight, the demons show Guthlac the 'norðdæl heofones' (northern part of heaven), the traditional site of the rival kingdom which cradled the angelic rebellion.[3] They taunt Guthlac, accusing him of apostasies worthy of the torments of hell:

> 'Us is miht seald þe to scufanne on ðas witu þysse neowolnesse, ⁊ her is þæt fyr þæt ðu sylfa in þe bærndest, ⁊ for þinum synnum helle duru ongen þe openað'.[4]

['To us is given the power to thrust you into the torments of this abyss, and here is the fire that you yourself kindled within you, and for your sins the hell-doors will open towards you'.]

The demons both physically and verbally assault the former military man turned hermit, stating that they might easily 'scufanne' (thrust) him into the fury of a hellish abyss.

The poet of *Guthlac A* modifies the aerial destination of the demons in Vercelli 23 and, in the process, invokes a more earthly, domestic, and familiar cradle of imagined rebellion. Attempting to reveal Guthlac's own capacity for sinfulness as a religious man, they show him the pride and materialism to be found in English religious houses,[5] filled with the 'idlum æhtum' (idle possessions) of a corrupt sacred space:

> Hy hine þa hofun   on þa hean lyft,
> sealdon him meahte   ofer monna cynn,
> þæt he fore eagum   eall sceawode
> under haligra   hyrda gewealdum
> in mynsterum   monna gebæru,
> þara þe hyra lifes   þurh lust brucan,
> idlum æhtum   oferwlencum,
> gierelum gieplicum, swa bið geoguðe þeaw,
> þær þæs ealdres   egsa ne styreð. (ll. 412–20)

[Then they lifted him high in the air, and gave him might over all of humankind so that before his eyes he beheld all the actions of men in the minster under the rule of holy pastors, those who enjoyed their lives according to desire, with idle possessions, pride, ostentatious clothing, as is the custom of youth when fear of the elder does not rule.]

Here, the demons order Guthlac to 'sceawode' (behold) the 'idlum æhtum ⁊ oferwlencum' (idle possessions and pride) of 'in mynsterum monna' (men in the minster) so that he may contemplate his own capacity for laxity. This unusual sequence has raised some critical debate.[6] Patrick Conner finds there to be no close analogue for this scene in any of the Guthlac materials that have come down to us. Furthermore, owing to this episode, Conner proposes that the poem may be a product of the Benedictine Reform period, a movement especially concerned with the 'problem of forming young monks' and, as demonstrated in the previous chapter, imagined rebellious religious communities.[7] While the Exeter copy could be contemporary with events of the Benedictine Reform, there is little reason to dismiss the poet's insistence that the deeds he recounts took place in his living memory, which the linguistic and metrical evidence supports. Furthermore, the demons regale Guthlac with a vision of material wealth and worldly desires cultivated by the rebellious monasteries; this perfectly resonates with the hermeneutic outlook established by Bede, who decried the waning of ecclesiastical values in his *Letter to Ecgbert* and saw in the decline of holy spaces an earthly copy of the first fracture of heavenly space.

Yet while these monks behaving badly are reminiscent of those condemned by Bede, the poet's attitude towards them is strikingly different. Instead of comparing them to rebel angels, the poet has rebel angels tempt Guthlac to self-righteousness in condemning the young men and taking pride in his own asceticism. Tellingly, Guthlac actively resists seeing the men living by 'rume regulas' (lax rules, l. 489) as evil. As Stephanie Clark notes, 'the monks are not in active rebellion against God, and they do have a hope of salvation ... [there is] hope that these same young men will achieve sanctity as they grow in the wisdom of age'.[8] Whether the poem was composed within living memory of the time of Guthlac (as the poet claims in lines 876–8), and thus during or closely following the age of Bede, or two centuries later during the Benedictine Reform, as Conner would have it, the text demonstrates a marked resistance to the narrative of rebel clerics. For both the youthful rebels and the once sacred spaces they inhabit, the poem would suggest, the possibility of reform remains. Guthlac uses the narrative of the fall of the angels as a weapon not against lax clergy, but against the demons themselves. As this chapter will show, *Guthlac A* and several Old English hagiographical poems endow the narrative with a powerful apotropaic quality that saints deploy to vanquish fallen angels and their temptations. Moreover, whereas the Benedictine reformers sought to consolidate their territories and retake contested sites, *Guthlac A* is a poem that reveals the difficulties that lie behind landed claims. Lindy Brady has recently argued that *Guthlac A* 'depicts both the land and its possession in more ambivalent ways' than critics have seen in the past, quite possibly 'reflecting the fluid boundaries of Mercia, and of the Welsh borderlands'.[9]

In Old English prose and poetry, saints appear specially armed with the ability to articulate the terms of this devotion, particularly when threatened by demons. The poems I examine in this chapter reveal a concern with spatial, geographical, and bodily protections against demons. Close encounters with the devil (or demons, as seen in the story of Guthlac) are common in episodes recounting the perfecting of a saint.[10] Whether it is their first interaction with the devil or one of many, 'a common instinct of the saints',[11] as C. Grant Loomis has remarked, is the ability to identify or clearly recognise the devil even when others cannot. The saints in the Old English poems *Elene*, *Andreas*, *Guthlac A*, and *Juliana* all demonstrate a common verbal strategy: each recites the story of the angelic rebellion, thereby identifying, silencing, and dispelling the devil.[12] The revelation of the angelic rebellion in these poems is typically accomplished through a display of 'wisdom questions' that resemble the question-and-answer dialogues found in texts such as *Solomon and Saturn I*. In this way, the narrative of the fall of the angels acquires a powerful defensive or apotropaic status within the symbolic world of Anglo-Saxon saints' lives.

In each of the four poems I examine here, a saints' articulation of the fall of the angels similarly serves as a protective ritual written across both bodies and landscapes. Guthlac, for instance, disarms his tormentors by defending his *beorg* and proclaiming his eventual inheritance of their formerly forfeited heavenly territories. Just as Anglo-Saxon charms master something threatening by defining and reciting its name, properties, and origins, so too, in *Elene* and *Juliana*, do Cynewulf's saintly protagonists Judas Cyriacus and Juliana master their demons by identifying them and their sins. In *Andreas* the fall of the angels is linked to the protective power of the baptismal *sphragis* that safeguards Christians against the devil. It would appear that Anglo-Saxon authors understood the fall of the angels as having a variety of narrative applications beyond a simple capacity to inspire Christian obedience. By viewing the fall of the angels as a speech act within the context of *galdra* ('charms'), we can see how a popular literary tradition troubles the boundaries between learned doctrine and popular religion. As saints' lives are meant to demonstrate ideals of Christian behaviour, these poems offer an arresting glimpse into how Anglo-Saxon Christians might understand sanctity and their capacity for heavenly inheritance.

The present chapter thus proposes that a saint's rehearsal of the angelic rebellion might operate at the level of the 'charm', invested with talismanic and miraculous properties. Karen Jolly's important work on charms informs our understanding of how popular folkloristic rituals and beliefs interacted with Christianity in Anglo-Saxon England. Jolly writes that in charms 'we find elements of Christianity and survivals of paganism, miracle and magic, and liturgy and folklore, all united through a holistic view of the world in which physical and spiritual realities were inter-

The angels' share

twined and interdependent'.[13] In addition to charms representing a nexus of beliefs and practices in Anglo-Saxon England, Jolly usefully argues that 'verbal formulas' or 'speech acts' serve a highly performative function wherein the 'assumption behind [a charm's] performance was that action and words combined have the power to change things'.[14] When a saint reiterates the story of the fall of the angels in the presence of a demon it has both a performative and perlocutionary force.[15] This perlocutionary act manifests both psychological and physical consequences. In the first place, the saint's utterance forces the demon to recall something from his dark past; what is more, these words allow the saint to effectively banish their demon. These verbal performances share striking similarities with both Anglo-Saxon protective charms and wisdom literature, genres that reveal a marked interest in uncovering the ultimate origin of a thing. Peter Dendle's incisive work on early medieval demonology has shown that Anglo-Saxons viewed the fall of the angels narrative as a historical event impacting the present with the devil figured as a concrete participant.[16] These poems reveal that the fall of the angels operates as a site of sacred import in Old English hagiographical poems; when saints recite the fall of the angels narrative, it thus achieves a powerful apotropaic status.[17]

In martyrdoms (or *passiones*) and *vitae*,[18] the notion that the devil must be clearly identified in order to be silenced and dispelled is crucial.[19] According to Rosemary Woolf, 'the commonest patristic definition of martyrdom was that of a conquest of the devil'.[20] Stories of saints who encountered demons were popular in the long tradition of hagiography beginning with the *Vitae Patrum*. For example, in the fourth-century *Vita Antonii* of Athanasius (PG 26), Anthony's encounter with the devil is fundamental to his process of sanctification.[21] As Dendle observes, 'demons frequently serve a critical structural function in tracing the development of the saint's progress. Saints are loners, and the devil often winds up as their oldest and most consistent acquaintance.'[22] Similar interactions can be seen in the prose lives of Saint Margaret and Saint Nicholas.[23] In an episode bearing striking similarities to Juliana's tussle with the devil, the author of the Life of Margaret describes how '[she] grabbed the devil by the hair and threw him to the ground and she put out his right eye and shattered all his bones and she set her right foot over his neck and said to him, "Leave my virginity alone! Christ is helping me, for his name shines in eternity"'.[24] When a dove tells Margaret to 'ask him [the devil] whom you have under your feet about his deeds', Margaret demands to know, 'what is your name, you unclean spirit?'.[25] While the redactor of the Life of Margaret in CCCC 303 also shows an interest in Margaret's quest to know the former deeds of the devil, those details are not fully borne out in either version of the text. In both Lives of Margaret, the devil successfully evades Margaret's questions by turning them back on her and interrogating her faith.[26] Ultimately, she simply silences the devil and forces him to retreat to hell: 'be silent now, for I do not want to hear one more word from your mouth'.[27]

Although the saintly protagonists of these Old English prose texts successfully identify the devil, there is little discussion of his origins or past crimes. These origins, however, are of principle interest to Cynewulf and the authors of *Andreas* and *Guthlac A*. This revelation is typically accomplished through an elaborate display of what folklorists call 'wisdom questions'.[28] One literary example of this perlocutionary function can be seen in the well-known charm from *Solomon and Saturn I* in which the anatomised *Pater Noster* physically overcomes the devil. The power of words is literalised in this poem as the fully embodied prayer acquires an imposing physical presence and shakes the 'feond be ðam feaxe' (fiend by the hair, l. 100a), strews his 'toðas / geond helle heap' (teeth throughout the crowd of hell, ll. 114b–5a),[29] all to the benefit of 'Cristes cempan' (Christ's warrior, l. 139a). The poet explains that

> Mæg simle se Godes cwide   gumena gehwylcum
> ealra feonda gehwane   fleondne gebrengan
> ðurh mannes muð,   manfulra heap,
> sweartne geswencan,   næfre hie ðæs syllice
> bleoum bregdað. (ll. 146–50a)

[The utterance of God can always for everyone put each and every fiend to flight through the mouth of man, the host of wicked ones, can vex the black one, even if they change their forms ever so strangely.]

A 'cwide' (utterance) issued 'ðurh mannes muð' (through the mouth of man), much like a charm or the *Pater Noster* prayer, can possess an apotropaic force. The *Solomon and Saturn* poet continues:

> Forðon nænig man scile
> oft orðances   ut abredan
> wæpnes ecgge,   ðeah ðe him se wlite cweme –
> ac symle   he sceal singan. (ll. 163b–6a)

[Therefore no man must draw out the weapon's edge without forethought, though its appearance is pleasing to him – but ever must he sing.]

The idea presented here is that the best protection against the devil is 'singing'. This connects with Jolly's characterisation of charms as a kind of 'song ... or incantation ... in the way a healer [might] sing a psalm or prayer'.[30] As Jolly notes, the very word *galdor* ('charm') comes from *galan* 'to sing or chant' and implies a kind of ritualised or formal performance.[31]

Scholars have identified and discussed non-verbal 'weapons' used against demons in Anglo-Saxon texts, noting the protective properties of crosses and the baptismal *sphragis* wherein the body is literally 'sealed' by the sign of the Cross.[32] According to David F. Johnson, saints use the *sphragis* 'for protective purposes, sometimes to guard themselves against danger, sometimes to protect others'.[33] In perhaps its most well-known poetic appearance, Andreas is 'protected by the mark ... a token which protects not only Andreas but baptised Christians everywhere'.[34] In his survey of the *crux usualis*, Johnson also notes that 'the efficacy of the [cross] may be ... wielded by the ordinary believer'.[35] Thomas D. Hill has reviewed the apotropaic effects of 'exsufflation', or sacred breath, also connected to the sacrament of baptism, suggesting that spiritual protection need not always be perceptible.[36] From material objects to signs to performative gestures, Anglo-Saxons possessed a host of demon repellants, 'protective shield[s]' or 'offensive weapon[s]',[37] to defend against malicious spiritual forces. To these we may add a further weapon against the devil to the Anglo-Saxon arsenal: the narration of the angelic rebellion. When uttered by a holy man or woman, this narrative literally disarms and expels the devil, serving as a guard against the physical presence of the demon and acting as a signifier of sainthood.[38]

Uncovering origins

Two of Cynewulf's rune-signed poems contain stories of saints who face demons.[39] *Juliana* and *Elene* are respectively set during the reigns of the pagan Maximian (286–305 CE) and his converted Christian son-in-law Constantine the Great (306–37 CE). As Jill Frederick and others have pointed out, *Juliana* is the only known Old English text 'that renders into poetry the *passio* of a female saint'.[40] The *passio* of Juliana was widely known in Anglo-Saxon

England. Bede mentions Juliana in his *Martyrologium* (PL 94, cols. 843–4) and her martyrdom is likewise narrated in the *Cotton-Corpus Legendary*.[41] The cult of Juliana was based on 'the *Passio S. Iulianae*, a text which was arguably composed in the later sixth century, or even in the seventh'.[42]

Juliana narrates the young woman's broken relationship with her father, Heliseus, and would-be suitor, Affricanus. When Juliana refuses to marry Affricanus, she endures four tortures: she is beaten with a rod, hanged by her hair, tied to a fiery wheel, and dipped in molten lead. When these tortures prove ineffective, Juliana is imprisoned, only to be visited by a demon in 'engles hiw' (the form of an angel, l. 244b).[43] Juliana immediately suspects he is 'se aglæca' (the adversary, l. 246b) and a 'wuldres wiþerbreca' (opponent, l. 269a). In the *Acta*, after making the sign of the Cross, Juliana seizes the demon and demands to know, 'who sent you to me?'.[44] As with Saint Margaret, a heavenly voice instructs Juliana to

'Forfoh þone frætgan   ond fæste geheald,
oþþæt he his siðfæt   secge mid ryhte,
ealne from orde,   hwæt his æþelu syn'. (ll. 284–6)

['Seize the perverse one and hold him fast, until he tells you his journey rightly, entirely from the beginning, what his origins may be'.]

This command to uncover the devil's origins does not appear in the *Passio S. Iulianae* or the *Acta*.[45] Cynewulf's modification makes Juliana's endeavour to expose the demon's 'æþelu' (origins) a divinely sanctioned act of recovery; narration thus becomes part of the process of expelling the demon from her presence.

Scholars have observed that this episode modulates between a variety of genres, ranging from penitentials to fairy tales. Allen Frantzen has argued that the poem imitates the process of confession, wherein 'the demon impersonates a penitent who has been forced to confess'.[46] Although the demon is eventually forthcoming about his past, his confession is neither apologetic nor sincere. As Frantzen observes: 'The demon's performance ... offered Anglo-Saxon Christians a glimpse of the theatricality of their spiritual lives: using language and words prescribed by the penitentials, he demonstrates both insincere confession and feigned sorrow for sins'.[47] Although focusing primarily on how this episode resonates with the structure of fairy tales, Rolf Bremmer Jr. mentions the similarities between this scene and the homiletic topos known as

'The Devil's Account' in which a devil tells an anchorite about heaven and hell.[48] Also demonstrating Cynewulf's presentation of speech acts, John P. Hermann has observed that this sequence contained a distinct 'question-and-answer' mode recalling texts such as *Adrian and Ritheus*, *Solomon and Saturn*, and the *Joca Monachorum*.[49] Hermann does not pursue this point further, but I think it productive to consider how Cynewulf deploys this mode, allowing Juliana to gain the upper hand through her knowledge of the demon's identity and past crimes.

Juliana begins questioning the devil in a direct manner with the command *Saga* ('Say'). This resembles the performative aspect of the question-and-answer dialogues we see in *Solomon and Saturn*. Indeed, one question from *Solomon and Saturn II* begins with Saturn saying, 'Saga ðu me ...' (Tell me ...) and ends with Solomon's extended account of the fall of the angels (ll. 273–97).[50] Juliana's entire demand reads:

> 'Saga, earmsceapen,   unclæne gæst,
> hu þu þec geþyde,   þystra stihtend,
> on clænra gemong?   Þu wið Criste geo
> wærleas wunne   ond gewin tuge,
> hogdes wiþ halgum.   Þe wearð helle seað
> niþer gedolfen,   þær þu nydbysig
> fore oferhygdum   eard gesohtes.
> Wende ic þæt þu þy wærra   weorþan sceolde
> wið soðfæstum   swylces gemotes
> ond þy unbealdra,   þe þe oft wiðstod
> þurh wuldorcyning   willan þines'. (418–28)

['Say, wretched one, unclean spirit, how you associated yourself, a ruler of darkness, among a pure company? You formerly strove faithless against Christ and brought about strife, conspired against the holy one. For you a hell pit was dug below, where harassed by misery because of your pride you sought out this dwelling. I expected that you might have been more wary and less bold over such an encounter with a righteous one, who often withstood your will through the king of glory'.]

While Cynewulf has already identified the devil as the 'fyrnsynna fruman' (author of ancient sins, l. 347),[51] in articulating her knowledge that the demon 'wið Criste geo wærleas wunne' (faithless, formerly strove against Christ), Juliana reveals her familiarity with the demon's ultimate origin, the war in heaven, and the litany of punishments the rebel angels received.

The devil averts Juliana's question, however, and (as in the story of Saint Margaret) tries to turn the questions back on her with 'þu me ærest saga' (you tell me first, l. 430b). Marie Nelson points out that the devil makes demands 'when he is not in a position to do so'.[52] Juliana remains persistent until the demon concedes that her speech is too powerful for him: 'Nu ic þæt gehyre þurh þinne hleoþorcwide, / þæt ic nyde sceal niþa gebæded / mod meldian, swa þu me beodest, / þreaned þolian' (Now I hear through your eloquence, that I out of necessity, constrained by afflictions, must reveal my mind, just as you bid me, and suffer punishing affliction, ll. 461–4a). The flyting between the saint and devil reveals Juliana's mastery over her adversary through the perlocutionary force that accompanies narratives of origin.

The demon then says he must 'mod meldian' (reveal his mind).[53] Expanding his Latin source, Cynewulf's demon recounts his misdeeds from the temptation of Adam and Eve (l. 500), to the beheading of John the Baptist (l. 293), to the betrayal and crucifixion of Christ (ll. 289–306), and the deaths of Peter, Paul, and Andrew (ll. 302–11).[54] Amid his catalogue of persecutions, we learn that Juliana's demon is, like the demon who tempts Adam and Eve in *Genesis B*, a mere subordinate sent from hell by his 'fæder' (father, l. 321a) whom he describes as 'hellwarena cyning' (king of the inhabitants of hell, l. 322a). This idea of the 'stay-at-home king' who sends his 'þegnas' (thanes, l. 333a) into the world, according to Jill Frederick, would have struck Anglo-Saxons in a particularly negative way.[55] These reflections on Satan as a kind of absentee king serve as a reminder that, as Dendle puts it, 'a physical entity chained in hell called Satan, a silent and distant prop serving only as a mute memorial to a failed rebellion long ago'.[56] Juliana subtly coaxes her demon to confess his crimes, beginning with the time when 'siþþan furþum wæs / rodor aræred' (the firmament was first lifted up, ll. 497b–8a).[57] In an attempt to regain face and entice Juliana, the demon sets about describing his treacherous professional accomplishments:

'Hwæt sceal ic ma riman
yfel endeleas?   Ic eall gebær,
wraþe wrohtas   geond werþeode,
þa þe gewurdun   widan feore
from fruman worulde   fira cynne,
eorlum on eorþan.   Ne wæs ænig þara
þæt me þus þriste,   swa þu nu þa,
halig mid hondum,   hrinan dorste,
næs ænig þæs modig   mon ofer eorþan

The angels' share

>   þurh halge meaht,   heahfædra nan
>   ne witgena.   Þeah þe him weoruda god
>   onwrige, wuldres cyning,   wisdomes gæst,
>   giefe unmæte,   hwæþre ic gong to þam
>   agan moste.   Næs ænig þara
>   þæt mec þus bealdlice   bennum bilegde,
>   þream forþrycte,   ær þu nu þa
>   þa miclan meaht   mine oferswiðdest,
>   fæste forfenge,   þe me fæder sealde,
>   feond moncynnes,   þe he mec feran het,
>   þeoden of þystrum,   þæt ic þe sceolde
>   synne swetan'. (ll. 505b–25a)

['Why must I recount more of my endless evil? I brought forth it all, evil crimes throughout nations of people, which have befallen humankind forever, people on earth, since the creation of the world. There were none who dared thus boldly to lay hold of me with hands, the way you do now, holy one, nor any man so courageous on earth through holy might, neither the patriarchs nor the prophets. Although the God of hosts, the king of glory, revealed the spirit of wisdom to them and innumerable graces, still I might possess access to them. Not one of them has so boldly surrounded me with shackles as this, overwhelmed with punishments, before you now overcame with firm grasp my great power that my father gave me, the enemy of humankind, who commanded me to journey out of darkness so that I might make sins sweet to you'.]

In rehearsing his crimes, the demon claims that he is the source who 'eall gebær' (brought forth it all, l. 506b). Speech becomes Juliana's own protective weapon,[58] as she reveals that she cannot be charmed by the devil because of her knowledge of salvation history.

Cynewulf introduces the idea of the demon turned 'melda' (informant, betrayer) against his fellow retainers in that he exposes their secrets. Shortly before Juliana is to be executed, the demon returns and exclaims, 'Gyldað nu mid gyrne, þæt heo goda ussa / meaht forhogde, ond mec swiþast / geminsade, þæt ic to meldan wearð' (Repay her now with earnest, that she despised the might of our gods, and grievously degraded me, such that I became an informer, ll. 619–21). Bosworth-Toller defines *melda* in two ways: first as 'a narrator, an informer, announcer' and second as 'betrayer'.[59] The related verb *meldian* means 'to declare, announce, tell' and 'inform against, accuse', or, alternatively as 'reveal' and it has distinct legalistic undertones.⁶⁰ In becoming a *melda*, the demon exposes his arts of temptation. But in this wisdom contest, Juliana reveals how a saint might prevail against adversaries simply through historical insight. In rehearsing this demon's origin, Juliana shows that speech and knowledge are sufficient weapons for combating spiritual enemies when one has no material objects or signs at one's disposal.

The devil's cut

Elene recounts the famous angelic vision granted to the Emperor Constantine and his subsequent victory over the armies of Maxentius (312 CE). The poem follows Constantine's triumphant return to Rome and his attempt to discover the meaning behind the *tacen* ('token') that led him to victory. Most of the poem, however, focuses on the emperor's mother and the apocryphal story of her *inventio* ('discovery') of Christ's Cross in the Holy Land. The man whom Elene enlists to help her in her quest to find the Cross is Judas Cyriacus, a Jew described by Cynewulf as 'gidda gearosnotor' (wise in lore, l. 418a) and 'wordes cræftige' (skilled in words, l. 419a). When Elene first meets Judas, he and the other Jews are described as 'modblinde' (spiritually blind, l. 306a). Cynewulf's poem traces the process of Judas's coerced conversion to the Christian faith.

Throughout the early stages of the poem, Elene aggressively mines the depths of Judas's knowledge about the history and lore of the Cross. When he refuses to reveal his knowledge regarding its whereabouts, Elene places Judas in an earthen pit and starves him. Suffering and hungry, Judas eventually agrees to help. While in search of the buried Cross (*goldhord*), Judas is seized upon by the devil. In order to banish the devil, and disassociate himself from his former 'spiritual blindness', Judas effectively utilises the fall of the angels narrative as an apotropaic weapon; he both identifies the devil and banishes him in a verbalised performance of his newly acquired Christian faith.

Elene is a poem about the recovery of knowledge with spiritual value.⁶¹ This reclamation process is initiated by Elene, who attempts to extract wisdom from Judas in a manner that resembles Juliana's interrogation of the devil. When trying to discover the location of the Cross, she goads Judas with the formulaic phrases 'saga, gif ðu cunne' (say, if you can, l. 856b) and 'saga ricene me' (tell me quickly, l. 623b). According to John Damon, 'Elene performs a role of domination and physical coercion often reserved in hagiography for the persecutors of martyrs'.⁶² Unlike Juliana, whose aim is the revelation of the devil's persecutions against humanity, Elene's interrogations are aimed at uncovering the hidden knowledge and lore concealed by the Jews in the poem, but in that sense they also resemble 'wisdom questions'.

Initially, Judas actively suppresses his knowledge of the location of the Cross. Robert Bjork asserts that Judas 'rhetorically and figuratively conceals' its whereabouts.⁶³ Nathan Breen similarly suggests that Judas desires to control 'the narration of the history of the Jews' through this act of concealment.⁶⁴ In the presence of the Jewish council, Judas affirms that the Cross must stay hidden for the security of the Jewish nation:

'Þæt wæs þrealic geþoht!   Nu is þearf mycel
þæt we fæstlice   ferhð staðelien,
þæt we ðæs morðres   meldan ne weorðen
hwær þæt halige trio   beheled wurde
æfter wigþræce,   þy læs toworpen sien
frod fyrngewritu   ond þa fæderlican
lare forleten'. (ll. 426–32a)

['That (the crucifixion) was a bad idea! Now there is great need that we are steadfast in our spirits, that we do not become informants of that murder, or as to where that holy tree was hidden after the violence of war, in case that the old writings be overturned and the laws of our fathers forsaken'.]

In this context, the Jews suppress evidence of their culpability in the death of Christ. While as Elizabeth Tyler notes the 'halige trio' (holy tree) is only figuratively a *goldhord*,⁶⁵ it is a form of plunder buried away after a violent engagement. In reference to *The Battle of Maldon*, Michael Cherniss suggests that 'a tribe's sense of its own worthiness depends heavily upon the treasure which it holds'.⁶⁶ A similar association could be made here; Judas insists that the Jews must not become 'meldan' (informants, betrayers) of their former crimes, which means that the Cross must remain buried for the maintenance and continuance of the Jewish people. As Scheil observes, Cynewulf works within a tradition suggesting that the Jews were responsible for Christ's death; he sees Judas as 'representative of the antagonistic Jew ... [who] killed Christ because [he] did not recognize him as the son of God'.⁶⁷ Moreover, 'by hiding the location of the cross', according to Scheil, 'the Jews are, in a sense, reenacting the crucifixion, extending their original crime'.[68] Becoming a *melda* would not only mean personal shame for Judas but also a betrayal and the overturning of Jewish traditions embodied in the 'frod fyrngewritu' (old writings) and 'fæderlican lare' (laws of our fathers).

We find this manner of *melda* who shares a connection to a hoard in *Beowulf*. When the ancient hoard is breached and the dragon awoken, the poet describes how 'him to bearme cwom / maðþumfæt mære þurh ðæs meldan hond' (a precious vessel had come to him [the lord] through the informer's hands, ll. 2404b–5).[69] Judas treats his knowledge as treasure but, like the treasure in *Beowulf*, this hoard becomes 'a symbol of everything wrongly hidden away, possessed in darkness, spell-bound by evil thought'.[70] As John Hill notes, 'buried treasure elicits a sense of uselessness'.[71] Like the 'unnyt' (useless, l. 3168) treasure hoard that is interred within Beowulf's barrow, the Cross has become unusable and remains shrouded in mystery. In both cases, the infiltration of a hoard amassed 'æfter wigþræce' (after the violence of war), with a *melda* acting as intermediary, threatens cultural rupture and radical change.

Cynewulf's *melda* in *Juliana* (the demon) openly claims responsibility for Christ's crucifixion (ll. 289–306). In evoking the idea of a *melda* in a slightly different context here, Cynewulf subtly associates the Jews not only with the crime of Christ's crucifixion but also with those of the devil. He reinforces this by characterising the Jews with phrases and formulae typically reserved for the rebel angels. He says that they have 'nið ahofun' (raised up enmity, l. 837a) and, like the rebels angels, they 'hyrdon' (listened) to 'leahtra fruman' (the author of sins, l. 838). Through their deliberate act of concealment, Cynewulf suggests that the Jews aid in the accumulation of the devil's own 'plunder' in the form of un-Christianised souls.

With his imprisonment and starvation in the earthen pit, Judas's own body becomes an emblem for buried wisdom. John Damon notes similarities between this sequence and the temptation of Juliana, stating that the women in both texts keep an 'informant held captive until he will reveal the secrets he holds'.[72] It is possible that Cynewulf draws upon Roman treasure laws and *thesaurus inventus* customs which call for those implicated in the concealment of a hoard to be subjected to torture. In his consideration of *Beowulf*, Earl R. Anderson observes that under Roman law, 'anyone who conceals [treasure] was regarded as a thief, subject to ordeal'.[73] Judas gives in to his hunger on the seventh day when he announces that he is prepared to reveal the secret location of the Cross. Upon his emergence from the pit, Judas says a prayer in 'Ebrisc' (Hebrew). In this prayer he begins to reveal his trove of spiritual knowledge, beginning with a history of angelic creation. He praises God (l. 725), evokes both the good angels (ll. 734b–59) and the fallen angels (ll. 759b–71), and anticipates Christ's rule on earth through the power of the Cross:[74]

'Þæs ðu, god dryhten,
wealdest widan fyrhð, ond þu womfulle
scyldwyrcende sceaðan of radorum
awurpe wonhydige. Þa sio werge sceolu
under heolstorhofu hreosan sceolde
in wita forwyrd, þær hie in wylme nu
dreogaþ deaðcwale in dracan fæðme,
þeostrum forþylmed. He þinum wiðsoc
aldordome. Þæs he in ermðum sceal,
ealra fula ful, fah þrowian,
þeowned þolian. Þær he þin ne mæg
word aweorpan, is in witum fæst,
ealre synne fruma, susle gebunden'. (ll. 759b–71)

['This you, Lord God, will rule forever, and you cast out the guilty sinful evil-doers from heaven, the foolish ones. Then that cursed troop had to fall down into dark abodes in the destruction of punishments, where they now undergo agonies in that surge of fire in the dragon's embrace, wrapped in darkness. He rebelled against your authority. For that, he must in misery, full of every foulness, suffer guilty, endure bondage. There he may not reject your word, he is bound fast in torment and punishment, the originator of all sin'.]

This prayer reveals that Judas's identity has changed; for Cynewulf, Judas is beginning to narrate a release from his own form of rebellion against the 'aldordome' (authority) of God. Judas asks that God reveal to him the *goldhord* 'þæt yldum wæs / lange behyded' (which has long been hidden from men, ll. 791–92a) by making smoke arise from that spot 'of ðam wangstede ... rec astigan', ll. 793a–94b) where the Cross is buried. In associating Christ's Cross with a *goldhord*, Cynewulf invokes the idea that buried treasure, like spiritual knowledge, is being placed back into circulation.

There follows a dramatisation of a dispute over the ownership of a hoard, competition for a space deemed sacred and valuable to Christians and demons alike. To become fully Christian, Judas must reclaim a *goldhord*, the contested space that the devil believes his own possession. Once the Cross has been unearthed and authenticated through a miraculous sign (ll. 859–97), a devil appears to Judas: 'on lyft astah lacende feond' (a demon leapt up there, hovering in the air, l. 899). The devil tells Judas that his hoard has been unjustly plundered and that he has been robbed of his 'cut' (a reference to the 'doctrine of the devil's rights').[75] Referencing Judas Iscariot and Judas Cyriacus simultaneously, the devil describes how a Judas formerly ('Iudas ær', l. 921b) brought him hope but now through a Judas ('þurh Iudas', l. 923b) he has been deprived of goods ('goda geasne', l. 923a). In becoming a *melda* for Christ, Judas has undone the devil's monopoly on souls (ll. 902–10) and transferred ownership of the *goldhord*.

Elene overhears Judas sparring with the 'ealre synne fruma' (originator of all sins, ll. 952b–61a), when the devil demands to know who 'iceð ealdne nið, æhta strudeð' (increases old strife, by plundering my possessions, l. 904). In the *Acta Cyriaci*, Cynewulf's major source for the Old English poem, Judas simply states: 'May Christ who raised the dead damn you to the abyss of everlasting fire'.[76] Significantly, Cynewulf expands this statement to demonstrate Judas's extensive knowledge of the fall of the angels:

> 'Ne þearft ðu swa swiðe,   synna gemyndig,
> sar niwigan   ond sæce ræran,
> morðres manfrea,   þæt þe se mihtiga cyning
> in neolnesse   nyðer bescufeð,
> synwyrcende,   in susla grund
> domes leasne,   se ðe deadra feala
> worde awehte.   Wite ðu þe gearwor
> þæt ðu unsnyttrum   anforlete
> leohte beorhtost   ond lufan dryhtnes,
> þone fægran gefean,   ond on fyrbæðe
> suslum beþrungen   syððan wunodest,
> ade onæled,   ond þær awa scealt,
> wiðerhycgende,   wergðu dreogan,
> yrmðu butan ende'. (ll. 939–52a)

['You need not, mindful of sins, so strongly renew sorrow and raise strife, wicked ruler of crime, because the mighty king thrust you down into the depth, sinful one, in the abyss of torments, lacking in glory, he who by his word raised many of the dead. You know the more clearly that you through folly forsook the fairest light and the love of the Lord, that beautiful joy, and ever since have dwelled on a fire-bath bound with torments, burned on a pyre, and there in your rebel-mindedness, you shall always suffer damnation and misery without end'.]

Here, Judas is able to clearly identify both the devil and his former status as an angel. Having been recently raised from his own abyss, Judas succinctly separates his identity from that of the devil, affirming his sanctity through revealed knowledge and by articulating the same terms of faith spoken by catechumens at baptism. Whereas the devil's speech to Judas is a complaint about his lost monopoly on souls (ll. 902–19a), Judas's apotropaic articulation of the angelic fall is a reminder of his primal forfeiture.

Judas thus banishes the devil in a highly ritualised sacral performance of his new Christian faith, echoing the renunciation of Satan found in the baptismal liturgy. Whereas before, Judas was *modblinde*, he is now described as overcoming 'blindness of heart'. We might compare a Gallican baptismal prayer from the Stowe Missal recounting Mark 3:5 and Eph. 4:18, which says catechumens must expel 'blindness of heart' as they 'loose the bonds of Satan ... Take from the devil all occasion of triumph'.[77] Following Judas's prayer, the poem describes how 'of ðære stowe steam up aras / swylce rec' (steam rose up from the place just like smoke, ll. 802–3a). This image is also reminiscent of the baptismal language and imagery found in the Stowe Missal quoting John 4:14: 'goeth down therein there may be a *well of water springing up unto eternal life*'.[78] The rising steam prefigures Judas's full entrance into the Church through baptism and his eventual salvation. Catherine A. Regan's study of the poem stresses the symbolic level of Judas's torture and conversion; she proposes that Cynewulf dramatises the relationship between the Church and the soul of a catechumen in preparation for baptism (ll. 1032b–5a, 1043–6a).[79] Regan suggests Judas's utterance serves as a kind of verbal commitment and that he 'is prepared now to enter the Christian community through the sacrament'.[80] Building on Regan's conclusions, Johnson convincingly identifies Judas's demon as a 'liturgical' devil (in contrast to the 'subordinate' demon that appears to Juliana).[81] This distinction, Johnson argues, links 'the episode to the liturgy of Baptism and [foregrounds] the figurative, symbolic dimension of the narrative's meaning'.[82]

While these critics address the crucial symbolic level of *Elene*, others such as John P. Hermann rightly caution against readings that privilege this level of the narrative, occluding the fundamentally violent nature of the torture which brings about Judas's conversion. Referring to Judas's enclosure in the pit as an 'inverted passion', Hermann argues that 'torture cannot simply be read as emblematic of the relationship between the church and the soul of a catechumen since torture in the name of a Higher Truth is not the same as fasting voluntarily chosen'.[83] Hermann contends that the poem is concerned with torturing the Jews into submission so that the Cross may become 'a weapon for advancing the reign of Christianity'.[84] He convincingly problematises *Elene* as 'a poetic celebration of forced cultural change'.[85] Although Judas's knowledge of Jewish lore guides him to the hoard, there remains an undeniable element of violence throughout it all. Objects taken from a *goldhord*, although they may serve as a positive reminder of past victories and of productive future distributions, can also act as visible reminders of past (and potentially future) violence and even cultural erasure.

The *Beowulf* poet's account of the discovery of the dragon's hoard and the transaction between the *melda* and his lord is fragmented and ambiguous. As Frederick M. Biggs has suggested, it is unclear whether the *melda* is the thief or an intermediary lord.[86] If we take the 'thief' in *Beowulf* to be the *melda* (as Theodore Andersson has),[87] and also the 'guide' who leads his lord to the dragon's lair, the role of the *melda* parallels Cynewulf's characterisation of Judas as the guide to the Cross who undoes his own capacity for 'theft' against his lord, owing to his lengthy concealment of a treasure trove.[88] Much as the *melda* who plunders the hoard in *Beowulf* plays a crucial role as a catalyst for a dramatic turn of events, so Judas, by reopening the hoard, is a catalyst for radical change which 'eventually engulfs everyone' as it physically widens the geographic scope of the Christian world.[89] In becoming a *melda* for Christ, and revealing true ownership of the *goldhord*, Judas increases the spiritual capital and burgeoning spaces of Constantine's Christian empire through newly circulating knowledge of Christ and the origin of his adversaries.

Narrative and bodily protection

The Old English *Andreas* traces the mission of the apostle Andrew (Andreas) to rescue Matthew from the cannibals of Mermedonia. The story of Andreas and his apostolic exploits derives from a Greek source known as the *Acta Andreae et Matthiae apud anthropophagos* ('The Acts of Andrew and Matthias in the Land of the Cannibals'), which is often referred to as the *Πράξεις* (*Praxeis*).[90] This Greek tradition influenced numerous Latin accounts, including the *Recensio Casanatensis* and *Recensio Vaticana*.[91] The *Praxeis* remains the closest approximation to the Old English poem, although the poet probably used a lost Latin redaction as his source.

Two Old English prose pieces recount the story of Andreas's adventures and his encounter with the devil. Blickling Homily 19 contains a fragment of the story of Andreas and a longer version is contained in CCCC 198.[92] The prose version describes how the devil disguises himself in 'cnihtes onlicnysse' (the likeness of a youth).[93] Andreas easily recognises and rebukes him, saying 'Ana þu heardeste stræl to æghwilcre unrihtnesse; þu þe simle fihtest wið manna cyn. Min Drihten Hælend Crist þe gehnæde in helle' (O you arrow hardened to all wickedness. You that ever fights against mankind! My Lord Saviour Christ has humbled/vanquished you in hell).[94] Andreas obliquely evokes the fall of the angels when he states that Christ 'þe gehnæde in helle' (has humbled/vanquished you in hell). This utterance, however, has no clear apotropaic effect. The devil later returns (with back up) to torment Andreas further:

> Þæt deofol þa genam mid him oþre seofon deoflo, þa þe [se] haliga Andreas þanon afliemde, and ingangende on þæt carcern hie gestodon on gesihþe þæs eadigan Andreas, and hine bismriende mid myclere bismre, and hie cwædon, 'Hwæt is þæt þu her gemetest? Hwilc gefreolseð þe nu of urum gewealde? Hwær is þin gilp and þin hiht?' Þæt deofol þa cwæð to þam oðrum deoflum, 'Mine bearn, acwellað hine, forþon he us gescende and ure weorc'. Þa deofla þa blæstan hie ofer þone halgan Andreas, and hie gesawon Cristes rodetacen on his onsiene; hi ne dorston hine genealæcan, ac hraðe hie on weg flugon.

[Then took the devil with him seven other devils, which the holy Andreas had put to flight from there, and stalking into the prison they stood in the sight of the blessed Andreas, and mocking him with great mockery they said, 'What is it you have found here? Who shall deliver you now from our power? Where is your boasting and your trust?' Then said the devil to the other devils, 'My children, slay him, for he has shamed us and our works'. Then the devils hurled themselves upon the holy Andreas, and they saw the sign of Christ's cross upon his countenance; they dared not approach him, but they quickly fled away.][95]

The devils' attack upon Andreas, however, reveals his counter-attack in the form of the *sphragis*, or the 'baptismal seal' upon his forehead. Although we see the baptismal seal performing its apotropaic function, it is important to note that Andreas is essentially silent in this homily. The 'mære tacen' (famous token, l. 1338b) of 'Cristes rode on his mægwlite' (Christ's rood on his face, ll. 1337a–8b) is enough to drive his demons away. On the contrary, in *Andreas*, the devil flees when Andreas reminds him of the fall of the angels and how he 'fæhðo iu wið god geara grimme gefremede' (formerly perpetrated a grim feud with God). The *sphragis* similarly appears in the Old English poem, but Andreas's utterance of the narrative of the fall of the angels is the catalyst for the devil's flight. In a poem concerned with the place of magic, miracles, and signs with talismanic properties, *Andreas* reveals that the knowledge of salvation history also supplies bodily protection.

The *Andreas* poet does not appear to have used either of the Old English prose pieces as sources.[96] Upon Andreas's arrival in Mermedonia, the apostle (who is miraculously made invisible) successfully frees the imprisoned Matthew, upsetting the dinner plans of the hungry Mermedonians. As in the prose, the devil appears to the Mermedonians disguised as a young man. The poet describes how 'Ongan þa meldigan morþres brytta, / hellehinca,[97] þone halgan wer / wiðerhycgende' (The dispenser of evil, the hobbler of hell, began to inform against the holy man with hostile intent, ll. 1170–2a).[98] The devil begins to 'meldigan' (inform against) Andreas, making the apostle's presence public knowledge.

The Mermedonians discover and seize Andreas and, at the urgings of the devil,[99] proceed to torture him in a way that emulates Christ's Passion.[100] However, his punishments also come to resemble those suffered by the devil after his fall from heaven. According to Nathan Breen, 'the punishment and suffering that the Devil advocates for Andreas is eerily similar to the punishment that Satan himself faced after rebelling against God'.[101] As with the prose account of Andreas, the devil's actions initiate the process of revealing both the visible and psychological reminders of his own status as fallen and damned. Merging the events of sacred and nonsacred time, the devil experiences a second fall through the miraculous sign inscribed upon Andreas's body.[102] After the devil reveals Andreas's presence and identity, Andreas, in turn, succinctly identifies the devil:

> 'Wæst þe bæles cwealm,
> hatne in helle,   ond þu here fysest,
> feðan to gefeohte.   Eart ðu fag wið god,
> dugoða demend.   Hwæt, ðu deofles stræl,
> icest þine yrmðo.   Ðe se ælmihtiga
> heanne gehnægde,   ond on heolstor besceaf,
> þær þe cyninga cining   clamme belegde,
> ond þe syððan a   Satan nemdon,
> ða ðe dryhtnes a   deman cuðon'. (ll. 1186b–94)

['You yourself know of the hot torment of flames in hell, and you compel a troop, a company to fight. You are hostile against God, judge of hosts. Listen, you devil's dart, you increase your own misery. The Almighty one humiliated you, and trust you into darkness, where the king of kings fettered you with a chain and ever since those who know how to proclaim the law of God have called you Satan'.]

When Andreas names his adversary the devil recedes, he must still contend with the hungry Mermedonians who beat him and leave him out in the cold. Andreas prays to God, asking him for protection against 'banan manncynnes, / facnes frumbearn' (the slayer of mankind, the first-born of evil, ll. 1293b–4a). Andreas is again imprisoned by the Mermedonians and again visited by the 'wærloga' (oath-breaker, l. 1297a):[103]

> Þa com seofona sum   to sele geongan,
> atol æglæca[104]   yfela gemyndig,
> morðres manfrea   myrce gescyrded,
> deoful deaðreow   duguðum bereafod. (ll. 1311–14)

[Then the terrible adversary, as one among seven came stalking into the hall, mindful of evil, wicked ruler of sin shrouded in darkness, the devil murderously cruel deprived of retainers.]

In a manner reminiscent of Grendel's approach to Heorot, the devil, 'yfela gemyndig' (mindful of evil), finds Andreas at his most vulnerable.[105] As with the prose version, 'seofona' (seven) demons come to persecute him. The significance of seven could, on the one hand, be meant as an inversion of the 'seven gifts of the Holy Spirit' or a reference to the seven deadly sins. There is also a tradition of 'sin demons' which can be found in Aldhelm's *De laudibus virginitatis*. Morton Bloomfield proposes that 'attacking demons were conceived as sins'.[106] This image of the seven demons could possibly come from Prudentius's *Psychomachia*, which refers to the 'Seven heathen nations that help Satan in his battle',[107] making these demons reflective of heathen Mermedonia itself.

On the close association between the *sphragis* and 'the renunciation of Satan', Jean Daniélou writes that 'one of the points most frequently brought out by the Fathers of the Church concerning the *sphragis* is that it makes the Christian fearful to demons'.[108] Scholars such as Thomas D. Hill have pointed out the liturgical echoes running through this sequence. Hill suggests that since a candidate who receives the *sphragis* obtains the power to combat Satan 'Andreas's *mægwlite* ... is by itself enough to defeat the devil and his hosts'.[109] Hill observes that the Gregorian Sacramentary contains a prayer over males at baptism in which 'the priest again invokes Satan and tells him that he has again been defeated, commanding him to depart and never trouble the candidate'.[110] The *Andreas* poet suggests that Satan's band of 'dugoða' (veteran warriors) are unusually inexperienced, and this leads them to flee their lord in battle when they perceive 'Cristes rode on his mægwlite, mære tacen' (Christ's cross on [Andreas's] countenance, the famous sign, ll. 1337b–8).[111] Once abandoned by his troop, Satan, like Grendel, 'ongan ... hearmleoð galan' (began to sing a song of sorrows, l. 1342b).[112] The role of utterance in conjunction with this baptismal imagery has implications for our understanding of this episode since it is Andreas's speech that then causes the devil to depart:

>'Hwæt, me eaðe   ælmihtig god,
>niða neregend,   se ðe in niedum iu
>gefæstnode   fyrnum clommum!
>Þær ðu syððan a,   susle gebunden,
>in wræc wunne,   wuldres blunne,
>syððan ðu forhogedes   heofoncyninges word.
>Þær wæs yfles or,   ende næfre
>þines wræces weorðeð.   Ðu scealt widan feorh
>ecan þine yrmðu.   Þe bið a symble
>of dæge on dæg   drohtaþ strengra'.
>Ða wearð on fleame   se ðe ða fæhðo iu
>wið god geara   grimme gefremede. (ll. 1376–87)

['Listen, Almighty God can free me, the saviour of men, can easily (free me), he who formerly fastened you in fiery chains! There ever since you have dwelled in exile, bound with torments, forfeit of glory, after you despised the word of God. That was the origin of evil (but) there will never be an end to your exile. You shall increase your misery eternally. Your way of life will always be more severe day by day'. Then he was put to flight, the one who formerly perpetrated the grim feud with God.]

As in the aforementioned hagiographical poems, a saint must properly render events in salvation history.[113] The order of salvation history has been restored through Andreas and his sanctity is written upon his face.

Andreas's sanctity has, in a sense, already been confirmed in a dream vision experienced by his disciples during his sea voyage.[114] His companions describe how eagles 'sawle abrugdon' (drew out our souls) as they slept, allowing them to witness 'wlitig weoroda heap' (a shining throng of celestial hosts):

'Swylce we gesegon   for suna meotudes,
æðelum ecne,   eowic standan,
twelfe getealde,   tireadige hæleð.
Eow þegnodon   þrymsittende,
halige heahenglas.   Ðam bið hæleða well
þe þara blissa   brucan moton.
Þær wæs wuldres wynn,   wigendra þrym,
æðelic onginn,   næs þær ænigum gewinn.
Þam bið wræcsið witod,   wite geopenad,
þe þara gefeana sceal   fremde weorðan,
hean hwearfian,   þonne heonon gangaþ'. (ll. 881–91)

['Also in the presence of the Lord's Son, we saw you standing, richly endowed with noble virtues, twelve all told, men blessed with glory. Holy archangels dwelling in majesty ministered to you. It will be well for the men who are allowed to enjoy those delights. The joy of heaven was there, the splendour and noble intention of the warriors, no dissension was there. Banishment will be ordained and torment opened up for those who shall become alienated from those pleasures, and depart in misery, when they go hence'.]

They describe those encircled around Christ as thanes around their Lord among the 'dugoð domgeorne' (company eager for glory, line 878a) with Andreas among them. According to Magennis, hagiography often seeks to portray the saint as poised between an earthly and heavenly threshold or community.[115] The poet utilises internal rhyme as he describes the joys awaiting Andreas and all those who will one day share in 'þara blissa' (those delights). This vision prefigures the Last Judgement when Andreas and his *dugoð* will replace the angels who forfeited their place at the table. At the same time, by collapsing sacred and earthly temporalities, the vision also prefigures events within the narrative itself by anticipating Andreas's 'wræcsið' (banishment) of the devil following the visual and verbal manifestations of the protective talismans that keep the devil at bay.

Idle possessions

Unlike the saints' lives I have discussed so far, in which holy men and women are visited by a single enigmatic devil or seven devils, Guthlac's story is unique in that he is assailed by a troop of demons. In accounts of desert fathers and hermits meeting devils, the saint's success at banishing them often hinges upon his or her ability to speak. According to Joyce Hill, in one account of the Life of Anthony 'there is one exceptional physical incident when the saint is so violently assaulted that he is left unable to speak'.[116] Similarly, in Gregory's *Dialogues*, Benedict spars with 'se ealda feond' (the old fiend). Here, Hill notes, 'the conflict is verbal', but Benedict comes to find that the devil 'can be overcome by prayers'.[117] *Guthlac A* is similarly concerned with utterances and their ability to banish demons from discrete places. One famous eleventh-century translation of Felix found in MS Cotton Vespasian D.xxi recounts how Guthlac verbally outmanoeuvres *bryttisc* ('Welsh') speaking demons.[118]

Guthlac A focuses on issues of angelology and salvation. Laurence K. Shook observes that the opening of the poem is primarily concerned with 'the function of angels in the salvation of man's soul'.[119] Upon Guthlac's eremitic retreat into the fens, the poet describes how he 'Christianizes the landscape' through a series of apotropaic gestures;[120] he blesses his 'wong' (plain, l. 178b) and raises 'Cristes rode' (Christ's cross, l. 180a). These gestures and materials reveal Guthlac fighting 'gæstlicum / wæpnum' (with spiritual weapons, l. 177b–8a). According to Hill, 'like Beowulf, [who] renounces the use of the sword in his fight against his foes Guthlac does not need swords because he believes God will protect him'.[121] Guthlac's arsenal of spiritual weapons proliferates as he is accosted by the demons. He uses both his knowledge of the fall of the angels and his understanding of the replacement doctrine to defend himself. Guthlac demonstrates that the 'idel gylp' (idle speech, l. 662) of devils can be overpowered and undone through an expression of his faithful expectation that he will be one of their replacements in heaven.

The story of Saint Guthlac's life in the Crowland fens appears in several Anglo-Saxon texts.[122] Felix's eighth-century Latin *Vita Guthlaci* (*c.* 730–49) was written for Ælfwald, king of East Anglia.[123] In the *Vita*, Felix recounts the life of Guthlac (*c.* 674–714), a Mercian warrior turned hermit.[124] Felix's *Vita* is loosely based on Athanasius's Life of Saint Anthony in the Latin translation of Evagrius.[125] Finding that these demons operate at an allegorical or psychological level, Benjamin Kurtz describes how they reflect the 'principal faults against which the monk had to struggle'.[126] The branch of the Guthlac legend I wish to turn to can be found in the Exeter Book,[127] which contains the poems known as *Guthlac A* and *B*. *Guthlac A* mainly comprises the saint's temptation, whereas *Guthlac B* offers an account of his death. Whether the *Guthlac A* poet knew the *Vita Antonii* has been debated, but the poet certainly does riff on motifs stemming from the Evagrian tradition.[128] Of particular importance to the poet are the *sedes* ('seats') of the fallen angels, which Evagrius describes as having been forfeited through 'ex proprio mentis arbitrio' (their [the demons'] own choice and intention). *Guthlac A*'s opening prologue discusses heaven (ll. 1–29), earth (ll. 30–59), humankind (ll. 60–80), and the life of the ascetic (ll. 81–92).

The *Guthlac A* poet demonstrates a marked interest in the physicality of Guthlac's battle with the demons as well as their infringement upon his sacred territory. Anglo-Saxon Christian charms such as the 'Field Remedy', which perform a purgative function similar to Rogationtide perambulations, were aimed at cleansing land believed to be possessed by demons. According to Jolly, 'the ritual allowed the participants to connect with [the] spiritual realm through the material reality' of the land and 'the potency of the mysteriously spoken words'.[129] Guthlac's highly ritualised verbal performance resembles a charm and his utterances allow him to connect his geographic surroundings with the spiritual realm.

The poem begins with a meeting between an angel and a soul (l. 2a) and discusses 'five prominent virtues' as identified by Bjork: angels, souls, light, homelands, and obedience.[130] We learn that Guthlac is imbued with the gift of 'engelcunde' (angelic grace, l. 101a) and that God has sent a 'weard' (guardian, l. 105b) to protect him. God reveals a home to Guthlac, a *beorg* ('hill', or perhaps 'barrow') which is described as a space awaiting a proper resident.[131] We also learn that Guthlac 'upp gemunde / ham in heofonum' (was mindful of the home in heaven, l. 97b–8a). Soon after his arrival at the *beorg*, Guthlac is beset by 'ealdfeondas' (old fiends), whom the poet describes as 'teonsmiðas' (slander-smiths, i.e. calumniators, l. 205a).

The assault on Guthlac, his homeland, and his claim to sanctity are central to the poem. The theme of Guthlac's homeland (both his earthly *beorg* and his heavenly homeland) is an issue that numerous scholars have addressed. Smith calls attention to the ways in which the land becomes a metaphor for salvation and inheritance in the heavenly kingdom.[132] For Smith, the fens serve as a vacation destination for the demons, who are described as having 'no rest for their limbs' (ll. 221–2).[133] In this same vein, Johnson notes that Guthlac's rightful possession of the land signals 'the heavenly homeland towards which Guthlac is proceeding',[134] and Patrick W. Conner suggests that Guthlac's *beorg* 'signifies the fundamental trope of Christianity, the heavenly *burh*, the eternal Jerusalem'.[135] The assaults of the demons threaten the very geography of the land Guthlac attempts to sanctify for God.

Building on Conner's work, Christopher A. Jones considers how the poet represents Guthlac's vocation.[136] Jones asks why the life of a solitary hermit might appeal to later Anglo-Saxon readers during an era when communal lifestyles (the *vita communis*, or *cenobium*) were becoming increasingly popular.[137] He contends that the poet's concern with vainglory and other common monastic sins suggests that 'the monastic spirituality of *Guthlac A* belongs more properly to the *cenobium* than to the hermitage'.[138] In this way, he argues, the *beorg* becomes a nexus for ideas of *cenobium* and heavenly community. The poet's choice of words to describe Guthlac's sacred land supports this assertion. Guthlac's home is set upon a *getimbru* ('foundation', ll. 18, 584), a term most often reserved for heavenly or sacred foundations and a prominent Anglo-Saxon metaphor for building that features in Alfred's Preface to the *Soliloquies* and *Genesis B* (as discussed in Chapter 2). The poet also employs common imagery used to describe the heavenly thrones and territories that await human occupants at the Last Judgement. The *beorg* is thus an *eðel* ('homeland', ll. 67, 656, 801) and a *setl* ('seat', ll. 244, 278, 383, 785).[139] There is a clear lexical resonance between Guthlac's *eorðlic eþel* (l. 261) and the 'selt on swegle' (seat in heaven, l. 785a) that Guthlac will eventually inherit. In this way, the terminology used to describe Guthlac's home bridges earthly and divine categories.

The angels' share

Guthlac maintains that he needs no material weapons in his fight against the demons (ll. 302–4). In challenging the demons, Guthlac initially identifies himself as an obedient 'servant':

'Þæt is in gewealdum   wuldorcyninges,
se eow gehynde   ond in hæft bidraf
under nearone clom,   nergende Crist.
Eom ic eaðmod,   his ombiehthera,
þeow geþyldig.   Ic geþafian sceal
æghwær ealles   his anne dom
ond him geornlice   gæst gemyndum
wille wideferh   wesan underþyded,
hyran holdlice   minum hælende
þeawum ond geþyncðum   ond him þoncian
ealra þara giefena   þe God gescop
englum ærest   ond eorðwarum,
ond ic bletsige   bliðe mode
lifes leohtfrum   ond him lof singe
þurh gedefne dom   dæges ond nihtes,
herge in heortan   heofonrices weard.
Þæt eow æfre ne bið   ufan alyfed
leohtes lissum   þæt ge lof moten
dryhtne secgan   ac ge deaðe sceolon
weallendne wean   wope besingan,
heaf in helle,   nales herenisse
halge habban   heofoncyninges'. (ll. 596–617)

['That is under the control of the king of heaven, the saviour Christ, who condemned you and drove you into captivity under a narrow fetter. I am his humble and dutiful servant, his obedient one. I shall wholly submit in every case to his sole judgement and my spirit eagerly will be subservient to him in my thoughts, and loyally obey my Lord in virtue and appearance and thank him for all the gifts which God created first for angels and for earth-dwellers, and happy in heart I will bless the author of light, and praise him lovingly through fitting glory day and night, and acclaim in my heart the ruler of the heavenly kingdom. Never from above will you be given the grace of light that you might speak praise of the Lord but you shall sing weeping in the surging torment, you will have mourning in hell, not at all will you have praise for the holy king of heaven'.]

In denouncing the demons, Guthlac constructs his identity against their own. He suggests that they were once disloyal, but he remains Christ's 'ombiehthera' (obedient one). Whereas the fallen angels rejected the gifts of God, Guthlac describes how he is mindful 'him þoncian ealra þara giefena' (to thank him for all the gifts). Like the 'singing devil' Andreas banishes, Guthlac reminds these demons that throughout eternity they will 'wope besingan' (sing weeping) in hell. Guthlac then directly relates the story of their downfall:

> 'Sindon ge wærlogan,   swa ge in wræcsiðe
> longe lifdon,   lege biscencte,
> swearte beswicene,   swegle benumene,
> dreame bidrorene,   deaðe bifolene,
> firenum bifongne,   feores orwenan,
> þæt ge blindnesse   bote fundon.
> Ge þa fægran gesceaft   in fyrndagum,
> gæstlicne goddream,   gearo forsegon,
> þa ge wiðhogdun   halgum dryhtne.
> Ne mostun ge a wunian   in wyndagum,
> ac mid scome scyldum   scofene wurdon
> fore oferhygdum   in ece fyr
> ðær ge sceolon dreogan   deað ond þystro,
> wop to widan ealdre; næfre ge þæs wyrpe gebidað'. (ll. 623–36)

['You are oath-breakers: just as you have lived long in exile, sunk in the fire, miserably deceived, removed from happiness, deprived of joys, consigned to death, surrounded by sins, without hope of life, that you would find a remedy for blindness. In former days long ago you renounced the fair creation, and spiritual godly joys, when you set yourself against the holy Lord. Now you are not permitted to dwell in days of gladness, but shamefully with guilt because of your pride you were thrust into eternal fire because of your pride where you must suffer death and darkness, weeping forever; never will you experience relief from that'.]

Here, Guthlac catalogues the punishments of the 'wærlogan' (oath-breakers) with a great deal of alliterative and rhythmical flourish.[140] They are 'biscencte' (sunk), 'beswicene' (deceived), 'benumene' (removed), 'bidrorene' (deprived), 'bifolene' (consigned), and 'bifongne' (surrounded) by sins without hope of finding a 'bote' (remedy). Smith persuasively argues that 'the saint's own entitlement is achieved through [the fallen angels'] deprivation' of land and title.[141] Just as Edgar revoked the landed privileges of the secular clerics during the Benedictine Reform, Smith proposes that the demons in the poem serve as a parallel to any sovereign's 'dual power to entitle or deprive' land just as 'God punishes the rebel angels by casting them out of their seats in heaven'.[142] Guthlac's charm-like iteration of the demons' dispossession seals and protects both the borders of the *beorg* and Guthlac's status as an inheritor of the demon's heavenly 'eðel' (homeland):

'ðær eow næfre   fore nergende
leohtes leoma   ne lifes hyht
in Godes rice   agiefen weorþeð
for þam oferhygdum   þe eow in mod astag
þurh idel gylp   ealles to swiðe.
Wendum ge ond woldum   wiðerhycgende,
þæt ge scyppende   sceoldan gelice
wesan in wuldre.   Eow þær wyrs gelomp,[143]
ða eow se waldend   wraðe bisencte
in þæt swearte susl   þær eow siððan wæs
ad inæled   attre geblonden,
þurh deopne dom,   dream afyrred,
engla gemana.   Swa nu awa sceal
wesan wideferh,   þæt ge wærnysse
brynewylm hæbben,   nales bletsunga.
ne þurfun ge wenan,   wuldre biscyrede,
þæt ge mec sunfulle   mid searocræftum
under scæd sconde   scufan motan
ne in bælblæsan   bregdon on hinder,
in helle hus,   þær eow is ham sceapen,
sweart sinnehte,   sacu butan ende,
grim gæstcwalu,   þær ge gnornende
deað sceolon dreogan,   ond ic dreama wyn
agan mid englum   in þam uplican
rodera rice,   þær is ryht cyning,
help ond hælu   hæleþa cynne,
duguð ond drohtað'. (ll. 658–84a)

['there before the saviour you will never experience the radiance of light nor hope of life in God's kingdom because of the pride which often arose in your mind through idle speech. You rebelliously thought and desired that you would be like the creator in glory. It turned out worse for you when the ruler wrathfully thrust you into that dark torment where a pyre mingled with venom was afterwards prepared for you through that profound judgement, expelled from the joy and the companionship of angels. Now and always it will be so that you have the burning flood of damnation, not at all blessings; you need not imagine, deprived of glory, that you sinful ones might through cunning devices thrust me shamefully under the shadow nor drag me down into the blazing fire into the hell house, where a home is made for you, dark unending night, pain without end, grim death of the soul, where you mournfully must suffer death and I will possess joys of bliss among the angels in the kingdom of heaven above where the true king is, help and healing for humankind, company and fellowship'.]

Guthlac creates a clear contrast between the 'idel gylp' (idle speech) of the demons, who 'wiðerhycgende' (rebelliously) desired a divine status, and his own efficacious protective rhetoric. He notes how Christ once thrust the demons into darkness, and maintains that they will never be able to 'under scæd sconde scufan' (thrust me shamefully under the shadow) (as the demons of Vercelli 23 threatened). Whereas the demons once desired to be *gelice* ('like') God, in gesturing towards his eventual status as their heavenly replacement, Guthlac articulates his desire to be 'mid englum' (among the angels). Guthlac's speech legitimises and affirms his saintly status. Arthur Groos observes that the *Guthlac A* poet is concerned with typologically linking the beginning and end of salvation history with the necessity for 'men to re-establish their equality with ... those faithful guardians whose depleted ranks saints such as Guthlac are now destined to fill'.[144] The devils are ultimately driven away from the land they had hoped to possess. Clark has convincingly argued that the *beorg* dispute replicates the devils' loss of their heavenly seats.[145] In this way, Guthlac's rehearsal of the fall of the angels and the doctrine of replacement secures and protects the status of both his earthly and heavenly 'setl' (seat). Guthlac's charm is an expression of his future destination among the 'duguð ⁊ drohtað' (company and fellowship) of angels.

Anglo-Saxon authors understood the fall of the angels and its corollary doctrines as having a variety of narrative applications beyond simply its capacity to inspire Christian obedience. The fall of the angels was not strictly a cosmological event: it infringed upon physical earthly space, as well as liturgical, hagiographical, and spiritual planes. In the saints' lives I have examined here, the very narration of the fall of the angels inspires martyrdom, conversion, and the ideals of Christian behaviour while affording the speaker protection against evil spirits. As a performative utterance that functions much like *galdra* ('charms'), infused with both apotropaic power and doctrinal significance, the narrative of the fall of the angels crosses the boundary between highly learned and popular modes of belief.[146] Significantly, Jolly notes that medieval *galdra* were often associated 'with demonic or evil practices'.[147] There was even a sense that charms were originally evil spells that came from the devil, leading them to be condemned by religious leaders.[148] Nevertheless, what we see in these hagiographical poems are saints reappropriating the devil's monopoly upon utterances and spells as they transform the devil's own history into a weapon to be used against him. That the fall of the angels is used as a protective utterance in verse saints' lives for bodily and geographical safeguarding suggests that there was perhaps a wider tradition of seeing the narrative as a cohesive verbal ritual, a powerful and performative manifesto of Anglo-Saxon Christian belief.

Notes

1 N. R. Ker, *Catalogue of Manuscripts Containing Anglo-Saxon* (Oxford: Clarendon Press, 1957), no. 29.
2 *The Vercelli Homilies*, ed. Scragg, 390.115–18.
3 Jane Roberts, 'The Old English Prose Translation of Felix's *Vita sancti Guthlaci*', in *Studies in Earlier Old English Prose*, ed. Paul E. Szarmach (Albany: State University of New York Press, 1986), pp. 363–79 (p. 374). On the transition between the Guthlac Homily and *Elene* in its manuscript context, see Éamonn Ó Carragáin, 'How did the Vercelli Collector Interpret *The Dream of the Rood?*' in *Studies in English Language and Early Literature in Honour of Paul Christophersen*, ed. P. M. Tilling, Occasional Papers in Linguistics and Language Teaching 8 (Colerain: The University of Ulster, 1981), pp. 63–104 (pp. 75–8).
4 *The Vercelli Homilies*, ed. Scragg, 391.132–4.
5 On Guthlac's temptations, see Charles D. Wright, 'The Three Temptations and the Seven Gifts of the Holy Spirit in *Guthlac A*, 160b–169', *Traditio*, 38 (1982), 341–3. See also Stephanie Clark, 'A More Permanent Homeland: Land Tenure in *Guthlac A*', *ASE*, 40 (2012), 75–102.
6 Patrick W. Conner argues that the poem can be read as a kind of manual for the training of the monastic soul; see 'Source Studies, the Old English *Guthlac A* and the English Benedictine Reformation', *Revue Bénédictine*, 103 (1993), 380–413 (p. 386). See also Thomas D. Hill, 'The Age of Man and the World in the Old English *Guthlac A*', *JEGP*, 80 (1981), 13–21; Hill references *De duodecim abusiuis saeculi*, which emphasises the importance of leaders in monastic settings with young monks in need of guidance (p. 17).
7 Conner, 'Source Studies', p. 407.
8 Clark, 'A More Permanent Homeland', p. 101.
9 Lindy Brady, *Writing the Welsh Borderlands in Anglo-Saxon England* (Manchester: Manchester University Press, 2017), pp. 53–70 (p. 53).
10 Ibid., p. 50.
11 C. Grant Loomis, *White Magic: An Introduction to the Folklore*

of *Christian Legend* (Cambridge, MA: The Medieval Academy of America, 1948), p. 74.

12 Quotations from *Elene* and *Andreas* are from *The Vercelli Book*, ed. George Philip Krapp, ASPR II (New York: Columbia University Press, 1932). See also *Cynewulf's Elene*, ed. P. O. E. Gradon (Exeter: University of Exeter Press, 1977) and *Andreas and The Fates of the Apostles*, ed. Kenneth R. Brooks (Oxford: Clarendon Press, 1961); quotations from *Juliana* and *Guthlac A* are from *The Exeter Book*, ed. Krapp and Dobbie. See also *Juliana*, ed. Rosemary Woolf (New York: Appleton-Century-Crofts, 1966) and *The Guthlac Poems of the Exeter Book*, ed. Jane Roberts (Oxford: Oxford University Press, 1979).

13 Karen Louise Jolly, *Popular Religion in Late Anglo-Saxon England: Elf Charms in Context* (Chapel Hill: The University of North Carolina Press, 1996), p. 97.

14 Jolly, *Popular Religion*, p. 99.

15 For more on 'perlocutionary acts' or 'perlocution', see J. L. Austin, *How To Do Things with Words*, ed. J. O. Urmson and Marina Sbisá (2nd ed. Oxford: Oxford University Press, 1976), pp. 101–9. In Austin's words, a speech act will 'produce certain consequential effects upon the feelings, thoughts, or actions of the audience, or of the speaker, or of other persons' (p. 101).

16 According to Peter Dendle, Origen established Satan as a proud, rebel figure 'in contrast to the image of a lustful "watcher angel" more popular in earlier sources' (*Satan Unbound*, p. 10).

17 The standard definition is 'having or reputed to have the power of averting evil influence or ill luck' (*Oxford English Dictionary*, s.v. 'apotropaic').

18 Rolf H. Bremmer Jr., 'Changing Perspectives on a Saint's Life: *Juliana*', in *Companion to Old English Poetry*, ed. Henk Aertsen and Rolf H. Bremmer Jr. (Amsterdam: VU University Press, 1994), pp. 201–16 (p. 201).

19 See Donald G. Bzdyl, '*Juliana*: Cynewulf's Dispeller of Delusion', *NM*, 86 (1985), 165–75.

20 Rosemary Woolf, 'Saints' Lives', in *Continuations and Beginnings: Studies in Old English Literature*, ed. E. G. Stanley (London and Edinburgh: Nelson, 1966), pp. 37–66 (p. 42).

21 Athanasius's work was known in Anglo-Saxon England through Evagrius's Latin translation, *Vita Beati Antonii Abbatis*, ed. Rosyde, PL 73 (Paris: Garnier Frères, 1879), cols. 125–69. One of the topics he discusses is the doctrine of *discretio spirituum* (the discernment of spirits), that is, the joy experienced in the present of a good spirit and the fear experienced upon being visited by an evil spirit. We also know that this text influenced Felix's *Vita Sancti Guthlaci* and perhaps the *Two Lives of Cuthbert*; see *Felix's Life of Saint Guthlac*, ed. and trans.

Bertram Colgrave (Cambridge: Cambridge University Press, 1956) and *Two Lives of Saint Cuthbert: A Life by an Anonymous Monk of Lindisfarne and Bede's Prose Life*, ed. and trans. Bertram Colgrave (Cambridge: Cambridge University Press, 1940), pp. 96–7 and pp. 214–15. Also popular was the 'devil and the anchorite' or 'Theban legend' (Wright, *The Irish Tradition*, p. 174ff). See also Dendle's latest work on the subject: Peter Dendle, *Demon Possession in Anglo-Saxon England* (Kalamazoo, MI: Medieval Institute Publications, 2014).

22 Dendle, *Satan Unbound*, p. 42.
23 Margaret's *passio* is contained in Cotton Tiberius A.iii and CCCC 303. See Claudia Di Sciacca, 'The Old English Life of St Margaret in London, British Library, Cotton Tiberius A.iii: Sources and Relationships', forthcoming in *JEGP*; see *The Old English Life of St Nicholas with the Old English Life of St Giles*, E. M. Treharne, Leeds Texts and Monographs New Series 15 (Otley, West Yorkshire: Smith Settle, 1997).
24 Mary Clayton and Hugh Magennis, *The Old English Lives of St Margaret*, CSASE 9 (Cambridge: Cambridge University Press, 1994), p. 125.
25 Ibid.
26 *Lives of St Margaret*, p. 167 and pp. 208–9.
27 Margaret's command 'Vade ex me' (Go away from me) (*Lives of St Margaret*, pp. 210–11), echoes Christ's defeat of Satan in the wilderness (Mk. 8:33: 'vade retro me Satana').
28 See Charles D. Wright, 'From Monks' Jokes to Sages' Wisdom: The *Joca monachorum* Tradition and the Irish *Imacallam in dá Thúarad*', in *Spoken and Written Language: Relations between Latin and the Vernacular in the Earlier Middle Ages*, ed. Mary Garrison and Marco Mostert (Turnhout: Brepols, 2013), pp. 199–225 (p. 210).
29 On this passage see John P. Hermann, *Allegories of War: Language and Violence in Old English Poetry* (Ann Arbor, MI: University of Michigan Press, 1989), pp. 32–6. In both *Juliana* and *Solomon and Saturn I*, the devil's 'sword' is inscribed with 'bealwe bocstafas' (harmful letters, l. 162a).
30 Ibid., pp. 98–9. DOE, *galdor*, sense 1, 'poem, song, incantation, charm; spell'; *(a)galan*, sense 2, 'to chant an incantation, sing a charm'; sense 3, 'divination, soothsaying, prophesying'.
31 Jolly notes that *galdor* typically glosses the Latin terms *carmen, cantio*, or *incantation* (*Popular Religion*, p. 99).
32 David F. Johnson, 'The *Crux Usualis* as Apotropaic Weapon in Anglo-Saxon England', in *The Place of the Cross in Anglo-Saxon England*, ed. Catherine E. Karkov, Sarah Larratt Keefer, and Karen Louise Jolly (Woodbridge: Boydell, 2006), pp. 80–95 (p. 82); Charles D. Wright, 'Jewish Magic and Christian Miracle in *Andreas*', in

Imagining the Jew in Anglo-Saxon England, ed. Samantha Zacher (Toronto: University of Toronto Press, 2016), pp. 167–93.
33   Johnson, 'The *Crux Usualis*', p. 85.
34   Thomas D. Hill, 'The Sphragis as Apotropaic Sign: *Andreas* 1334–44', *Anglia*, 101 (1983), 147–51 (p. 150).
35   Johnson, 'The *Crux Usualis*', p. 84.
36   T. D. Hill, 'The Sphragis as Apotropaic Sign', pp. 147–51 and Thomas D. Hill, 'When God Blew Satan out of Heaven: The Motif of Exsufflation in *Vercelli Homily XIX* and Later English Literature', *LSE*, 16 (1985), 132–41.
37   Johnson, 'The *Crux Usualis*', p. 82.
38   Ibid., p. 92.
39   On the dating of Cynewulf, see R. D. Fulk, 'Cynewulf: Canon, Dialect, and Date', in *Cynewulf: Basic Readings*, ed. Robert E. Bjork (New York: Psychology Press, 1996), pp. 3–21; Patrick W. Conner, 'On Dating Cynewulf', in *Cynewulf: Basic Readings*, ed. Robert E. Bjork (New York: Psychology Press, 1996), pp. 23–55; John M. McCulloh, 'Did Cynewulf Use a Martyrology? Reconsidering the Sources of *The Fates of the Apostles*', *ASE*, 29 (2000), 67–83.
40   Jill Frederick, 'Warring With Words: Cynewulf's *Juliana*', in *Readings in Medieval Texts: Interpreting Old and Middle English Literature*, ed. David F. Johnson and Elaine Treharne (Oxford: Oxford University Press, 2005), pp. 60–74 (p. 61). For more on Juliana's cult, see Michael Lapidge, 'Cynewulf and the *Passio S. Iulianae*', in *Unlocking the Wordhord: Anglo-Saxon Studies in Memory of Edward B. Irving Jr.*, ed. Mark C. Amodio and Katherine O'Brien O'Keeffe (Toronto: Toronto University Press, 2003), pp. 147–71 (pp. 147–8).
41   Michael Lapidge, 'The Saintly Life in Anglo-Saxon England', in *The Cambridge Companion to Old English Literature*, ed. Malcolm Godden and Michael Lapidge (Cambridge: Cambridge University Press, 1986), pp. 243–63 (p. 260).
42   Lapidge, 'Cynewulf and the *Passio S. Iulianae*', p. 149. Lapidge is credited with discovering the redaction of the *Passio S. Iulianae* used by Cynewulf, now preserved in Paris, Bibliothèque nationale de France, lat. 10861 (fols. 113^v–21^r).
43   Woolf views this angelic disguise alongside the biblical (2 Cor. 11:14) and hagiographical motif of the 'angel of light' motif popularised by Gregory the Great ('Saints' Lives', p. 44). This episode stands juxtaposed to Cynewulf's representation of an authentic angelic messenger. See my article, '*Angelus Pacis*: A Liturgical Model for the Masculine "fæle friðowebba" in Cynewulf's *Elene*', *MÆ*, 83 (2014), 189–209.
44   Allen and Calder, *Sources and Analogues*, p. 126.
45   A leaf is missing in *Juliana* where the devil recites some of his later history.
46   Allen J. Frantzen, 'Drama and Dialogue in Old English Poetry: The

Scene of Cynewulf's *Juliana*', *Theatre Survey*, 48 (2007), 99–119 (p. 110).
47 Ibid., p. 113.
48 Bremmer, 'Changing Perspectives', p. 210. See also Wright, *The Irish Tradition*, p. 175ff.
49 Hermann, *Allegories of War*, p. 168.
50 For more on this episode, see Anlezark, 'The Fall of the Angels in *Solomon and Saturn II*', 121–33.
51 See John P. Hermann, 'Language and Spirituality in Cynewulf's *Juliana*', *Texas Studies in Literature and Language*, 26 (1984), 263–8; Hermann writes, 'They are "ancient," or "former" because they stem from a conflict between God and Satan, who is the *hostis antiquus*' (p. 267).
52 Marie Nelson, '*The Battle of Maldon* and *Juliana*: the Language of Confrontation', in *Modes of Interpretation in Old English Literature: Essays in Honour of Stanley B. Greenfield*, ed. Phyllis Rugg Brown, Georgia Ronan Crampton, and Fred C. Robinson (Toronto: University of Toronto Press, 1986), pp. 137–50 (p. 147).
53 On the demon's highly stylised rhetoric, see Antonina Harbus, 'Articulate Contact in *Juliana*', in *Verbal Encounters: Anglo-Saxon and Old Norse Studies for Roberta Frank*, ed. Antonina Harbus and Russell Poole, Toronto Old English Series (Toronto: University of Toronto Press, 2005), pp. 183–200.
54 Robert E. Bjork, *The Old English Verse Saints' Lives: A Study in Direct Discourse and the Iconography of Style*, McMaster Old English Studies and Texts 4 (Toronto: University of Toronto Press, 1985).
55 Frederick, 'Warring With Words', p. 69.
56 Dendle, *Satan Unbound*, p. 102.
57 This appears to reflect the exegetical tradition concerning the 'firmness' of the angels who did not rebel (Wright, 'The Confirmation of the Angels', p. 25 and p. 34, n. 25).
58 Harbus, 'Articulate Contact', p. 193.
59 Bosworth-Toller, *melda*, senses 1 and 2.
60 Bosworth-Toller, *meldian*, senses 1 and 2.
61 Nathan Alan Breen, 'The Voice of Evil: A Narratological Study of Demonic Characters in Old English Literature', PhD dissertation, University of Illinois at Urbana-Champaign, 2003 (p. 58).
62 John Edward Damon, *Soldier Saints and Holy Warriors: Warfare and Sanctity in the Literature of Early England* (Aldershot: Ashgate, 2004), p. 95.
63 Bjork, *Old English Verse Saints' Lives*, p. 80.
64 Breen, 'The Voice of Evil', p. 61.
65 Elizabeth Tyler, *Old English Poetics: The Aesthetics of the Familiar in Anglo-Saxon England* (Woodbridge: York Medieval Press, 2006), p. 28.

66 Michael Cherniss, *Ingeld and Christ: Heroic Concepts and Values in Old English Christian Poetry* (The Hague: Mouton, 1972), p. 98.
67 Scheil, *The Footsteps of Israel*, p. 219.
68 Ibid., p. 226.
69 This noun most probably refers to the thief or the thief's lord (*Klaeber's Beowulf*, n. to line 2405b). See also Earl R. Anderson, 'Treasure Trove in *Beowulf*: A Legal View of the Dragon's Hoard', *Mediaevalia*, 3 (1977), 141–64.
70 J. Hill, *The Cultural World in Beowulf*, p. 137.
71 Ibid., p. 122.
72 Damon, *Soldier Saints and Holy Warriors*, p. 117.
73 Anderson, 'Treasure Trove in *Beowulf*', p. 146. Anderson observes that 'in twelfth-century England, fraudulent concealment of a treasure trove was considered theft, and also treason against the king' (p. 146).
74 In the *Acta*, Judas says, 'You cast the unbelieving angels into deep Tartarus' (Allen and Calder, *Sources and Analogues*, p. 65).
75 According to the doctrine of the devil's rights, Satan controlled the destiny of humankind after the fall of Adam and Eve until Christ's sacrifice. For a synopsis, see David F. Johnson, 'Hagiographical Demon or Liturgical Devil? Demonology and Baptismal Imagery in Cynewulf's *Elene*', in *Essays for Joyce Hill on Her Sixtieth Birthday*, ed. Mary Swan, LSE, 37 (Leeds: University of Leeds, 2006), 9–29 (12ff). See also C. William Marx, *The Devil's Rights and the Redemption in the Literature of Medieval England* (Cambridge: D. S. Brewer, 1995); Robert Boenig, *Saint and Hero: "Andreas" and Medieval Doctrine* (Lewisburg, PA: Bucknell University Press, 1991), who addresses the 'Diabolus-model of Atonement' (p. 82).
76 Allen and Calder, *Sources and Analogues*, p. 66.
77 *Documents of the Baptismal Liturgy*, ed. E. C. Whitaker (London: Society for Promoting Christian Knowledge, 1970), p. 216.
78 Ibid., p. 218.
79 Catharine A. Regan, 'Evangelicalism as the Informing Principle of Cynewulf's *Elene*', *Traditio*, 29 (1973), 27–52 (p. 33ff.). Regan likens Judas's fasting (ll. 611–6a) to Christ's fasting in the wilderness; on this episode, see also Thomas D. Hill, 'Sapiential Structure and Figural Narrative in the Old English *Elene*', in *Cynewulf: Basic Readings*, ed. Robert E. Bjork (New York: Garland, 1996), pp. 207–28.
80 Regan, 'Evangelicalism', p. 52.
81 Johnson, 'Hagiographical Demon', p. 9.
82 Ibid., p. 16.
83 Hermann, *Allegories of War*, p. 106 and p. 108.
84 Ibid., p. 111.
85 Ibid., p. 115.
86 Frederick M. Biggs, '*Beowulf* and Some Fictions of the Geatish

Succession', *ASE*, 32 (2003), 55–77 (p. 62); Biggs considers whether the *melda* represents the 'thief' or the 'intermediary lord' (p. 63).
87 Theodore M. Andersson, 'The Thief in *Beowulf*', *Speculum*, 59 (1984), 493–508.
88 Anderson, 'Treasure Trove in *Beowulf*', p. 146. Gustav Neckel suggested that the 'thief' in *Beowulf* was a 'Judas-figure'. See Gustav Neckel, 'Sigmunds Drachenkampf', *Edda*, 13 (1920), 122–40; 204–9 (p. 126).
89 Andersson, 'The Thief in *Beowulf*', p. 493.
90 Daniel Anlezark, *Water and Fire: The Myth of the Flood in Anglo-Saxon England* (Manchester: Manchester University Press, 2006), p. 211.
91 The *Recensio Casanatensis* is printed by Franz Blatt, along with the Greek edited by M. Bonnet in the *Acta Apostolorum Apocrypha*, vols. 1–2 (Leipzig: Mendelssohn, 1898), 65–116; the poetic *Recensio Vaticana* can be found in *Die lateinischen Bearbeitungen der Acta Andreae et Matthiae apud anthropophagos*, ed. Franz Blatt, *Beihefte zur Zeitschrift für die neutestamentliche Wissenschaft*, 12 (Giessen: Töpelmann, 1930), pp. 32–148.
92 Morris reconstructs the missing portions of the homily in his edition (*Blickling Homilies*, pp. 236–49).
93 In the *Casanatensis* the devil appears as an 'old man' (Allen and Calder, *Sources and Analogues*, p. 30).
94 *Blickling Homilies*, ed. and trans. Morris, p. 241.
95 Ibid., p. 243. I have modified Morris's translation somewhat here.
96 Brooke, *Andreas*, p. xvi.
97 See Thomas D. Hill, 'Satan's Pratfall and the Foot of Love: Some Pedal Images in *Piers Plowman* A, B, C', *Yearbook of Langland Studies*, 14 (2000), 157–8.
98 The devil in *Elene* (l. 951a) is similarly referred to as 'perverse of mind' (*wiðerhycgende*).
99 Scheil likens this to Anti-Judaic traditions suggesting that the Jews put Christ to death because of the promptings of the devil (*The Footsteps of Israel*, p. 228).
100 Frederick M. Biggs, 'The Passion of Andreas: *Andreas* 1398–1491', *SP*, 85 (1988), 413–27 (p. 417).
101 Breen, 'The Voice of Evil', p. 194.
102 Hermann, *Allegories of War*, p. 134.
103 Jewish elders in *Elene* are also called 'wærlogan' (oath-breakers, l. 613a).
104 This same formula is used to describe the devil in *Elene* (l. 898a).
105 The devil in *Elene* is also described as *yfela gemyndig* (l. 901).
106 Morton Bloomfield, *The Seven Deadly Sins: An Introduction to the History of a Religious Concept, with Special Reference to Medieval English Literature* (East Lansing: Michigan State College Press,

1962), p. 108. Bloomfield notes that Evagrius discusses 'sin demons' (p. 59).
107 Ibid., p. 64.
108 Jean Daniélou, *The Bible and the Liturgy* (Notre Dame, IN: University of Notre Dame Press, 1966), p. 59; on the *sphragis*, see 54ff.
109 T. D. Hill, 'The Sphragis as Apotropaic Sign', pp. 147–51.
110 Ibid., pp. 148–9.
111 T. D. Hill argues, 'The sign of God's power clearly has baptismal resonances ... the imposition of the sphragis itself precedes baptism' ('The Sphragis as Apotropaic Sign', p. 150).
112 *Beowulf*, ll. 786–7a; the devil in *Juliana* also 'hearm galan' (sings of misery, l. 629).
113 The *Casanatensis* draws upon *The Book of the Secrets of Enoch* stating that 'you entered the hearts of God's sons, made them lie with women; and their sons were made into giants on the earth' (Allen and Calder, *Sources and Analogues*, p. 26).
114 This episode appears briefly in chapter seventeen of the *Casanatensis* and the *Praxeis* (Brooke, *Andreas*, p. xvi).
115 Magennis, *Images of Community*, p. 10.
116 Joyce Hill, 'The Soldier of Christ in Old English Prose and Poetry', *LSE*, 12 (1981), 57–80 (p. 63).
117 Ibid., p. 63.
118 Ker, *Catalogue of Manuscripts*, no. 5. This was edited by Paul Alfred Gonser, *Das angelsächsische Prosa-Leben des hl. Guthlac*, Anglistische Forschungen 27 (Heidelberg: C. Winter, 1909) who presents the two prose texts (the other one found in the Vercelli Book) side by side to demonstrate their derivation from a common source. In the prose *Guthlac*, the demons famously speak 'Welsh' (*bryttisc sprecende*) (6.8) deriving from Felix, whose demons *verba loquentis vulgi Brittanicaque* (34.110).
119 Laurence K. Shook, 'The Prologue of the Old-English *Guthlac A*', *Mediaeval Studies*, 23 (1961), 294–304 (p. 295).
120 Jolly, *Popular Religion*, p. 31.
121 Hill, 'The Soldier of Christ', p. 68.
122 Smith, *Land and Book*, p. 192.
123 See Thomas D. Hill, 'Drawing the Demon's Sting: A Note on a Traditional Motif in Felix's "Vita Sancti Guthlaci"', *N&Q*, 23 (1976), 388–90; Alaric Hall, 'Constructing Anglo-Saxon Sanctity: Tradition, Innovation and Saint Guthlac', in *Images of Medieval Sanctity: Essays in Honour of Gary Dickson*, ed. Debra Higgs Strickland, Visualising the Middle Ages 1 (Leiden: Brill, 2007), pp. 207–35 (p. 208).
124 On Guthlac's earlier career as a warrior, see Damon, *Soldier Saints and Holy Warriors*.
125 Benjamin Kurtz traces the parallels between Felix's *Vita Guthlaci* and the Latin *Vita Antonii* in 'From St. Anthony to St. Guthlac: A

Study in Biography', *University of California Publications in Modern Philology*, 12 (1926), 103–46.
126 Ibid., p. 109.
127 Helmut Gneuss and Michael Lapidge, *Anglo-Saxon Manuscripts: A Bibliographical Handlist of Manuscripts and Manuscript Fragments Written or Owned in England up to 1100* (Toronto: University of Toronto Press, 2014), no. 257; and Ker, *Catalogue of Manuscripts*, no. 116; Ker dates the Exeter Book to the second half of the tenth century, Gneuss and Lapidge to its third quarter. Roberts suggests slightly earlier (*Guthlac Poems*, pp. 48–63; p. 70), which is supported by R. D. Fulk, *A History of Old English Meter* (Philadelphia: University of Pennsylvania Press, 1992), p. 400. Conner proposes a date closer to c. 960–70 ('Source Studies', pp. 409–10).
128 For an overview, see Stephanie Clark, '*Guthlac A* and the Temptation of the Barrow', *Studia Neophilologica*, 87 (2015), 48–72, who argues that 'while we cannot state for certain that the *Guthlac A* poet did not know Felix's *Vita*, we can confidently state that he did not use it' (p. 50).
129 See Jolly, *Popular Religion*, p. 23ff.
130 Bjork, *Old English Verse Saints' Lives*, p. 32.
131 See Clark, '*Guthlac A* and the Temptation of the Barrow', who concludes that the evidence for the *beorg* as a 'barrow' is weak. Manish Sharma, 'A Reconsideration of the Structure of *Guthlac A*: The Extremes of Saintliness', *JEGP* (2002), 185–200, considers the legal dimension of *edergong* ('thresholds'); see also Laurence K. Shook, 'The Burial Mound in *Guthlac A*', *MP*, 58 (1960), 1–10; Karl P. Wentersdorf, '*Guthlac A*: The Battle for the *Beorg*', *Neophil*, 62 (1978), 135–42; Alfred K. Siewers, 'Landscapes of Conversion: Guthlac's Mound and Grendel's Mere as Expressions of Anglo-Saxon Nation-Building', *Viator*, 34 (2003), 1–39; on the East Anglian setting, see Katherine O'Brien O'Keeffe, 'Guthlac's Crossing', *Quaestio*, 2 (2001), 1–26.
132 Smith, *Land and Book*, p. 198ff.
133 On the 'respite of the damned' motif, see Clark, 'A More Permanent Homeland', p. 86.
134 David F. Johnson, 'Spiritual Combat and the Land of Canaan in *Guthlac A*', in *Intertexts: Studies in Anglo-Saxon Culture Presented to Paul E. Szarmach*, ed. Virginia Blanton and Helene Scheck (Tempe, AZ and Turnhout: ACMRS with Brepols, 2009), pp. 307–18.
135 Conner, 'Source Studies', p. 403.
136 Christopher A. Jones, 'Envisioning the *cenobium* in *Guthlac A*', *Mediaeval Studies*, 57 (1995), 259–91 (p. 260).
137 Ibid., p. 263.
138 Ibid., p. 264.
139 Clark notes that '*eþel* connotes the emotional idea of home, family,

security, belonging, and an amorphous set of rights to protection and sustenance' ('A More Permanent Homeland', p. 83 n. 34). Alaric Hall considers Scandinavian parallels concerned with driving away monsters ('Constructing Anglo-Saxon Sanctity', p. 216ff).

140 For an assessment of the complex rhyme in this passage, see Smith, *Land and Book*, p. 204.
141 Ibid., p. 192.
142 Ibid., p. 194.
143 Variations upon this phrase appear in *Christ and Satan* (l. 24b; l. 174, l. 246) and in *Genesis B* (l. 259a).
144 Arthur Groos, 'The "Elder" Angel in *Guthlac A*', *Anglia*, 101 (1983), 141–6 (p. 146).
145 Clark, 'A More Permanent Homeland', p. 76.
146 Jolly, *Popular Religion*, p. 96ff.
147 Ibid., p. 101.
148 Ibid., p. 75.

5
A homeland as a possession

Medieval saints' lives sometimes include brief episodes in which a holy figure measures the boundaries of a designated sacred site or hallowed landscape.[1] For instance, the *Leabhar Breac* homily on St Patrick describes how Patrick, accompanied by an angel and Ireland's elders, consecrates the borders of Armagh at its founding: 'and they marked out the city in his presence, and the place of the temple and of the kitchen and of the guest-house. And [the angel] went right-hand-wise round the rampart, and Patrick behind him'.[2] A similar version of events is recounted in the *Vita tripartita Sancti Patricii* or *Bethu Phátraic*:

> Patrick blessed Armagh out of his two hands. The way in which Patrick measured the rath was this – the angel before him and Patrick behind the angel; with his household and with Ireland's elders, and Jesu's Staff in Patrick's hand ... In this wise, then, Patrick measured the *Ferta*.[3]

Precise measurements for the *rath* ('enclosure, property') then follow. Just as Patrick carefully measures the *ferta* ('site') of Armagh and Guthlac establishes the defensive parameters of his *beorg*, the ritualised demarcation of boundaries can also be seen across the spaces of hell at the end of the Old English *Christ and Satan*.[4]

Scholars frequently characterise this final poem of the Junius Manuscript as obscure or even confused because it follows an unorthodox chronology in placing the Harrowing, Ascension, and Last Judgement before Christ's Temptation in the wilderness. Furthermore, the poem concludes with a peculiar, unsourced episode in which Christ orders Satan to measure the *ymbhwyrft* ('circuit') of hell with his hands.[5] Not long after Satan embarks on his measurements, the manuscript closes resolutely with the phrase, 'Finit Liber II. Amen'.[6] Nineteenth-century scholars such as John Josias Conybeare, Benjamin Thorpe, and Bernhard ten Brink assumed that the poem was fragmentary and that it must have been arranged in a piecemeal or even arbitrary fashion.[7] Friedrich Groschopp likewise saw structural incompatibilities in the poem owing to its blending of narrative-dramatic and hortatory-homiletic elements.[8] These perceived shortcomings were reiterated in the twentieth century by scholars such as C. Abbetmeyer.[9]

The sheer number of metrical and textual irregularities would suggest that the version of *Christ and Satan* that survives in the Junius Manuscript is a vestige of a much earlier work, its defects accumulating as the poem underwent several stages of imperfect transmission at the hands of several separate scribes. In one case, the poem was altered by an individual known today only by the somewhat unfortunate moniker, 'the Corrector', who, at the expense of meter and basic sense, attempted to conform the text to the West Saxon dialect.[10]

Aside from the poem's internal idiosyncrasies, the very status of *Christ and Satan* within Oxford, Bodleian Library, Junius 11 has been a persistent topic of scholarly debate. Quite unlike some of the vibrantly illustrated Genesis poems that precede it, *Christ and Satan* lacks illustrations and shows signs of heavy use and wear. These physical disparities have led some scholars to conclude that the poem was not originally meant for inclusion in Junius 11. Peter Lucas, for instance, proposed that *Christ and Satan* once circulated independently as a booklet within a monastic milieu before being bound in the manuscript.[11] Following Barbara Raw's persuasive codicological study of the manuscript, however, it is generally agreed that *Christ and Satan* was expressly copied for Junius 11, but as 'a fairly early afterthought' in the codex's late tenth- or early eleventh-century compilation.[12]

The poem's likely status as a late addition, its numerous poetic defects, interspersed homiletic passages,[13] unusual structure, and New Testament subject matter do make *Christ and Satan* the odd one out following the Old Testament poems *Genesis A*, *Genesis B*, *Exodus*, and *Daniel*. So whose 'fairly early afterthought' brought *Christ and Satan* into a codex primarily devoted to Old Testament poetry? What kind of audience did they envision for its message? How might this poem make a fitting end to the compilation? The mysterious inclusion of *Christ and Satan* serves as an important reminder that both the poem (and the manuscript as a whole) is no mere one-off, but a remnant of a long, complex transmission history: within Junius 11's many pages are whispers of poetry undoubtedly hailing from different geographic corners of England, of artists of various talents and backgrounds, and of ideological preoccupations from diverse social contexts during the lengthy Anglo-Saxon period. Just as the embeddedness of *Genesis B* reveals a compiler's desire to tell an unbroken account of the wee moments in creation history, the later physical grafting of *Christ and Satan* indicates a further evolution, perhaps even a repurposing, of the manuscript, as well as an expansion of the mythos of the angelic rebellion.

Although several studies have productively traced unifying themes through the Junius poems from start to finish,[14] *Christ and Satan* is still occasionally characterised as awkwardly 'disjointed' at worst and 'meandering' at best.[15] The poem's most recent editor, Robert Emmett Finnegan, rightly suggests that if we are to regard *Christ and Satan* as 'one poem rather than a series of fragments, it should be possible to demonstrate a thematic progression' through each of the poem's subsections: heavenly creation (ll. 1–21), the tortured memories of the fallen angels (ll. 22–364), the Harrowing of Hell (ll. 378–440), Ascension (ll. 557–63a), Last Judgement (ll.579–641), and the abrupt time-warp to Christ's Temptation in the wilderness (ll. 665–729).[16] Among the scholars who have sought to reconcile this nonlinear chronology and discover unifying principles within the poem are Alois Brandl, Israel Gollancz, and M. D. Clubb.[17] Bernard Huppé, and later Thomas D. Hill, similarly argue that the narrative's trajectory is neither problematic nor capricious because Christ's wilderness temptation anticipates 'the final defeat of Satan at the Last Judgement'.[18] Although these typological readings are convincing, the thematic sequence is nevertheless complicated when, in the closing lines of the poem, Christ commands Satan to measure the *ymbhwyrft* ('circuit', l. 701a) of hell 'mid hondum' (by hand, l. 699b) before 'twa ... tida' (two hours, l. 708) have passed. No scriptural, apocryphal, or exegetical source has been identified for either Christ's bizarre demand or the image of Satan's enfeebled procession through his 'merced hus' (appointed dwelling, l. 709a).

The undeniable structural and chronological incongruities of *Chris and Satan* may make better sense if we consider not only the Bible as a source but the Anglo-Saxon liturgy as well – specifically, the feast of Rogationtide. The three-day Rogation observances were an integral part of the Anglo-Saxon liturgical cycle. The attendant practices were geared towards affirming community, demarcating territorial boundaries, and purifying both physical spaces and the human soul through fasting, vigils, prayers, and, most significantly, processions throughout the countryside. Just as a saint might trace a circuit at the founding of a monastery or holy place to signal the site's devotedness to God, medieval Christian communities routinely participated in similar ambulatory rituals across their parish boundaries. The poem's conclusion – Satan's perambulation of the boundaries of hell – can be productively understood as an inversion of the penitential and spatial rituals associated with Rogationtide, making his punishment a demonic parody of the communal 'circuit' that lies at the centre of the feast. By evoking the symbolic geography of Rogationtide and presenting his audience with a demonic imitation of a popular communal practice, the *Christ and Satan* poet invites his audience to contemplate the rituals that sanctify earthly spaces and secure the advance of faithful Christians to heavenly spaces.

In this way, the *Christ and Satan* poet also dramatises contemporary liturgical and spatial rituals that were popular from the mid-eighth century onward, and during the time of Junius 11's compiling. If Christ's command that Satan measure hell's *ymbhwyrft* alludes to the Rogation 'circuit' (*ymbgang* or *ymbhwyrft*),[19] the poem then provides a lexical and thematic framework through which Anglo-Saxon readers might recognise the distinction between the penance earned through liturgical practice and the punishment afforded to those who fail to recognise Christ's sovereignty. The poet's concern with salvific inheritance not only places *Christ and Satan* into direct conversation with the lived spiritual world of its Anglo-Saxon readers, but also allows its New Testament material to illuminate the preceding Old Testament poems by furthering the codex's guiding themes of repentance and the promise of divine inheritance.[20]

The thematic centrality of the organisation of space and borders in *Christ and Satan* is signalled at the beginning of the poem in a tableau that reshapes the war in heaven into a dispute between rival lords concerned with power, rank, and territorial possession. Whereas *Genesis A* and *Genesis B* depict Satan's pre-lapsarian desire to surpass God's sovereignty, *Christ and Satan* offers several retrospective accounts of Satan's failed attempt to *towerpan* ('overthrow', l. 85a) his sovereign, Christ, and seize control of heavenly territories. That the *Christ and Satan* poet recasts Christ as the Lord who crushes Satan's rebellion – six hundred years before John Milton locates Christ as the heroic defender of heaven in Book V of *Paradise Lost*[21] – is somewhat surprising and innovative. Satan, a veteran retainer, violates his obligations to his young lord through his desire for status and landed supremacy, crimes that would have immediate political relevance in Anglo-Saxon England. The idea of a heavenly rivalry between Christ and Satan is thus fraught with ideological implications, and is as rare in patristic traditions as it is in the Anglo-Saxon record.[22] References to Christ as arbiter of Satan's banishment occur only fleetingly in Anglo-Saxon texts, including Felix's *Life of Saint Guthlac*,[23] and in three Exeter Book poems.[24] A twelfth-century copy of an Old English Antichrist homily (*c.* 1120) from MS Vespasian D. XIV states that the devil claimed 'þæt he mihte rixigen ofer heofones and beon gelic Godes sune' (that he might rule over heaven and be like God's son).[25] In his Commentary on Jude 6 (CCSL 121.68),[26] Bede remarks that the rebel angels' punishment was administered by Christ:

> Iesu dominus noster praeuaricatores angelos puniuit ... et a principio superbientes angelos ita sub caligine aeris huius damnauit ut eosdem in die iudicii grauiores reseruet ad poenas.
>
> [Jesus our Lord punished the angels who transgressed ... and from the beginning so condemned the proud angels in the darkness of this air that he might keep the same for greater punishment on the day of judgement.][27]

Here, Bede invokes the typological connection between Christ's expulsion of 'praeuaricatores angelos' (the angels who transgressed) at the beginning of time and the final defeat of Satan on the Day of Judgement. These events at the origin and end of creation history were fused in the Anglo-Saxon theopolitical imaginary because both reinforce the idea that membership in the community of the saved is earned by those who remain loyal.

Despite all its oddities, the fact remains that *Christ and Satan* is a poem that grapples with many fundamental questions concerning space, territory, and authority: the geography of hell; the internalisation of space and boundaries; the terror of disinheritance and exile; and the nature of sovereignty and kingship. Satan's primary lament, which reverberates throughout the poem, is that he has lost *eðel to æhte* ('a homeland as a possession' l. 278a). Like *Genesis A* and *Genesis B* before it, landed supremacy and the competition for power lead to the fall of the angels at the start of the poem. The poet is careful to point out that Satan's attempts to disrupt Christ's authority in both heavenly and earthly territories accordingly results in the forfeiture of his lands, his exclusion from heaven, and his exile to the chaotic spaces of hell. These topics reassert themselves at the end of *Christ and Satan* during Christ's Temptation in the wilderness.

Just as the *Christ and Satan* poet canvasses the whole scheme of salvation history from the angelic rebellion through Last Judgement, Rogation rituals re-enact this same drama across earthly space, from the original purification of heaven to the final eschatological inclusions and exclusions of Doomsday. The poet demonstrates the contrast between heavenly spaces, defined by their stability and inheritability, and the chaotic spaces of hell, which lack order and true sovereignty despite Satan's presence there. While the feast of Rogationtide encourages participants to focus annually on a deferred heavenly investiture, the poet shows how Satan's treachery results in his exile to a homeland that cannot be mapped and a space where sacral ritual has lost all potency. By situating his poem within established semantic and cultural categories of liturgical and localised practice, the poet appeals to an audience readily familiar with the primary goals of Rogationtide, namely, the purification of earthly boundaries in the interest of making oneself a suitable heir to otherworldly geographies.

Gangdagas and *gebeddagas*

Scholars have long noted the influence of the Anglo-Saxon liturgy throughout Junius 11. Paul G. Remley, for example, positively reappraised and extended James W. Bright's suggestion that the language and imagery found during the Crossing of the Red Sea in *Exodus* parallels the Holy Saturday liturgy derived from the Gelasian lection tradition.[28] Phyllis Portnoy observed the influence of Holy Saturday lections in *Christ and Satan*,[29] while Geoffrey Shepherd and Judith N. Garde have gone so far as to propose that the entire Junius codex may have been related to the lectionaries of the Anglo-Saxon Church.[30] To my knowledge, however, the feast of Rogationtide has not previously been put forward as a possible influence on any of the Junius poems. My aim here is not to argue for the presence of specific textual echoes, but rather to suggest that an echo of liturgical practice reverberates through hell in *Christ and Satan*.

We can glean basic insights into the practices associated with Rogationtide through a handful of anonymous homilies as well as nine sermons written by Ælfric of Eynsham for the feast.[31] Homilies associated with Rogationtide give us an unusually concrete picture of how the laity would have engaged with a popular liturgical feast. In order to demonstrate how the *Christ and Satan* poet invokes Rogation rituals, it will be necessary first to provide a brief overview of its history and accompanying festivities. In England, Rogationtide was officially recognised at the Council of Clofesho (d. 747).[32] Canon 16 under *De diebus litaniarum* distinguishes between two festivals: one according to the rite of the Roman Church referred to as *litania major* (on 25 April), and another based upon 'the custom of our forefathers, three days before the Ascension of our Lord into the heavens'.[33] Translating Latin *rogare* ('to ask'), vernacular witnesses refer to the three Rogation days as *gangdagas* ('walking days') or *gebeddagas* ('prayer days') that reflect the two central observances of the feast: perambulations (or processions) and stationed penitential prayer.[34]

Milton McCormick Gatch refers to Rogationtide as a 'favorite season of Anglo-Saxon sermon writers',[35] and Rogationtide material is indeed prevalent in the Anglo-Saxon corpus.[36] Helen Gittos describes Rogation processions (later called 'beating the bounds'[37]) as among 'the most public and revered features of early medieval liturgy'.[38] At once a very formulaic tradition, Rogation was also a very pliable and adaptable one that incorporated new emphases in the hands of different homilists. According to M. Bradford Bedingfield, Rogation rituals were overtly penitential and involved fasting, prayers, and processions both within the church and throughout the parochial countryside as 'evidence of repentance'.[39] Bazire and Cross Homily 1 offers a detailed description of how the congregation should process:

> Us is georne to witanne and to gehlystenne for hwilcum þingum we þas gangdagas healdon and barefote gangen þus on geares fyrste … We hi sceolon healdan on micelre eadmodnysse and on micclum geþylde and on soðre lufe and on ealre clænnysse, lichaman and sawle, and on godum wæccum and nytweorðum and on fæstenum and on halgum gebedum and on ælmysdædum.[40]

[We ought eagerly to know and to hear for what reasons we keep these Rogation Days and go barefoot in this way every year … We ought to keep them in great humility and in great patience and in charity and in all purity of body and soul, and in good and useful vigils, and in fasts and in holy prayers and in almsdeeds.]

Stephen F. Harris notes that these customs were in perfect concert with the liturgical texts designated for the feast, which invoked 'suffering, resignation, wisdom, and joy. A celebrant moves from place to place, moment to moment, prayer to prayer, in a constant ritual peregrination.'[41] The three Rogation days were solemn occasions designed to call attention to a penitent's status as an earthly pilgrim and the parish as a unified community of pilgrims.[42] As Hugh Magennis writes, this enables the liturgy to serve as 'a reflection of the heavenly community on earth', making Rogation an important occasion for communal worship and identity formation.[43] Although Christ's Temptation is not directly connected with Rogationtide in the liturgical cycle, Christ's wilderness fasting is occasionally referenced in various homilies rubricated for the feast. Vercelli Homily 12, for instance, contains admonitions about the importance of keeping fasts as Christians prepare 'gangan ymb ure land' (to go around [their] land, l. 31), suggesting that fasting strengthens one's ability to overcome the 'constunga' (temptations) of the devil:

> Þurh þæt fæsten dryhten diofles miht abræc ⁊ his costunga oferswiðde ⁊ mancynne ecne sige forgeaf, þæt manna gehwylc mæg diofol oferswiðan.[44]

[Through that fast the Lord broke the might of the devil and conquered his temptations, and gave to mankind eternal victory so that each of men may conquer the devil.]

Likewise, Ælfric's CH I.19 ('Feria III De Dominica Oratione') reflects on how fasting affords one a greater proximity to God (ll. 146–77), serving as a model for both the clergy and the laity on the path to salvation.

Rogationtide practices are attested from the mid-eighth century onward, particularly the circuit made by the community of believers. One such circuit is mentioned in the *Epistola Cuthberti de obitu Baedae*, in which he describes how he and the monks briefly departed from the bedside of Bede (who died just before Ascension Thursday) and how 'ambulauimus' (we walked) in procession according to the precepts of the feast.[45] Vercelli Homily 12 likewise refers to the 'gedefelice gange' (fitting procession) as central to the festival's symbolic geography.[46] As Alexandra Walsham observes, the circuit constituted an engrained cultural practice in early Christian England 'designed to imprint ... geographical boundaries upon the mind' and reinforce 'the map that divided neighboring communities'.[47] Likewise, Stephen Hindle suggests that the feast was not 'merely a ritual of incorporation [but] implied

... demarcation'.⁴⁸ In this way, the circuit defines particular communities of the faithful by way of exclusion.

Bedingfield proposes that processions were often symbolic amalgams of several key moments in salvation history such as Christ's Harrowing and Ascension.⁴⁹ Through this synthesis, ideas of Christ's ascent and descent would have been firmly fixed in the Anglo-Saxon imagination. Christ, in a sense, beats the bounds of his own territory, perambulating from the depths of hell to the heights of heaven just as Rogation-goers perambulate horizontal boundaries all the while imagining a vertical dimension to the ritual. Johanna Kramer, in her work on Ascension theology, argues that both Ascension and Rogationtide are fundamentally liminal phenomena 'linked by their common concern with boundaries and borders: both feasts ... are all spatial processes, whether physical movements through space or a boundary crossing Christological event'.⁵⁰ Inasmuch as Rogation was focused on the consecration of land, Bedingfield also points out that the purification of souls was critical to 'the upcoming Ascension, where [Christians] can either join Christ's elevation of humanity to heaven or fall under his divine punishment'.⁵¹ In turn, Rogation was about envisioning earth as a threshold where one can work to attain heavenly inheritance and avoid the deprivations of hell. Consequently, Rogationtide homilies often allude to the fall of the angels and the eventual reunification of heaven, suggesting that it was a theme of recurring interest for Rogation sermon writers.⁵² Not only is the fall of the angels invoked textually, but it is also recalled in the dramatic performativity of the processions. Of the common themes that appear in Rogation sermons, Bedingfield suggests that the most prominent are penance, care of the soul, and the incantatory casting-out of demons.⁵³

Eamon Duffy's authoritative work on early modern religious practice suggests that the material objects associated with Rogation – bells, crosses, banners – were all directed at driving out demons.⁵⁴ We see prototypes of these traditions in the Anglo-Saxon period when apotropaic crosses and holy relics would have marked off God's territory by, in Bedingfield's words, delineating a *gemotstow* ('sacred space'), or a 'pocket of God's presence'.⁵⁵ Perambulating supplicants would claim physical territory as sacred 'by infusing it' with God's divinity.⁵⁶ This transformation of earthly space into a signifier for heavenly space is key because, as Bedingfield further notes, 'unity with this space ... allows [believers'] approach to heaven'.⁵⁷ Through these practices Anglo-Saxons define themselves as a mobile community of faithful Christians, perambulating and purifying the boundaries, while anticipating their eventual inclusion among the heavenly order.

The seriousness of these rituals is evident in the severity of the punishments associated with failure to participate in earnest. The anonymous homily Bazire and Cross 4 emphasises the importance of fasting by recalling the three-day fast of the Ninevites, before explaining the need for penitents to walk barefoot while undertaking observances. The homilist explains how the neglect of proper processions in life means that one will be doomed to process in hell:

> And se man þe nele nu þas þry dagas mid Godes halgan reliquian bærfot gangan, þurh þa nigon helle he sceal ær domesdæge eal swa feola siðan swa he her fotspora gesceod eode ofer þæs prestes bebod.[58]

[And the man who does not wish to now go barefoot with God's holy relics during these three days, must go through the nine hells before Doomsday just as many times as he here walked footpaces shod against the priest's command.]

That a quasi-Rogation might also occur within the vast confines of hell is crucial; it suggests that one may choose to process earthly boundaries as a means of penance or otherworldly boundaries as a form of interim punishment.[59] The homily goes on to explain that the unshod sinner will traverse the nine hells or compartments, touring each 'stow' (place) furnished for different types of sinners, including the chamber intended for 'hlafordswicon' (lord-betrayers, l. 59). The transgressor's punishment in Bazire and Cross 4 is enacted across the vast structures of hell just as Satan's at the end of *Christ and Satan*. The man who fails at his Rogation duties, rather than abide in a particular compartment, must navigate the entirety of the nine houses for every misstep he took in life. Rogation thus demarcates not only the boundaries of a spiritual community but also of a damned community, partitioning the faithful from the unfaithful, revealing, as Harris notes, 'the limits of the Church' and enemies worthy of exclusion from it.[60]

While Rogation days would have signalled the possibility of a heavenly inheritance to Anglo-Saxon Christians, both Bazire and Cross Homily 4 and, as I will argue, *Christ and Satan*, suggest that the feast may also invoke the converse: the threat of a hellish inheritance. These themes of inheritance, processing, claiming space, coming to know the limits of one's community, and visualising

Judgement Day all have bearing upon our understanding of *Christ and Satan*. The poet emphasises the unification of heavenly space through the image of Christ as judge who invites the righteous to 'gongan' (go, l. 613) into the heavenly 'burh' (city, l. 612b),[61] while delineating a space fit for sinners like the man in Bazire and Cross Homily 4 who must go through the spatially inexpressible vastness of hell.

Eðel to æhte

While Rogationtide encourages a kind of spiritual mobility, its rituals would have also served as a reminder that securing heavenly inheritance is a privilege open only to the faithful and contrite. *Christ and Satan* begins with a uniquely represented fall of the angels narrative which allows the poet to elaborate upon these themes of loyalty and betrayal. Since Israel Gollancz first demonstrated some of the striking doctrinal anomalies in the poet's account of heavenly creation, the issue of Satan's manifold betrayals has generated scholarly debate.[62] To begin with, the opening lines suggest that Satan and Adam may have coexisted in heaven simultaneously (ll. 19–20), an unconventional idea found in Irish traditions influenced by the apocryphal *Life of Adam and Eve*:[63] 'Dreamas he gedelde, duguðe and geoguþe, / Adam ærest, and þæt æðele cyn, / engla ordfruman, þæt þe eft forwarð' (He distributed joys, divided the young troop and the old, first Adam and that noble race, the chief of the angels who afterwards fell).[64] At line 19b, the manuscript reads *geþeode*, which Finnegan and others persuasively emend to *geoguðe* owing to the phrase's formulaic status.[65] At first glance, these lines appear to equalise Adam and Satan as heavenly comrades. However, as David F. Johnson points out, the poet obliquely suggests that Adam, although he is head of the *geoguðe* ('young troop'), appears to outrank Lucifer, the presumed head of the *duguðe* ('veteran troop'). Johnson suggests that the poet thus invites readers to associate with the *geoguðe*, the young troop that aspires 'to join the ranks of the *duguþe*' whose former crimes are 'rendered all the more perfidious because of [Lucifer's] status as the leader of the tried and trusted veteran retainers'.[66] Furthering this tension, the poet also reveals that the treacherous *duguþe* believed that 'hie weron seolfe swegles brytan, / wuldres waldend' (they themselves might be the rulers of heaven, lords of glory, ll. 23–4a), though it is not until after the fall of the angels that we learn more about what drove the rebels to insurrection. That the fledgling *geoguðe* must earn their place among the higher ranks of the heavenly order suggests that the poet imagines humankind as poised to inherit the former stature and possessions forfeited by the angels who rebelled. For Anglo-Saxon Christians, the prospect of a heavenly inheritance had a doctrinal basis and would have been at the forefront of the minds of believers during Rogationtide.

An even more complex picture concerning this heavenly power struggle unfolds in the complaints of the recently banished *duguðe*. Here, the rebels accuse Satan of fraud claiming that they were fooled into believing that he was 'halig god / scypend seolfa' (holy God, the creator himself, ll. 56b–7a), and that his son, presumably meaning Christ, would be the Lord of mankind: 'Segdest us to soðe þæt ðin sunu wære / meotod moncynnes' (You said to us in truth that your son would be the measurer of mankind, ll. 63–4a).[67] As a result, the dissidents feel no loyalty towards him. His betrayal (and punishment) is manifold in that he betrayed his fellow angels and conspired to betray Christ. Even in hell, Satan is viewed by the other fallen angels as their betrayer. We also learn that Satan's fall was not a consequence of his aversion to worshipping Adam (as is the case in Irish versions concerning the fall, as discussed in Chapter 2), but rather a result of his desire to seize lands, power, and glory from the young Lord, Christ, who, eventually 'afirde' (exiled, l. 67b) the troop of rebels.[68] Initially, Satan laments a time when heaven was ordered, unified, and part of angelic possession:

> 'Hwær com engla ðrym,
> þe we on heofnum   habban sceoldan? ...
> Hwæt, we for dryhtene iu   dreamas hefdon,
> song on swegle   selrum tidum,
> þær nu ymb ðone æcan   æðele stondað,
> heleð ymb hehseld,   herigað drihten
> wordum and wercum,   and ic in wite sceal
> bidan in bendum,   and me bættran ham
> for oferhygdum   æfre ne wene'. (ll. 36b–7; 44–50)

['What has become of the glory of angels, which we should have possessed in heaven? ... Listen! We once enjoyed pleasures before the Lord, singing in heaven in better times, where now noble ones stand around the eternal one, heroes around the high seat, they worship the Lord with words and deeds, while I in torment must wait in chains, and never know a better home for myself because of pride'.]

These lines express traditional Germanic heroic imagery as Satan reminisces about the former 'engla ðrym' (glory of angels) and the

A homeland as a possession

bonds of loyalty among the 'æðele' (noble ones) in heaven (presumably the unfallen angels or humankind),[69] who have inherited his former place at the heavenly table where holy heroes still stand. Satan identifies his banishment from heaven as a 'tacen sutol' (clear sign).[70] Like 'Grendles grape' (Grendel's claw), which is detached and hung 'under geapne hrof' (under the vaulted roof, l. 836b) for all to see, Satan's expulsion from heaven similarly signifies a severance both permanent and visible within the poem. The consequences of these actions are manifested in Satan's physical displacement from heaven and unstable embodiment in hell: he 'spearcade' (spit sparks, l. 78a) as he speaks and is 'ealle ... ungelice' (entirely ... unlike, l. 149) his former angelic self, who once possessed 'wlite and weorðmynt' (beauty and worth, l. 151a). Satan's former desire for sole possession of heaven becomes more pronounced in the next lines:

'Þa ic in mode   minum hogade
þæt ic wolde towerpan   wuldres leoman,
bearn helendes,   agan me burga gewald
eall to æhte,   and ðeos earme heap
þe ic hebbe to helle   ham geledde.
Wene þæt tacen sutol   þa ic aseald wes on wærgðu,
niðer under nessas   in ðone neowlan grund.
Nu ic eow hebbe to hæftum   ham gefærde
alle of earde.   Nis her eadiges tir,
wloncra winsele,   ne worulde dream,
ne ængla ðreat,   ne we upheofon
agan moten'. (ll. 84–95a)

['Then in my heart I thought that I wanted to overthrow the light of glory, the son of the saviour, to have rule of the cities entirely unto myself, along with this wretched troop which I have led home to hell. I think that was a clear sign when I was sent into condemnation, deep under the chasms in this deep abyss. Now I have led you all home as captives out of your native land. There is no triumph of the blessed one here, wine halls of proud men, nor joy of the world, nor troop of angels, nor might we possess heaven above'.]

By transgressing the boundaries of Christ's 'burga' (cities), Satan finds himself in 'wærgðu' (condemnation), having been expelled from one territory to another. Discussion of Satan's rebellion against Christ is more than a mere postscript; bemoaning his fate as a warrior bereft of his hall, Satan's lament is strikingly reminiscent of elegiac poems recounting the pains of exile:[71]

> 'Eala þæt ic eam ealles leas   ecan dreames,
> þæt ic mid handum ne mæg   heofon geræcan,
> ne mid eagum ne mot   up locian,
> ne huru mid earum ne sceal   æfre geheran
> þære byrhtestan   beman stefne!
> Ðæs ic wolde of selde   sunu meotodes,
> drihten adrifan,   and agan me þæs dreames gewald,
> wuldres and wynne,   me þær wyrse gelamp
> þonne ic to hihte   agan moste.
> Nu ic eom asceaden   fram þære sciran driht,
> alæded fram leohte   in þone laðan ham ...
> þæs ðe ic geþohte adrifan   drihten of selde,
> weoroda waldend;   sceal nu wreclastas
> settan sorhgcearig,   siðas wide'. (ll. 167–77; 186–8)

['Alas, that I am entirely cut off from eternal joy, that I may not reach heaven with my hands, nor may I look upwards with my eyes, nor afterwards shall I even hear with my ears the sound of the clearest trumpet! Because I desired to drive the Lord, the son of the creator, from his throne, and to possess for myself rule of that joy, of wonder and bliss, it turned out worse for me than I might have hoped. Now I am separated from the shining company, exiled from light in that loathly home ... because I thought to drive the Lord from his throne, the ruler of hosts; I shall now with sorrowful care tread paths of exile, far journeys'.]

Significantly, amid the catalogue of woes, Satan cites his loss of dexterity, stating that he 'may not reach heaven with [his] hands'. He repeats multiple times that he sought 'to drive the Lord from his throne',[72] and recalls rallying his troops 'on geardagum' (in days of old, l. 367) with the allure of sole custody over heaven: 'Uta oferhycgan helm þone micclan, / weroda waldend, / agan us þis wuldres leoht, / eall to æhte' (Let us renounce that great protector, the ruler of hosts, and possess for ourselves this glory of heaven, entirely as our own possession, ll. 250–2a). Yet Satan's wish to *adrifan* ('drive away' or 'expel') Christ only leads to his own banishment.[73] Since the revolt in heaven is featured as a grab for territory and supremacy, it is appropriate that the poet presents Christ as the powerful lord who severs would-be usurpers from their heavenly inheritance. Satan's former promise to provide 'langsumne ræd' (enduring counsel) to his fellow angels highlights the fact that he continues to provide false and unreliable counsel from hell. This speech also situates territory and Satan's desire for singular possession of heaven at the heart of the fallen angels' reflections.

Forms of possession necessarily carry obligations and, with his speech, Satan cancels the bonds of desirable reciprocity and equal share that existed within the heavenly polity. In her discussion of the poem, Fabienne Michelet has argued that 'what is at stake in the struggle is the appropriation and the control of space'.[74] The fallen angels recognise that their defeat means they have lost their *eðel* ('homeland', l. 278a) for good.[75] Smith has noted how Old English poets often represent Satan's crimes in legal terms, and that in late Anglo-Saxon England landed possession could easily 'be revoked by the issuing authority'.[76] Such is the case with *Christ and Satan*, as Satan's territorial ambitions result in a forfeiture of the possessions once granted to him within the heavenly polity. The new space Satan and his fellow rebels inherit necessitates permanent separation from God. Howe aptly traces the idea of homelands and 'geographical specificity' throughout Junius 11, noting Satan's musings on his absent *eðel*, his physical dislocation, and Christ's role as 'the guide to the homeland, a figure who fulfils but also completes Moses because he is allowed to finish his journey and that of his followers'.[77]

In her analysis of the poet's use of measured time, Constance D. Harsh notes that the demons reflect on the same subjects, especially their lost homeland, in a continuous circuit: '[they lament] their former joys as angels, their sin, their present suffering, their lack of hope, and their assertion of continued hostility to Christ'.[78] In failing to relate properly to narrative time, the fallen angels also fail to understand the eschatological outcomes set in motion by their crimes. This finds its clearest expression in their unconventional wish to be redeemed one day:[79]

'Ic her geþolian sceal   þinga æghwylces,
bitres niðæs   beala gnornian,
sioc and sorhful,   þæs ic seolfa weold,
þonne ic on heofonum   ham staðelode,
hwæðer us se eca   æfre wille
on heofona rice   ham alefan,
eðel to æhte,   swa he ær dyde'. (ll. 272–8)

['Here, I must forfeit everything, bemoan the bitter enmity of evils, sick and sorrowful, which I myself possessed, when I held a home in heaven, whether the eternal one will ever grant us a home in the heavenly kingdom, a homeland as a possession, just as he did before'.]

As he laments an *eðel to æhte* ('a homeland as a possession') Satan reveals that both eschatological time and the divine plan are occluded in hell. Satan and the fallen angels also fail to understand the eschatological outcomes set in motion by their crimes.

While Howe observes that exilic displacement requires continuous movement towards a homeland where one can stop moving, the *Christ and Satan* poet implies that, for sinners, hell is both a physical and internalised space: 'fyr bið ymbutan / on æghwylcum, þæh he uppe seo' (fire surrounds each one, though he may be on high, ll. 263b–4).[80] Carrying hell-fires inside of them, the rebel angels' sundering from the ordered spaces of heaven is literalised as they 'hweorfan' (roam about, l. 340a) in a disorderly and purposeless way; their endless motion, then, is altogether futile.

Unlike the single-minded Satan we are presented with in *Genesis B*, who without an *œðel to œhte* is bent on the ruin of Adam and Eve, this devil appears to have lost all focus and resolve, as his laments return again and again to his dispossession:

> 'Ne mot ic hihtlicran   hames brucan,
> burga ne bolda,   ne on þa beorhtan gescæft
> ne mot ic æfre ma   eagum starian.
> Is me nu wyrsa   þæt ic wuldres leoht
> uppe mid englum   æfre cuðe,
> song on swegle,   þær sunu meotodes
> habbað eadige bearn   ealle ymbfangen
> seolfa mid sange'. (ll. 137–44a)

['I might not possess a more joyous home, nor cities nor halls, nor might I ever gaze with my eyes upon that bright creation. It is now worse for me that I ever knew that light of glory above with angels, singing in heaven, where the blessed children have themselves wholly surrounded the son of the creator with singing'.]

The imagery of kinship, love, and praise continues as he describes the former intimacy that he and the other angels once shared with Christ. Whereas the figure of Satan in *Genesis B* announces his contempt for God, here, Satan is represented as nostalgic for former times:

> 'Ealle we syndon   ungelice
> þonne þe we iu in heofonum   hæfdon ærror
> wlite and weorðmynt.   Ful oft wuldres sweg
> brohton to bearme   bearn hælendes,
> þær we ymb hine utan   ealle hofan,

leomu ymb leofne,   lofsonga word,
drihtne sædon'. (ll. 149–55a)

['We are entirely unlike that beauty and esteem which we formerly enjoyed in heaven. Often the sons of the saviour brought the song of glory to his bosom, when we entirely around him, limbs about the loved one, raised hymns of praise, spoken to the Lord'.]

Satan's remembrance of his former proximity to Christ only underscores his current separation from him. In referencing the 'bearn' (sons) formerly encircled around the 'bearme' (bosom) of the 'leofne' (loved one), the language and imagery subtly anticipates the 'broad stones' the devil will bring 'to bearme' (to the bosom) of Christ in the final Temptation sequence. Despite the individual part he played in the rebellion, however, Satan is careful to remind his fellow demons that the decision to drive the 'cyning of cestre' (king from his city) was a communal one and that it is therefore fitting that the punishment befalls them all:

'Ða gewearð usic   þæt we woldon swa
drihten adrifan   of þam deoran ham,
cyning of cestre.   Cuð is wide
þæt wreclastas   wunian moton,
grimme grundas.   God seolfa him
rice haldeð.   He is ana cyning,
þe us eorre gewearð,   ece drihten,
meotod mihtum swið'. (ll. 254–61a)

['Then it was agreed among us that we wished thus to drive the Lord out of that dear home, the king from his city. It is known widely that we must dwell on the paths of exile, the grim depths. God holds the kingdom for himself. He alone is king, who became angry with us, the eternal Lord, the creator strong in might'.]

In a manuscript so deeply concerned with how the soul can find a permanent place within a community,[81] the treachery of the fallen angels is accordingly punished with exclusion to a community where bonds of loyalty find no place. Unlike *Genesis B*, where Satan musters his loyal thanes for the temptation of Adam and Eve (ll. 409–34), the *Christ and Satan* poet suggests that fidelity cannot be forged in hell. In turning to the poem's conclusion, the poet explains that Christ will separate righteous from wicked souls on Judgement Day (ll. 579–641) and banish those who are excluded from heaven with the words, 'Astigað ... in þæt witehus' (Descend

... into that house of pain, l. 626). As Howe states: 'From these judgments, there can be no further recourse, no further motion. Place is fixed within the eternal scheme of God's will.'[82] For the devils, of course, this finality threatens erasure and means that their geographic and salvific displacement is forever sealed.

Fearful circuitry

That the final episode of *Christ and Satan* turns on the issue of space and territory is appropriate as it duplicates Satan's opening wish to surpass Christ's authority and attain singular possession of heaven. In other words, with a highly controlled envelope pattern, the poet subtly evokes the original crisis of the poem at the end. Abruptly following a description of the Ascension (ll. 557–63a), is an image of Christ's condemnation of sinners at Judgement Day (ll. 626–7), then the flashback to the Temptation (an episode loosely based on Matthew 4:3–11)[83] which brings the narrative back from the brink of eternal time into historical time, traversing both earthly and salvific time.

After providing several exhortations to right Christian living (ll. 642–64), the poet abruptly turns to Christ's forty days of fasting and confrontation in the wilderness:

> Þa gewearð þone weregan,   þe ær aworpen wæs
> of heofonum   þæt he in helle gedeaf,
> þa costode   cyning alwihta.
> Brohte him to bearme   brade stanas,
> bæd him for hungre   hlafas wyrcan–
> 'gif þu swa micle   mihte hæbbe'. (ll. 667–72)

[Then it happened to the wretched one, he who was cast out of heaven before, that he sank down into hell, when he tempted the almighty king. He brought to his bosom broad stones, urged him because of his hunger to turn them into loaves– 'if you possess such great power'.]

Here, the poet reverses Satan's prior nostalgia for the 'bearme' (bosom) of his Lord, instead describing how he places 'brade stanas' (broad stones, l. 670b) upon Christ's bosom as a sign of provocation, entreating him to 'hlafas wyrcan' (turn them into loaves, l. 671b). This gesture is reminiscent of *Beowulf*, as when Hunlaf's son challenges Hengest to avenge his lord; he lays 'billa selest on bearm' (the best of swords on his lap, ll. 1144). In this light,

A homeland as a possession

an Anglo-Saxon reader might see Satan's gesture as a symbolic threat to Christ's honour, a sign of goading, just as the kinsman's gesture ties an intensely personal object to Hengest's sense of worth: a weapon symbolising honour for a hero and the transfiguration of bread for Christ. Unlike Hengest, however, whose subsequent actions resurrect a feud, Christ repels Satan's provocation.

The poet also makes subtle yet significant modifications to Satan's temptation which, as Finnegan notes, '[magnify his] offense'.[84] Here, Satan seizes Christ *mid hondum* (l. 679b) and, slinging him upon his shoulders, sets him atop a mountain. Satan offers Christ an inheritance consisting of lands and nobility:

> 'Ic þe geselle   on þines seolfes dom
> folc and foldan.   Foh hider to me
> burh and breotone   bold to gewealde,
> rodora rices,   gif þu seo riht cyning
> engla and monna,   swa ðu ær myntest'. (ll. 684–8)

['I will give you people and land according to your own judgement. Receive from me here the city and the spacious hall into your control, the kingdom of heaven, if you are a rightful king of angels and men, as you thought before'.]

Satan's offer that Christ might inherit a 'burh' (city) and 'breotone bold' (spacious palaces) replicates Satan's primal failure to recognise Christ's sovereignty. In many ways, his proposition parallels Hygelac's ceremonial presentation of gifts and land to Beowulf.[85]

> he on Biowulfes   bearm alegde,
> ond him geselade   seofan þusendo,
> bold ond bregostol.   Him wæs bam samod
> on ðam leodscipe   lond gecynde,
> eard eðelriht,   oðrum swiðor
> side rice   þam ðær selra wæs. (ll. 2194–9)

[He laid the sword in Beowulf's lap, and gave him seven thousand (hides of land), a hall and prince-throne. The pair of them held inherited land in that nation, a home and native rights, but the wider rule was reserved for the better one.]

Just as Hygelac places 'the heirloom of Hrethel' upon the hero's lap and confers ancestral lands upon him (ll. 2194–9), Satan's offer of lands might, on the surface, look like an overdue recognition of Christ's claim to sovereignty or an invitation for joint rulership. Frederick M. Biggs has convincingly demonstrated that the *Beowulf* poet models two different kinds of rulership, one of which envisions Beowulf as co-ruler with Hygelac (a traditionally Germanic form of rulership), while the other envisions a singular sovereign (modelled after emergent Christian forms of kingship). Biggs states that, [a]s close kin, Beowulf and Hygelac appear to designate each other king, the one using the royal treasure he has received in Denmark, the other an heirloom of his father and Beowulf's grandfather, Hrethel'.[86] If Satan is, in fact, tempting Christ to accept an outmoded form of kingship wherein nobles share the right to realm and rule, Christ emerges as an exemplar of a new Christian model of succession, a distinct feature of the later Anglo-Saxon period with its evolving ideas of sovereignty. Nevertheless, by enticing Christ with symbols of rulership appropriate for a proven retainer, Satan means to lure him unwittingly into accepting subordinate status. Investiture turns back on Satan as Christ, acting as king, compels him to take possession of his own wholly undesirable fiefdom, reinforcing his status as an ignoble vassal.[87]

After resisting Satan's temptations, Christ commands him back to hell in a striking manner:

'Cer ðe on bæcling!
Wite þu eac, awyrgda,   hu wid and sid
helheoðo dreorig,   and mid hondum amet.
Grip wið þæs grundes;   gang þonne swa
oððat þu þone ymbhwyrft   alne cunne,
and ærest amet   ufan to grunde,
and hu sid seo   se swarta eðm.
Wast þu þonne þe geornor   þæt þu wið god wunne,
seoððan þu þonne hafast   handum ametene
hu heh and deop   hell inneweard seo,
grim græfhus.   Gong ricene to,
ær twa seondon   tida agongene,
þæt ðu merced hus   ameten hæbbe'. (ll. 697–709)

['Turn yourself back! Know too, you cursed one, how wide and spacious the dreary hell-hall is, and measure it with your hands. Seize hold of that abyss; then go until you know the whole circuit, and first measure from top to bottom, and how vast the dark air is. Then you will know the better that you fought with God, after you have measured with your hands how high and deep hell, the grim grave, is inside. Go quickly, before two hours are gone, so that you have measured the dwelling appointed for you'.]

Despite this episode's obscurities, it has nonetheless occasioned several productive explications. Thomas D. Hill, focusing on biblical scenes of 'measurement',[88] observes that the Old English term *metod* ('measurer') is frequently synonymous with God's act of 'measuring' creation.[89] He notes that Satan's wish to overthrow the legitimate *metod* turns him into 'the measurer of the only realm that is truly his'.[90] Ruth Wehlau draws attention to identity construction and suggests that measuring 'functions as a graphic figuring of self-knowledge'.[91] She posits that by placing the Temptation at the end, the poet offers a 'model that the human reader might be able to emulate' in Christ.[92]

Building on Hill's work, Harsh argues that this sequence reveals the 'incommensurate might' of Christ, who travels a clear path from creation to Judgement and is repeatedly defined by 'His ability to comprehend by enumeration'.[93] The poet thus contrasts Christ's forward momentum and the fallen angels' retrograde obsession with their former bliss. Janet Ericksen observes similar numerological concerns, noting the poem's affinities with the genre of wisdom literature found in *Joca Monachorum*, the *Collectanea pseudo-Bedae*, and *Solomon and Saturn*, where riddles and *enigmatae* activate rumination upon creation itself.[94] Finding Christ's impossible challenge reminiscent of this genre, Ericksen proposes that Satan simply 'recognizes the vastness of the task and not the lesson'.[95]

The spiritual drama of Rogationtide and the circuitry associated with holy spaces can further illuminate the poet's aims. He translates Christ's command *vade retro* 'Go back' with 'Cer ðe on bæcling' ('Turn yourself back'), with the verb *cyrran* signalling physical motion.[96] Invoking prominent features of the Rogationtide lexis, Christ uses the imperative *gang* ('Go!'), from the verb *gangan*, which is regularly used to denote 'processing about' during Rogationtide.[97] While *gangan* is one of the most common verbs, it is the immediate context of Satan's 'going' along the boundaries of hell that invokes a connection to the *gangdagas*. According to the *DOE*, in homilies and elsewhere, *gangan* commonly has the force of 'to go round, make a circuit of, visit all parts of',[98] figuratively referencing the 'path, way, or course' one follows in life.[99] This moment is also reminiscent of line 629b, which describes how damned souls *hwyrftum scripað* ('go turning') after Christ dismisses them.[100] Harsh and Hill have both posited a connection between this passage and Psalm 11:9, which describes how *In circuitu impii ambulant* ('the wicked walk round about').

Harsh, for instance, notes that like the *impii* of the psalm, the demons have 'an aimless, static existence, and the structure of their laments reflects this fact'.[101] While Ælfric translates this psalm in CH I.34 with 'Ða arleasan turniað on ymbhwyrfte',[102] there are no fewer than eight psalters that gloss 11:9 with forms of *gangan* and *ymbhwyrft* (the Vespasian Psalter and Stowe Psalter among others). Hill, suggesting that the 'immediate gloss for *hwyrft* is *circuitus*',[103] also remarks that, for Augustine, the *impii* sever themselves from heaven by '[attempting] to find final satisfaction in "*temporalia*"',[104] reminding readers of Rogationtide's purpose in reorienting a processant's focus away from the temporal and transient and towards that which is timeless and eternal.

In addition to literalising this psalm, however, Satan is ordered to gain an intimate familiarity with his *ymbhwyrft*. While this term occurs most often in the context of divine creation, in Bazire and Cross Homily 5, *ymbhwyrft* twice describes the perambulations associated with Rogation (ll. 124 and 141). In her influential work on the consecration of Anglo-Saxon cemeteries, Gittos notes the evolution of 'a spatial dimension' to sanctity in the late tenth century when Anglo-Saxons ritually bounded and sanctified 'specific areas for burial'.[105] Like Rogation rituals, she observes, such ceremonies culminated with '[a] procession around the perimeters of the space, sprinkling holy water, [and] prayers'.[106] This 'spiritualizing of property',[107] as Barbara H. Rosenwein similarly argues, may derive from texts such as the influential Romano-Germanic Pontifical, which describes how to transfigure sites through holy psalms and circuits.[108]

Analogously, Satan must process through the spatial boundaries of his homeland, yet his is a space that cannot be sacralised. He is ordered to 'ymbhwyrft alne cunne' (know the whole circuit) as a Rogation processant would be asked to do. Yet Christ orders Satan to do this with his hands rather than with his bare feet. Reminding readers of his prior lamentation that he cannot reach heaven *mid handum* (l. 168), this detail means that Satan must be bent over to perform his task in a contorted, extreme penitential posture that denotes his perversion and the severity of his crimes as he travels in both horizontal and vertical dimensions throughout hell. In addition to echoing the Rogation circuit, this *ymbhwyrft* echoes the *ymblyt* or 'circuit' that describes God's act of measuring in the opening lines of the poem, creating an envelope pattern: 'Deopne ymblyt clene ymbhaldeð / meotod on mihtum' (the measurer in his might, entirely embraces the deep circuit, ll. 7–8a).[109] Satan's wicked and partial embrace of his homeland's terrain contrasts sharply with God's 'clene' (completed) embrace of the earth.

Hands also served highly performative functions in Anglo-Saxon culture. Anglo-Saxons, as Allen J. Frantzen observes, spoke the 'language of hands'.[110] Christ's command that Satan physically measure woe and punishment also recalls a brief episode from the Harrowing when Eve is forced to render a confession before she can exit hell. After admitting that she once 'abealh' (angered, l. 408a) the Lord when she took fruit *mid handum* (l. 415), Eve's hands become her vehicle for forgiveness as she 'Ræhte þa mid handum to heofencyninge' (then reached out with her hands to the heavenly king, l. 435) and proceeds 'up to eðle' (up to the homeland, l. 459a). By contrast, Satan's hands can offer him no such expiation. In Germanic traditions 'the hero's hand or handgrip', as John M. Hill writes, 'is a synecdoche for his embodied strength, heart, and courage ... a guarantor of rightful governance'.[111] In legal contexts, the *mund* ('hand', 'right of protection') often indicates 'rightful possession'.[112] In this way, Satan's hands seal and legitimate his investiture of the spaces of hell.

Christ's request that the *ymbhwyrft* be completed within two hours likewise alludes to Rogationtide, a ritual ordered by the passing of fixed time. In Bazire and Cross Homily 6 the perambulations are described as commencing at Terce (the 'third hour') and ending at Nones (the 'ninth hour'): 'forlætan ... þa woruldlican weorc on þa ðriddan tid dæges, þæt is on undern sylfne, and forðgan mid þam halgum religuium oþ þa nigoðan tid, þæt is oð non' (forsake ... worldly works on the third hour of the day, that is at Terce, and process with the holy relics until the ninth hour, that is until Nones, ll. 36–7). The homily suggests that penitents go about their usual business during Matins and Lauds, the night and dawn offices preceding the holy procession. Within the context of the poem, at the end of his two hours, Satan will have failed Christ's challenge within the same amount of time that Christian penitents have to process from Terce until Nones. Their Rogations are to be complete, measured, and bounded, whereas Satan's are impossible.

Infinite spaces at the end of the Junius Manuscript

Although a reoccurring concern among scholars has been the poem's lack of thematic progression, *Christ and Satan*'s 'meandering' form accords with the final message concerning Satan's peripatetic wanderings. Just as the boundary rituals associated with Rogationtide are enacted across earthly space while encouraging participants to imagine both heavenly space and time, the end of the poem plays out in spatial and temporal metaphors. Satan's fraught time-management only underscores his inability to perambulate in an ordered manner:

> Hwilum mid folmum mæt
> wean and witu.   Hwilum se wonna læg
> læhte wið þes laþan.   Hwilum he licgan geseah
> hæftas in hylle.   Hwilum hream astag,
> ðonne he on þone atolan   eagum gesawun. (ll. 712b–16)

[At times with his hands he would measure its woes and punishments. At times the dark fire would surge up against the loathsome one. At times he would gaze upon the captives lying in hell. At times a cry would go up, when they saw the terrible one with their eyes.]

The poet's repetition of 'hwilum' (at times) underscores Satan's disordered movements within time and space. We see Satan coming into contact with his community in hell, yet it is a community that abhors his presence. That the 'wonna læg' (dark fires) occasionally 'læhte wið' (surge up against) him suggests that his own geography works against him as hell itself attempts to stymie Satan's dark procession.

The poet ultimately presents readers with two contrasting models of wandering that might be compared to those found in *The Seafarer* and *The Wanderer*. One is figured through Christ's wandering in the wilderness, the emblem of the spiritual pilgrim seeking unity with God. Like the Germanic exile, however, Satan's wandering is 'never voluntary', as Johnson puts it; he suffers 'separation from one's native land and the protection of one's lord'.[113] *Christ and Satan* juxtaposes Christ, whose orderly spiritual peregrinations expel demons, and Satan, whose aimless wandering in exile maps his original breach within the heavenly community across the geography of hell. In this way, the Temptation sequence is a confrontation between Christian and Germanic models of earthly

A homeland as a possession

power, inheritance, and, ultimately, one's relation to earthly space. Rather than bring him closer to God, Satan's movements only take him further from his *eðel*:

> Þa him þuhte þæt þanon wære
> to helleduru hund þusenda
> mila gemearcodes, swa hine se mihtiga het
> þæt þurh sinne cræft susle amæte.
> Ða he gemunde þæt he on grunde stod.
> Locade leas wiht geond þæt laðe scræf,
> atol mid egum, oððæt egsan gryre
> deofla mænego þonne up astag. (ll. 719–26)

[Then it seemed to him that from there to the door of hell was a hundred thousand miles in measure, just as the mighty one had commanded him that through his own power he might measure his torment. Then he was aware that he stood on the bottom. The false creature looked, the hideous one, with eyes across the hateful cavern, until an awful terror rose up with the multitude of devils.]

Satan eventually 'gemunde' (became aware) that penance is not possible for him as he measures out his own 'susle' (torment). His inability to 'measure' his ambit in hell recalls the inexpressibility topoi often employed to describe it. In Vercelli Homily 4, for example, hell is 'ungemet' (immeasurable, ll. 51, 54), and in Vercelli Homily 8 it is likewise 'unmætan' (l. 83). In Vercelli Homily 9, the devil can neither expressly define nor describe hell.[114]

Whereas Rogationtide establishes spiritualised, bounded space, its inverse is characterised by a terrifying endlessness as Satan's *merced hus* only evokes fear and anxiety in contrast with the positive associations the poet ascribes to the limitless 'brade lond' (broad lands, l. 214b) in the kingdom of heaven. At the end of the poem, Satan embodies his own exclusion and condition of lordlessness, dramatising his sinfulness through the logic of Rogation perambulation. In this way, the poet literalises hell's inexpressibility and immeasurability for readers in Satan's unambiguous failure to ascertain his boundaries, making him a paradigm for that which is to be excluded, an exclusion perennially re-enacted by the communal rituals of Rogation. The end of the Junius Manuscript also reveals the true protagonist of the biblical story. Although the patriarchs (Noah and Abraham) and the prophets (Moses and Daniel) dominate major portions of the manuscript, the final poem establishes Christ as the hero who frees these Old

Testament figures from hell at the Harrowing and restores order to heaven.

Would Anglo-Saxon readers have recognised the links between Satan's procession and their own Rogation rituals within the confined spaces of churches or throughout the sweeping countryside? Bedingfield describes Rogation as a 'polyvalent festival' capable of incorporating new emphases in the hands of different homilists and writers.[115] The *Christ and Satan* poet vividly illustrates how the world of the liturgy might inform imagined literary spaces, offering us a glimpse into the communal, performative, and spatial world of later Anglo-Saxon England. Like the liturgical verse examined by Sarah Larratt Keefer, *Christ and Satan* similarly encourages 'interactions between private and public, personal and communal' as 'poets invite their audiences to ponder' important 'spiritual paradoxes'.[116] The poet somewhat boldly moves outside of the spaces of catechetical tradition in *Christ and Satan* to demonstrate the contrast between heavenly spaces, defined by their stability and inheritability and the chaotic spaces of hell that lack order and true sovereignty. The *ymbhwyrft* at the end of the poem signifies more than a walkabout; for an Anglo-Saxon audience, this echo of their own communal rituals would have stood as a *bysne* ('example', l. 195a),[117] challenging them to be worthy of the heavenly community by perambulating earthly boundaries in this life so that they will not wander lordless after Judgement Day. In this sense, appealing to their deeply rooted cultural traditions, the poet offers readers a means to touch with their hands and tread with their feet a path towards redemption and the heavenly homeland.

Notes

1 A version of this chapter appears as 'Measuring Hell by Hand: Rogation Rituals in *Christ and Satan*', *RES*, 68 (2017), 1–22. For the consecrating of ecclesiastical sites, especially churches and cemeteries, see Helen Gittos, 'Creating the Sacred: Anglo-Saxon Rites for Consecrating Cemeteries', in *Burial in Early Medieval England and Wales*, ed. Sam Lucy and Andrew Reynolds, The Society for Medieval Archaeology Monograph Series 17 (London: Society for Medieval Archaeology, 2002), pp. 195–208 (pp. 201–5).

2 *The Tripartite Life of Patrick with Other Documents Related to that Saint*, ed. and trans. Whitley Stokes (London: Eyre and Spottiswoode 1887), pp. 473–5.

3 Ibid., pp. 237–8.

4 The poem acquired its title from Christian W. M. Grein, *Bibliothek der angelsächsischen Poesie in kritisch bearbeiteten Texten und mit vollständigem Glossar herausgegeben*, vols. 1–2 (Göttingen: Georg H. Wigand, 1857; 1858). All citations of *Christ and Satan* are taken from *The Junius Manuscript*, ed. George Krapp. For a recent translation, see *Old English Poems of Christ and His Saints*, ed. and trans. Mary Clayton, Dumbarton Oaks Medieval Library (Cambridge, MA: Harvard University Press, 2013).

5 For an overview concerning the unity and fitt divisions of *Christ and Satan*, see Emily Thornbury, *Becoming a Poet in Anglo-Saxon England* (Cambridge: Cambridge University Press, 2014), p. 163ff. See also Charles Sleeth, *Studies in Christ and Satan*, McMaster Old English Studies and Texts 3 (Toronto: Toronto University Press, 1982), p. 3ff. On the language and date, see Finnegan, *Christ and Satan*, pp. 56–63 and Sleeth, *Studies in Christ and Satan*, pp. 27–49. Finnegan suggests *c*. 792–802 (p. 60) and Clubb proposes *c*. 790–830 (p. lx). Fulk, however, cites only the difficulty in dating the poem with any accuracy (*A History of Old English Meter*, p. 396).

6 *Christ and Satan* ends with the explicit 'Finit Liber II' although there is no corresponding 'Liber I' in the manuscript.

7 Conybeare, *Illustrations of Anglo-Saxon Poetry*, p. 189; Benjamin Thorpe, *Caedmon's Metrical Paraphrase of Parts of the Holy Scriptures in Anglo-Saxon: with an English Translation, Notes, and Verbal Index* (London: Society of Antiquaries of London, 1832), p. xiv; Bernhard ten Brink, *History of English Literature*, trans. Horace M. Kennedy, vol. 1 (New York: Henry Holt and Company, 1883), pp. 86–8.

8 Groschopp, 'Das angelsächsische Gedicht *Christ und Satan*', PhD dissertation, University of Leipzig (Halle: E. Karras, 1883).

9 Abbetmeyer, *Old English Poetical Motives*, pp. 17–18.

10 Thornbury thinks that the poem is the work of at least two individuals, one who was highly trained and another aspiring 'would-be poet' working in isolation (*Becoming a Poet*, p. 174 and pp. 180–1).

11 Peter J. Lucas, 'On the Incomplete Ending of *Daniel* and the Addition of *Christ and Satan* to MS Junius 11', *Anglia*, 97 (1979), 46–59.

12 Raw, 'The Construction of Oxford, Bodleian Junius 11', p. 191ff; Ker, *Catalogue of Manuscripts*, pp. 406–8 (no. 334) assigns the first part of the manuscript to 's.x/xi' and 'Liber II' to 's.xi[1]'; Lockett proposes *c*. 960–90 (Lockett, 'An Integrated Re-examination', pp. 141–73) and states that 'the execution of Liber II occurred no earlier than the first years of eleventh century' with a '*terminus ante quem* of *c*. 1010' (p. 158).

13 On the poem's homiletic qualities, see Finnegan, *Christ and Satan*, pp. 19–25, and Trilling, *The Aesthetics of Nostalgia*, p. 109.

14 The most influential of these being Hall, 'The Old English Epic of Redemption', pp. 20–52; see also Joyce Hill, 'Confronting *Germania*

Latina: Changing Responses to Old English Biblical Verse', in *The Poems of Junius 11: Basic Readings*, ed. R. M. Liuzza (New York and London: Routledge, 2002), pp. 1–19 (p. 12).
15 Remley, *Old English Biblical Verse*, p. 5.
16 Finnegan, *Christ and Satan*, p. 17.
17 Alois Brandl, *Geschichte der altenglischen Literatur* (Strassburg: Trübner, 1908); see also Clubb, *Crist and Satan*, pp. xlviii–lv; Neil D. Isaacs, *Structural Principles in Old English Poetry* (Knoxville: University of Tennessee, 1968), pp. 127–44.
18 See T. D. Hill, 'The Fall of Satan', p. 323; Huppé, *Doctrine and Poetry*, pp. 227–31; Finnegan, *Christ and Satan*, pp. 35–6); Sleeth, *Studies in Christ and Satan*, pp. 24–6.
19 See *Eleven Old English Rogationtide Homilies*, ed. Joyce Bazire and James E. Cross (Toronto: University of Toronto Press, 1982), p. 73 (l. 124 and l. 141).
20 On the themes of homeland and inheritance, see Howe, 'Falling into Place', pp. 14–37; Smith, 'Faith and Forfeiture', pp. 593–615.
21 For connections to *Paradise Lost*, see Albert C. Labriola, 'The Begetting and Exaltation of the Son: The Junius Manuscript and Milton's *Paradise Lost*', in *Milton's Legacy*, ed. Kristin A. Pruitt and Charles W. Durham (Selinsgrove, PA: Susquehanna University Press, 2005), pp. 22–32.
22 According to Thomas D. Hill, the *Divine Institutes* of Lactantius (CPL 85) suggests a heavenly rivalry between Christ and Satan ('The Fall of Satan', p. 317).
23 *Felix's Life of Saint Guthlac*, ed. and trans. Colgrave, pp. 116–17.
24 These are *Juliana* (ll. 420–4), *Guthlac A* (ll. 596–8), and *Resignation* (ll. 52b–6); see also Ælfric's *Letter to Sigeweard*, in *Libellus*, ed. Marsden, p. 203, ll. 74–5.
25 Max Föster, 'Kleinere mittelenglische Texte', *Anglia*, 42 (1918), 145–224 (p. 222, ll. 12–14).
26 Finnegan, *Christ and Satan*, p. 40.
27 *In epistulas VII catholicas*, ed. and trans. Hurst, p. 244.
28 James W. Bright, 'The Relation of the Cædmonian *Exodus* to the Liturgy', *Modern Language Notes*, 27 (1912), 97–103; Remley, *Old English Biblical Verse*, pp. 170–220.
29 Phyllis Portnoy, 'Remnant and Ritual: The Place of *Daniel* and *Christ and Satan* in the Junius Epic', *ES*, 75 (1994), 408–22. See also Joyce Hill, 'Confronting *Germania Latina*', pp. 71–88.
30 Geoffrey Shepherd, 'Scriptural Poetry', in *Continuations and Beginnings: Studies in Old English Literature*, ed. E. G. Stanley (London and Edinburgh: Nelson, 1966), pp. 1–36 (p. 24); Judith N. Garde, *Old English Poetry in Medieval Christian Perspective: A Doctrinal Approach* (Cambridge: D. S. Brewer, 1991), p. 49ff; see also

Catherine E. Karkov, 'The Sign of the Cross: Poetic Performance and Liturgical Practice in the Junius 11 Manuscript', in *The Liturgy of the Late Anglo-Saxon Church*, ed. Helen Gittos and M. Bradford Bedingfield, HBS (Woodbridge: Boydell, 2005), pp. 245–65.

31 Stephen J. Harris, 'The Liturgical Context of Ælfric's Homilies for Rogation', in *The Old English Homily: Precedent, Practice, and Appropriation*, ed. Aaron J. Kleist (Turnhout: Brepols, 2007), pp. 143–69 (p. 150).

32 The origins are traditionally traced back to Mamertus, Bishop of Vienne (d. 470) and the springtime *Robigalia* or *Ambarvalia* festival (*Eleven Rogationtide Homilies*, ed. Bazire and Cross, pp. xxi–xxii).

33 *Eleven Rogationtide Homilies*, ed. Bazire and Cross, p. xvi.

34 For the distinction between the 'Minor Litany' and the 'Major Litany', see J. Hill, 'The *Litaniae maiores* and *minores* in Rome, Francia, and Anglo-Saxon England: Terminology, Texts, and Traditions', *Early Medieval Europe*, 9 (2000), 211–46.

35 Milton McCormick Gatch, *Preaching and Theology in Anglo-Saxon England: Ælfric and Wulfstan* (Toronto: University of Toronto Press, 1977), p. 201 (n. 37).

36 Ker lists twenty-four Rogation homilies (*Catalogue of Manuscripts*, p. 259; pp. 460–4 (no. 394); see also *Eleven Rogationtide Homilies*, ed. Bazire and Cross, pp. xix–xx and pp. 39–40. There are arguably eight Rogationtide homilies in *The Vercelli Book* (c. 950–99) though not all are rubricated. Vercelli Homilies 11, 12, 13 are explicitly rubricated and Homily 10 is linked to this group. Its Blickling analogue (Homily 9) is a Rogation homily. There is also evidence that Vercelli Homilies 19, 20, and 21 form a Rogation unit. On this point, see Michael Fox, 'Vercelli Homilies XIX–XXI, the Ascension Day Homily in CCCC 162, and the Catechetical Tradition from Augustine to Wulfstan', in *New Readings in the Vercelli Book*, ed. Samantha Zacher and Andy Orchard (Toronto: University of Toronto Press, 2009), pp. 254–79. For more, see Donald G. Scragg, 'An Old English Homilist of Archbishop Dunstan's Day', *Words, Texts, and Manuscripts: Studies in Anglo-Saxon Culture Presented to Helmut Gneuss on the Occasion of his Sixty-Fifth Birthday*, ed. Michael Korhammer (Cambridge: Cambridge University Press, 1992), pp. 181–92. Vercelli Homily 14 also has sources and analogues intended for Rogationtide.

37 On boundary-clauses, see John Hunter Blair, *The Church in Anglo-Saxon Society* (Oxford: Oxford University Press, 2005), p. 486. Boundary-clause perambulations have been explored in relation to *Christ and Satan* by Kevin Caliendo, 'Land Grants in Old English Poetry: Beating the Boundaries of Hell in *Christ and Satan*', 125th MLA Annual Convention, Philadelphia, December 2009.

38 Helen Gittos, *Liturgy, Architecture, and Sacred Places in Anglo-Saxon*

England (Oxford: Oxford University Press, 2013), pp. 134–49 (p. 145).

39 An influential study of liturgical drama is M. Bradford Bedingfield, *The Dramatic Liturgy of Anglo-Saxon England* (Woodbridge: Boydell, 2002), pp. 191–209 (p. 194).
40 *Eleven Rogationtide Homilies*, ed. Bazire and Cross, p. 18 (ll. 57–8; 61–4).
41 Harris, 'The Liturgical Context of Ælfric's Homilies for Rogation', p. 169.
42 On the temporal connection between Christ's Ascension and Harrowing see Bedingfield, *The Dramatic Liturgy*, p. 199.
43 Magennis, *Images of Community*, p. 10.
44 *The Vercelli Homilies*, ed. Scragg, 228.22–5.
45 *Bede's Ecclesiastical History*, ed. and trans. Colgrave and Mynors, pp. 584–5.
46 *The Vercelli Homilies*, ed. Scragg, 228.14.
47 Alexandra Walsham, *The Reformation of the Landscape: Religion, Identity, and Memory in Early Modern Britain and Ireland* (Oxford: Oxford University Press, 2011), p. 256.
48 Steve Hindle, 'Beating the Bounds of the Parish: Order, Memory, and Identity in the English Local Imagination, c. 1500–1700', in *Defining Community in Early Modern Europe*, ed. Michael J. Halvorson and Karen E. Spierling (Burlington, VT: Ashgate, 2008), pp. 205–27 (p. 206).
49 Bedingfield, *The Dramatic Liturgy*, p. 191.
50 Johanna Kramer, *Between Earth and Heaven: Liminality and the Ascension of Christ in Anglo-Saxon Literature* (Manchester: Manchester University Press, 2014), p. 148.
51 Bedingfield, *The Dramatic Liturgy*, p. 197.
52 *Eleven Rogationtide Homilies*, Bazire and Cross, p. 134 (ll.119–21) explains that fasting can drive out the devil.
53 Bedingfield, *The Dramatic Liturgy*, p. 191.
54 Eamon Duffy, *The Stripping of the Altars: Traditional Religion in England 1400–1580* (New Haven, CT: Yale University Press, 2005), p. 217.
55 Bedingfield, *The Dramatic Liturgy*, p. 201.
56 Ibid., p. 200.
57 Ibid., p. 202.
58 *Eleven Rogationtide Homilies*, pp. 62–3 (ll.38–40).
59 The 'nine hells' may refer to 'the nine meanderings of the Styx' or derive from apocryphal sources like the *Visio S. Pauli* (*Eleven Rogationtide Homilies*, ed. Bazire and Cross, p. 58).
60 Harris, 'The Liturgical Context of Ælfric's Homilies', p. 156. On this same point, see Kramer, *Between Earth and Heaven*, pp. 171–2.

61 Kramer suggests that the return to the doors of the church corresponds to the symbolic arrival at 'the gates of heaven' (*Between Earth and Heaven*, p. 172).
62 Gollancz, *The Cædmon Manuscript*, p. ciii.
63 *Vita Latina Adae et Evae*, 1:304–14. For further discussion of this tradition, see Wright, 'Apocryphal Lore and Insular Tradition', pp. 124–45.
64 This difficult syntax has been discussed by Finnegan (*Christ and Satan*, ns. 92–3) and Krapp (*The Junius Manuscript*, p. 232). On the doctrinal implications, see Morey, 'Adam and Judas in the Old English *Christ and Satan*', pp. 397–409.
65 On the emendation to *geoguþe*, see Finnegan, *Christ and Satan*, pp. 92–3; see also David F. Johnson, 'Old English Religious Poetry: *Christ and Satan* and *The Dream of the Rood*', in *A Companion to Old English Poetry*, ed. Henk Aersen and Rolf H. Bremmer Jr. (Amsterdam: VU University Press, 1994), pp. 159–87 (pp. 167–7).
66 Johnson, 'Old English Religious Poetry', p. 167.
67 Thomas D. Hill proposes connections to Antichrist traditions ('The Fall of Satan', pp. 323–4).
68 This idea is echoed several times (ll. 81–7; 168–75; 340–7).
69 Clubb suggests that these lines refer to both angels and men (*Christ and Satan*, p. 58), but Finnegan disagrees (*Christ and Satan*, p. 94 (ns. 46–7)).
70 A 'clear sign' is a common formulaic phrase: *Andreas* (l. 742), *Beowulf* (ll. 141; 833b), *Daniel* (l. 486), and *The Paris Psalter* (73.8); *Genesis B* (ll. 886b–7a).
71 Johnson usefully discusses this sequence in terms of the 'poet's inherited Germanic repertoire' ('Old English Religious Poetry', pp. 162–75).
72 Satan could be referring to either the 'God the Father' or the 'Son' here. On the unitary perspective of the Trinity and pre-incarnate Christ, see Wright, '*Genesis A* ad Litteram', p. 148 and p. 154.
73 *DOE*, *adrifan*, sense 1, 'drive away, expel, banish'; sense 1b, 'cast out, exorcise'; sense 1d, 'evict'.
74 Michelet, *Creation, Migration, and Conquest*, pp. 67–8.
75 Words for 'home' appear throughout the poem with *ham* (twenty-six times), *eard* (seven times), and *eðel* (ten times). Satan consistently refers to his former dwelling in heaven as an 'eðel', which Sleeth glosses as lands passed on through 'heredity', 'birthright', or 'inheritance' (*Studies in Christ and Satan*, pp. 100–4).
76 Smith, *Land and Book*, p. 233.
77 Howe, 'Falling into Place', p. 32.
78 Constance D. Harsh, '*Christ and Satan*: The Measured Power of Christ', *NM*, 90 (1989), 243–53 (p. 246).
79 Shook notes that in *The Life of St Brendan*, St Brendan comes upon

fallen angels who expect to re-enter heaven one day, 'the so-called neutral angels who did not fall as deeply' ('The Burial Mound', p. 9 n. 72).

80 For a discussion of Satan's paradoxical binding in hell and mobility, see Johnson, 'Old English Religious Poetry', p. 162ff.
81 On this point, see Howe, 'Falling into Place', pp. 14–37.
82 Ibid., p. 33.
83 DiNapoli identifies the following homilies on this pericope: 'Blickling Homily 3 for the first Sunday of Lent, *CH* I.11 for the first Sunday of Lent, Supp 11a.128–32, Vercelli Homily 12 for the second day of Rogation' (*An Index of Theme and Image*, p. 78).
84 Finnegan, *Christ and Satan*, p. 34.
85 For more on this episode, see Frederick M. Biggs, 'The Politics of Succession in *Beowulf* and Anglo-Saxon England', *Speculum*, 80 (2005), 709–41 and David C. Van Meter, 'The Ritualized Presentation of Weapons and the Ideology of Nobility in *Beowulf*', *JEGP*, 95 (1996), 175–89.
86 Biggs, 'The Politics of Succession', p. 710. For examples of joint rule, see pp. 714–5.
87 On this point, see Finnegan, *Christ and Satan*, p. 65.
88 Hill, 'The Measure of Hell: *Christ and Satan* 695–722', *PQ*, 60 (1982 for 1981), 409–14 (p. 410). See also Hugh Keenan, 'Some Vagaries of Old English Poetic Composition', *Studies in Medieval Culture*, 5 (1975), 25–32, who identifies biblical passages concerning measurement: Revelation 11:1–2, Ezekiel 40:3–49, 41;42, Zechariah 2:1–2, and Numbers 35:4–5 which features 'an angel [who] marks out the dimensions of the Holy City using a reed for a measuring stick' (p. 32). To this list, we might also add Job 38:5. In the Welsh *Taliesin*, the first address of Taliesin reads 'What is the measure of hell? How thick its covering? How wide its jaws? How many its stones?' See Taliesin, *The Poems of Taliesin*, ed. Ifor Williams and trans. J. E. Caerwyn Williams (Dublin: Dublin Institute for Advanced Studies, 1968).
89 Hill, 'The Measure of Hell', p. 411.
90 Ibid., p. 412.
91 Ruth Wehlau, 'The Power of Knowledge and the Location of the Reader in *Christ and Satan*', in *The Poems of Junius 11: Basic Readings*, ed. R. M. Liuzza (New York and London: Routledge, 2002), pp. 287–301 (p. 291).
92 Ruth Wehlau, 'The Power of Knowledge', pp. 287–301 (p. 291); Wehlau proposes that the 'measuring of hell is thus a literalization of a [Gregorian] metaphor' ('The Power of Knowledge', p. 292)
93 Harsh, 'The Measured Power of Christ', pp. 243–5.
94 Janet Schrunk Ericksen, 'The Wisdom Poem at the end of MS Junius 11', in *The Poems of Junius 11: Basic Readings*, ed. R. M. Liuzza (New York and London: Routledge, 2002), pp. 302–26 (p. 306).

95 Ericksen, 'The Wisdom Poem at the end of MS Junius 11', pp. 311–13.
96 On this phrase, see Malcolm Godden, *Ælfric's Catholic Homilies: Introduction, Commentary, and Glossary*, EETS ss 18 (Oxford: Oxford University Press, 2000), pp. 84–94 (p. 90).
97 *DOE, gangan*, sense 6.5b.
98 Ibid., sense 6.13.
99 Ibid., sense 1.3c.
100 Regarding the damned who 'go turning' at Judgement Day, see Thomas D. Hill, '"Hwyrftum scriþað": *Beowulf*, l. 163', *Mediaeval Studies*, 33 (1971), 379–81.
101 Harsh, 'The Measured Power', p. 247.
102 *Ælfric's Catholic Homilies*, 472.211.
103 Hill, 'Hwyrftum scriþað', p. 380.
104 Ibid., p. 381.
105 Gittos, 'Creating the Sacred', pp. 195–208 (p. 208).
106 Ibid., p. 196. See also Barbara H. Rosenwein, *Negotiating Space: Power, Restraint, and Privileges of Immunity in Early Medieval Europe* (Ithaca, NY: Cornell University Press, 1999).
107 Rosenwein, *Negotiating Space*, p. 166.
108 Ibid., p. 179.
109 Krapp emends manuscript *ybmlyt* to *ymblyt* (*The Junius Manuscript*, p. 231), a hapax legomenon with a meaning somewhat analogous to *ymbhwyrft* 'circuit, circle, circumference'. On the poem's metrical irregularities, see Finnegan (*Christ and Satan*, pp. 31–4).
110 Frantzen, 'Drama and Dialogue in Old English Poetry', p. 103.
111 John M. Hill, 'The Sacrificial Synecdoche of Hands, Heads, and Arms in Anglo-Saxon Heroic Story', in *Naked Before God: Uncovering the Body in Anglo-Saxon England*, ed. Benjamin C. Withers and Jonathan Wilcox (Morgantown: West Virginia University Press, 2003), pp. 116–37 (p. 127).
112 John M. Hill, 'The Sacrificial Synecdoche', p. 124; see also David D. Day, 'Hands across the Hall: The Legalities of Beowulf's Fight with Grendel', *JEGP*, 98 (1999), 313–24.
113 Johnson, 'Old English Religious Poetry', p. 168. For common tropes of exile, see Stanley B. Greenfield, 'The Formulaic Expression of the Theme of 'Exile' in Anglo-Saxon Poetry', *Speculum*, 30 (1955), 200–6.
114 Wright, *The Irish Tradition*, p. 180.
115 Bedingfield, *The Dramatic Liturgy*, p. 207.
116 Sarah Larratt Keefer, *Old English Liturgical Verse: A Student Edition* (Buffalo, NY: Broadview, 2010), p. 16.
117 See also the homiletic admonition at *Christ and Satan*, ll. 193–4: 'Therefore each of men shall think on how not to provoke the Son of the ruler.' Trilling notes that sermon-like admonitions such as

this one 'encourage [the audience] to ... choose devotion to God over selfish desires, and earn a place in the *eðel* of heaven' (*The Aesthetics of Nostalgia*, p. 110).

6
A new *praedestinati* in Wulfstan's *Sermo Lupi ad Anglos*?

In 1009, a call for a cycle of penitential rituals was issued in the king's name as a response to the invasion of Thorkell the Tall and his 'micelle here' (great army). Archbishop Wulfstan's appeal for this very public penance was meant to refocus the English nation and the souls of its wayward Christian inhabitants. This act of penance (documented in VII Æthelred) would coincide with the three-day Rogationtide festival.[1] The edict reads: 'Et instituimus, ut omnis Christianus, qui etatem habet, ieiunet tribus diebus in pane et aqua et herbis crudis' (And we have decreed that every Christian who has reached adulthood is to fast for three days with bread, water, and raw herbs).[2] According to Andrew Rabin, this great 'penance here [served] as an ideological instrument designed to unify the community in the face of a common threat and to emphasise the moral dimensions of the struggle'.[3] The vernacular account (VIIa Æthelred) offers subsequent guidelines for penitents:

> ⁊ cume manna gehwilc bærfot to circan buton golde ⁊ glæncgum, ⁊ ga man to scrifte. ⁊ gan ealle ut mid halidome ⁊ clipian inweardre heortan georne to Criste.[4]

[And everyone is to come to church barefoot, without gold or ornaments, and they are to go to confession. And all are to process out with holy relics and fervently call upon Christ with their innermost hearts.]

Throughout his career, Wulfstan demonstrated an interest in re-sanctifying the borders of his polity. The communal ritual of Rogationtide (as discussed in the previous chapter) offered Anglo-Saxon Christians one avenue for self-reflection in the face of threats and pressures both *inne ond ute* ('at home and abroad') (one of Wulfstan's favourite verbal formulae).[5] Alongside his interest in preserving the spiritual wholeness of his realm, Wulfstan frequently evokes well-entrenched ideas about biblical lore and salvation history in an effort to convey his message to the English Christian community at large.

Whereas the earliest Benedictine reformers sought to establish a religious identity for themselves as 'replacements' by seizing lands and reclaiming spaces from 'rebel' clerics in the name of a holier English monasticism, the writings of Wulfstan and other late Anglo-Saxon authors betray a different set of concerns. As discussed in Chapter 3, during the reign of King Edgar, reformers such as Æthelwold appealed to the replacement doctrine to position the secular clergy as a rebellious *cuneus* ('troop') incapable of ensuring that English Christians would realise their place in the scheme of salvation history. Drawing upon Augustinian and Bedan analogies for fallen clerical identity, Edgar's reign overcame this perceived threat to English Christianity by associating the conduct of the secular clerics with that of *superbentium angelorum* ('pride-filled angels').

By rehearsing the doctrine of replacement in texts such as the New Minster Charter, and removing the secular canons from the ecclesiastical hierarchy, the early reformers promoted the idea that the way to heaven would be reopened under the spiritual protection of a reformed monasticism by monks who saw the task of preparing Christian souls for salvation as their special duty. In addition to the narrative of replacement, the fall of the angels was used to explain the pastoral crisis within the ecclesiastical hierarchy and legitimate the expulsion of those canons residing in the city of Winchester. In a sense, Edgar and the monastic reformers, 'cleansed' the city and estates long occupied by the canons by choreographing their very own fall of the angels across earthly space.[6]

In 978, after decades of relative peace, the state of regal affairs in England began to change in dramatic ways.[7] The *ASC* (the Peterborough Manuscript) tells us that on 18 March the young king Edward was 'ofslagen on æfentide æt Corfesgeate' (killed in the evening ... at Corfesgeate). There follows a poetic account of the heinous deed:

> Ne wearð Angelcynne nan wyrse dæd gedon
> þonne þeos wæs, syððon hi ærest Brytonland gesohton.
> Menn hine ofmyrðredon, ac God hine mærsode.
> He wæs on life eorðlice cing;
> he is nu æfter deaðe heofonlic sanct.

A new *praedestinati*

Hyne noldon his eorðlican magas wrecan,
ac hine hafað his heofonlica fæder swiðe gewrecen.⁸

[There was no worse deed done than this among the English, since they first sought the land of Britain. Men murdered him, but God glorified him. He was in life an earthly king; he is now after death a heavenly saint. His earthly kin did not wish to avenge him, but his heavenly father has greatly avenged him.]

After lavishing praises upon Edward (now, Edward 'the Martyr') and accusing his 'eorðlican banan' (earthly slayers) of treachery (and his kin of cowardice), the chronicler notes that his brother, Æthelred 'feng ... to rice' (Æthelred succeeded to the kingdom). The C version of the *ASC* tells us that just two years later, a 'norðscipherige' (northern fleet) unleashed its fury upon both Southampton and Cheshire. Subsequent viking raids receive further documentation and increased attention from then on: through Maldon in 991, the sacking of London in 994, to the 'Danish taking possession of the place of slaughter' outside of Rochester in 997.⁹ In 994, Æthelred served as Olaf Tryggvason's baptismal sponsor in the hopes that Christianising Danes might alleviate the violence. The Danish incursions thus become an annual fixture amid succeeding annals as chroniclers register their impressions of shock, horror, and despair. The entry for 1016 in the D Manuscript recalls Cnut's great victory at Ashingdon:¹⁰

Þa common þa scipo to Grenawic to þam Gandagum ⁊ binnon lytlum fæce wendon to Lundene ⁊ dulfon þa ane mycele dic on ða suðhealfe ⁊ drogon heora scipa on westhealfe þære brycge ⁊ bedicodon syððon þa burh uton þet nan mann ne mihte ne inn ne ut ⁊ oftrædlice on ða burh fuhton.¹¹

[Then at the Rogation Days the ships came to Greenwich and within a short time turned towards London and then dug a great ditch on the south side and dragged their ships to the west side of the bridge and then afterwards surrounded the town with a dike so that no one could get in or out, and frequently attacked the town.]

In this way, the *ASC* author suggestively depicts the Danish entrenchment as a kind of terrible Rogation procession with the army encircling the parameters of the city and claiming the boundaries of their new landed and maritime possessions. It is certainly possible that the Danes hoped everyone would be caught unawares (and unarmed) amid their processing. Was Cnut's army at Ashingdon simply capitalising upon or disrupting English Rogationtide festivities? Or do various *ASC* authors imply that the incoming Danes were poised to tread the footsteps of Christian believers with their own encircling of the landscape?

This chapter addresses one of the latest pre-Conquest evocations of the fall of the angels and the ways in which the narrative of the angelic rebellion and the replacement doctrine shifted dramatically in the early eleventh century, owing to the waves of Danish intrusions and the unstable sovereignty associated with the reigns of Æthelred and Cnut. While Edgar had justified the seizing of lands of disobedient clerics in an effort to restore the polity, Wulfstan faced an authentic crisis of borders with the viking assault on what he viewed as a disobedient English nation. Wulfstan, however, remaps the terms of replacement, expanding the narrative to encompass the entire Christian body politic and urging them not to cede to the vikings their earthly and heavenly inheritances, or their providential role in salvation history.

Wulfstan's views on the creation and fall of the angels have, by and large, been overshadowed by critical interest in his numerous eschatological homilies and vivid accounts of Antichrist. Nevertheless, in order to better understand Wulfstan's views on future events, we must also consider how he grappled with originary ones. Wulfstan, unlike other authors of the Benedictine Reform period such as Æthelwold or Abbo of Fleury, avoids direct comparisons between the sins of the rebel angels and perceived threats to the nation (wicked clerics, marauding vikings, or otherwise). Rather than locating the source of evil as external to the ideal Christian self and thereby promoting Anglo-Saxon spiritual identity against a rebellious 'other', Wulfstan treats the disloyalty and pride of the rebel angels as potential sins within any English Christian. In Wulfstan's *Sermo* 6, for example, we are given a rare glimpse of the archbishop's conception of events surrounding both angelic creation and the crimes that set biblical history in motion. *Sermo* 6 reveals how Wulfstan (and anonymous Old English homilists who imitated him) adapted the fall of the rebel angels narrative for pastoral contexts to elaborate upon the responsibilities of clergyman facing unprecedented challenges.

Wulfstan saw the role of the Church as vital, even as he overturned the Æthelwoldian figuration of the replacement doctrine. Instead of envisioning the English as replacements – as they are majestically portrayed in the New Minster Charter – Wulfstan suggests that both Anglo-Saxon and Anglo-Danish Christians alike have come to resemble the prideful and rebellious order that may be destined to a fall rather than salvation through the logic of replacement. Wulfstan viewed the English Christian community as mired in a state of rebellion resulting from a collective failure to recognise the proper sovereign status of the throne, the altar and, by extension, God. Wulfstan locates the source of this crisis not with the viking menace or within the ecclesiastical hierarchy, but within the English Christian *þeod* ('people') at large.

Much can be gained by looking at Wulfstan's body of work holistically. In all likelihood, Wulfstan wrote *Sermo* 6 around the turn of the eleventh century, and I will demonstrate how he evokes and expands upon the core concerns of the narrative of the angelic rebellion roughly a decade later in his most famous litany of civil disorders, *Sermo Lupi ad Anglos*, as a way to address the shortcomings of the polity. One of the chief concerns of Wulfstan's career was promoting proper relations to authority in both sacred and secular spheres. His engagement with this subject is clear in his admonition against the English people in *Sermo Lupi*. Wulfstan not only suggests that the English nation is teetering on the verge of a fall of biblical proportions, but also that it is about to forfeit its role in a salvation narrative stretching back to the Germanic migrations from the Continent.

In *Sermo* 6, Wulfstan directly alludes to the replacement doctrine, noting God's intent for humankind to *gefyllan ⁊ gemænigfyldan* ('fill up and multiply') what was diminished in the heavens. Like many Anglo-Saxon authors before him, Wulfstan aims to illustrate how humankind was created to properly recognise God's sovereignty and thus rectify the loss incurred in heaven after the angelic rebellion. Wulfstan's later works, however, reveal the flexibility of the doctrine by, somewhat surprisingly, aligning morally depraved Anglo-Saxon Christians with the rebel order of angels. I propose that in *Sermo Lupi* Wulfstan summons this complex doctrinal parallel through his evocation of the British writer Gildas (who claimed that the pagan Anglo-Saxons had providentially replaced the Christian Britons). Like the *Genesis A* poet, who depicts Abraham and Lot wresting control of their 'promised land' from 'heathen' rulers (ll. 1960–2172), Wulfstan implies that the rebellious Anglo-Saxons might in turn be replaced by pagan vikings. Through his citation of Gildas, then, Wulfstan reimagines similar patterns of rebellion, invasion, and conversion as active in his own time. His conflation of the English and the dissolute Britons suggests, not that the vikings were forerunners of Antichrist (a position commonly held by scholars),[12] but that the vikings would likely supplant the English as the rightful Christian rulers of their 'promised land'. Much like the heathens that migrated from the Continent only to become Christianised Anglo-Saxons, Wulfstan suggests that the inbound vikings could become what Augustine called the *praedestinati* ('predestined ones'). Read in this way, *Sermo Lupi* represents not just a view of conquest, but of an impending fall of a Christian people and their replacement by colonisers destined for heavenly seats.

The fall of the angels was, of course, a popular homiletic theme, as this chapter will demonstrate.[13] After offering an overview of how different homilists of Wulfstan's time adapted the narrative, I will illuminate Wulfstan's unique doctrinal and ideological preoccupations surrounding the fall of the angels before suggesting that we can see the influence of this narrative in *Sermo Lupi*. Of particular importance for this analysis will be the extensive writings of Ælfric of Eynsham on the fall of the angels. Wulfstan's own engagement with this narrative suggests a rich intertextual relationship with Ælfric. I think it likely that Wulfstan was familiar with some of his counterpart's writings on the angelic rebellion, an enduring topic of interest for Ælfric.

Integrating Wulfstan's views on theological matters and political events suggests that he feared the English had lost sight of God's ultimate sovereignty. Re-envisioning the role of churchmen like himself, Wulfstan proposes that the clergy must act as counsellors to both the king and the body politic to encourage proper obedience to the law of the land.[14] As his era was one of volatile sovereignty, Wulfstan appeals to God's law as the ultimate source of sovereign authority and encourages secular and ecclesiastical leadership alike to do the same if they are to avert their own exclusion as rebels in God's eyes. Rather than revoking lands or concentrating power in the hands of a king (as the Benedictine reformers did under the aegis of Edgar), both Wulfstan and Ælfric argue that Christian subjects are responsible for bringing themselves back from the brink of rebellion, or accepting the consequences of their disobedience. Reinstituting the spatial rituals of the Rogation period would be the first step.

The next generation's rebel angels

In the decades following the Benedictine Reform, when there emerged what David Dumville calls 'a socio-ecclesiastical polity',[15] external threats to the stability of England increased. Writing after the death of Edgar and the 'anti-monastic reaction',[16] both Ælfric of Eynsham and Wulfstan of York differ from their predecessors in their respective treatments of the fall of the angels. Both tend to emphasise Lucifer's interiority and agency prior to his fall and expulsion from heaven. Ælfric wrestled time and again in his writings with the fall of the angels. Despite his allegiance to scriptural authority and his concession in his 'Preface to *Genesis*' that the Bible 'ne spricð na be þærra engla gesceapenisse' (does not say anything about the creation of the angels),[17] Ælfric examines the fall of the angels as a crucial link in the chain of creation history in no fewer than six of his major works. The narrative features in his translations of Alcuin's *Interrogationes Sigwulfi Presbiteri* and the *Exameron Anglice*, as well as in several of his *Catholic Homilies*, notably in CH I.1 (*De Initio Creaturae*).[18]

He also mentions the fall twice in his correspondence – in his *Letter to Sigeweard*,[19] and his *Letter to Wulfgeat of Ylmandun* (*c.* 1005–6); the latter begins with a proem in the style of a catechetical *narratio* describing the rebel angels' collective failure to recognise God's lordship. As I noted in Chapter 1, Wulfgeat was one of Æthelred's favourite thanes whose lands and possessions were seized in 1006 (S 918 accounts for this confiscation of property).[20] Ælfric's letter opens with salutations to the rebel Wulfgeat before the vignette describing the fall of the angels:

> Englas he gesceop on ænlicre fægernysse
> manega þusenda, on micelre strengðe,
> þæt hi mihton geseon godes mærða mid him
> and mid munian on his ecum wuldre.
> Hi nabbað nænne lichaman, ac hi libbað on gaste
> ungesewenlice us, þe on synnum lybbað.
> And þa halgan englas, þe on heofonum wuniað,
> ne worhton nane synne, ne hi synnian ne magon,
> buton þam anum, þe þanon afeollon
> for heora modignysse ongean þone ælmihtigan god.
> and hi wurdon awende to awyrigedum deoflum,
> forðam þe hi noldon habban heora scyppend him to hlaforde.[21]

[He shaped angels in singular beauty, many thousands, with great strength, that they might be able to see the glories of God through him and be mindful of his eternal glory. They have no bodies, but they live as spirits invisibly to us, who live in sin. And the holy angels, who dwell in heaven, did not commit any sin, nor are they able to sin, except those alone, who fell from there because of their pride against the Almighty God. And they were turned into accursed devils, because they would not have their creator as their lord.]

The story of the fall of the angels is clearly meant to mirror Wulfgeat's own political troubles. We know that Wulfgeat was once beloved by Æthelred before being accused of 'injusta judicia' (unjust judgements) and 'superba ... opera' (arrogant deeds).[22] Ælfric continues:

> Ða ne mihte he wunian on þære micclan mærðe,
> ne eac his gegadan, butan godes mihte,
> ac wurdon þa asyndrode fram þam soðum gode,
> forþam ðe hi forletan his hlafordscipe
> ealle swyðe unwislice, fram him ascyrede,
> mid andan afyllede and mid orwennysse
> ælcere miltsunge, manfulle gastas.

[Then he might no longer dwell in that great glory, nor afterwards may his cohort, without God's power, but they were separated from the true God, because they forsook His lordship altogether unwisely, divided from Him, filled with malice and with anger despair of any mercy, the wicked spirits.]

In thinking of themselves as separate from God, the rebel angels literally find themselves 'asyndrode' (sundered) from heaven and all ties to God's 'hlafordscipe' (lordship). Ælfric's interest in the fall of the angels has received a fair amount of critical attention. Using as a point of departure Paul Szarmach's observations about Ælfric's tendency to establish a 'narrative impulse',[23] Michael Fox explains that Ælfric 'places his distinctive narrative account of angelic history at the appropriate point ... and then proceeds to establish its relevance to the material which follows'.[24] While perhaps not as didactic as Ælfric in developing a 'narrative impulse' in his discussion of the fall of the angels, Wulfstan also understands this event as a critically important moment in the mythology of his Christian nation. Although Wulfstan's engagement with the fall of the angels has received considerably less attention, I will demonstrate that he appears to have come into contact with one or more of Ælfric's renditions of the event sometime prior to his composition of *Sermo Lupi*.

We know very little about Wulfstan's early life,[25] and of the time before he rose to the status of Archbishop of York (1002–23) and of Worcester (1002–16).[26] He was a public figure in England during one of the most tumultuous eras in its history. By the time of his death in 1023, Wulfstan had served under both Æthelred II (978–1013; 1014–16) and Cnut (1016–35).[27] Scholars such as Dorothy Whitelock and Patrick Wormald have characterised Wulfstan as a dynamic eleventh-century state-builder.[28] Wormald has gone so far as to argue that Wulfstan, even more so than Alfred or Bede, might be called the architect of the 'world's most enduring polity'.[29] According to Simon Keynes, the attacks of Thorkell's army in the last decade of Æthelred's reign 'reached unprecedented levels of ferocity'.[30] It was about this time that Wulfstan's political influence peaked; Keynes suggests that *Sermo Lupi* springs from this historical moment.

The first king that Wulfstan served, Æthelred, went into exile under the protection of the Church, at which time the Danes assumed political control for the first time in England. From this historical perspective, in Wulfstan we see a politically minded figure addressing a series of national upheavals during a time of ill-defined sovereignty.[31] Swein Forkbeard came to power in 1013 with the support of the Danelaw regions.[32] With Swein's unexpected death in 1014 there followed an uneasy tension over whether Cnut would ascend to the throne or if Æthelred would return.[33] Jonathan Wilcox proposes that a gathering of the nation's top councillors at York in February 1014, soon after the death of Forkbeard but before Æthelred's return from Normandy, is the most likely context for the public performance of Wulfstan's provocative sermon.[34] Ultimately, Æthelred temporarily regained his kingship. We have evidence that Wulfstan continued to write and revise *Sermo Lupi* throughout this period at least up to the death of Æthelred and the ascendancy of Cnut in 1016.

In addition to Wulfstan's involvement in early English statecraft, Joyce Hill stresses the importance of seeing Wulfstan as a prominent voice on theological matters during Benedictine Reform movement.[35] Although Wulfstan's letters are no longer extant, we know that he and Ælfric corresponded frequently, and that Wulfstan appears to have viewed Ælfric as the voice of authority on a range of theological questions.[36] The level of intertextuality between the writings of the abbot and the archbishop is crucial. It suggests that they shared concerns regarding the function of ecclesiastical authority and the instruction of the laity in Anglo-Saxon England. Their correspondence, which has been examined by critics such as Hill and Godden, provides evidence of Wulfstan's sustained interest in issues from the celebration of mass to the extent of episcopal authority.[37] Granted, not all of their correspondence is extant. Nevertheless, it is likely that homilies, socio-political works, and even Wulfstan's legal writings could have passed back and forth between the two, deeply impacting their thinking about contemporary topics.

Despite their lines of communication, in a larger sense Wulfstan lived worlds away from Ælfric. Wulfstan was an eyewitness to the threats posed by the Danish invaders. Their assaults on the north made Wulfstan highly conscious of both sacred and secular institutions as well as his responsibility in maintaining them. As Renée Trilling observes, 'Wulfstan combined the religious authority of the bishop with the secular authority of the royal adviser, and he played an active role in the administration of both secular and ecclesiastical society'.[38] Wulfstan was at the forefront of engaging with these challenges, especially when Cnut ascended the throne. Joyce Tally Lionarons suggests that, for Wulfstan, the coming of Cnut 'signaled a reprieve and a chance to rebuild the English nation into Wulfstan's vision of a holy society'.[39]

Like Ælfric, Wulfstan demonstrates a highly developed sense of authorship. While my interest in this chapter lies mainly in Wulfstan's homiletic corpus, it is important to note that he also wrote numerous legal tracts, law codes, social prescriptions, a commonplace book, and paraliturgical material.[40] Scholars frequently note the considerable overlap between his works in these different genres.[41] According to Christopher A. Jones, Wulfstan 'is one of the few early medieval figures ... for whom the sources reveal the deep affinities between liturgy, law, and preaching as media to proclaim the ordinances of God and, simultaneously, the authority of his pontifical messengers'.[42]

The task of reconstructing Wulfstan's canon has been underway for well over a century.[43] Arthur S. Napier's 1883 edition of homilies attributed to Wulfstan comprised no fewer than sixty-two,[44] four of which contain accounts of the fall of the rebel angels (Napier 2, Napier 29, Napier 30, and Napier 58). Thanks to Karl Jost's *Wulfstanstudien* (1950), and subsequent editions of Wulfstan's homilies by Dorothy Whitelock (1937) and Dorothy

Bethurum (1957), we know that only one of these four is authentically Wulfstanian (Napier 2 = Bethurum 6), which Bethurum characterised as a work on 'The Christian Faith'.

Nevertheless, the 'pseudo-Wulfstan' homily, Napier 30, also warrants some consideration. A variety of authoritative and apocryphal homiletic models for the fall of the angels circulated during the late tenth and early eleventh centuries, and analysing variant treatments of the subject can illuminate the doctrinal interests, exegetical attitudes and, most importantly, the ideological preoccupations of different Anglo-Saxon homilists. In what follows, I will briefly compare the handling of the fall of the angels motif by several anonymous homilists against Wulfstan's *Sermo* 6 (as well as the works of Ælfric) to highlight each author's theological and pastoral concerns. These can shed light on how Wulfstan and his contemporaries understood the first sin in heaven, God's response to it, and the subsequent motivation for the creation of humankind.

No throne to sit upon nor kingdom to stand upon

Pseudo-Wulfstan's account of the fall of the angels has, surprisingly, occasioned more comment than the genuine Wulfstan homily, *Sermo* 6.[45] Since it contains certain passages with highly poetic qualities, special attention has been devoted to its metrical nature. Angus McIntosh referred to Napier 30 a 'curiously complicated pastiche' and suggested that it had a 'Wulfstan ring to it'.[46] The portion of Napier 30 that discusses the fall of the angels stresses the importance of rejecting pride:

> Þurh ða ofermodignesse mære englas on heofonum wurdon geo forsceapene to atelicum deoflum ⁊ besceofene on helle grund, þære hi sceolon ecelice witu þolian, for ðam þe hi forhogedon þone ecan drihten ⁊ him sylfum þær rice mynton. Ac him se ræd ne geþeah, ac se stiðmoda cyning, drihten ælmihtig, awearp of ðam setle þone modigan feond ⁊ of ðam wuldre eac þæs heofonlican rices. ⁊ ealle þa ðe mid him æt ðam ræde wæron, hi wiston þe geornor, witum besette on þære byrnendan helle, wið hwæne hi winnon ongunnon.[47]

[Through that pride glorious angels in heaven were once transformed into terrible devils and thrusted down into the abyss of hell, where they must suffer torments eternally, because they despised the eternal Lord and intended to make for themselves a kingdom there. But the plan did not succeed for them, but the resolute king, the almighty Lord, cast the proud demon from that seat and likewise from the glory of the kingdom of heaven. And all those who were in league with him, they knew all the more surely, placed in torments in burning hell, against whom they had set out to fight.]

Scragg compiled parallels between Napier 30 and passages found in Vercelli Homilies 4, 9, and 21.[48] This connection has been thoroughly examined by Wright, who argues that the corresponding passage in Vercelli 21 is a (defective) quotation from a lost Old English poem. While cleaving closely to its source, as Wright has shown, Napier 30 nevertheless somewhat 'dilutes [the] metrical and alliterative form' found in Vercelli 21,[49] which in Wright's tentative reconstruction of its poetic form reads as follows:

> Þurh oferhyg<e>d<ness>e wurdon englas iu
> forsceapene to deoflum   ⁊ bescofene eac
> on helle grund,   þær hie sceolon
> on worulda woruld   witu þolian,
> for ðam þe hie forhogedon   heofona wealdend
> <⁊> sigora syllend,   ⁊ him sylfum þær
> rice mynton.   Ac him se ræd ne geþah,
> ac se stiðmoda cyning,
> <æl>mihtig dryhten,   þone modigan feond
> awearp of ðam setle   ⁊ of ðam wuldre eac
> <þæs> heofon<lic>an rices   ealle þa þe <mid him> æt ðam ræde
>   wæron.
> Hie wiston þe geornor,   witum besette
> on þære byrnendan helle,
> wið hwæne hie   winnan ongunnon.

[Through pride angels were once transformed into devils and also thrust down into the abyss of hell, where they must forever suffer torments, because they despised the ruler of the heavens, giver of victories, and intended to make for themselves a kingdom there. But that plan did not succeed for them, but the resolute king, the mighty Lord, cast the proud demon from his seat and likewise from the glory of the kingdom of heaven all those who were in league with him. Placed into torments in burning hell, they knew the more surely against whom they had set out to fight.][50]

With just a few slight variations, these two texts strike upon similar themes such as Satan's contempt for God, his desire to create a 'rice' (kingdom) for himself, the bad 'ræd' (counsel) given to the other angels, and the subsequent banishment from the 'setle' (seat) of heaven. Both accounts describe the process of de-throning the 'modigan feond' (proud demon) and explain how the rebel angels were 'bescofene' (thrust down) by God into hell.⁵¹

Wulfstan's influence upon Napier 30 has also been documented by Scragg,⁵² who found that the homily incorporates passages from Wulfstan's *Sermo* 10, the *Institutes of Polity* 25, the law tract *Grið* (as Jost had already noted), as well as an excerpt from *Sermo* 6 on the birth of Christ.⁵³ While the author of Napier 30 demonstrates a liking in places for Wulfstan's style, notably his use of intensifiers, and also substituted Wulfstan's word for 'pride' (*ofermodignys*) for *oferhygednesse*, little else in *Sermo* 6 (including a passage concerning the replacement doctrine) appears to have interested him. In turning to Wulfstan's *Sermo* 6, we might ask why pseudo-Wulfstan opted for the version of the fall of the angels in Vercelli 21 as his model, when he had Wulfstan's account at his disposal.

While Wulfstan may well have been familiar with these anonymous works, I suggest that his representation of the *principium* of salvation history is fundamentally different from that in the Vercelli and Napier homilies and more in line with Ælfric's treatment of events. Wulfstan's *Sermo* 6 contains an outline of Christian history, encompassing angelic creation, the fall of Lucifer, the creation and fall of Adam and Eve, Noah and the Flood, the Babylonian Captivity, Christ's birth, death, and resurrection, before concluding with Ascension, Antichrist, and Last Judgement.⁵⁴ *Sermo* 6 is, strictly speaking, more doctrinal and less vivid than the anonymous homilies in its representation of the fall of the angels. Bethurum suggests that Wulfstan composed this homily in the 'period before 1008' and Patrick Wormald has narrowed that window, proposing that it was written in 1002, shortly after Wulfstan became Archbishop of York.⁵⁵ Thomas N. Hall characterises *Sermo* 6 as 'an outline of Christian history addressed to priests which ... warns that on Judgment Day they will be held personally responsible for the souls of wicked men' whom they failed to save.⁵⁶ Wulfstan opens with a direct address to his audience, stating:

> Gyf ðu þonne þæt ne dest ac forsuwast hit ⁊ nelt folce his þearfe gecyðan, þonne scealt þu ealra þæra sawla on domesdæg gescead agyldan þe þurh þæt losiað, þe hy nabbað þa lare ⁊ ða mynegunge þe hy beðorfton.⁵⁷

[If you do not do this but pass over it in silence and fail to alert the people to their need, then you will be forced to render an account to God on Doomsday for all those souls who are lost because they have not received the instruction and warning they need.]

After this emphasis on 'lar' (instruction) and the 'mynegung' (warning) that faithful Christians must hear, Wulfstan says that he has a good deal of biblical history to cover, and will therefore be discussing everything 'scortlice' (briefly).[58] Wulfstan's first episode, concerning the creation and fall of the angels, reads as follows:

> An is ece God þe gesceop heofonas ⁊ eorðan ⁊ ealle gesceafta, ⁊ on fruman he gelogode on þære heofonlican gesceafte, þæt is, on heofona rice, engla weredu mycle ⁊ mære. Ða wearð þær an þæra engla swa scinende ⁊ swa beorht ⁊ swa wlitig þæt se wæs Lucifer genemned. Þa þuhte him þæt he mihte beon þæs efengelica ðe hine gescop ⁊ geworhte; and sona swa he þurh ofermodignysse þæt geðohte, þa hreas he of heofonum ⁊ eall þæt him hyrde, ⁊ hy gewurdan of englum to deoflum gewordene, ⁊ heom wearð hyll gegearwod, ⁊ hi ðær wuniað on ecan forwyrde.[59]

[One is eternal God who created the heavens and earth and created all things, and in the beginning he placed in that heavenly creation, that is, in the kingdom of heaven, troops of angels mighty and splendid. Then one of those angels was so shining and so bright and so fair that he was called Lucifer. Then it seemed to him that he might be equal to him who created and made him; and as soon as he thought that through pride, then he and all who obeyed him fell out of heaven, and they became changed from angels to devils, and hell was made ready for them, and they dwell there in eternal ruin.]

In this passage, we see several telltale marks of Wulfstan's style. There is a repetition of *an* first in reference to 'ece God' (eternal God) as 'one' and then in reference to 'an þæra engla' (one of those angels). We see Wulfstanian alliterative hallmarks such as *mycle ⁊ mære* and *gewurdan ... gewordene*. Wulfstan passes over many of the essential elements of the narrative that are given prominence in the other homilies: he omits Lucifer's contempt for God and the implication that he gave questionable 'ræd' (advice) to the soon-to-be fallen angels.[60]

Wulfstan's overview of salvation history has invited comparisons with Ælfric's *Sermo De Initio Creaturae* (CH I.1) and even the extended biblical verse epic *Genesis B*.[61] However, such comparisons must be carefully qualified. If CH I.1 was Wulfstan's primary influence, it is clear that he was highly selective in his borrowing, since Ælfric's account of the fall of Satan (discussed below) is anything but *scort*. Lionarons has pointed out that Wulfstan's discussion is half the length of Ælfric's.[62] Jost suggested that an alternative source for Wulfstan was the *Scarapsus* of Abbot Pirmin of Reichenau.[63] The *Fontes Anglo-Saxonici* database suggests that Wulfstan most likely conflated the two, using Pirmin for lines 24–7, CH I.1 for lines 29–30, Pirmin again for lines 30–2 and, finally, CH I.1 for 32–3.[64]

Ælfric, Pirmin, pseudo-Wulfstan, and the Vercelli homilist incorporate even more details into their respective accounts, describing everything right down to the sinful thoughts, words, and deeds of Lucifer. Wulfstan ideologically grounds his narrative by reducing Lucifer's sin to a singular prideful breach centred on the failed recognition of God as sovereign. The creation sequence in the *Dicta abbatis Pirmi* can further illustrate the divide between Wulfstan and other available sources:

> But he said he was equal [*simile*] to him, and for this pride, with many other angels, who consented to him, he was thrown down from that celestial throne into that air, which is under heaven, [and] he became the devil. In the same way, those angels, who were in league with him, were cast down from heaven with him, losing their splendor, were made demons. After the fall of the angels God formed man of the dust of the earth, so that, if he kept the precept of our Lord, he could advance without death into that heavenly place, from which those angels fell from refuge; but if he should break the command of God, he shall die.[65]

Whereas Pirmin uses *simile* to describe how Lucifer conceives of himself in relation to God, and many other vernacular accounts of this primal insurrection use *gelic*, Wulfstan suggests that Lucifer desired to be *efengelica* ('co-equal'). For Wulfstan's clerical audience, *efengelica* would have had distinctly Trinitarian connotations as it was commonly used to gloss *aequalis* and *coaequalis* in copies of the Athanasian Creed in Anglo-Saxon psalters. Finally, Wulfstan offers his own personal touch on how Lucifer comes to fall out of heaven. Whereas many anonymous homilies recounting this episode describe how God forcibly 'thrusts', 'blows', or 'hurls' Lucifer from heaven (as seen in Napier 30, Vercelli 19, and Vercelli 21), for Wulfstan, Lucifer's mere thought of 'co-equality' causes him and his retinue to drop from the heavens. Lucifer's mental status projects itself upon his surroundings, signalling disarray within the heavenly order. For Wulfstan, then, rebellion originates in the mind and emanates outward, impacting the very landscape of heaven.

Reading as an extended version of his *Letter to Wulfgeat*, Ælfric's dramatic version of events in CH I.1 can further illuminate this matter:

> Þæt teoðe werod abreað ⁊ awende on yfel; god hi gesceop ealle gode. ⁊ let hi habban agenne cyre. Swa hi heora scyppende lufedon ⁊ filidon. swa hi hine forleton; þa wæs teoðan weredes ealdor swiðe fæger ⁊ wlitig gesceapen. swa þæt he wæs gehaten leohtberend. Þa began he to modigeanne for ðære fægernysse. Þe he hæfde. ⁊ cwæð on his heortan. þæt he wolde ⁊ eaðe mihte beon his scyppend gelic. ⁊ sittan on ðam norðdæle heofonan rices. ⁊ habban anweald ⁊ rice ongean gode ælmihtigum; Þa gefæstnode he þisne ræd wið ðam werode þe he bewiste. ⁊ hi ealle to ðam ræde gebugon; Þa ða hi ealle hædon þisne ræd betwux him gefæsnod. Þa becom godes grama ofer him eallum. ⁊ hi ealle wurdon awende of ðam fægeran hiwe þe hi on gescapene wæron. To laðlicum deoflum; And swiðe rihtlice him swa getimode. Þa ða he wolde mid modinysse beon betera þonne he gesceapen wæs. ⁊ cwæð þæt he mihte beon þam ælmihtigum gode gelic. Þa wearð he ⁊ ealle his geferan. Forcuþran ⁊ wyrsan þonne ænig oðer gesceaft. ⁊ þa hwile þe he smeade hu he mihte dælan rice wið god. Þa hwile gearcode se ælmihtiga scyppend him ⁊ his geferan hellewite. ⁊ hi ealle adræfde of heofonan rices myrihðe. ⁊ let befeallan on þæt ece fyr þe him gegearcod wæs for heora ofermettum.[66]

[The tenth host rebelled and turned to evil. God created them all good, and let them have their own choice, whether they would love and follow their creator, or would forsake him. Now the prince of the tenth host was formed very fair and beauteous, so that he was called Light-bearer. Then he began to grow proud because of the beauty he had, and he said in his heart that he intended and might easily be equal to his creator and sit in the northern part of heaven's kingdom, and have power and command over God Almighty. Then he confirmed this resolve with the host over which he ruled, and they all submitted to that advice. When they all had confirmed this resolve among themselves, God's anger came over all of them, and they were changed to devils from the beautiful form in which they were created. And very rightly it befell him, when in pride he intended to be better that he was created, and said that he might be equal to Almighty God. Then he and his troop became more wicked and worse than any other creature. And while he meditated on how he might divide the kingdom with God, the

Almighty creator prepared hell-torments for him and his troop, and drove them from all the joy of heaven's kingdom, and caused them to fall into the eternal fire that was prepared for them on account of their pride.]

Here, Ælfric mentions Lucifer's desire to 'sittan' (sit) upon the throne of a rival kingdom in the 'norðdæle' (northern part) of heaven. He calls attention to the themes of pride, the desire for dominance, and disobedience to the will of God. He uses different terms for 'pride' with *ofermetto* or *modi(g)nys* (whereas Wulfstan uses *ofermodignys*).[67] Yet Wulfstan and Ælfric agree on one essential feature of the narrative: rebellion is first a psychological and then physical movement away from God:

> Swa mihton eac þa oðre þe ðær feollon. dón gif hi woldon. for ði þe god hi geworhte to wlitegum engla gecynde. ⁊ let hi habban agenne cyre ⁊ hi næfre ne gebigde ne ne nydde mid nanum þingum to ðam yfelan ræde. ne næfre se yfela ræd ne com of godes geþance. ac com of ðæs deofles. swa swa we ær cwædon; Nu þencð mænig man ⁊ smeað hwanon deoful come; þonne wite he þæt god gesceop to mæran engle þone þe nu is deoful. ac god ne sceop hine na to deofle. ac þa ða he wæs mid ealle fordón ⁊ forscyldgod þurh ða miclan upahefednysse ⁊ wiðerweardnysse þa wearð he to deofle awend. se ðe ær wæs mære engel geworht.[68]

[So might also the others who fell have done if they had been willing, because God had made them in the beautiful nature of angels, and let them have their own choice and would never have inclined or forced them in any way to that evil counsel. Nor did the evil counsel ever come from God's conception, but came from the devil's as we said before. Now many a man will think and inquire from whence the devil came; now let him understand that God created as a glorious angel the one who is now the devil, but God did not create him as the devil. But when he was wholly corrupted and guilty through that arrogance and rebelliousness, then he who was before created as a glorious angel became changed into a devil.]

For the second time in his discussion of angelic free will Ælfric uses the phrase '⁊ let hi habban agenne cyre' (and let them have their own choice).[69] Both Ælfric and Wulfstan appear to agree that the rebel angels simply exercised (or rather squandered) the divine gift of *cyre* ('choice').[70]

Katherine O'Brien O'Keeffe has explored how Ælfric differentiates between *agen cyre* (or 'free choice', *liberum arbitrium*) and *agen willa* (or 'free will', *libera uoluntas*), with *agen* having the force of 'self'. She argues that 'Ælfric is considerably more interested in the pragmatics of choice than in the metaphysics of free will'.[71] Ælfric, breaking from traditional Augustinian modes of interpretation, views the *cyre* given by God as the 'capacity by which man is responsible for his every behavior, behavior that is judged by the degree to which man is obedient to God'.[72] In this particular episode in CH I.1, O'Brien O'Keeffe asserts that God endows all created beings with *agen cyre* and thus 'the point of his excursus on the angelic behavior [improper choice] is the defense of human freedom to choose'.[73] Whereas many other accounts of the angelic rebellion trace Lucifer's wish for spatial expansion of his realm or a division of heaven territories, both Ælfric and Wulfstan explore the underlying psychological origin of those desires. For them, the domain of the mind is not unlike a physical space which, as Lefebvre might say, undergoes the same careful structuring, organising, and governing. Ælfric's Lucifer 'smeade' (from 'asmeagan') or 'meditated' ('to think, meditate, contemplate') about dividing his realm *with* God but without reference to God's sovereignty, as any monk in spiritual training, catechumenate, or faithful Christian ought not do. For both homilists, then, Lucifer's violation is an abuse of God's gift of agency followed by the creation of perils that did not originate with God. In rejecting the sacred mores of heaven, the rebel angels create new impious ways of thinking and relating to authority. Through their own exercise of free choice, their embodied status is also changed (*awend*) from angelic to demonic.

But what is the experience of falling from heaven like? Ælfric takes up this perplexing issue in his *Libellus de veteri testamento et novi* or *Letter to Sigeweard*. In the *Libellus*, Ælfric states that God's newly created angels are 'ealle lichamlease' (entirely bodiless).[74] In this sense, their spirits do not require a bodily *–ham* ('home') because their home is heaven. He also calls attention to their inexpressible beauty. They are 'swa wlitiges gecindes swa we secgan ne magon' (of so beautiful a nature that we cannot express, ll. 60–1), as Ælfric puts it.

Ælfric next turns to Lucifer's personal recognition of his singular beauty: 'gesceawode se an engel, þe þær ænlicost wæs, hu fæger he silf wæs and hu scinende on wuldre, and cunnode his mihte þæt he mihtig wæs gesceapen, and him wel gelicode his wurðfulniss þa' (one angel, who was most peerless there, beheld how beautiful he himself was and how shining in glory, and knew his power that he was created mighty, and then his magnificence pleased him very much, ll. 65–8). Beyond emphasising Lucifer's fixation on his outward appearance and beauty with terms such as 'ænlicost' (most splendid), 'ænlic' (singular), 'fæger' (fair), and 'wlitig' (beautiful),[75] Ælfric begins to mobilise a constellation of psychological motivations surrounding Lucifer's fall in this context, including the angel's fascination with his own power:

> Ða þuhte him to huxlic þæt he hiran sceolde ænigum hlaforde, þa he swa ænlic wæs, and nolde wurðian þone þe hine geworhte and him þancian æfre ðæs þe he him forgeaf, and beon him underðeodd þæs ðe swiþor geornlice for þære micclan mærðe þe he hine gemæðegode. He nolde þa habban his scippend him to hlaforde, ne þurhwunian on ðære soþfæstnisse ðæs soðfæstan Godes sunu, þe gesceop fægerne, ac wolde mid riccetere him rice gewinnan and þurh modignisse hine macian to Gode.[76]

[Then it seemed to him too shameful that he should obey any lord, since he was so peerless, and did not desire to worship the one who made him and afterwards thank him for what he had given him, nor would he be willingly subservient to him for the great splendour with which he had honoured him. He did not desire to have his maker as his lord, nor to be steadfast or true to God's son, who created him so fair, but he desired to attain a kingdom for himself by force and through pride make himself into a god.]

Here, we get a glimpse of Lucifer's delight in his own beauty and his perception that his status as subject is 'huxlic' (shameful). Just as Wulfstan's *Sermo* 6 establishes that the condition of being 'an' (singular) is one normally reserved for God, Ælfric shows that Lucifer's sense of his own 'ænlic' (singular or peerless) qualities leads him astray. These thoughts culminate in his radical desire to 'gewinnan' (attain) a rival kingdom and 'macian' (make) himself into a god. Lucifer desires to assert ownership over space and claim separate sovereignty 'mid riccetere' (by force).

Ælfric's interest in the spatial schematics of heaven continues. In fact, heaven appears to acquire a kind of agency all its own as the material surroundings appear to reject Lucifer's ambitions. In what could be described as perhaps the most cinematic account of Lucifer's fall, Ælfric draws on Augustine's trope of the 'foot of the soul' or the 'foot of love' (*Enarrationes in Psalmos* 9:15 [PL 36.124] and 120:5 [PL 37.1608]),[77] which describes how the soul can either ascend towards love of God or descend towards hell. In this case, Ælfric literalises the topos, depicting Satan's lost foothold:

Ða næfde he nan setl hwær he sittan mihte, for ðan ðe nan heofon nolde hine aberan ne nan rice næs þe his mihte beon ongean Godes willan, þe geworhte ealle ðinc. Ða afunde se modiga hwilce his mihta wæron, þa þa his fet ne mihton furðon ahwar standan, ac he feoll ða adun.[78]

[Then he had no throne where he might sit, because heaven would not bear him nor was there any kingdom which might be his against the will of God, who created all things. Then the proud one discovered what kind of powers were his, when his feet might not even stand anywhere, but then he fell downward.]

By depicting Lucifer's construction of the self and his embodiment as simultaneous, Ælfric is able to imagine heaven as unable to support his weight alongside his vanishing throne and kingdom (*nan setl ... nan rice*). Ælfric then describes how the remaining good angels, in a manner reminiscent of a monk's constant contemplation, 'æfre beoð ymbe þæt an, hu hi magon Gode gehyrsumian, and him gecweman' (are only ever meditating about how they may obey God and be acceptable to him, l. 50). In both Wulfstan and Ælfric's versions, Lucifer's sin causes its own punishment; the fall of the angels is a personal undoing of angelic identity with the very space of heaven assisting in their expulsion. The spatial 'rice' (kingdom) of heaven thus becomes a manifestation of God's laws and sovereign will. Both homilists thus magnify the spatial consequences associated with rebellious thought. God has no need to forcibly or aggressively intervene; their imagined heavenly polities simply cannot bear rebellious behaviour.

Wulfstan and Ælfric have similar accounts of the next event in creation history. In the *Libellus*, Ælfric briefly touches upon replacement, stating that Adam and Eve 'sceoldon habban, and heora ofspring mid him, þa fægeran wununge þe se feond forleas, gif hi gehirsumedon heora scippende on riht' (were to have, and their offspring with them, that fair dwelling place that the enemy lost, if they obeyed their creator rightly, ll. 86–7). Wulfstan's rehearsal of the doctrine of replacement similarly expresses the view that humankind has the potential to repair the heavenly polity:

And to ðam hy gesceop God ælmihtig, þæt hy 7 heora ofspring scoldan gefyllan 7 gemænigfyldan þæt on heofonum gewanad wæs; þæt wæs ungerim þæt ðænon þurh deofles ofermodignesse into helle behreas. Ac sona swa deofol ongeat þæt mann to ðam gescapen wæs,

A new *praedestinati*

þæt he scolde ⁊ his cynn gefyllan on heofonum þæt se deofol forworhte ðurh his ofermodignesse, þa wæs him þæt on myclan andan, ongann þa beswican ⁊ gelæran þæt se man abræc Godes bebod.[79]

[And God almighty created them, so that they and their offspring should fill up and multiply what was diminished in the heavens; that was a countless number which fell from there into hell through the pride of the devil. But as soon as the devil learned that man had been created for that purpose, that he and his kin were to replenish in heaven that which the devil forfeited through his pride, then that was a great source of envy to him, and he began to deceive and teach that man how to break God's command.]

Formulating the replacement doctrine in a way that echoes God's command to Adam and Eve to increase and 'multiply' (Gen. 1:28), Wulfstan states that God intends for humankind to 'gefyllan ⁊ gemænigfyldan' (fill up and multiply) 'what was diminished in the heavens' with their offspring. Wulfstan describes the fallen inventory of angels as *ungerim* ('countless, numberless, innumerable'),[80] an image that fittingly contrasts with the *an* ('singular') angel who precipitated the fall. By Wulfstan's reckoning, heaven's emptying is impossible to quantify.

Wulfstan's *Sermo* 6 engages with the consequences of failing to recognise the proper sovereignty of God paired with his anxiety over the failure of churchmen to adequately convey this relationship to Christians. Lionarons suggests that Wulfstan intends to demonstrate how God punishes 'the disobedient without remorse … [using] the alternation of sin and punishment to transform his homily into a vehicle for moral exhortation'.[81] She adds that this structure suggests that 'Wulfstan was already thinking of the English in terms of both the Old and New Testament paradigms that he uses to much greater rhetorical effect in *Sermo Lupi*'.[82]

It is fair to say that Ælfric's various descriptions of the fall of the angels and the emergent space he imagines for God's sovereignty is more developed than Wulfstan's *Sermo* 6. Although both homilists attempt to work through the connections between sovereignty, space, and choice, Wulfstan's *Sermo* 6 perhaps represents only his earliest thinking about these subjects. He will pick up these threads to a far greater extent as his career progresses and his interest in sovereignty and the law deepens.[83] If we are to discover Wulfstan's fullest articulation of the relationship between sovereignty and space we must turn to *Sermo Lupi*, where the homilist powerfully connects the themes of pride, disloyalty, and displacement while calling upon the necessity for choice, action, and obedience in a very overt way. O'Brien O'Keeffe argues that the concept of 'free choice' in Anglo-Saxon England involves 'an explicit form of self-fashioning, inward looking, yet institutionally framed' process, which paradoxically means that one only discovers 'freedom in obedience'.[84] O'Brien O'Keeffe therefore suggests that for Anglo-Saxon Christians the highest attainment of freedom accords perfectly with obedience to the will of God.

As this survey demonstrates, Ælfric and Wulfstan show a strong and evolving interest in the nature of obedience as seen through the story of the fall of the angels. In what follows, I will propose that Wulfstan's understanding of the originary sin in salvation history extends to his most historically oriented homily, *Sermo Lupi*. By recounting the widespread perversions of hierarchical relations and also qualifying the English downfall as one freely brought upon themselves, Wulfstan implicitly envisions the vikings as possible 'replacements' for the English who would become landless owing to their rebelliousness towards God. Unlike the early Benedictine reformers who reaffirmed the destiny of the English as replacements, Wulfstan calibrates the English as the subjects who thwart sovereign authority, situating them disturbingly among the rebel 'weredu' (troops) that reject God's grace.

Redefining the doctrine of replacement in *Sermo Lupi ad Anglos*

Wulfstan's representation of the fall of the angels and its corollary doctrine of replacement in *Sermo* 6 shares a connection to his later elaboration upon the depravities of the English nation in his wellknown *Sermo Lupi*. The replacement doctrine – first elaborated upon by Augustine and later Gregory the Great – is crucial to understanding Wulfstan's portrayal of the English people (both Anglo-Saxon and Anglo-Danish Christians) and the vikings. Whereas scholars have read Wulfstan's representation of the vikings in his *Sermo Lupi* as the stereotypical immoral and demonic enemies of the English or even heralds of Antichrist, viewing their role through this doctrinal framework suggests that Wulfstan had a more nuanced understanding of the viking menace. Wulfstan sees the vikings not as Antichrists, but as possible Christians and potential 'replacements', just as the originally pagan Anglo-Saxons supplanted the sinful Christian Britons.

Authors from Bede to Ælfric frequently correlated the narrative of the fall of the rebel angels with the doctrine of replacement as a way to describe the heavenly territories that await faithful Christians. This doctrine was derived from treatises such as Augustine's *De Civitate Dei* 22.1 (CCSL 48.807), which states:

> [Q]ui de mortali progenie merito iusteque damnata tantum populum gratia sua colligit, ut inde suppleat et instauret partem, quae lapsum est angelorum, ac sic illa dilecta et superna ciuitas non fraudentur suorum numero ciuium, quin etiam fortassis et uberiore laetetur.

[For out of this mortal progeny, so rightly and justly condemned, God by his grace is gathering a people so great that from them he may fill the place of the fallen angels and restore their number. And thus that beloved Heavenly City will not be deprived of its full number of citizens; it may perhaps rejoice in a still more abundant population.][85]

In his *Enchiridion*, Augustine expresses how the loss of angels is replenished 'from among men' whom he calls *praedestinati* ('predestined ones'). Augustine's view of the replacement doctrine is also inextricably linked with his conception of reform.[86] Augustine suggests that the Church must be filled with 'men capable of reform' who 'will replenish the angelic host whose number was depleted by the fall of the rebel angels'.[87] According to Gerhart Ladner, for Augustine reform should always be oriented towards repopulating the forfeited spaces in heaven by continually perfecting the Church on earth.

Scholars frequently trace the source of this replacement ideology in Anglo-Saxon England back to Gregory the Great's missionary endeavours, especially to his famous anecdote concerning pagan boys from 'Anglia', who should become coheirs of the *angeli* in heaven. His *Homiliae in Evangelia* 34 (CCSL 141A), which explicates Luke 15:8 (the parable of the ten drachmas), was therefore a widely known and cited source for replacement theology. Gregory characterises the angelic parties in heaven as 'orders' (as seen in Ælfric's CH I.1), explaining how the original ten turned to nine after the fall of the rebellious lot. Bede closely follows Gregory's metric in his *In Lucae Euangelium Expositio* (CCSL 120A.285ff) and in his commentary *In Tobiam* (CCSL 119B) where he states that 'Having been led to the heavenly homeland, humanity's [elect] will be welcomed by God ... and also by the angels whose number they will complete'. This sense that Anglo-Saxons could become *coheredes* ('co-heirs', *æfenerfeweardas* in the Old English Bede) and that heavenly territories await would-be inheritors fundamentally informs conceptions of early English Christian identity and the Anglo-Saxons' understanding of their unique role in salvation history.

To fully appreciate Wulfstan's use of the replacement doctrine we need to recognise how he transforms the way it was used by earlier generations. The New Minster Charter, as we have seen, portrays the secular clerics at Winchester as a subversive threat to English ecclesiastical unity by aligning their sinful behaviour with that of the rebel angels. What makes the connection with the laxity of the secular clerics more than mere polemics is the implication that the compromise of their earthly properties affects the destiny of the English, who are to number among the intended replacements. New earthly caretakers are needed if the English are to become heavenly inheritors, and so privileges must be revoked to safeguard those eternal spaces. Following the proem, the New Minster Charter describes the thrones of heaven, which will stand idle until God 'should make good the number of angels driven out, full of pride, from the dwellings of Heaven'.[88] The document suggests that the reformers alone, by ushering out one 'order' (*cuneus*) and installing a new one, could resecure the role of the English people as 'replacements'. Wulfstan would almost certainly have been familiar with this reformist propaganda, yet he sought to redefine its terms as he called upon his audience (who faced a very different kind of crisis) to hold fast to their place in salvation history through obedience to God. Wulfstan's depiction of replacement in *Sermo* 6 can shed light on the underlying 'Old Testament logic' (to borrow Patrick Wormald's phrase) of *Sermo Lupi*.

Sermo Lupi continues to fascinate scholars, primarily because of Wulfstan's alignment of legal and theological discourses. *Sermo Lupi* (Bethurum 20; Napier 33) exists in five manuscripts in three different versions.[89] Versions E and I, which include passages referring to the Danish attacks, begin with the Latin rubric *Quando Dani Maxime Persecuti Sunt Eos Quod Fuit Anno Millesimo XIIII* ('When the Danes greatly persecuted them which was in the year 1014').[90] This has led many scholars to assume that these two versions represent Wulfstan's revisions. Version C also comments upon these attacks, while the two other versions do not.[91] E and I also contain unique references to Gildas's *De Excidio Brittannia*, which Wulfstan translated by way of Alcuin.[92]

According to Stephanie Hollis, '[t]he central theme of the sermon can be summarised as the nation's progression to disaster'.[93] Raachel Jurovics similarly observes that Wulfstan is most dismayed by the diminishing bonds of loyalty that have allowed men to 'betray their kinsmen, their kings, their fellow Christians'.[94] The clear breakdown of fidelity between God and the human community is conveyed in Wulfstan's description of various waning social structures:[95]

> And eac syndan wide, swa we ær cwædan, þurh aðbricas ⁊ þurh wedbrycas ⁊ þurh mistlice leasunga forloren ⁊ forlogen ma þonne scolde ⁊ freolsbricas ⁊ fæsten brycas wide geworhte oft ⁊ gelome. And eac her syn on earde apostatan abroþene ⁊ cyrichatan hetole ⁊ leodhatan grimme ealles to manege, ⁊ oferhogan wide godcundra rightlaga ⁊ cristenra þeawa, ⁊ hocorwyrde dysige æghwær on þeode oftost on þa þing þe Godes bodan beodaþ ⁊ swyþost on þa þing þe æfre to Godes lage gebyriað mid rihte.[96]

[And, as we said before, we are widely ruined through oath-breaking and through pledge-breaking and through various lies more than one should and through forsaking festivals and fast-breaking that occurs widely often and again. And also here in the land there are all too many wicked apostates and hostile haters of the Church and too many grim tyrants, and those who scorn godly laws and Christian practices are widespread, and everywhere in the nation are those who foolishly and often deride things which the messengers of God command, and especially things which ever belong to God's law by right.]

Wulfstan calls attention to the neglect of Christian 'freolsbricas' (festivals) and 'fæsten' (fasts) (quite possibly a reference to Rogationtide practices). This failure to observe ritualised aspects of Christian spiritual life suggests that, for Wulfstan, the fundamental borders of Christian obligation and identity are breaking down. He constructs the sin of the nation as not only the failure to uphold proper social relations, but the active inversion of them, one that occurs on both spiritual and secular levels.[97] His castigation of this sorry state of affairs centres primarily on the breaking of oaths and pledges ('aðbricas' and 'wedbrycas'), a sin that resonates with the 'oath-breaking' of the rebel angels found in *Genesis A*.

Lucifer's oath-breaking is also a dominant theme in a mid-thirteenth-century Old Norse treatise known as *Konungs Skuggsjá* (the *Speculum Regale* or 'Mirror for Kings').[98] Written in Norway, the *Skuggsjá* is stylised as a question-and-answer session between a father and son containing wisdom lessons from biblical stories. The text depicts Lucifer and the rebel angels as consenting to God's laws only to later default on their pledges. Unsatisfied with the limitations of their 'ríkis' (kingdom), the angels knowingly break God's 'lögbrot' (law) and engage in a 'uppreist' (rebellion) against heaven. Just as this treatise is meant to hold up a mirror to the society and the individual, Wulfstan's homily similarly compels his Anglo-Saxon (and Anglo-Danish) audiences to look inward.

Although Wulfstan addresses his sermon to a single *þeod* ('people') his listeners would have most likely consisted of those who would have self-identified as Danish, many of whom would have been profiled as *hæþen* ('heathen') just a few generations earlier.[99] When Wulfstan uses the term *þeod*, he most likely refers to Christian people living in England, whether Anglo-Saxons or Christianised Danes who had been settled in England for some time.[100] Wulfstan gives some indication of his views on what it means to be *hæþen* in II Cnut 5.2, where he characterises *hæðenscipe* as the worship of idols and false gods. In *Sermo Lupi*, he suggests that practising unchristian behaviours, not one's ethnic or national identity, makes one *hæþen*. As Stephen Harris importantly observes, Wulfstan ultimately proposes that Christians are just as capable of brutish *hæþen* behaviour, while 'Vikings are capable of Christian behavior'.[101] For Wulfstan, as Harris states, identity has its basis in 'legal and moral foundations, rather than ethnic ones'.[102] Moreover, Wulfstan says that 'on hæþenum þeodum ne dear man forhealdan lytel ne micel þæs þe gelagod is to gedwolgoda weorðunge' (among heathen peoples one does not dare withhold little or much of that which is appointed for the worship of false gods, ll. 27–9). In other words, he sees heathens as proficient in exercising their own form of piety and even more steadfast in their devotions, unlike the lapsed English, whom he chides.

Lionarons observes that in his enumeration of sins Wulfstan returns 'repeatedly to two particularly invidious categories of sin: inversions of the proper order of society and the world, and treachery against lords, family, and nation'.[103] Sinfulness, for Wulfstan, is not simply a failure to uphold proper social relations, but the active inversion of them:

> Forþam her syn on lande ungetrywþa micle for Gode ⁊ for worolde, ⁊ eac her syn on earde on mistlice wisan hlafordswican manege. And ealra mæst hlafordswice se bið on worolde þæt man his hlafordes saule beswice; ⁊ ful micel hlafordswice eac bið on worolde þæt man his hlaford of life forræde oððon of lande lifiendne drife.[104]

[For there are here in the land great disloyalties towards God and before the world, and there are also many here in this land who are lord-betrayers in diverse ways. And the worst betrayal of one's lord in the world is that a man betray his lord's soul; and likewise it is a very great lord-betrayal in the world that a man should plot against the life of his lord or drive him, while living, from his land.]

Wulfstan describes how 'ungetrywþa' (disloyalty) has permeated the nation. He focuses on 'hlafordswice' (lord-betrayal) in both the earthly and spiritual realm by creating a parallel between God and one's secular *hlaford*. He notes his revulsion towards 'forræde' (plotting) and the desire to 'drife' (drive) one's lord 'of lande' (from the land), two of the chief ideas used to express Lucifer's heinous disloyalty in other representations of the fall of the angels. As in Ælfric's *Libellus*, it is as though the land itself could reject its inhabitants. On the ramifications of lord-betrayal, Fred Robinson succinctly observes, 'loyalty in pre-Conquest society was the *sine qua non* ... Satan emerges ... as an unworthy thane whose disloyalty to God introduced disorder and evil into the world. To Christians elsewhere, the primal sin of Lucifer was pride; to the Christian Anglo-Saxon it seems ... to have been disloyalty'.[105] Robinson explains further: 'Wulfstan's most famous sermon is in large part a catalogue of the horrors that befall a people once the principle of loyalty is forgotten'.[106] These horrors include viking invaders, who nonetheless are made 'swa strange þurh Godes þafunge' (so strong through God's consent) and become the beneficiaries of English disloyalty.[107] By identifying the English nation as fallen and qualifying the English downfall as self-inflicted, Wulfstan depicts the vikings as poised to displace the English, poised to enact a grim parody of replacement.

Fall of the Britons, Fall of the Angels

Like Alcuin before him, Wulfstan attempts to frame the viking onslaughts of his time within God's providential design for the Anglo-Saxons. While scholars such as Lionarons ultimately read the function of Wulfstan's many 'inversions of the proper order' in *Sermo Lupi* as emblematic of Antichrist, 'the reversal of good and evil',[108] in what follows I suggest that these inversions can be traced back to *Sermo* 6, where Wulfstan represented disloyalty and rebellion through Lucifer's desire to be co-equal with God. Along with Lionarons, Stephanie Hollis characterises the vikings as heralds of the apocalypse, suggesting that the 'imminent historical event is the conquest of England by the vikings, which for Wulfstan coalesces with the eschatological event'.[109] Although Hollis argues that the vikings are not only 'precursors to the advent of Antichrist, but [rendered] "antichrists" themselves', Lionarons has cautioned that 'Wulfstan never explicitly identifies the Vikings with Antichrist (or as "antichrists")'.[110] Nevertheless, the conflation of vikings with Antichrist has been a fixture in Wulfstan studies, and it has a bearing upon our understanding of Christian (and heathen) identity. I want to question some firmly entrenched assumptions that enable this conflation and propose an alternative reading for how Anglo-Saxons might have conceived of 'divine punishment' for their sins.

As I mentioned earlier, Wulfstan at times appears to characterise the vikings as exemplars of piety, albeit heathen piety. Had he wished to conflate viking identity with either Satan or Antichrist, there would have been ample precedent for him to follow. Wulfstan might, for example, have drawn upon Abbo of Fleury's reflections on the viking incursions in his *Passio S. Eadmundi*.[111] Abbo was a Continental monk who taught at Ramsey from 985 to 987 before returning to Fleury in 988, where he wrote down his reflections on the martyrdom of Edmund. According to James Earl,[112] 'The monks at Ramsey urged Abbo of Fleury to produce his *Passio S. Eadmundi*, on Edmund, king of the East Angles, killed by the Danes in 869'.[113] Drawing upon imagery from the Book of Jeremiah 1:14, Isaiah 14:12–15, Isidore's *Etymologies* (9.2.132), and Revelation 20:4, Abbo equates the viking homeland with the northern seat of Lucifer's kingdom and implies that their coming signals the Last Judgement. The relevant portion of Jeremiah reads 'And the Lord said to me: from the north shall an evil break forth upon all the inhabitants of the land'. In his description of the arrival of the vikings, Abbo draws upon these regional distinctions as he writes,

> Nec mirum, cum uenerint indurati frigore suae malitiae ab illo terrae uertice quo sedem suam posuit qui per elationem Altissimo similis esse concupiuit. Denique constat iuxta prophetae uaticinium quod ab aquilone uenit omne malum, sicut plus aequo didicere, perperam passi aduersos iactus cadentis tesserae, qui aquilonalium gentium experti sunt seuitiam.

[It is no wonder, since they will come hardened by the cold of their malice from that polar region in which he who desired through pride to be like the Most High placed his seat. Indeed it is well known in the prediction of the prophet that all evil comes from the north, as they have learned all too well who, suffering to their cost adverse cases of the die, have experienced the ferocity of the northern nations.]114

Abbo's audience in the early tenth century faced a comparable enemy in Scandinavians hailing from the North Sea, yet his response differs radically from Wulfstan's. While Patrick Wormald has noted that both Abbo and Wulfstan 'shared the view that the emergencies of the time demanded more concentrated attention to the Law of God and His Church',115 and while Abbo's residency on the Continent may have led him to have a similarly vexed relationship with the northern peoples of Scandinavia, Wulfstan nonetheless eschews characterisation of the vikings as icy devils 'indurati frigore' (hardened by cold),116 instead casting the English as the prime agents of their own undoing. When Wulfstan presents us with images of the vikings, his purpose is to demonstrate how the English go about subverting the natural order of things:

> And la, hu mæg mare scamu þurh Godes yrre mannum gelimpan þonne us deð gelome for agenum gewyrhtum? Ðeah þræla hwylc hlaforde ætleape ⁊ of cristendome to wicinge weorþe, ⁊ hit æfter þam eft geweorþe þæt wæpengewrixl weorðe gemæne þegene ⁊ þræle, gif þræl þænne þegen fullice afylle, licge ægylde ealre his mægðe.117

[And, alas, how can more shame befall men through the wrath of God than frequently happens to us on account of our own deeds? If any thrall escape from his lord and forsaking Christendom becomes a viking, and after that it happens that an armed encounter occurs between the thane and thrall, if the thrall should then slay the thane entirely, he will lie without compensation to any of his family.]

Wulfstan's purpose here is to show the frailty of allegiances and perhaps the fragility of the national identity of a people altogether. Furthermore, it significant that Wulfstan calls attention to men's 'agenum gewyrhtum' (own deeds) as the greatest source of their disorder and 'scamu' (shame) in society.

There is further reason to believe that Wulfstan may have wished to characterise the vikings more neutrally than Abbo. Earl explains: 'For two and a half centuries the Vikings shared more than just the slaughter-field with the Anglo-Saxons. They also shared, increasingly from the ninth-century on, a national culture.'118 Earl suggests that there was perhaps more assimilation and understanding between the two cultures than we might initially expect.

Wulfstan's role in the court of Cnut and his part in formulating the king's law codes may have made him more inclined to see similarities between the communities of the Anglo-Danes and the Anglo-Saxons. Wulfstan and others were beginning to see, rather than two different peoples, 'a single English people before God'.[119] As Godden notes, we get a much more nuanced view of the vikings from Wulfstan, in whose hands 'Anti-Christ and the vikings seem in fact to be very differently presented'.[120] Godden finds that Wulfstan's homily deliberately avoids registering eschatological undertones in favour of 'the longer and continuing movement of history'.[121] He ultimately suggests that Wulfstan differentiates between 'divine anger [which] is directed against a particular nation for particular sins' and apocalypse, which involves the whole world.[122] Such a characterisation bears on our understanding of the Gildas material. Godden is right, to my mind, when he suggests that through Gildas '[Wulfstan] was turning to a story which allowed for eventual acceptance of the invaders within the fold of religion and civilization'.[123]

Since we have several versions of *Sermo Lupi* that vary in length, there has been debate about whether the sermon underwent a process of 'abbreviation' or 'expansion'.[124] While some suggest that the E and I versions represent Wulfstan's final stage of revision, others argue that it must be the other way around and that Wulfstan must have derived his shorter versions from these longer renditions. Overall, critical interest tends to cluster around versions E and I because of the augmented Gildas material. As Joyce Hill has remarked, E and I reveal Wulfstan's heightened interest in setting his homily within 'the wider framework for God's plan for the whole of mankind'.[125] Lionarons suggests that the Gildas passage, in fact, recalls *Sermo* 6 in demonstrating 'a continuing cycle of sin, punishment, atonement, and redemption ... [as] he compares the conquest of the Britons ... to the impending conquest of the English by the Danes'.[126] Howe characterises events in a similar way, suggesting that, for Wulfstan, 'the English are about to follow the British into the margin of history'.[127] Howe argues that Wulfstan makes use of what he terms the Anglo-Saxon 'migration myth', that is, 'the idea that God has guided the Israelites to the promised land, so he guided the Anglo-Saxons to the promised land of Britain'.[128] I agree with Howe's thesis, and would extend its implications and suggest that the replacement doctrine and migration myth operate in tandem in the Anglo-Saxon imagination. Wulfstan is, in other words, interested in the 'afterlife' of

A new *praedestinati*

the 'migration myth', that is, the conversion of the English and their consequent role as Christian souls destined to migrate to the heavenly kingdom as alluded to in *Sermo* 6.

Roughly two centuries earlier, in response to the viking raid upon Lindisfarne in 793, Alcuin addressed Æthelhard, Archbishop of Canterbury (792–805), in his *Epistula Albini leuitae ad Aeðelhardum archiepiscopum* (II 10.107–17):

> I say this because of the scourge that has recently happened in parts of our island which for almost three hundred and forty years our parents inhabited. We read in the book of Gildas, the wisest of Britons, that those same Britons lost their homeland because of the excess and greed of princes, because of the violence and injustice of judges, on account of indolence and idleness of the bishops preaching, on account of the extravagance and bad more of the people. Let us take care that these same vices do not grow up in our times, that the divine blessing should keep our country in the good prosperity which it has deigned to grant us in its mercy.[129]

Alcuin sees the viking scourge through the prism of Gildas, who thought that the Britons fell to the invading Saxons because of their 'auaritia' (greed), 'iniustitia' (injustice), and widespread 'luxuria' (laziness), among other vices. This passage most likely struck a chord with Wulfstan owing to Alcuin's sense that the 'patria' (homeland) could be lost. The possibility of a lost homeland, of course, resonates with the core concern in narratives about the angelic rebellion: more than divine authority, splendour, or happiness, the fallen angels are most frequently depicted as missing the 'eard' (homeland) they forfeited through their sinfulness. Turning to older patterns to make sense of his contemporary one, Wulfstan draws upon Alcuin's reference to Gildas's *De Excidio Britanniae*. He writes:

> An þeodwita wæs on Brytta tidum Gildas hatte. Se awrat be heora misdædum hu hy mid heora synnum swa oferlice swyþe God gegræmedan þæt he let æt nyhstan Engla here heora eard gewinnan ⁊ Brytta dugeþe fordon mid ealle.[130]

[There was a historian in the time of the Britons called Gildas. He wrote about their misdeeds how by their sins they angered God so very excessively that finally he let the army of the English conquer their land and destroy the nobility of the Britons altogether.]

There are several aspects of this passage that parallel Anglo-Saxon ideas surrounding falls and replacements. The way in which

Wulfstan describes this conquest is reminiscent of his description of the Babylonian Captivity in *Sermo* 6, in which the Israelites became so sinful before God 'þæt he let faran hæþenne here forhergian eall þæt land' (that he let the heathen army go forth and destroy all that land). Here, God simply 'let' (let) the 'hæþenne here' (heathen army) take over.[131] Moreover, as I demonstrated, in sermons by both Ælfric and Wulfstan we see the alignment in their thinking about how Lucifer's crime results in a fall because God simply allows it to unfold; the Israelites similarly choose exclusion from their homeland.

Wulfstan's rendition of the replacement doctrine in *Sermo* 6 most closely resembles Augustine's views from the *Enchiridion ad Laurentium* 62 and 29 (CCSL 46.82; CCSL 46.65) and *De Civitate Dei* 22.1 (CCSL 48.807). In Ch. 62 of the *Enchiridion*, Augustine writes:

> Et utique nouerunt angeli sancti, docti de deo cuius ueritatis aeterna contemplatione beati sunt, quanti numeri supplementum de genere humano integritas illius ciuitatis exspectat ... Instaurantur quippe quae in caelis sunt, cum id quod inde in angelis lapsum est ex hominibus redditur; instaurantur autem quae in terris sunt, cum ipsi homines qui praedestinati sunt in aeternam uitam a corruptionis uetustate renouantur.

[And certainly, the holy angels, taught by God, who are blessed in the eternal contemplation of truth, know how great a number the completeness of that city requires as supplement from the human race ... For the things which are in heaven are restored when what was lost there from angels is returned from among men; but the things on earth are restored, when those who are predestined to eternal life are renewed from their old corruption.][132]

In light of the doctrine, Wulfstan's correlation of the English with the Britons suggests not that the vikings were forerunners of Antichrist, but that their descendants could replace the English as the rightful Christian rulers of their promised land, just as the Christian English were descended from pagan ancestors who had supplanted the Christian Britons. The still unconverted English were, in Gregory's famous conceit, like angels destined to become members of the community of elect who would restore the loss incurred at the fall of the rebel angels. Of course, by 1016 many of the most powerful noblemen had shifted their loyalties to Cnut. As Harris observes: 'Given the conversion to Christianity of earlier

A new *praedestinati*

waves of Danish settlers, it is not beyond imagination that Wulfstan conceived of the possibility of Viking conversion.'[133] Thus, the vikings could become, in Augustinian terms, 'praedestinati' (those who are predestined) for a homeland.

Since Augustine's notion of the doctrine of replacement is inextricably linked with his conception of reform, it makes sense that Wulfstan includes a reproach against lazy priests – one of his favourite topics – in versions E and I. His admonishment reads:[134]

> And þæt wæs geworden þæs þe he sæde, þurh ricra reaflac 7 þurh gitsunge wohgestreona, ðurh leode unlaga 7 þurh wohdomas, ðurh biscopa asolcennesse 7 þurh lyðre yrhðe Godes bydela þe soþes geswugedan ealles to gelome 7 clumedan mid ceaflum þær hy sceoldan clypian. Þurh fulne eac folces gælsan 7 þurh oferfylla 7 mænigfealde synna heora eard hy forworhtan 7 selfe hy forwurdan.[135]

[And as (Gildas) said that came about through theft by the powerful and through the desiring of wrongful acquisitions, through the lawlessness in a land and through unjust judgements, through the idleness of bishops and through the cowardice of God's ministers who all too often refrained from proclaiming the truth and instead mumbled with their jowls where they should have cried out. Likewise through the foul wantonness of the people and through gluttony and manifold sins they destroyed their country and they themselves perished.]

The inclusion of this passage, too, is tied to Wulfstan's interest in the role of the clergy in the schematics of replacement. According to Ladner, Augustine's view is that clergy are responsible for '[replenishing] the angelic host whose number was depleted by the fall of the rebel angels'.[136] This passage registers the same concerns Wulfstan outlined at the start of *Sermo* 6 (as well as those expressed by the anonymous homilist of Blickling 4) when he said that priests would be held accountable and 'ealra þæra sawla on domesdæg gescead agyldan þe þurh þæt losiað' (render an account to God on Doomsday for all those souls who are lost).[137] Thus, Wulfstan characterises the clergy as duly responsible for replenishment and accountable for loss. Significantly, instead of admonishing the English 'gefyllan 7 gemænigfealdan' (to fill and multiply) heaven, as Wulfstan describes in *Sermo* 6, in the Gildas passage Wulfstan ominously echoes and inverts the positive valences of this phrase, suggesting that, like the Britons, they are actively undoing this potential through 'oferfylla 7 mænigfealde synna' (gluttony and manifold sins) nature.[138] Their role as replacements was a defining feature of English Christian identity from Gregory's pun on *Angli* right down to Wulfstan's *Sermo ad Anglos*.[139] I think that Wulfstan relies on the long-standing intertextual nature of the fall of the Britons tradition from Gildas to Bede to Alcuin, which enables him to leave his rehearsal of the replacement doctrine and the fall of the angels implicit in his homily.

Wulfstan reinforces the idea that English history is filled with rebellion against both divine and temporal authority. According to Trilling, the Gildas passage was initially picked up by Bede 'as a source for the history of pre-Conversion England'.[140] Trilling observes, however, that 'Bede turns the model on its head and interprets them instead as God's sanction of the Anglo-Saxons as replacements for the dissolute Britons … [reconstruing] the *adventus Saxonum* as God's designation of a chosen people'.[141] The key concept for this progression, and for Wulfstan's figuration of the vikings not as Antichrists, but as possible Christians, lies in his observance of the replacement doctrine. As Howe puts it, from Gildas to Wulfstan, 'history repeats itself – or threatens to repeat itself – because God works through the same pattern: the island must be cleansed of its sinful inhabitants by heathen outsiders'.[142] As we saw, for Abbo, the vikings were proud, violent, rebellious, and demonic. But for Wulfstan, matters were not so cut and dried. On the subject of viking and Anglo-Saxon relations, Earl observes: 'The Vikings were too much a part of Anglo-Saxon culture to be conveniently demonised … The two groups evolved an awkward, intimate antagonism. North and south defined themselves partly in relation to each other, as they still do.'[143] Szarmach similarly suggests that in the many texts that focus on Christian-heathen conflict, the vikings often become a psychological mirror to hold up to a country's own moral corruption.[144] In texts such as *The Battle of Maldon*, for instance, 'conflict operates within a set of narrative expectations … [existing] within a definable yet unfixed horizon'.[145] Wulfstan similarly situates *Sermo Lupi* firmly within this framework. By avoiding direct comparisons between the invaders as bloodthirsty barbarians, idol-worshipers, and wolf-like marauders, Wulfstan's characterisation of the vikings defies conventional literary expectations as he works to disrupt and alter expectations about viking identity through the well-known matrix for the conversion of the English, the migration myth, and, here, the evocation (via Gildas) of the replacement doctrine.

Wulfstan, moreover, rewrites the 'horizon of expectations' for the topos of the fall of the angels. Edgar and Æthelwold linked the rebel angels with the secular canons at Winchester at the start of the Benedictine Reform. In their writings, the rebel angels become mirrors for English Christian identity at large and an image of what will happen if the English relinquish their divinely envisioned position within salvation history. Once used to characterise secular clerics such as himself, Wulfstan resituates the narrative onto the body politic, calling upon the English not to lose their role as replacements in his own historical moment. According to Trilling, 'Wulfstan offers a path to salvation in place of the expected apocalypse – especially in light of the coming millennium. His rhetorical stance reinscribes England, on the verge of conquest, into the larger identity of Christendom, and thus preserves a sense of England's integrity at a moment of crisis'.[146] In this way, *Sermo Lupi* is not only a warning about a specific crisis, but also a reminder of earlier periods of turmoil that the converted English are meant to rectify through their faith and obedience to God.

Wulfstan's inclusion of the narrative of the fall of the Britons warns the English that their disloyalty and disorder threatens them with the same fate, but also offers them a chance to reaffirm loyalty to God's sovereignty. Living in a time of renewed viking devastation, he calls upon the English to reaffirm their role as steadfast Christians in the final lines of *Sermo Lupi*:

> And utan word ⁊ weorc rihtlice fadian ⁊ ure ingeþanc clænsian georne ⁊ að ⁊ wed wærelice healdan ⁊ sume getrywða habban us betweonan butan uncræftan.[147]

[And let us set in order words and works aright, and earnestly cleanse our conscience, and carefully keep oaths and pledges, and have some loyalty between us without deceit.]

Here, Wulfstan reveals the overlap between personal obedience, social order, and divine order. He deploys a rich lexicon of verbs denoting penance in thought, word, and deed, calling upon the English to 'beþencan' (consider), 'don' (act), 'gebugan' (submit), 'betan' (atone), 'lufian' (love), 'fylgean' (follow), 'gelæstan' (practice), 'fadian' (set in order), 'clænsian' (cleanse), 'healdan' (keep) oaths and pledges, and 'geearnian' (earn) their place in the kingdom of heaven.

As an Anglo-Saxon bishop and author who was deeply connected to political spheres, Wulfstan was concerned about the place of God's law and the law of the land.[148] His interest in the law and its role in the lives of Christians was a career-long preoccupation, and what emerges in his works is a distinct way of imagining the return to order through adherence to the law and the sacred. 'Homilies', as Andrew Rabin puts it, provide a model for ordering 'social relations ... [producing] the self-reflection necessary to re-internalize the rule of God'.[149] Wulfstan maintains that, like the fallen angels, individuals are capable of radically undoing themselves through improper recognition of sovereign authority.[150] If we can read Lucifer's desire to be *efengelica* in *Sermo* 6 as related to Wulfstan's distress over his nation's disobedience in *Sermo Lupi*, it would suggest that Wulfstan used this originary moment to better comprehend the dangers he saw in his contemporary world.

It is important to recognise the trace of the narrative of replacement in *Sermo Lupi*, and Wulfstan's sense that the English were actively erasing their place within salvation history. As Paul Kahn explains, 'when the narrative of a polity disappears, when all that we have left are broken remains of buildings and shards of artifacts, the human is reduced to the material'.[151] In this regard, we might think of the bleak and foreboding landscapes in *The Wanderer* and *The Ruin* as what Wulfstan fears will be the fate of his polity if English Christians lose their connection to God's sovereignty. While other Anglo-Saxon homilies provide vivid accounts of the fall of the rebel angels, Wulfstan isolated aspects of the story that informed his thinking about the fate of his nation at a time of crisis involving disloyalty, pride, ruin, and a precarious replacement. Furthermore, we see Wulfstan attentively engaging with Christian doctrine in order to frame his argument. Such a complex deployment of theological ideas leads me to disagree with Greenfield and Calder when they state that '[Wulfstan's] approach is hortatory and topical, and his sermons minimise doctrinal and intellectual concerns'.[152] On the contrary, Wulfstan utilises doctrine to conceptualise his community's dominant narrative. Wulfstan picks up the doctrine of replacement, already a proven ideological weapon, where the early reformers left off, urging Anglo-Saxon Christians not to lose their foothold upon the land.

Critics have often characterised Wulfstan's *Sermo Lupi* as the rendition of a 'divine punishment', yet we might think of this homily as the re-enactment of a 'divine replacement'. For Anglo-Saxons, patterns of conquest and invasion were also cycles of falls and replacements. Old English texts from *Maxims* to the *Elegies* to *Beowulf* betray this curious taste for dramatic reversals of fortune. The fall of the angels was perhaps the original and, one could argue, the most popular in the Anglo-Saxon imagination. Wulfstan exploits this taste to the fullest measure, challenging the *þeod* not to let their own reversal come full circle.

Notes

1 Simon Keynes, 'An Abbot, an Archbishop, and the Viking Raids of 1006–7 and 1009–12', *ASE*, 36 (2007), 151– 220 (pp. 181–3). Several homiletic adaptations refer to the edict: Napier 35 'On Various Misfortunes'. Andrew Rabin has recently edited Napier 35 in *The Political Writings of Archbishop Wulfstan of York* (Manchester: Manchester University Press, 2015), pp. 131–2.
2 Liebermann, *Gesetze*, 2.
3 Rabin, *Political Writings*, p. 185.
4 Liebermann, *Gesetze*, 2.1; see Keynes 'An Abbot, an Archbishop', pp. 186–7; Pauline Stafford, *Unification and Conquest: A Political and Social History of England in the Tenth and Eleventh Centuries* (London: Edward Arnold, 1989) suggests that the increased number of viking attacks led to a 'raised historical consciousness' (p. 11).
5 This formula recurs throughout *Sermo Lupi ad Anglos* (ll. 29; 31; 55; 112).
6 To this point, see Barrow, 'The Ideology of the Tenth-Century English Benedictine "Reform"', pp. 141–54.
7 On the date, see Keynes, *The Diplomas of King Æthelred*, p. 167.
8 *The Anglo-Saxon Chronicle: A Collaborative Edition, Volume 7: MS E*, ed. Susan Irvine (Cambridge: D. S. Brewer, 2004), pp. 59–60. On the death of Edward, see Nicole Marafioti, *The King's Body: Burial and Succession in Late Anglo-Saxon England* (Toronto: University of Toronto Press, 2014), pp. 161–91.
9 *The Anglo-Saxon Chronicle: A Collaborative Edition, Volume 5: MS C*, ed. Katherine O'Brien O'Keeffe (Cambridge: D. S. Brewer, 2001).
10 *The Anglo-Saxon Chronicle: A Collaborative Edition, Volume 6: MS D*, ed. G. P. Cubbin (Cambridge: D. S. Brewer, 1996), p. 62.
11 *ASC MS E*, ed. Irvine, p. 73.
12 Among critics who have taken up this question are Stephanie Hollis, 'The Thematic Structure of the *Sermo Lupi ad Anglos*', *ASE*, 6 (1977), 175–95 and Joyce Tally Lionarons, *The Homiletic Writings of Archbishop Wulfstan: A Critical Study* (Woodbridge: Boydell, 2010). For an alternative to reading, see Malcolm R. Godden, 'Apocalypse and Invasion in Late Anglo-Saxon England', in *From Anglo-Saxon to Early Middle English: Studies Presented to E. G. Stanley*, ed. Malcolm Godden, Douglas Gray, and Terry Hoad (Oxford: Clarendon Press, 1994), pp. 130–62.
13 For a list of homilies containing material on the fall of the angels see Robert DiNapoli, *An Index of Theme and Image*, p. 41.

14 Renée R. Trilling, 'Sovereignty and Social Order: Archbishop Wulfstan and the *Institutes of Polity*', in *The Bishop Reformed: Studies of Episcopal Power and Culture in the Central Middle Ages*, ed. John S. Ott and Anna Trumbore Jones (Burlington, VT: Ashgate, 2007), pp. 58–85 (p. 69).
15 David N. Dumville, *Wessex and England from Alfred to Edgar: Six Essays on Political, Cultural, and Ecclesiastical Revival*, Studies in Anglo-Saxon History 3 (Woodbridge: Boydell, 1992), p. 145.
16 Fisher, 'The Anti-Monastic Reaction', 254–70.
17 *The Old English Heptateuch*, ed. Marsden, pp. 3–7.
18 See Stoneman, 'A Critical Edition', and MacLean, 'Ælfric's Version of *Alcuini Interrogationes Sigeuulfi*'; Ælfric, *Exameron*, ed. S. J. Crawford, *Exameron Anglice or The Old English Hexameron*, Bibliothek der angelsächsischen Prosa 10 (Hamburg: Grand, 1921); *Ælfric's Catholic Homilies: The First Series. Text*, ed. Peter Clemoes, EETS ss 17 (Oxford: Oxford University Press, 1997).
19 *The Old English Heptateuch*, ed. Marsden, pp. 201–30.
20 The story of Wulfgeat appears in the *ASC* (E) in the year 1006 and S 934. Wulfgeat most likely lived at Ilmington (roughly 30 miles from Eynsham, where Ælfric was serving as a newly elected abbot).
21 *Angelsächsische Homilien und Heiligenleben*, ed. Assman, pp. 1–12.
22 Keynes, *The Diplomas of King Æthelred*, p. 211.
23 Paul Szarmach, 'Ælfric as Exegete: Approaches and Examples in the Study of the *Sermones Catholici*', in *Hermeneutics and Medieval Culture*, ed. P. Gallacher and H. Damico (Albany, NY: SUNY Press, 1989), pp. 237–47 (p. 241).
24 Fox, 'Ælfric on the Creation and Fall of the Angels', p. 176.
25 Patrick Wormald, 'Archbishop Wulfstan: Eleventh-Century State-Builder', in *Wulfstan, Archbishop of York*, ed. Townend, SEMA 10 (Turnhout: Brepols, 2004), pp. 9–27 (p. 12); Keynes, 'An Abbot, an Archbishop', p. 170.
26 Jonathan Wilcox, 'The Wolf on Shepherds: Wulfstan, Bishops, and the Context of the *Sermo Lupi ad Anglos*', in *Old English Prose*, ed. Paul E. Szarmach, Basic Readings in Anglo-Saxon England 5 (New York: Garland, 2000), p. 395.
27 Andy Orchard, 'Wulfstan as Reader, Writer, and Rewriter', in *The Old English Homily: Precedent, Practice, and Appropriation*, ed. Aaron J Kleist, SEMA 17 (Turnhout: Brepols, 2007), pp. 157–82.
28 Dorothy Whitelock, 'Archbishop Wulfstan, Homilist and Statesman', in *Transactions of the Royal Historical Society*, 24 (1942), 24–45; Wormald, 'Archbishop Wulfstan', pp. 9–27.
29 Wormald, 'Archbishop Wulfstan', p. 25.
30 Keynes, 'An Abbot, an Archbishop', p. 154.
31 Dorothy Bethurum, 'Wulfstan', in *Continuations and Beginnings:*

Studies in Old English Literature, ed. E. G. Stanley (London and Edinburgh: Nelson, 1966), pp. 210–44 (pp. 210–11).
32 On Swein's objectives, see Stafford, *Unification and Conquest*, p. 66.
33 Ibid., p. 379.
34 Jonathan Wilcox, 'Wulfstan's *Sermo Lupi ad Anglos* as Political Performance: 16 February 1014 and Beyond', in *Wulfstan, Archbishop of York*, ed. Townend, SEMA 10 (Turnhout: Brepols, 2004), pp. 373–96 (p. 378).
35 Joyce Hill, 'Archbishop Wulfstan: Reformer?', in *Wulfstan, Archbishop of York*, ed. Townend, SEMA 10 (Turnhout: Brepols, 2004), pp. 309–24.
36 These letters have been edited in Whitelock, *Councils and Synods*, pp. 242–302.
37 J. Hill, 'Archbishop Wulfstan: Reformer?', pp. 313–4; Malcolm Godden, 'The Relations of Wulfstan and Ælfric: A Reassessment', in *Wulfstan, Archbishop of York*, ed. Townend, SEMA 10 (Turnhout: Brepols, 2004), pp. 353–74.
38 Trilling, 'Sovereignty and Social Order', p. 59.
39 Lionarons, *Homiletic Writings*, p. 163. Bethurum observes that 'Wulfstan was apparently very much occupied with problems attendant upon the victory of the Danes' especially 'the tutoring of Cnut and assisting in his transformation from a Viking war-lord to a model Christian king' ('Wulfstan', p. 214).
40 For a helpful overview and chronology of Wulfstan's works, see Wormald's Appendix, 'Archbishop Wulfstan', pp. 26–7.
41 Orchard, 'Wulfstan as Reader', p. 319.
42 Christopher A. Jones, 'Wulfstan's Liturgical Interests', in *Wulfstan, Archbishop of York*, ed. Townend, SEMA 10 (Turnhout: Brepols, 2004), pp. 325–52 (p. 350).
43 See Andy Orchard, 'Re-editing Wulfstan: Where's the Point?', in *Wulfstan, Archbishop of York*, ed. Townend, SEMA 10 (Turnhout: Brepols, 2004), pp. 63–91 and Andy Orchard, 'On Editing Wulfstan', in *Early Medieval Texts and Interpretations: Studies Presented to Donald G. Scragg*, ed. Elaine Treharne and Susan Rosser (Tempe: ACMRS, 2003), pp. 311–40. Bethurum accepted Napier 23, 24, 25, 35, 36, 39, 50, 51, 52, 59, and 61 as authentic although she did not print them in her edition. Orchard says that this has left these Napier homilies in a kind of 'limbo' ('Re-editing', p. 318).
44 *Wulfstan: Sammlung der ihm zugeschriebenen Homilien nebst Untersuchungen über ihre Echtheit*, ed. Arthur S. Napier (Berlin: Weidmann, 1883; repr. Dublin and Zürich: 1967); see also Patrick Wormald, 'Archbishop Wulfstan and the Holiness of Society', in *Anglo-Saxon History: Basic Readings*, ed. David A. E. Pelteret (New York: Garland, 2000), pp. 191–224 (p. 191).
45 C. F. R. Becher, *Wulfstans Homilien* (Leipzig: Sturm and Koppe,

1910); Karl Jost, *Wulfstanstudien*, Swiss Studies in English 23 (Bern: Francke, 1950); Angus McIntosh, 'Wulfstan's Prose', *Proceedings of the British Academy*, 34 (1949), pp. 109–42; repr. in *British Academy Papers on Anglo-Saxon England*, ed. E. G. Stanley (Oxford: Oxford University Press, 1990), pp. 111–44; Leslie Whitbread, 'Wulfstan's Homilies XXIX, XXX, and Some Related Texts', *Anglia*, 81 (1963), 347–64; Donald G. Scragg, 'Napier's 'Wulfstan' Homily XXX: Its Sources, its Relationship to the Vercelli Book and its Style', *ASE*, 6 (1977), 197–211; Wright, 'More Old English Poetry', pp. 245–62.

46 McIntosh, 'Wulfstan's Prose', p. 143 (n. 29).
47 *The Vercelli Homilies*, ed. Scragg, Appendix (397.54–62).
48 Scragg, 'Napier's "Wulfstan" Homily', p. 198.
49 Wright, 'More Old English Poetry', p. 258.
50 Ed. and trans. Wright, 'More Old English Poetry', corresponding to *The Vercelli Homilies*, ed. Scragg, 357.141–9.
51 Vercelli 19 says that God 'with his breath blew' Satan out of heaven (*The Vercelli Homilies*, ed. Scragg, 316.15). For further discussion see Thomas D. Hill, 'When God Blew Satan out of Heaven', pp. 132–41.
52 Scragg suggests that Napier 30 was made in Canterbury and that the author may have had access to the same exemplars as the Vercelli compiler ('Napier's "Wulfstan" Homily', p. 210).
53 Jost, *Wulfstanstudien*, pp. 208–19.
54 On the technique, see Day, 'Catechetical *narratio*', pp. 51–61.
55 Wormald, 'Archbishop Wulfstan', p. 26.
56 Thomas N. Hall, 'Wulfstan's Latin Sermons', in *Wulfstan, Archbishop of York*, ed. Townend, SEMA 10 (Turnhout: Brepols, 2004), pp. 93–139 (p. 102).
57 Wulfstan, *The Homilies of Wulfstan*, ed. Dorothy Bethurum (Oxford: Clarendon Press, 1957), 142–3.10–4. References to Wulfstan's homilies are by page number and line number.
58 Ibid., 143.24.
59 Ibid., 143–4.24–33.
60 The M version (British Library, Cotton Otho B.x) reads that Lucifer 'wolde dalan rice wið God ælmihtigne'. See Jonathan Wilcox, 'The Dissemination of Wulfstan's Homilies: The Wulfstan Tradition in Eleventh-Century Vernacular Preaching', in *England in the Eleventh Century: Proceedings of the 1990 Harlaxton Symposium*, ed. Carola Hicks, Harlaxton Medieval Studies 2 (Stamford: Paul Watkins, 1992), pp. 199–217 (p. 209).
61 Hall, 'The Old English Epic of Redemption', pp. 20–52, and 'Twenty-Five-Year Retrospective', pp. 53–68.
62 Lionarons, *Homiletic Writings*, p. 83.
63 Jost, *Wulfstanstudien*, pp. 55–61. Lionarons notes that Pirmin often excerpts from sermons by Caesarius of Arles, Martin of Braga's *De*

correctione rusticorum, and the Benedictine Rule (*Homiletic Writings*, p. 93).
64 See S. J. Hollis, 'The Sources of Wulfstan of York Homily 6 (Cameron C.B.2.2.1)', 2002, *Fontes Anglo-Saxonici: World Wide Web Register*, http://fontes.english.ox.ac.uk/, accessed July 2017.
65 *Die Heimat des Hl. Pirmin des Apostels der Alamannen*, ed. Gall Jecker, Beiträge zur Geschichte des alten Mönchtums und des Benediktinerordens 13 (Munich: Aschendorff, 1927).
66 CH I.1.26–45. Translations of the *Catholic Homilies* are Benjamin Thorpe's, with minor alternations.
67 On these modifications, see Scragg, 'Napier's "Wulfstan" Homily XXX', p. 208. On the Old English word-field for 'pride' see W. Hofsetter, 'Winchester and the Standardization of Old English Vocabulary', *ASE*, 17 (1988), 139–61.
68 CH I.1.51–61.
69 For the legal usages of this phrase, see Karl Jost, 'The Legal Maxim in Ælfric's Homilies', *ES*, 36 (1955), 204–5; Malcolm Godden, 'Ælfric and Anglo-Saxon Kingship', *The English Historical Review*, 102 (1987), 911–15.
70 For a discussion of *agen cyre*, see O'Brien O'Keeffe, *Stealing Obedience*, pp. 9–54.
71 Ibid., p. 15.
72 Ibid., p. 21.
73 Ibid., p. 22.
74 *Ælfric's Libellus*, ed. Marsden, p. 203, l. 59.
75 Fox notes that this sequence derives from Martin of Braga's description of Lucifer's self-recognition ('Ælfric on the Fall of the Angels', p. 185); see *Martin von Bracara's Schrift De correctione rusticorum*, ed. Carl Paul Caspari (Oslo: Gedruckt in der Mallingsche Buchdruckerei, 1883).
76 *Ælfric's Libellus*, ed. Marsden, p. 203, ll. 69–77.
77 On this point, see Thomas D. Hill, 'Satan's Pratfall and the Foot of Love', pp. 157–8.
78 *Ælfric's Libellus*, ed. Marsden, p. 203, ll. 78–82.
79 *The Homilies of Wulfstan*, ed. Bethurum, 144–5.36–44. Translation draws upon Haines, 'Vacancies in Heaven', with minor alterations.
80 Bosworth-Toller, *ungerim*, sense 1.
81 Lionarons, *Homiletic Writings*, p. 85.
82 Ibid.
83 On Wulfstan's self-fashioning as a 'fiery preacher', see Andy Orchard, 'Crying Wolf: Oral Style and the *Sermones Lupi*', *ASE*, 21 (1992), 239–64.
84 O'Brien O'Keeffe, *Stealing Obedience*, p. 14.
85 *The City of God*, trans. Henry Bettenson (London: Penguin, 2003), p. 1023.

86 On Augustinian notions of replacement and reform, see Ladner, *The Idea of Reform*, pp. 126 and 240–1.
87 Ibid., p. 277.
88 *Property and Piety*, ed. and trans. Rumble, p. 75.
89 On the varying versions, see Godden, 'Apocalypse and Invasion', pp. 144–62; Lionarons, *Homiletic Writings*, pp. 43–74; and Andrew Rabin, 'The Wolf's Testimony to the English: Law and the Witness in the *Sermo Lupi ad Anglos*', *JEGP*, 105 (2006), 388–414.
90 *The Homilies of Wulfstan*, ed. Bethurum, 271.100–28.
91 Hollis, 'Thematic Structure', p. 176.
92 Gildas, *The Ruin of Britain and Other Works*, ed. and trans. Michael Winterbottom (Sussex: Phillimore, 1978).
93 Hollis, 'Thematic Structure', p. 177.
94 Raachel Jurovics, '*Sermo Lupi* and the Moral Purpose of Rhetoric', in *The Old English Homily and Its Background*, ed. Paul E. Szarmach and Bernard F. Huppé (Albany: University of New York Press, 1978), pp. 203–20 (p. 213).
95 Howe, *Migration and Mythmaking*, p. 4ff.
96 *The Homilies of Wulfstan*, ed. Bethurum, 272.138–46.
97 On the recurrence of lord-rebellion during the eleventh century, see *Sermo Lupi ad Anglos*, ed. Dorothy Whitelock (London: Methuen, 1963), who observes that 'the frequency of references to treachery is one of the most striking features of the records of this period ... there is mention of an Essex conspiracy, as early as 994, to accept Swegn as king ... and in 1006 the Berkshire estates of a king's thegn, Wulfgeat, were forfeited because he leagued with the king's enemies. In 1009 Wulfnoth the South Saxon is in open rebellion and before 1012 a certain Leofric, in Wiltshire, had forfeited his lands for rebelling against the king's troops. Treachery towards one's lord incurs the death penalty in the laws' (Af 4, II As 4, III Edg 7.3, II Cn 57, 64, 77; V Atr (28–31)' (pp. 55–6, n. 73).
98 See *Konungs skuggsiá*, ed. Ludvig, Holm-Olsen, Gammelnorske tekster 1 (Oslo: Norsk Historisk Kjeldskrift-Instituutt, 1945; repr. 1983).
99 Of course, many Danes had converted to Christianity by Wulfstan's time. For a helpful overview, see Audrey L. Meaney, 'Old English Legal and Penitential Rituals for "Heathenism"', in *Anglo-Saxons: Studies Presented to Cyril Roy Hart*, ed. Simon Keynes and Alfred P. Smyth (Dublin: Four Courts Press, 2006), pp. 127–58. See also Lesley Abrams, 'The Conversion of the Danelaw', in *Vikings and the Danelaw: Select Papers from the Proceedings of the Thirteenth Viking Congress*, ed. James Graham-Campbell, Richard Hall, Judith Jesch, and David N. Parsons (Oxford: Oxbow Books, 2001), pp. 31–44. On Wulfstan's representation of ethnic identity, see especially Stephen J. Harris, *Race and Ethnicity in Anglo-Saxon Literature* (New York: Routledge, 2003), pp. 107–30.

100 Harris, *Race and Ethnicity*, p. 126.
101 Ibid., p. 126.
102 Ibid., p. 108.
103 Lionarons, *Homiletic Writings*, p. 159.
104 *The Homilies of Wulfstan*, ed. Bethurum, 270.71–5.
105 Fred Robinson, 'God, Death, and Loyalty in *The Battle of Maldon*', in *The Tomb of Beowulf and Other Essays on Old English* (Cambridge, MA: Blackwell, 1993), pp. 105–21 (pp. 119–20).
106 Ibid., p. 119.
107 *The Homilies of Wulfstan*, ed. Bethurum, 271.111–12.
108 Lionarons, *Homiletic Writings*, p. 159.
109 Hollis, 'Thematic Structure', p. 185.
110 Lionarons, *Homiletic Writings*, p. 157.
111 James Earl, 'Violence and Non-Violence in Anglo-Saxon England: Ælfric's "Passion of St. Edmund"', *PQ*, 78 (1999), 125–49.
112 On the differences between Ælfric's and Abbo's account of St Edmund, see Earl ('Violence and Non-Violence', p. 132).
113 Ibid., p. 128.
114 Abbo of Fleury, *Passio Sancti Eadmundi*, in *Three Lives of English Saints*, ed. Michael Winterbottom (Toronto: PIMS, 1972), 71.8–14. I thank Charles D. Wright for his assistance with translating this passage in particular.
115 Wormald, 'Archbishop Wulfstan', p. 17.
116 Godden, 'Apocalypse and Invasion', p. 152.
117 *The Homilies of Wulfstan*, ed. Bethurum, 271.100–5.
118 Earl, 'Violence and Non-Violence', p. 126.
119 Harris, *Race and Ethnicity*, p. 109.
120 Godden, 'Apocalypse and Invasion', p. 153; Godden, *Relations of Wulfstan and Ælfric*, p. 374.
121 Ibid., p. 152.
122 Ibid., p. 154.
123 Godden, 'Apocalypse and Invasion', p. 156.
124 On the transmission of the three versions, see Stephanie Dien, '*Sermo Lupi ad Anglos*: The Order and Date of the Three Versions', *NM*, 76 (1975), 561–70; Godden, 'Apocalypse and Invasion', pp. 130–62; Wilcox, '*Sermo Lupi ad Anglos* as Political Performance', pp. 375–96; Keynes, 'An Abbot, an Archbishop', pp. 151–220; Lionarons, *Homiletic Writings*, pp. 43–74.
125 J. Hill, 'Archbishop Wulfstan: Reformer?', p. 234.
126 Lionarons, *Homiletic Writings*, p. 157.
127 Howe, *Migration and Mythmaking*, p. 18.
128 Ibid., p. 16.
129 *Two Alcuin Letter-Books*, ed. and trans. Colin Chase, Toronto Medieval Latin Texts 5 (Toronto, PIMS, 1975), 74.107–17.
130 *The Homilies of Wulfstan*, ed. Bethurum, 274.176–9.

131 Ibid., 149.116–17. Godden suggests that Wulfstan's '[e]mphasis gradually shifted from the apocalyptic crisis to the national one' ('Apocalypse and Invasion', p. 154).
132 My translation draws upon Haines's as it appears in 'Vacancies in Heaven', p. 151.
133 Harris, *Race and Ethnicity*, p. 122.
134 On this topoi, see Wilcox, 'The Wolf on Shepherds', pp. 395–418. According to Wilcox, the sermon uses the image of a lax cleric as a bad shepherd (p. 399).
135 *The Homilies of Wulfstan*, ed. Bethurum, 274.180–186.
136 Ladner, *The Idea of Reform*, p. 277.
137 *The Homilies of Wulfstan*, ed. Bethurum, 142–3.11–3.
138 Wulfstan uses *gælsan* ('wantonness') to describe the sins of the Britons. Variants appear as *gal* and *galscipe* in *Genesis B*, ll. 327a, 341a with reference to the sins of the rebel angels (see Doane, *The Saxon Genesis*, n. 267).
139 Howe suggests that Gildas, Bede, Alcuin, and Wulfstan were the central figures in the 'process of mythmaking' for Anglo-Saxon England (*Migration and Mythmaking*, p. 2).
140 Trilling, *The Aesthetics of Nostalgia*, p. 136.
141 Ibid., p. 138.
142 Howe, *Migration and Mythmaking*, p. 12.
143 Earl, 'Violence and Non-Violence', p. 142.
144 Paul Szarmach, 'The (Sub-) Genre of *The Battle of Maldon*', in *The Battle of Maldon Fact and Fiction*, ed. Janet Cooper (London: The Hambledon Press, 1993), pp. 43–61.
145 Ibid., p. 61.
146 Trilling, *The Aesthetics of Nostalgia*, p. 149.
147 *The Homilies of Wulfstan*, ed. Bethurum, 275.195–7.
148 Trilling, 'Sovereignty and Social Order', p. 77.
149 Rabin, 'The Wolf's Testimony to the English', p. 408.
150 Hollis suggests that repentance must take the form of the restoration of *lagu* and *riht* ('Thematic Structure', p. 181).
151 Paul W. Kahn, *Political Theology: Four New Chapters on the Concept of Sovereignty* (New York: Columbia University Press, 2011), p. 108.
152 Greenfield and Calder, *A New Critical History*, p. 89.

Afterword

Considering its prevalence in the Anglo-Saxon corpus, the narrative of the fall of the angels might be all too easily dismissed as a literary or liturgical commonplace. The present study, however, has traced its diverse literary and political implications and uses in elite and popular contexts, in Old English and Anglo-Latin poetry and prose. These tell us that the ancient myth of the fall of the angels and its core repertoire of themes inflected Anglo-Saxon ideas about physical space, about early Christian identity, and about the sacralisation of political authority and demonisation of rebellion. Another way of putting it: adaptations of the fall of the angels narrative were shaped by and, in turn, shaped both the ecclesiastical and wider social worlds of early medieval England.

The story of the fall of the angels in Anglo-Saxon England is, then, the story of a popular exegetical and apocryphal teaching turned rich literary tradition.[1] I began this study with a consideration of the Christian-Latin traditions and apocryphal comparanda that found a residence in the minds and works of medieval men and women who subsequently fashioned for it an improbable literary legacy. From Bede's *In Genesin* to Werferth's *Dialogues* and the translated works of Alfred's circle, to the documents recording the dissensions and proclaiming the triumphs of Benedictine Reform, to the sermons of Ælfric, and the biblical poetry of the Junius Manuscript, we see how the fall of the angels muscularly crisscrossed literary, theological, and political spheres, revealing the porous boundaries between them. Along the way, I have argued that Anglo-Saxon authors used this extra-biblical narrative to construct and interrogate institutional modes of authority by rendering the fall of the angels in spatially, temporally, and culturally legible terms. They converted esoteric doctrinal matters into a symbolic language that addressed contemporary concerns, supplying lessons from salvation history to early English readers and auditors who saw themselves as participants within an ongoing biblical narrative.

The narrative perhaps had its most secure and enduring foothold in the ecclesiastical world. It is therefore unsurprising that authors such as Æthelwold and the anonymous homilist of Blickling 4 use the story to explain corruption and decay within the Church. In their hands, the fall of the angels becomes a didactic tool encouraging the reform of lapsed religious communities and errant priestly behaviours. With its complex hermeneutic Latin, Æthelwold's New Minster Charter propagandises the story of the fallen angels, fixing it as the mythical origin and backdrop for the most significant Church reforms of the age. This foundational historical document offers us flashes of insight into the men and women to whom this story mattered, not just as a vivid yet remote moment in salvation history, but as a potent leverage in contemporary polemics. The charter's lengthy witness list even gives us the names of those who would have been familiar with its content, even though Æthelwold's arcane and highly stylised Latin would have deliberately occluded meaning for some.

Nevertheless, the story of the angelic rebellion was not solely intended for religious men in high places and inner circles. Some of the earliest accounts of the fall of the angels in the British Isles were written for women. Aldhelm addresses his *Carmen de virginitate* to Abbess Hildelith and the nuns at Barking Abbey. Both his prose and poetic works on the virtue of chastity discuss the best methods for counteracting the deadly pride that led to the fall of the angels. In his poetic account, Aldhelm describes Satan as a 'Monster' who took his 'beginnings on the high summits of heaven ... [he] eagerly desired to promote his own greatness from the north and in his wickedness vowed to be like the Lord'.[2] Adorned with a necklace of gemstones, Lucifer conceives his crimes by saying that 'he might be equal to the Lord with his own powers'. Aldhelm proposes that chastity means little if one succumbs to pride and vanity, which he often figures as a fierce, tyrannical queen.[3] Aldhelm's theory of the fall reveals the narrative's capacity for reaching a wide audience, even an exclusively female community. And he was not alone. The twelfth-century *Ancrene Wisse* – a handbook also intended for women – similarly places emphasis on the inherent dangers of vanity and sight. The author states that when Lucifer saw himself and 'biheold on him-seolf his ahne feiernesse', he immediately 'leop into prude ant bicom of engel eatelich deovel'.[4]

Afterword

The ecclesiastical legacy of the fall of the angels became the narrative's primary offshoot in the post-Conquest period. A version of Ælfric's homily 'De Initio Creaturae' can be found in the twelfth-century Vespasian D. xiv.[5] The story of the fall of the angels also later appears in *Cursor Mundi* and the Auchinleck MS *Life of Adam*. In addition to the *Pearl* poet's account in *Cleanness*, a further example can be found in the prose *Life of Adam and Eve* in the Vernon Manuscript,[6] and a poem on the 'Fall and Passion' preserved in London, British Library, MS Harley 913. The Vernon Manuscript was most certainly meant for use in a religious context as an instructional tract for clerics. The text describes how angels are called upon to participate in the exaltation of Adam. But when they convene to honour him, Lucifer refuses. In front of the entire company of angels, Lucifer makes his complaint: 'I was er Adam!' before the booming voice of God then interrupts with, 'I was er then thou'. Whereas Vernon focuses on the vexed relationship between Lucifer and humankind, as well as the question of seniority, the *Pearl* poet emphasises the fraught relationship between Lucifer and God in *Cleanness*, which describes how Lucifer (the 'falce fende') and the rebel angels fall from heaven like a powerful snowstorm ('snaw þikke'):

> For þe fyrste felonye þe falce fende wroȝt
> Whyl he watz hyȝe in þe heuen houen vpon lofte,
> Of alle þyse aþel aungelez attled þe fayrest:
> And he vnkyndely, as a karle, kydde a reward.
> He seȝ noȝt bot hymself how semly he were,
> Bot his Souerayn he forsoke and sade þyse wordez:
> 'I schal telde vp my trone in þe tramountayne,
> And by lyke to þat Lorde þat þe lyft made.'
> With þis worde þat he warp, þe wrake on hym lyȝt:
> Dryȝtyn with His dere dom hym drof to þe abyme,
> In þe mesure of His mode, His metz neuer þe lasse.
> Bot þer He tynt þe type dool of His tour ryche. (ll. 205–15)

The poet suggests that in fixating upon his radiant appearance, Lucifer's offence is the transgressive emulation of authority.[7] The association between God and Lucifer in the poem and the cycle dramas of the later Middle Ages resembles the kind of relationship to be found between a sovereign lord and foolish noble who oversteps the bounds of a clearly defined social hierarchy.[8] In many of these later medieval contexts, the fall of the angels appears to reinforce purity, obedience, and teach the dangers of self-love. Fallen away, to a certain extent, are the connections to issues of lordship and laws, crime and punishment, and the struggle for landed supremacy, all of which were of central importance to the poets of texts like *Genesis B*.

The narrative also found a powerful foothold in the Anglo-Saxon political and social imagination. Alfred was, for instance, interested in the structuring of the individual through diligent intellectual and spiritual work, the process whereby one becomes a suitable heir worthy of both material and otherworldly inheritances. Thus, his interest in the lessons of inheritance and disinheritance in the fall of the angels story is clear. Chapters 1 and 2 contextualised how the narrative of the angelic rebellion and its corollary doctrines were powerfully transformed to address questions of treachery, oath-breaking, and forfeiture, and how the proems of certain land charters and grants mirror some of the recurring themes of seizure and replacement found in poems like *Genesis A*. In the course of writing this book, it has become clear to me that the poems contained in the Junius Manuscript would have reinforced these social ideals of territorial inheritance and expected obedience, making the texts powerful commentaries upon Anglo-Saxon legal and cultural practices.

How the narrative moves and changes from genre to genre – exegesis, charter, liturgy, sermon, biblical poetry, hagiography – has been another concern in this book. Chapter 4 highlighted the fall of the angels narrative in poetic saints' lives wherein the story acquires the incantatory effect of a charm employed by saints imperiled by devils. Such moments reveal that learned exegetical and doctrinal ideas could readily intersect with the realm of popular folklore and belief. Similarly, the narrative could intersect with the cycles of liturgical practice, as I argue with *Christ and Satan*, a poem that imagines Satan's eternal punishment as a kind of defective or impossible Rogationtide procession.

As my last chapter illustrates, with Ælfric and Wulfstan, the fall of the angels again bridges religious and secular worlds. Wulfstan uses the narrative to advocate for the reform of both the spiritual self and the reinstitution of lordly obligations, evincing a marked resistance to the labelling of groups such as secular clerics or even vikings as rebel angels as had been characteristic of earlier generations. With these shifting tides of belief, we see a rejection of the idea that the English people remain pure souls or loyal servants of God under attack. Instead, Wulfstan's and Ælfric's theory of rebellion situates angelic treachery as a potential flaw within any English Christian. Their homiletic messages cut across the ecclesiastical and lay spheres to mobilise English Christians in defence of their lands and in defence of their souls.

A reoccurring theme among the texts under consideration in this book is that both worldly and otherworldly inheritances were often figured in spatially concrete terms, whether in the boundaries listed in a *bocland* charter or the mental and material terrains of Rogationtide. There are, I think, many other ways of elaborating upon this framework and further possibilities for understanding the fall of the angels narrative in the early medieval period that I have not covered here. Iconographic traditions and images associated with the fall of the angels represent just one area that merits even further exploration. Fol. 2r in *The Old English Hexateuch* (London, British Library, Cotton Claudius B.iv), presents hell with its fallen and falling host of angels as the visual inverse of heaven. Even though the story of the fall of the angels does not occur in the text, an illustrator (like so many of his contemporaries) thought it crucial and essential to depict the angelic demise and all its dramatic aftershocks. Anglo-Saxon authors possessed a highly complex, ever-changing, ever-adapting theory of the fall of the angels. The overall impression one gains from examining their work, then, is that the fall of the angels mythos – and the restructuring of the heavenly and earthly polities in its aftermath – gave the Anglo-Saxons a way to imagine the construction of their own earthly society, and a means to understand how they could chart clear paths to a heavenly one.

Notes

1 That tradition persisted in Middle English literature. Examples are inventoried by James Morey, *Book and Verse: A Guide to Middle English Biblical Literature* (Urbana, IL: University of Illinois Press, 2000), see "Angel(s), fall of", p. 396.
2 *Carmen de uirginitate*, pp. 316–17; trans. Lapidge and Rosier, *Aldhelm: The Poetic Works*, p. 163.
3 Ibid., p. 457; trans. Lapidge and Rosier, p. 67.
4 *Ancrene Wisse: A Corrected Edition of the Text in Cambridge, Corpus Christi College, MS 402 with variants from other manuscripts*, EETS os 325 (London: Oxford University Press, 2005), Book II, 46–7.
5 Warner, *Early English Homilies from the Twelfth Century*, p. 2.
6 *Middle English Religious Prose*, ed. N. F. Blake (London: Edward Arnold, 1972).
7 Sarah Stanbury suggests that Lucifer 'errs' by gazing admiringly upon himself; see 'In God's Sight: Vision and Sacred History in *Purity*', in

Text and Matter: New Critical Perspectives of the Pearl-Poet, ed. Robert Blanch, Miriam Youngerman Miller, and Julian Wasserman (Troy, NY: Whitson, 1991), pp. 105–16 (p. 110).

8 Robert W. Barrett *Fall of Lucifer* in *Against All England: Regional Identity and Cheshire Writing, 1195–1656* (Notre Dame, IN: Notre Dame Press, 2009) argues that the Tanner's 'Fall of Lucifer' dramatises exclusion from the body politic (pp. 81–2).

Bibliography

Primary sources

Abbo of Fleury, *Passio Sancti Eadmundi*, ed. Michael Winterbottom, *Three Lives of English Saints* (Toronto: PIMS, 1972).
Ælfric, *Ælfric's Catholic Homilies, The First Series*, ed. Peter Clemoes, EETS ss 17 (Oxford: Oxford University Press, 1997).
Ælfric, 'Ælfric's Version of *Alcuini Interrogationes Sigeuulfi in Genesin*', ed. G. E. MacLean, *Anglia*, 6 (1883), 425–73; 7 (1884), 1–59.
Ælfric, *Angelsächsische Homilien und Heiligenleben*, ed. Bruno Assmann, Bibliothek der Angelsächsischen Prosa 3 (Kassel: Wigand, 1889); repr. Peter Clemoes (Darmstadt: Wissenschaftliche Buchgesellschaft, 1964).
Ælfric, 'A Critical Edition of Ælfric's Translation of Alcuin's *Interrogationes Sigwulfi Presbiteri* and of the Related Texts *De creatore et creatura* and *De sex etatibus huius seculi*', ed. W. Stoneman, PhD dissertation, University of Toronto, 1983.
Ælfric, *Exameron*, ed. S. J. Crawford, *Exameron Anglice or The Old English Hexameron*, Bibliothek der angelsächsischen Prosa 10 (Hamburg: Grand, 1921).
Ælfric, *The Old English Heptateuch and Ælfric's Libellus de Veteri et Testamento et Novo*, ed. Richard Marsden, EETS os 330 (Oxford: Oxford University Press, 2008).
Ælfric, *The Old English Version of the Heptateuch, Ælfric's Treatise on the Old and New Testament and his Preface to Genesis*, ed. S. J. Crawford, EETS os 160 (London: Milford, 1922; repr. Oxford: Oxford University Press, 1969).
Ælfric, *Two Ælfric Texts: The Twelve Abuses and the Vices and Virtues*, ed. and trans. Mary Clayton (Suffolk: Boydell and Brewer, 2013).
Aethicus Ister, *The Cosmography of Aethicus Ister: Edition, Translation, Commentary*, ed. and trans. Michael W. Herren, Publications of the Journal of Medieval Latin 6 (Turnhout: Brepols, 2011).
Alcuin, *Alcuini epistolae*, ed. Ernst Dümmler, MGH Epistolae Karolini aevi 4 (Berlin: Weidmann, 1896).
Alcuin, *Interrogationes et responsiones in Genesin*, ed. J.-P. Migne, PL 101 (Paris: Garnier Frères, 1851), cols. 515–66.

Alcuin, *Two Alcuin Letter-Books*, ed. Colin Chase, Toronto Medieval Latin Texts 5 (Toronto: PIMS, 1975).
Aldhelm, *Carmen de uirginitate*, ed. Rudolf Ehwald, *Aldhelmi Opera Omnia*, MGH Auctores antiquissimi 15 (Berlin: Weidmann, 1919).
Aldhelm, *De uirginitate*, ed. Scott Gwara, *Aldhelmi Malmesbiriensis prosa de uirginitate cum glosa Latina atque anglosaxonixa*, CCSL 124A (Turnhout: Brepols, 2001).
Aldhelm: The Poetic Works, ed. and trans. Michael Lapidge and James L. Rosier (Suffolk: D. S. Brewer, 1985).
Aldhelm: The Prose Works, ed. and trans. Michael Lapidge and Michael Herren (Suffolk: D. S. Brewer, 1979).
Alfred, *King Alfred's Version of St. Augustine's Soliloquies*, ed. Thomas A. Carnicelli (Cambridge: Harvard University Press, 1969).
Alfred, *King Alfred's West Saxon Version of Gregory's Pastoral Care*, ed. H. Sweet, EETS os 45, 50 (London: Oxford University Press, 1871–2; repr. 1978).
Ancrene Wisse: A Corrected Edition of the Text in Cambridge, Corpus Christi College, MS 402 with variants from other manuscripts, ed. Barbara Millett, EETS os 325 (London: Oxford University Press, 2005).
Andreas and The Fates of the Apostles, ed. Kenneth R. Brooks (Oxford: Clarendon Press, 1961).
Das angelsächsische Prosa-Leben des hl. Guthlac, ed. Paul Alfred Gonser, Anglistische Forschungen 27 (Heidelberg: C. Winter, 1909).
Anglo-Saxon Charters, ed. and trans. A. J. Robertson (Cambridge: Cambridge University Press, 2009).
The Anglo-Saxon Chronicle, trans. Michael Swanton (New York: Routledge, 1998).
The Anglo-Saxon Chronicle: A Collaborative Edition, gen. ed. David N. Dumville and Simon Keynes (Cambridge: D. S. Brewer, 1983–).
The Anglo-Saxon Chronicle: A Collaborative Edition, Volume 3: MS A, ed. Janet Bately (Cambridge: D. S. Brewer, 1986).
The Anglo-Saxon Chronicle: A Collaborative Edition, Volume 5: MS C, ed. Katherine O'Brien O'Keeffe (Cambridge: D. S. Brewer, 2001).
The Anglo-Saxon Chronicle: A Collaborative Edition, Volume 6: MS D, ed. G. P. Cubbin (Cambridge: D. S. Brewer, 1996).
The Anglo-Saxon Chronicle: A Collaborative Edition, Volume 7: MS E, ed. Susan Irvine (Cambridge: D. S. Brewer, 2004).
Asser, *Asser's Life of King Alfred and Other Contemporary Sources*, trans. Simon Keynes and Michael Lapidge (London: Penguin, 1983).
Asser, *Asser's Life of King Alfred Together with the Annals of Saint Neots Erroneously Ascribed to Asser*, ed. W. H. Stevenson (Oxford: Clarendon Press, 1904; repr. 1959).
Augustine, *De catechizandis rudibus*, ed. I. B. Bauer, CCSL 46 (Turnhout: Brepols, 1969).

Bibliography

Augustine, *The City of God*, trans. Henry Bettenson (London: Penguin, 2003).
Augustine, *De ciuitate Dei*, ed. Bernahrd Dombart and Alfons Kalb, *Sancti Aurelii Augustini episcopi De Civitate Dei*, CCSL 47–8 (Turnhout: Brepols, 1955).
Augustine, *Confessiones*, ed. P. Knöll, *Sancti Aureli Augustini Confessiones*, CSEL 33 (Vienna, 1896).
Augustine, *Enchiridion ad Laurentium de fide et spe et caritate*, ed. E. Evans, *Sancti Aurelii Augustini opera*, CCSL 46 (Turnhout: Brepols, 1964).
Augustine, *De Genesi ad litteram*, ed. Joseph Zycha, *Sancti Aureli Augustini De Genesi ad litteram libri duodecim eiusdem libri capitula, De Genesi ad litteram imperfectus liber, Loctunionum in Heptateuchum libri septem*, CSEL 28.1 (Vienna: Tempsky, 1894).
Augustine. *The Literal Meaning of Genesis*, trans. John Hammond Taylor S. J., vol. 2, Ancient Christian Writers: The Works of the Fathers in Translation (New York: Newman Press, 1982).
Augustine, *St Augustine: The First Catechetical Instruction (De Catechizandis Rudibus)*, trans. Joseph P. Christopher (New York: Newman, 1946).
Bede, *Commentarius in epistolas VII catholicas*, ed. David Hurst, *Bedae Venerabilis Opera*, CCSL 121 (Turnhout: Brepols, 1983).
Bede, *The Commentary on the Seven Catholic Epistles of Bede the Venerable*, trans. David Hurst, Cistercian Studies Series 82 (Kalamazoo, MI: Cistercian Publications, 1985).
Bede, *Epiostola ad Ecgberhtum episcopum*, ed. and trans. Christopher Grocock and I. N. Wood, *Abbots of Wearmouth and Jarrow* (Oxford: Clarendon Press, 2013).
Bede, *In Genesin*, ed. C. W. Jones, *Bedae Venerabilis Opera*, CCSL 118A (Turnhout: Brepols, 1967).
Bede, *On Genesis*, trans. Calvin Kendall (Liverpool University Press, 2008).
Bede, *Historia ecclesiastica gentis Anglorum*, ed. and trans. Bertram Colgrave and R. A. B. Mynors (Oxford: Oxford University Press, 1969).
Bede, *Homelarium euangelii*, ed. David Hurst, *Bedae Venerabilis Opera. Pars IV: opera rhythmica*, CCSL 122 (Turnhout: Brepols, 1960), 1–378.
Bede, *In Lucae euangelium expositio*, ed. David Hurst, *Bedae Venerabilis Opera*, CCSL 120 (Turnhout: Brepols, 1960).
Bede, *In Tobiam*, ed. David Hurst, *Bedae Venerabilis Opera*, CCSL 119B (Turnhout: Brepols, 1983).
Benedict of Nursia, *The Rule of Saint Benedict*, ed. and trans. Bruce L. Venarde (Cambridge: Harvard University Press, 2011).
The Blickling Homilies of the Tenth Century, ed. R. Morris, EETS os 58, 63, 73 (London: Trübner, 1874–80).
The Blickling Homilies, ed. and trans. Richard J. Kelley (London and New York: Continuum, 2003).

Boniface. *De uirtutibus et uiitiis*, ed. and trans. Maria De Marco, *Collectiones aenigmatum merovingicae aetatis*, CCSL 133 (Turnhout: Brepols, 1968).

The Book of the Secrets of Enoch or I Enoch: A New English Translation with Commentary and Textual Notes, ed. and trans. Matthew Black (Leiden: Brill, 1985).

Bosworth, Joseph, *An Anglo-Saxon Dictionary, Based on the Manuscript Collections of the Late Joseph Bosworth-Toller*, ed. T. Northcote Toller (Oxford: Clarendon Press, 1882).

Byrhtferth of Ramsey, *Byrhtferth's Enchiridion*, ed. Peter S. Baker and Michael Lapidge, EETS ss 15 (London: Oxford University Press, 1995).

Byrhtferth of Ramsey, *Byrhtferth of Ramsey: The Lives of St Oswald and St Ecgwine*, ed. and trans. Michael Lapidge (Oxford: Clarendon Press, 2009).

The Cædmon Manuscript of Anglo-Saxon Biblical Poetry, Junius XI in the Bodleian Library, ed. Israel Gollancz (London: Oxford University Press, 1927).

Caedmonis monachi paraphrasis poetica Genesios ac praecipuarum sacrae pagina historiarum, ed. Franciscus Junius (Amsterdam: 1655); repr. Peter J. Lucas (Amsterdam: Rodopi, 2000).

Cartularium Saxonicum: A Collection of Charters Relating to Anglo-Saxon History, ed. Walter de Gray Birch (London: Whiting & Company, 1885–99).

Charters of the New Minster, Winchester, ed. Sean Miller, Anglo-Saxon Charters 9 (Oxford: Oxford University Press, 2001).

Christ and Satan: A Critical Edition, ed. Robert Emmett Finnegan (Waterloo, Ontario: Wilfrid Laurier University Press, 1977).

Christ and Satan: An Old English Poem Edited with Introduction, Notes and Glossary, ed. Merrel Dare Clubb (New Haven: Yale University Press, 1925).

Codex Diplomaticus Aevi Saxonici, ed. J. M. Kemble (London: Sumptibus Societatis, 1839–48).

Councils and Synods with Other Documents Relating to the English Church Volume I A.D. 871–1204, Part 1, ed. Dorothy Whitelock, Martin Brett, and Christopher N. L. Brook (Oxford: Clarendon Press, 1981).

Cynewulf, *Cynewulf's Elene*, ed. P. O. E. Gradon (Exeter: University of Exeter Press, 1977).

Cynewulf, *Juliana*, ed. Rosemary Woolf (New York: Appleton-Century-Crofts, 1966).

A Digital Facsimile of Oxford, Bodleian Library MS Junius 11, ed. Bernard J. Muir. Bodleian Library Digital Texts 1 (Oxford: Bodleian Library, 2004).

Dhuoda, *Handbook for William: A Carolingian Woman's Counsel for her Son by Dhuoda*, trans. Carol Neel (Washington, DC, Catholic University Press, 1991).

Dhuoda, *Dhuoda: Handbook for her Warrior Son. Liber Manualis*, ed. Marcelle Thiébaux, Cambridge Medieval Classics 8 (Cambridge: Cambridge University Press, 1998).
Documents of the Baptismal Liturgy, ed. E. C. Whitaker (London: Society for Promoting Christian Knowledge, 1970).
The Earliest Life of Gregory the Great, ed. and trans. Bertram Colgrave (Cambridge: Cambridge University Press, 1968).
The Early Charters of Northern England and the North Midlands, ed. C. R. Hart, SEEH 6 (Leicester: Leicester University Press, 1975).
Early English Homilies from the Twelfth Century MS. Vesp. D. XIV, ed. Rubie D-N. Warner. EETS os 152 (London: Trübner and Oxford University Press, 1917).
The Early Lives of St Dunstan, ed. and trans. Michael Winterbottom and Michael Lapidge (Oxford: Clarendon Press, 2012).
Eleven Old English Rogationtide Homilies, ed. Joyce Bazire and James E. Cross (Toronto, University of Toronto Press, 1982).
English Historical Documents, 500–1042, ed. and trans. Dorothy Whitelock, vol. 1 (2nd ed., Oxford: Oxford University Press, 1979).
Evagrius, *Vita Beati Antonii Abbatis*, ed. Roswyde, PL 73 (Paris: Garnier Frères, 1879).
The Exeter Book, ed. George Philip Krapp and Elliot Kirk Dobbie, ASPR III (New York: Columbia University Press, 1936).
Felix, *Felix's Life of Saint Guthlac*, ed. and trans. Bertram Colgrave (Cambridge: Cambridge University Press, 1956).
Florence of Worcester, *Chronicon: Florentii Wigorniensis monahi Chronicon ex Chronicis*, ed. Benjamin Thorpe (London: Kraus, 1848–9).
Fontes Anglo-Saxonici Project, ed., *Fontes Anglo-Saxonici: World Wide Web Register*, http://fontes.english.ox.ac.uk/.
Genesis A: A New Edition, ed. A. N. Doane (Madison, WI: The University of Wisconsin Press, 1978).
Genesis A: A New Edition, Revised, ed. A. N. Doane, Medieval and Renaissance Texts and Studies 435 (Tempe: ACMRS, 2013).
Die Gesetze der Anglesachsen, ed. Felix Liebermann, 3 vols. (Halle: Niemeyer, 1903–16).
Gildas, *The Ruin of Britain and Other Works*, ed. and trans. Michael Winterbottom (Sussex: Phillimore, 1978).
Gregory the Great, *Dialogues*, ed. Adalbert de Vogüé, Sources Chrétiennes 260 (Paris: Editions de Cerf, 1979).
Gregory the Great, *Gregory the Great: Forty Gospel* Homilies, trans. David Hurst, Cistercian Studies Series 123 (Kalamazoo, MI: Cistercian Publications, 1990).
Gregory the Great, *Homiliae in Evangelia*, ed. Raymond Étaix, CCSL 141 (Turnhout: Brepols, 1999).
The Guthlac Poems of the Exeter Book, ed. Jane Roberts (Oxford: Oxford University Press, 1979).

Haimo of Auxerre, *Homiliae de tempore CXIV*, ed. J.-P. Migne, PL 188 (Paris: Garnier Frères, 1851), col. 613.

Hymnar und Hymnem im Englischen Mittelalter, ed. Helmut Gneuss, *Studien zur Überlieferung, Glossierung und Übersetzung lateinischer Hymnem in England*, Buchreihe der Anglia 12 (Tübingen: Niemeyer, 1969).

The Irish Adam and Eve Story from Saltair na ran, ed. David Greene and Fergus Kelly, 2 vols. (Dublin: Dublin Institute for Advanced Studies, 1976).

The Junius Manuscript, ed. George Philip Krapp, ASPR I (New York: Columbia University Press, 1931).

The King's Mirror (Speculum Regale – Konungs skuggsjá), trans. Laurence Marcellus Larson (New York: Trayne, 1917).

Klaeber's Beowulf and the Fight at Finnsburg, ed. R. D. Fulk, Robert E. Bjork, and John D. Niles (4th ed., Toronto: University of Toronto Press, 2008).

Konungs skuggsiá, ed. Ludvig, Holm-Olsen, Gammelnorske tekster 1 (Oslo: Norsk Historisk Kjeldskrift-Instituut, 1945; repr. 1983).

Leabhar Breac, ed. and trans. Bartholomew Mac Carthy, *The Codex Palatino-Vaticanus, No. 830*, Todd Lecture Series 3 (Dublin: Royal Irish Academy, 1892).

Leabhar Gabhála Érenn: The Book of the Taking of Ireland, ed. and trans. R. A. S. Macalister, Early Irish Texts Society 34 (Dublin: Educational Company of Ireland, 1938).

Liber Eliensis: A History of the Isle of Ely from the Seventh Century to the Twelfth, trans. J. Fairweather (Woodbridge: Boydell, 2005).

Martin of Braga, *De correctione rusticorum*, ed. C. W. Barlow, *Martini Episcopi Bracarensis Opera Omnia* (New Haven: Yale University Press, 1950).

Martin of Braga. *Martin von Bracara's Schrift De correctione rusticorum*, ed. Carl Paul Caspari (Oslo: Gedruckt in der Mallingsche Buchdruckerei, 1883).

Middle English Religious Prose, ed. N. F. Blake (London: Edward Arnold, 1972).

The Old English Dialogues of Solomon and Saturn, ed. and trans. Daniel Anlezark, Anglo-Saxon Texts 7 (Cambridge: D. S. Brewer, 2009).

The Old English Life of St Nicholas with the Old English Life of St Giles, E. M. Treharne, Leeds Texts and Monographs New Series 15 (Otley, West Yorkshire: Smith Settle, 1997).

Old English Poems of Christ and His Saints, ed. and trans. Mary Clayton, Dumbarton Oaks Medieval Library (Cambridge: Harvard University Press, 2013).

The Old English Version of Bede's Ecclesiastical History of the English People, ed. and trans. Thomas Miller, EETS os 95 (London: Oxford University Press, 1890; repr. 1997).

The Old English Vision of St. Paul, ed. Antonette DiPaolo Healey, Speculum Anniversary Monographs 2 (Cambridge, MA: The Medieval Academy of America, 1978).

Pirmin of Reichenau, *Die Heimat des Hl. Pirmin des Apostels der Alamannen*, ed. Gall Jecker, Beiträge zur Geschichte des alten Mönchtums und des Benediktinerordens Heft 13 (Munich: Aschendorff, 1927).

Property and Piety in Early Medieval Winchester: Documents Relating to the Topography of the Anglo-Saxon and Norman City and its Minsters, ed. Alexander R. Rumble, Winchester Studies 4, Part 3 (Oxford: Clarendon Press, 2002).

Pseudo-Cyprianus, *De XII abusivis saeculi*, ed. Siegmund Hellmann, Texte und Untersuchungen zur Geschichte der altchristlichen Literatur 34 (Leipzig: J. C. Hinrichs, 1909).

Pseudo-Dionysius, *The Celestial Hierarchy*, ed. Günter Heil and Adolf Martin Ritter, *Corpus Dionysiacum II* (Berlin: de Gruyter, 1991).

Recensio Casanatensis, ed. M. Bonnet, *Acta Apostolorum Apocrypha*, vols. 1–2 (Leipzig: Mendelssohn, 1898).

Recensio Vaticana, ed. Franz Blatt, *Die lateinischen Bearbeitungen der Acta Andreae et Matthiae apud Anthropophagos*, Zeitschrift für die neutestamentliche Wissenschaft 12 (Giessen: Töpelmann, 1930).

Regularis Concordia: The Monastic Agreement of the Monks and Nuns of the English Nation, ed. Dom Thomas Symons (London: Thomas Nelson and Sons, 1953).

Saltair na Rann: A Collection of Early Irish Poems, ed. Whitley Stokes, Anecdota Oxoniensa, Mediaeval and Modern Series 1 (Oxford: Clarendon Press, 1883).

SASLC: The Apocrypha, ed. Frederick M. Biggs, Instrumenta Anglistica Mediaevalia 1, (Kalamazoo, MI: Medieval Institute Publications, 2007).

SASLC: Bede, Part 2, Fascicles 1–4, ed. George Hardin Brown and Frederick M. Biggs (Amsterdam: Amsterdam University Press, 2018).

The Saxon Genesis: An Edition of the West Saxon Genesis B and the Old Saxon Vatican Genesis, ed. A. N. Doane (Madison, WI: The University of Wisconsin Press, 1991).

Sources and Analogues of Old English Poetry: The Major Latin Texts in Translation, ed. and trans. Michael J. B. Allen and Daniel Calder (Cambridge: D. S. Brewer, 1976).

Tacitus, *Germania*, trans. M. Hutton, Loeb Library 35 (London: Loeb Classical Library, 1970).

Taliesin, *The Poems of Taliesin*, ed. Ifor Williams and trans. J. E. Caerwyn Williams (Dublin: Dublin Institute for Advanced Studies, 1968).

Tatwine, *Enigma XXV*, ed. and trans. Maria de Marco, *Collectiones aenigmatum merovingicae aetatis*, CCSL 133 (Turnhout: Brepols, 1968).

Three Lives of English Saints, ed. Michael Winterbottom (Toronto: PIMS, 1973).

The Tripartite Life of Patrick with Other Documents Related to that Saint, ed. Whitley Stokes (London: Eyre and Spottiswoode, 1887).
Two Lives of Saint Cuthbert: A Life by an Anonymous Monk of Lindisfarne and Bede's Prose Life, ed. and trans. Bertram Colgrave (Cambridge: Cambridge University Press, 1940).
The Vercelli Book, ed. George Philip Krapp, ASPR II (New York: Columbia University Press, 1932).
The Vercelli Homilies and Related Texts, ed. Donald G. Scragg, EETS os 300 (Oxford: Oxford University Press, 1992).
Vita Latina Adae et Evae, ed. Jean Pierre Pettorelli, Jean-Daniel Kaestli, et al., 2 vols, CCSA 18–19 (Turnhout: Brepols, 2012).
Werferth, *Bischofs Wærferth von Worcester Übersetzung der Dialoge Gregors des Grossen*, ed. Hans Hecht, Bibliothek der angelsächsischen Prosa 5 (Leipzig, 1900–7; repr. Darmstadt, 1965).
Wolfram von Eschenbach, *Parzival*, ed. Wolfgang Spiewok, 2 vols (Stuttgart: Reclam, 1981).
Wulfstan of Winchester, *The Life of St. Æthelwold*, ed. Michael Lapidge and Michael Winterbottom (Oxford: Clarendon Press, 1991).
Wulfstan of York, *The Homilies of Wulfstan*, ed. Dorothy Bethurum (Oxford: Clarendon Press, 1957; repr. 1998).
Wulfstan of York, *The Political Writings of Archbishop Wulfstan of York*, ed. Andrew Rabin (Manchester, Manchester University Press, 2015).
Wulfstan of York, *Sermo Lupi ad Anglos*, ed. Dorothy Whitelock (London: Methuen, 1963).
Wulfstan of York, *Wulfstan: Sammlung der ihm zugeschriebenen Homilien nebst Untersuchungen über ihre Echtheit*, ed. Arthur S. Napier (Berlin: Weidmann, 1883; repr. Dublin and Zürich: 1967).

Secondary sources

Abbetmeyer, C., *Old English Poetical Motives Derived from the Doctrine of Sin* (Minneapolis: H. W. Wilson Company, 1903).
Abels, Richard, *Alfred the Great: War, Kingship and Culture in Anglo-Saxon England* (London: Routledge, 1998).
Abels, Richard, 'Appendix on the Authenticity of Asser's *Life of King Alfred* and Alfred's Translations' (forthcoming with Routledge).
Abels, Richard, 'Bookland and *Fyrd* Service in Late Anglo-Saxon England', in *The Battle of Hastings: Sources and Interpretations*, ed. Stephen Morillo (Woodbridge: Boydell, 1996); repr. *Anglo-Norman Studies*, 7 (1984), 1–25.
Abels, Richard, *Lordship and Military Obligation in Anglo-Saxon England* (Berkeley: University of California Press, 1988).
Abrams, Lesley. 'The Conversion of the Danelaw', in *Vikings and the Danelaw: Select Papers from the Proceedings of the Thirteenth Viking*

Congress, ed. James Graham-Campbell, Richard Hall, Judith Jesch, and David N. Parsons (Oxford: Oxbow Books 2001), 31–44.

Anderson, Earl R., 'Treasure Trove in *Beowulf*: A Legal View of the Dragon's Hoard', *Mediaevalia*, 3 (1977), 141–64.

Andersson, Theodore M., 'The Thief in *Beowulf*', *Speculum*, 59 (1984), 493–508.

Anlezark, Daniel, 'Connecting the Patriarchs: Noah and Abraham in the Old English *Exodus*', *JEGP*, 104 (2005), 171–88.

Anlezark, Daniel, 'The Fall of the Angels in *Solomon and Saturn II*', in *Apocryphal Texts and Traditions in Anglo-Saxon England*, ed. Kathryn Powell and Donald G. Scragg (Cambridge: D. S. Brewer, 2003), 121–33.

Anelzark, Daniel, *Water and Fire: The Myth of the Flood in Anglo-Saxon England* (Manchester: Manchester University Press, 2006).

Austin, J. L., *How To Do Things with Words*, ed. J. O. Urmson and Marina Sbisá (2nd ed. Oxford: Oxford University Press, 1976).

Barrett, Robert W., *Against All England: Regional Identity and Cheshire Writing, 1195–1656* (Notre Dame, IN: Notre Dame Press, 2009).

Barrow, Julia, *The Clergy in the Medieval World: Secular Clerics, Their Families and Careers in North-Western Europe, c. 800–c. 1200* (Cambridge: Cambridge University Press, 2015).

Barrow, Julia, 'English Cathedral Communities and Reform in the Late Tenth and Eleventh Centuries', in *Anglo-Norman Durham, 1093–1193*, ed. David Rollason, Margaret Harvey, and Michael Prestwich (Woodbridge: Boydell, 1994), 25–39.

Barrow, Julia, 'The Ideology of the Tenth-Century English Benedictine "Reform"', in *Challenging the Boundaries of Medieval History: The Legacy of Timothy Reuter*, ed. Patricia Skinner, SEMA (Turnhout: Brepols, 2009), 141–54.

Bately, Janet M., 'Alfred as Author and Translator', in *A Companion to Alfred the Great*, ed. Nicole Guenther Discenza and Paul E. Szarmach, Brill's Companions to the Christian Tradition 58 (Leiden: Brill, 2015), 113–42.

Bately, Janet M., 'Did King Alfred Actually Translate Anything? The Integrity of the Alfredian Canon Revisited', *MÆ*, 78 (2009), 189–215.

Battles, Paul, '*Genesis A* and the Anglo-Saxon Migration Myth', *ASE* 29 (2000), 43–66.

Becher, C. F. R., *Wulfstans Homilien* (Leipzig: Sturm and Koppe, 1910).

Bedingfield, M. Bradford, *The Dramatic Liturgy of Anglo-Saxon England* (Woodbridge: Boydell, 2002).

Bethurum, Dorothy, 'Wulfstan', in *Continuations and Beginnings: Studies in Old English Literature*, ed. E. G. Stanley (London and Edinburgh: Nelson, 1966), 210–44.

Biddle, Martin, '*Felix Urbs Winthonia*: Winchester in the Age of Monastic Reform', in *Tenth-Century Studies: Essays in Commemoration of the Millennium of the Council of Winchester and Regularis Concordia*, ed.

David Parsons (London: Phillimore, 1975); repr. in *Anglo-Saxon History: Basic Readings*, ed. David A. E. Pelteret (New York: Garland, 2000), 289–316.

Biggs, Frederick M., '*Beowulf* and Some Fictions of the Geatish Succession', *ASE*, 32 (2003), 55–77.

Biggs, Frederick M., 'Edgar's Path to the Throne', in *Edgar, King of the English 959–975: New Interpretations*, ed. Donald Scragg (Woodbridge: Boydell, 2008), 124–42.

Biggs, Frederick M., '*Englum gelice: Elene* Line 1320 and *Genesis A* Line 185', *NM*, 86 (1985), 447–52.

Biggs, Frederick M., 'The Passion of Andreas: *Andreas* 1398–1491', *SP*, 85 (1988), 413–27.

Biggs, Frederick M., 'The Politics of Succession in *Beowulf* and Anglo-Saxon England', *Speculum*, 80 (2005), 709–41.

Binchy, D. A., 'Some Celtic Legal Terms', *Celtica*, 3 (1956), 221–31.

Bischoff, Bernhard, 'Paläographische Fragen deutschen Denkmäler der Karolingerzeit', *Frühmittelalterliche Studien*, 5 (1971), 101–34; repr. in *Mittelalterliche Studien: Ausgewählte Aufsätze zur Schriftkunde und Literaturgeschichte* (Stuttgart: A. Hiersemann, 1981), 73–111.

Bisson, Thomas N., *The Crisis of the Twelfth Century: Power, Lordship, and the Origins of European Government* (Princeton: Princeton University Press, 2009).

Bjork, Robert E., 'Digressions and Episodes', in *A Beowulf Handbook*, ed. Robert E. Bjork and John D. Niles (Lincoln: University of Nebraska Press, 1997), 193–212.

Bjork, Robert E., *The Old English Verse Saints' Lives: A Study in Direct Discourse and the Iconography of Style*, McMaster Old English Studies and Texts 4 (Toronto: University of Toronto Press, 1985).

Blair, John, *The Church in Anglo-Saxon Society* (Oxford: Oxford University Press, 2005).

Bloomfield, Morton, *The Seven Deadly Sins: An Introduction to the History of a Religious Concept, with Special Reference to Medieval English Literature* (East Lansing, MI: Michigan State College Press, 1962).

Boenig, Robert, *Saint and Hero: 'Andreas' and Medieval Doctrine* (Lewisburg, PA: Bucknell University Press, 1991).

Bosworth, Joseph, *An Anglo-Saxon Dictionary, Based on the Manuscript Collections of the Late Joseph Bosworth Toller*, ed. and enlarged by T. Northcote Toller (Oxford: Clarendon Press, 1882).

Boyd, Nina, 'Doctrine and Criticism: A Revaluation of "Genesis A"', *NM*, 83 (1982), 230–8.

Bracken, Damien, 'The Fall and the Law in Early Ireland', in *Ireland and Europe in the Early Middle Ages: Texts and Transmission*, ed. Próinséas Ní Chatháin and Michael Richter (Dublin: Four Courts, 2002), 146–69.

Brady, Lindy, *Writing the Welsh Borderlands in Anglo-Saxon England* (Manchester: Manchester University Press, 2017).

Brandl, Alois, *Die angelsächsische Literatur*, in *Grundriss der germanischen Philologie*, ed. Hermann Paul, 3 vols (Strassburg: Trübner, 1901–9).
Brandl, Alois, *Geschichte der altenglischen Literatur* (Strassburg: Trübner, 1908).
Bredehoft, Thomas A., *Early English Meter* (Toronto: University of Toronto Press, 2005).
Breen, Nathan Alan., 'The Voice of Evil: A Narratological Study of Demonic Characters in Old English Literature', PhD dissertation, University of Illinois at Urbana-Champaign, 2003.
Bremmer, Rolf H. Jr., 'Changing Perspectives on a Saint's Life: *Juliana*', in *Companion to Old English Poetry*, ed. Henk Aertsen and Rolf H. Bremmer, Jr. (Amsterdam: VU University Press, 1994), 201–16.
Bright, James W., 'The Relation of the Cædmonian *Exodus* to the Liturgy', *MLN*, 27 (1912), 97–103.
Brockman, Bennett A., '"Heroic" and "Christian" in *Genesis A*: The Evidence of the Cain and Abel Episode', *Modern Language Quarterly*, 35 (1974), 115–28.
Broderick III, Herbert R., 'The Iconographic and Compositional Sources of the Drawings in Oxford Bodleian Library, MS Junius 11', PhD dissertation, Columbia University, 1978.
Broderick III, Herbert R., 'Observations on the Method of Illustration in MS Junius 11 and the Relationship of the Drawings to the Text', *Scriptorium*, 37 (1983), 161–77.
Brooks, Nicholas, *Anglo-Saxon Myths: State and Church 400–1066* (London: Hambledon Press, 1998); repr. (London: Hambledon Continuum, 2003).
Bzdyl, Donald G., '*Juliana*: Cynewulf's Dispeller of Delusion', *NM*, 86 (1985), 165–75.
Caliendo, Kevin, 'Land Grants in Old English Poetry: Beating the Boundaries of Hell in *Christ and Satan*', 125th MLA Annual Convention, Philadelphia, December 2009.
Carey, John, *A New Introduction to Lebor Gabála Érenn*, Subsidiary Publication Series 1 (Dublin, Irish Texts Society, 1993).
Carney, James, 'The Dating of Early Irish Verse Texts, 500–1100', *Éigse*, 19 (1983), 177–216.
Chaney, William A., *The Cult of Kingship in Anglo-Saxon England: The Transition from Paganism to Christianity* (Manchester: Manchester University Press, 1970).
Chaplais, Pierre, 'The Origin and Authenticity of the Royal Anglo-Saxon Diploma', *Journal of the Society of Archivists*, 3 (1965), 48–61.
Charles-Edwards, T. M., *Early Christian Ireland* (Cambridge: Cambridge University Press, 2004).
Cherniss, Michael, 'Heroic Ideals and the Moral Climate of *Genesis B*', *Modern Language Quarterly*, 30 (1969), 479–97.

Cherniss, Michael, *Ingeld and Christ: Heroic Concepts and Values in Old English Christian Poetry* (The Hague: Mouton, 1972).

Clark, George, 'The Anglo-Saxons and *Superbia*: Finding a Word for It', in *Old English Philology: Studies in Honour of R. D. Fulk*, ed. Leonard Neidorf, Rafael J. Pascual, and Tom Shippey (Cambridge: D. S. Brewer, 2016), 172–89.

Clark, Stephanie, *Compelling God: Theories of Prayer in Anglo-Saxon England* (Toronto: University of Toronto Press, 2018).

Clark, Stephanie, '*Guthlac A* and the Temptation of the Barrow', *Studia Neophilologica*, 87 (2015), 48–72.

Clark, Stephanie, 'A More Permanent Homeland: Land Tenure in *Guthlac A*', *ASE*, 40 (2012), 75–102.

Clayton, Mary, '*De Duodecim Abusiuis*, Lordship and Kingship in Anglo-Saxon England', in *Saints and Scholars: New Perspectives on Anglo-Saxon Literature and Culture*, ed. Stuart McWilliams (Cambridge: D. S. Brewer, 2012), 141–63.

Clayton, Mary and Hugh Magennis, *The Old English Lives of St. Margaret*, CSASE 9 (Cambridge: Cambridge University Press, 1994).

Clemoes, Peter, 'King Alfred's Debt to Vernacular Poetry: The Evidence of *ellen* and *cræft*', in *Words, Texts, and Manuscripts: Studies in Anglo-Saxon Culture Presented to Helmut Gneuss*, ed. Michael Korhammer (Woodbridge: D. S. Brewer, 1992), 213–38.

Coates, Simon, 'Perceptions of the Anglo-Saxon Past in the Tenth-Century Monastic Reform Movement', in *The Church Retrospective: Papers Read at the 1995 Summer Meeting and the 1996 Winter Meeting of the Ecclesiastical History Society*, ed. R. N. Swanson, Studies in Church History 33 (Woodbridge: Boydell, 1997), 61–72.

Cohen, Adam S., 'King Edgar Leaping and Dancing Before the Lord', in *Imagining the Jew in Anglo-Saxon Literature and Culture*, ed. Samantha Zacher (Toronto: University of Toronto Press, 2016), 219–36.

Cole, Andrew, 'Jewish Apocrypha and Christian Epistemologies of the Fall: The *Dialogi* of Gregory the Great and the Old Saxon Genesis', in *Rome and the North: The Early Reception of Gregory the Great in Germanic Europe*, ed. Rolf H. Bremmer, Kees Dekker, and David F. Johnson (Paris: Peeters, 2001), 157–88.

Condren, Edward, '"Unnyt" Gold in "Beowulf" 3168', *PQ*, 52 (1973), 296–99.

Conner, Patrick W., 'On Dating Cynewulf', in *Cynewulf: Basic Readings*, ed. Robert E. Bjork, (New York: Psychology Press, 1996), 23–55.

Conner, Patrick W., 'Source Studies, the Old English *Guthlac A* and the English Benedictine Reformation', *Revue Bénédictine*, 103 (1993), 380–413.

Conybeare, John Josias, *Illustrations of Anglo-Saxon Poetry*, ed. William Daniel Conybeare (London: Hardin and Lepard, 1826).

Cubitt, C., 'Images of St. Peter: the Clergy and the Religious Life in

Anglo-Saxon England', in *The Christian Traditions in Anglo-Saxon England: Approaches to Current Scholarship and Teaching*, ed. P. Cavill, Christianity and Culture: Issues in Teaching and Research (Cambridge: D. S. Brewer, 2004), 41–54.

Dalbey, Marcia A., 'Hortatory Tone in the Blickling Homilies: Two Adaptations of Caesarius', *NM*, 70 (1969), 641–58.

Damon, John Edward, *Soldier Saints and Holy Warriors: Warfare and Sanctity in the Literature of Early England* (Aldershot and Brookfield, VT: Ashgate, 2004).

Daniélou, Jean, *The Bible and the Liturgy* (Notre Dame, IN: University of Notre Dame Press, 1966).

Davies, Wendy, 'Clerics as Rulers: Some Implications of the Terminology of Ecclesiastical Authority in Early Medieval Ireland', in *Latin and the Vernacular in Early Medieval Britain*, ed. Nicholas Brooks (Leicester: University of Leicester Press, 1982), 81–97.

Davis, Kathleen, 'Boredom, Brevity and Last Things: Ælfric's Style and the Politics of Time', in *A Companion to Ælfric*, ed. Hugh Magennis and Mary Swan (Leiden: Brill, 2009), 321–44.

Day, David D., 'Hands across the Hall: The Legalities of Beowulf's Fight with Grendel', *JEGP*, 98 (1999), 313–24.

Day, Virginia, 'The Influence of the Catechetical *narratio* on Old English and Some Other Medieval Literature', *ASE*, 3 (1974), 51–61.

DeGregorio, Scott, 'Texts, *Topoi* and the Self: A Reading of Alfredian Spirituality', *Early Medieval Europe*, 13 (2005), 79–96.

Dendle, Peter, *Demon Possession in Anglo-Saxon England* (Kalamazoo, MI: Medieval Institute Publications, 2014).

Dendle, Peter, *Satan Unbound: The Devil in Old English Narrative Literature* (Toronto: University of Toronto Press, 2001).

Derolez, R., '*Genesis*: Old Saxon and Old English', *ES*, 76 (1995), 409–23.

Electronic Dictionary of the Irish Language Based Mainly on Old and Middle Irish Materials: Compact Edition, ed. E. G. Quin (Dublin: Royal Irish Academy, 1983), online as eDIL, www.dil.ie.

Dictionary of Old English: A to H Online, ed. Angus Cameron, Ashley Crandell Amos, Antonette diPaolo Healey, et al. (Toronto: Dictionary of Old English Project, 2016).

Dien, Stephanie, '*Sermo Lupi ad Anglos*: The Order and Date of the Three Versions', *NM*, 76 (1975), 561–70.

DiNapoli, Robert, *An Index of Theme and Image to the Homilies of the Anglo-Saxon Church: Comprising the Homilies of Ælfric, Wulfstan, and the Blickling and Vercelli Codices* (Hockwold cum Wilton: Anglo-Saxon Books, 1995).

Discenza, Nicole Guenther, *Inhabited Spaces: Anglo-Saxon Constructions of Place* (Toronto: University of Toronto Press, 2017).

Discenza, Nicole Guenther, 'The Old English Boethius', in *A Companion* to *Alfred the Great*, ed. Nicole Guenther Discenza and Paul E. Szarmach (Leiden: Brill, 2014), 200–34.

Di Sciacca, Claudia, *Finding the Right Words: Isidore's Synonyma in Anglo-Saxon England* (Toronto: University of Toronto Press, 2008).

Di Sciacca, Claudia, 'The Old English Life of St Margaret in London, British Library, Cotton Tiberius A.iii: Sources and Relationships' (forthcoming in *JEGP*).

Dubs, Kathleen E., '*Genesis B*: a Study in Grace', *American Benedictine Review*, 33 (1982), 47–64.

Duffy, Eamon, *The Stripping of the Altars: Traditional Religion in England 1400–1580* (New Haven: Yale University Press, 2005).

Dumville, David N., 'Biblical Apocrypha and the Early Irish: A Preliminary Investigation', in *Proceedings of the Royal Irish Academy. Section C: Archaeology, Celtic Studies, History, Linguistics, Literature* (1973), 299–338.

Dumville, David N., *Wessex and England from Alfred to Edgar: Six Essays on Political, Cultural, and Ecclesiastical Revival*, Studies in Anglo-Saxon History 3 (Woodbridge: Boydell, 1992).

Dumville, David N., 'The West Saxon Genealogical Regnal List and the Chronology of Early Wessex', *Peritia*, 4 (1985), 21–66.

Dumville, David N., 'The West Saxon Genealogical Regnal List: Manuscripts and Texts', *Anglia*, 104 (1986), 1–32.

Earl, James W., 'Violence and Non-Violence in Anglo-Saxon England: Ælfric's "Passion of St. Edmund"', *PQ*, 78 (1999), 125–49.

Ericksen, Janet Schrunk, 'Lands of Unlikeness in *Genesis B*', *SP*, 93 (1996), 1–20.

Ericksen, Janet Schrunk, 'Legalizing the Fall of Man', *MÆ*, 74 (2005), 205–20.

Ericksen, Janet Schrunk, 'The Wisdom Poem at the End of MS Junius 11', in *The Poems of Junius 11: Basic Readings*, ed. R. M. Liuzza (New York and London: Routledge, 2002), 302–26.

Etchingham, Colmán, *Church Organisation in Ireland, A.D. 650–1000* (Maynooth: Laigin Publications, 1999).

Evans, J. M., '*Genesis B* and Its Background', *RES*, 14 (1963), 1–16; 113–23.

Evans, J. M., *Paradise Lost and the Genesis Tradition* (Oxford: Clarendon Press, 1968).

Fisher, D. J. V., 'The Anti-Monastic Reaction in the Reign of Edward the Martyr', *Cambridge Historical Journal*, 10 (1952), 254–70.

Fitzgerald, Jill M., '*Angelus Pacis*: A Liturgical Model for the Masculine "fæle friðowebba" in Cynewulf's *Elene*', *MÆ*, 83 (2014), 189–209.

Fitzgerald, Jill M., 'Measuring Hell by Hand: Rogation Rituals in *Christ and Satan*', *RES*, 68 (2017), 1–22.

Foot, Sarah, 'Anglo-Saxon Minsters: A Review of Terminology', in

Pastoral Care before the Parish, ed. J. Blair and R. Sharpe (Leicester: Leicester University Press, 1992), 212–25.

Foot, Sarah, *Monastic Life in Anglo-Saxon England, c. 600–900* (Cambridge: Cambridge University Press, 2006).

Förster, Max, 'Kleinere mittelenglische Texte', *Anglia*, 42 (1918), 145–224.

Fox, Michael, 'Ælfric on the Creation and Fall of the Angels', *ASE*, 31 (2002), 175–200.

Fox, Michael, 'Vercelli Homilies XIX–XXI, the Ascension Day Homily in CCCC 162, and the Catechetical Tradition from Augustine to Wulfstan', in *New Readings in the Vercelli Book*, ed. Samantha Zacher and Andy Orchard (Toronto: University of Toronto Press, 2009), 254–79.

Frank, Roberta, 'The *Beowulf* Poet's Sense of History', in *The Wisdom of Poetry: Essays in Early English Literature in Honor of Morton W. Bloomfield*, ed. Larry D. Benson and Siegfried Wenzel, Medieval Institute Publications (Kalamazoo, MI: Western Michigan University, 1982), 53–85.

Frantzen, Allen J., 'Drama and Dialogue in Old English Poetry: The Scene of Cynewulf's *Juliana*', *Theatre Survey*, 48 (2007), 99–119.

Frederick, Jill, 'Warring With Words: Cynewulf's *Juliana*', in *Readings in Medieval Texts: Interpreting Old and Middle English Literature*, ed. David F. Johnson and Elaine Treharne (Oxford: Oxford University Press, 2005), 60–74.

Fulk, R. D., 'Cynewulf: Canon, Dialect, and Date', in *Cynewulf: Basic Readings*, ed. Robert E. Bjork (New York: Psychology Press, 1996), 3–21.

Fulk, R. D., *A History of Old English Meter* (Philadelphia: University of Pennsylvania Press, 1992).

Garde, Judith N., *Old English Poetry in Medieval Christian Perspective: A Doctrinal Approach* (Cambridge: D. S. Brewer, 1991).

Garrison, Mary, 'The Social World of Alcuin: Nicknames at York and at the Carolingian Court', in *Alcuin of York: Scholar at the Carolingian Court, Proceedings of the Third Germania Latina Conference held at the University of Groningen May 1995*, ed. L. A. J. R. Houwen and A. A. MacDonald, Germania Latina III (Groningen: Forsten, 1998), 59–79.

Gatch, Milton McCormick, *Loyalties and Traditions: Man and his World in Old English Literature* (New York: Pegasus, 1971).

Gatch, Milton McCormick, *Preaching and Theology in Anglo-Saxon England: Ælfric and Wulfstan* (Toronto: University of Toronto Press, 1977).

Gatch, Milton McCormick, 'The Unknowable Audience of the Blickling Homilies', *ASE*, 18 (1989), 99–115.

Geary, Patrick J., 'Land, Language, and Memory in Europe 700–1100', *Transactions of the Royal Historical Society*, 9 (1999), 169–84.

Gittos, Helen, 'Creating the Sacred: Anglo-Saxon Rites for Consecrating

Cemeteries', in *Burial in Early Medieval England and Wales*, ed. Sam Lucy and Andrew Reynolds, The Society for Medieval Archaeology Monograph Series 17 (London: Society for Medieval Archaeology, 2002), 195–208.

Gittos, Helen, *Liturgy, Architecture, and Sacred Places in Anglo-Saxon England* (Oxford: Oxford University Press, 2013), 134–49.

Gneuss, Helmut, 'The Battle of Maldon 89: Byrtnoð's *ofermod* Once Again', *SP*, 73 (1976), 117–37.

Gneuss, Helmut and Michael Lapidge, Anglo-Saxon Manuscripts: A Bibliographical *Handlist of Anglo-Saxon Manuscripts and Manuscript Fragments Written or Owned in England up to 1100* (Toronto: University of Toronto Press, 2014).

Godden, Malcolm, 'Ælfric and Anglo-Saxon Kingship', *The English Historical Review*, 102 (1987), 911–15.

Godden, Malcolm, *Ælfric's Catholic Homilies: Introduction, Commentary and Glossary*, EETS ss 18 (Oxford: Oxford University Press, 2000).

Godden, Malcolm, 'Apocalypse and Invasion in Late Anglo-Saxon England', in *From Anglo-Saxon to Early Middle English: Studies Presented to E. G. Stanley*, ed. Malcolm Godden, Douglas Gray, and Terry Hoad (Oxford: Clarendon Press, 1994), 130–62.

Godden, Malcolm, 'Did King Alfred Write Anything?', *MÆ*, 76 (2007), 1–23.

Godden, Malcolm, 'Literature and the Old Testament', in *The Cambridge Companion to Old English Literature*, ed. Malcolm Godden and Michael Lapidge (Cambridge: Cambridge University Press, 1991), 206–26.

Godden, Malcolm, 'The Relations of Wulfstan and Ælfric: A Reassessment', in *Wulfstan, Archbishop of York: The Proceedings of the Second Alcuin Conference*, ed. Matthew Townend (Turnhout: Brepols, 2004), 353–74.

Greenfield, Stanley B., 'The Formulaic Expression of the Theme of "Exile" in Anglo-Saxon Poetry', *Speculum*, 30 (1955), 200–6.

Greenfield, Stanley B. and Daniel G. Calder, *A New Critical History of Old English Literature* (New York: New York University Press, 1986).

Grein, C. W. M., *Bibliothek der angelsächsischen Poesie in kritisch bearbeiteten Texten und mit vollständigem Glossar herausgegeben*, vols 1 and 2 (Göttingen: Georg H. Wigand, 1857–8).

Gretsch, Mechthild, *The Intellectual Foundations of the Benedictine Reform*, CSASE 25 (Cambridge: Cambridge University Press, 1999).

Groos, Arthur, 'The "Elder" Angel in *Guthlac A*', *Anglia*, 101 (1983), 141–6.

Groschopp, Friedrich, 'Das anelsächsische Gedicht *Christ und Satan*', PhD dissertation, University of Leipzig (Halle: E. Karras, 1883).

Haines, Dorothy, 'The Vacancies in Heaven: The Doctrine of Replacement and *Genesis A*', *N&Q*, 44 (1997), 150–4.

Hall, Alaric, 'Constructing Anglo-Saxon Sanctity: Tradition, Innovation

and Saint Guthlac', in *Images of Medieval Sanctity: Essays in Honour of Gary Dickson*, ed. Debra Higgs Strickland, Visualising the Middle Ages 1 (Leiden: Brill, 2007), 207–35.
Hall, J. R., 'The Old English Epic of Redemption', in *The Poems of Junius 11: Basic Readings*, ed. R. M. Liuzza (New York and London: Routledge, 2002), 20–52.
Hall, J. R., 'The Old English Epic of Redemption', *Traditio*, 32 (1976), 185–208.
Hall, J. R., '"The Old English Epic of Redemption": Twenty-Five-Year Retrospective', in *The Poems of Junius 11: Basic Readings*, ed. R. M. Liuzza (New York and London: Routledge, 2002), 53–68.
Hall, Thomas N., 'Preaching at Winchester in the Early Twelfth Century', *JEGP*, 104 (2005), 189–218.
Hall, Thomas N., 'Wulfstan's Latin Sermons', in *Wulfstan, Archbishop of York: The Proceedings of the Second Alcuin Conference*, ed. Matthew Townend (Turnhout: Brepols, 2004), 93–139.
Harbus, Antonina, 'Articulate Contact in *Juliana*', in *Verbal Encounters: Anglo-Saxon and Old Norse Studies for Roberta Frank*, ed. Antonina Harbus and Russell Poole, Toronto Old English Series (Toronto: University of Toronto Press, 2005), 183–200.
Harris, Stephen J., 'Bede and Gregory's Allusive Angles', *Criticism*, 44 (2002), 271–89.
Harris, Stephen J., 'The Liturgical Context of Ælfric's Homilies for Rogation', in *The Old English Homily: Precedent, Practice, and Appropriation*, ed. Aaron J Kleist (Turnhout: Brepols, 2007), 143–69.
Harris, Stephen J., *Race and Ethnicity in Anglo-Saxon Literature* (New York: Routledge, 2003).
Harsh, Constance D., '*Christ and Satan*: The Measured Power of Christ', *NM*, 90 (1989), 243–53.
Hauer, Stanley R, 'The Patriarchal Digression in the Old English *Exodus*, Lines 362–446', in *Eight Anglo-Saxon Studies*, ed. Joseph Wittig (Chapel Hill, NC: University of North Carolina Press, 1981), 77–90.
Heuchan, Valerie, 'God's Co-Workers and Powerful Tools: The Sources of Alfred's Building Metaphor in his Old English Translation of Augustine's *Soliloquies*', *N&Q*, 54.1 (2007), 1–11.
Hermann, John P., *Allegories of War: Language and Violence in Old English Poetry* (Ann Arbor, MI: University of Michigan Press, 1989).
Hermann, John P., 'Language and Spirituality in Cynewulf's *Juliana*', *Texas Studies in Literature and Language*, 26 (1984), 263–81.
Hieatt, Constance B., 'Divisions: Theme and Structure of *Genesis A*', *NM*, 81 (1980), 243–51.
Hill, John M., *The Cultural World in Beowulf* (Toronto: University of Toronto Press, 1995).
Hill, John M., 'The Sacrificial Synecdoche of Hands, Heads, and Arms in Anglo-Saxon Heroic Story' in *Naked Before God: Uncovering the Body*

in *Anglo-Saxon England*, ed. Benjamin C. Withers and Jonathan Wilcox (Morgantown, WV: University of West Virginia Press, 2003), 116–37.

Hill, Joyce, 'The Apocrypha in Anglo-Saxon England: The Challenge of Changing Distinctions', in *Apocryphal Texts and Traditions in Anglo-Saxon England*, ed. Kathryn Powell and D. G. Scragg (Cambridge, D. S. Brewer, 2003), 165–8.

Hill, Joyce, 'Archbishop Wulfstan: Reformer?', in *Wulfstan, Archbishop of York: The Proceedings of the Second Alcuin Conference*, ed. Matthew Townend (Turnhout: Brepols, 2004), 309–24.

Hill, Joyce, 'The Benedictine Reform and Beyond', in *A Companion to Anglo-Saxon Literature*, ed. Phillip Pulsiano and Elaine Treharne (Malden, MA: Blackwell, 2008), 151–68.

Hill, Joyce, 'Confronting *Germania Latina*: Changing Responses to Old English Biblical Verse', in *The Poems of Junius 11: Basic Readings*, ed. R. M. Liuzza (New York and London: Routledge, 2002), 1–19; repr. from *Latin Culture and Medieval Germanic Europe: Proceedings of the First Germania Latina Conference held at the University of Groningen, 26 May 1989*, ed. Richard North and Tette Hofstra (Groningen: E. Forsten, 1992), 71–88.

Hill, Joyce, 'The *Litaniae maiores* and *minores* in Rome, Francia, and Anglo-Saxon England: Terminology, Texts and Traditions', *Early Medieval Europe*, 9 (2000), 211–46.

Hill, Joyce, 'The Soldier of Christ in Old English Prose and Poetry', *LSE*, 12 (1981), 57–80.

Hill, Thomas D., 'The Age of Man and the World in the Old English *Guthlac A*', *JEGP*, 80 (1981), 13–21.

Hill, Thomas D., 'Drawing the Demon's Sting: A Note on a Traditional Motif in Felix's "Vita Sancti Guthlaci"', *N&Q*, 23 (1976), 388–90.

Hill, Thomas D., 'The Fall of Angels and Man in the Old English *Genesis B*', in *Anglo-Saxon Poetry: Essays in Appreciation, For John C. McGalliard*, ed. Lewis E. Nicholson and Dolores Warwick Frese (Notre Dame, IN: University of Notre Dame Press, 1975), 279–90.

Hill, Thomas D., 'The Fall of Satan in the Old English *Christ and Satan*', *JEGP*, 76 (1977), 315–25.

Hill, Thomas D., '"Hwyrftum scriþað": *Beowulf*, l. 163', *Mediaeval Studies*, 33 (1971), 379–81.

Hill, Thomas D., 'The Measure of Hell: *Christ and Satan* 695–722', *PQ*, 60 (1982 for 1981), 409–14.

Hill, Thomas D., 'Pilate's Visionary Wife and the Innocence of Eve: An Old Saxon Source for the Old English Poem *Genesis B*', *JEGP*, 101 (2002), 170–84.

Hill, Thomas D., 'Sapiential Structure and Figural Narrative in the Old English *Elene*', in *Cynewulf: Basic Readings*, ed. Robert E. Bjork, Basic Readings in Anglo-Saxon England 4 (New York: Garland, 1996), 207–28; repr. from *Traditio*, 27 (1971), 159–77.

Hill, Thomas D., 'Satan's Injured Innocence in *Genesis B*, 360–2; 390–2: A Gregorian Source', *ES*, 65 (1984), 289–90.
Hill, Thomas D., 'Satan's Pratfall and the Foot of Love: Some Pedal Images in *Piers Plowman* A, B, C', *Yearbook of Langland Studies*, 14 (2000), 153–61.
Hill, Thomas D., 'Some Remarks on "The Site of Lucifer's Throne"', *Anglia*, 87 (1969), 303–11.
Hill, Thomas D., 'The Sphragis as Apotropaic Sign: *Andreas* 1334–44', *Anglia*, 101 (1983),147–51.
Hill, Thomas D., 'The "Variegated Obit" as an Historiographic Motif in Old English Poetry and Anglo-Latin Historical Literature', *Traditio*, 44 (1988), 101–24.
Hill, Thomas D., 'When God Blew Satan out of Heaven: The Motif of Exsufflation in *Vercelli Homily XIX* and Later English Literature', *LSE*, 16 (1985), 132–41.
Hindle, Steve, 'Beating the Bounds of the Parish: Order, Memory, and Identity in the English Local Imagination, c. 1500–1700', in *Defining Community in Early Modern Europe*, ed. Michael J. Halvorson and Karen E. Spierling (Burlington, VT: Ashgate, 2008), 205–27.
Hofmann, Petra, 'Infernal Imagery in Anglo-Saxon Charters', PhD dissertation, University of St Andrews, 2008.
Hofsetter, W., 'Winchester and the Standardization of Old English Vocabulary', *ASE*, 17 (1988), 139–61.
Hollis, Stephanie, 'The Thematic Structure of the *Sermo Lupi ad Anglos*', *ASE*, 6 (1977), 175–95.
Hooke, Della, *The Landscape of Anglo-Saxon England* (Leicester: Leicester University Press, 1998).
Howe, Nicholas, 'Falling Into Place: Dislocation in the Junius Book', in *Unlocking the Wordhord: Anglo-Saxon Studies in Memory of Edward B. Irving, Jr.*, ed. Mark C. Amodio and Katherine O'Brien O'Keeffe (Toronto: University of Toronto Press, 2003), 14–37.
Howe, Nicholas, *Migration and Mythmaking in Anglo-Saxon England* (Notre Dame, IN: University of Notre Dame Press, 2001).
Howe, Nicholas. *Writing the Map of Anglo-Saxon England: Essays in Cultural Geography* (New Haven: Yale University Press, 2008).
Huppé, Bernard F., *Doctrine and Poetry: Augustine's Influence on Old English Poetry* (New York: State University of New York Press, 1959).
An Icelandic-English Dictionary, ed. Richard Cleasby and Gudbrand Vigfusson (Oxford: Clarendon Press, 1975).
Insley, Charles, 'Where Did All the Charters Go? Anglo-Saxon Charters and the New Politics of the Eleventh Century', *Anglo-Norman Studies*, 24 (2002), 109–27.
Irving, Edward B., Jr. *A Reading of Beowulf* (New Haven, CT: Yale University Press, 1968).

Isaacs, Neil D., *Structural Principles in Old English Poetry* (Knoxville: University of Tennessee Press, 1968).

Jager, Eric, 'Tempter as Rhetoric Teacher: The Fall of Language in the Old English *Genesis B*', *Neophil*, 72 (1988), 434–48.

Jaski, Bart, *Early Irish Kingship and Succession* (Dublin: Four Courts Press, 2000).

John, Eric, 'The Church of Winchester and the Tenth-Century Reformation', *Bulletin of the John Ryland's University Library of Manchester*, 47 (1965), 404–29.

John, Eric, *Land Tenure in Early England* (Leicester: Leicester University Press, 1964).

John, Eric, *Orbis Britanniae and Other Studies* (London: Leicester University Press, 1966).

John, Eric, 'The Sources of the English Monastic Reformation: A Comment', *Revue Bénédictine*, 70 (1960), 197–203.

Johnson, David F., 'The *Crux Usualis* as Apotropaic Weapon in Anglo-Saxon England', in *The Place of the Cross in Anglo-Saxon England*, ed. Catherine E. Karkov, Sarah Larratt Keefer, and Karen Louise Jolly (Woodbridge: Boydell, 2006), 80–95.

Johnson, David F., 'The Fall of Lucifer in *Genesis A* and Two Anglo-Latin Royal Charters', *JEGP* 97 (1998), 500–21.

Johnson, David F., 'Hagiographical Demon or Liturgical Devil? Demonology and Baptismal Imagery in Cynewulf's *Elene*', in *Essays for Joyce Hill on Her Sixtieth Birthday*, ed. Mary Swan, *LSE* 37 (Leeds: University of Leeds, 2006), 9–29.

Johnson, David F., 'Old English Religious Poetry: *Christ and Satan* and *The Dream of the Rood*', in *Companion to Old English Poetry*, ed. Henk Aertsen and Rolf H. Bremmer Jr. (Amsterdam: VU University Press, 1994), 159–87.

Johnson, David F., 'Spiritual Combat and the Land of Canaan in *Guthlac A*', in *Intertexts: Studies in Anglo-Saxon Culture Presented to Paul E. Szarmach*, ed. Virginia Blanton and Helene Scheck (Tempe and Turnhout: ACMRS with Brepols, 2009), 307–18.

Johnson, David F., 'Studies in the Literary Career of the Fallen Angels: The Devil and his Body in Old English Literature', PhD dissertation, Cornell University, 1993.

Johnson, David. F., 'Winchester Revisited: Æthelwold, Lucifer, and the Place of Origin of MS Junius 11' (forthcoming).

Jolly, Karen Louise, *Popular Religion in Late Anglo-Saxon England: Elf Charms in Context* (Chapel Hill: The University of North Carolina Press, 1996).

Jones, Christopher A., 'Envisioning the *cenobium* in *Guthlac A*', *Mediaeval Studies*, 57 (1995), 259–91.

Jones, Christopher A., 'Wulfstan's Liturgical Interests', in *Wulfstan,*

Archbishop of York: The Proceedings of the Second Alcuin Conference, ed. Matthew Townend (Turnhout: Brepols, 2004), 325–52.

Jost, Karl, 'The Legal Maxim in Ælfric's Homilies', *ES*, 36 (1955), 204–5.

Jost, Karl, *Wulfstanstudien*, Swiss Studies in English 23 (Bern: Francke, 1950).

Jurovics, Raachel, '*Sermo Lupi* and the Moral Purpose of Rhetoric', in *The Old English Homily and Its Backgrounds*, ed. Paul E. Szarmach and Bernard F. Huppé (Albany: University of New York Press, 1978), 203–20.

Kabir, Ananya Jahanara, *Paradise, Death, and Doomsday in Anglo-Saxon Literature*, CSASE 32 (Cambridge: Cambridge University Press, 2001).

Kahn, Paul W., *Political Theology: Four New Chapters on the Concept of Sovereignty* (New York: Columbia University Press, 2011).

Karkov, Catherine E., *Ruler Portraits of Anglo-Saxon England*, Anglo-Saxon Studies 3 (Woodbridge: Boydell, 2004).

Karkov, Catherine E., 'The Sign of the Cross: Poetic Performance and Liturgical Practice in the Junius 11 Manuscript', in *The Liturgy of the Late Anglo-Saxon Church*, ed. Helen Gittos and M. Bradford Bedingfield, HBS (Woodbridge: Boydell, 2005), 245–65.

Karkov, Catherine E., *Text and Picture in Anglo-Saxon England: Narrative Strategies in the Junius Manuscript*, CSASE 31 (Cambridge: Cambridge University Press, 2001).

Keefer, Sarah Larratt, *Old English Liturgical Verse: A Student Edition* (Buffalo: Broadview, 2010).

Keenan, Hugh. '*Christ and Satan*: Some Vagaries of Old English Poetic Composition', *Studies in Medieval Culture*, 5 (1975), 25–32.

Kelly, Fergus, *A Guide to Early Irish Law*, Early Irish Law Series 3 (Dublin: Dublin Institute for Advanced Studies, 1988).

Ker, N. R., *Catalogue of Manuscripts Containing Anglo-Saxon* (Oxford: Clarendon Press, 1957).

Keynes, Simon, 'An Abbot, an Archbishop, and the Viking Raids of 1006–7 and 1009–12', *ASE*, 36 (2007), 151–220.

Keynes, Simon, 'Charters and Writs', in *The Blackwell Encyclopedia of Anglo-Saxon England* ed. Michael Lapidge, John Blair, Simon Keynes, and Donald Scragg (Malden, MA: Blackwell, 2001).

Keynes, Simon, 'A Conspectus of the Charters of King Edgar, 957–75', in *Edgar, King of the English 959–975: New Interpretations*, ed. Donald Scragg (Woodbridge: Boydell, 2008), 60–82.

Keynes, Simon, *The Diplomas of King Æthelred 'The Unready' 978–1016: A Study in Their Use as Historical Evidence*, Cambridge Studies in Medieval Life and Thought Third Series 13 (Cambridge: Cambridge University Press, 1980).

Knowles, Dom David, *The Monastic Order in England: A History of Its Development from the Times of St Dunstan to the Fourth Lateran Council 943–1216* (Cambridge: Cambridge University Press, 1950).

Kramer, Johanna, *Between Earth and Heaven: Liminality and the Ascension of Christ in Anglo-Saxon Literature* (Manchester: Manchester University Press, 2014).

Kurtz, Benjamin P., 'From St. Anthony to St. Guthlac: A Study in Biography', *University of California Publications in Modern Philology*, 12 (1926), 103–46.

Labriola, Albert C., 'The Begetting and Exaltation of the Son: The Junius Manuscript and Milton's *Paradise Lost*', in *Milton's Legacy*, ed. Kristin A. Pruitt and Charles W. Durham (Selinsgrove: Susquehanna University Press, 2005), 22–32.

Ladner, Gerhart B., *The Idea of Reform: Its Impact on Christian Thought and Action in the Age of the Fathers* (Cambridge: Harvard University Press, 1959).

Lambert, Tom, *Law and Order in Anglo-Saxon England* (Oxford: Oxford University Press, 2017).

Lapidge, Michael, 'Æthelwold as Scholar and Teacher', in *Anglo-Latin Literature 900–1066* (London: Hambledon Press, 1993).

Lapidge, Michael, *The Anglo-Saxon Library* (Oxford: Oxford University Press, 2006).

Lapidge, Michael, 'B. and the *Vita Dunstani*', in *Anglo-Latin Literature 900–1066* (London: Hambledon Press, 1993).

Lapidge, Michael, 'Cynewulf and the *Passio S. Iulianae*', in *Unlocking the Wordhord: Anglo-Saxon Studies in Memory of Edward B. Irving Jr.*, ed. Mark C. Amodio and Katherine O'Brien O'Keeffe (Toronto: Toronto University Press, 2003), 147–71.

Lapidge, Michael, 'The Hermeneutic Style in Tenth-Century Anglo-Latin Literature', in *Anglo-Latin Literature 900–1066* (London: Hambledon Press, 1993).

Lapidge, Michael, 'The Saintly Life in Anglo-Saxon England', in *The Cambridge Companion to Old English Literature*, ed. Malcolm Godden and Michael Lapidge (Cambridge: Cambridge University Press, 1986), 243–63.

Lavezzo, Kathy, *Angels on the Edge of the World: The Geography of English Identity from Ælfric to Chaucer* (Santa Barbara: University of California, 1999).

Leclercq, Jean, et al., *The Spirituality of the Middle Ages* (New York: Burnes & Oates, 1986).

Lee, Alvin A., *The Guest-Hall of Eden: Four Essays on the Design of Old English Poetry* (New Haven: Yale University Press, 1972).

Lefebvre, Henri, *The Production of Space*, trans. Donald Nicholson-Smith (Oxford: Blackwell, 1991).

Le Goff, Jacques, 'Discorso di chiusura', in *Popoli e paesi nella cultura alltomedievale*, 2 vols., Settimane di studio del Centro italiano di studi sull'alto medioevo 29 (Spoleto: Presso la sede del Centro, 1983).

Lionarons, Joyce Tally, *The Homiletic Writings of Archbishop Wulfstan: A Critical Study* (Woodbridge: Boydell, 2010).
Lockett, Leslie, 'An Integrated Re-examination of the Dating of Oxford, Bodleian Library Junius 11', *ASE*, 31 (2002), 141–73.
Lockett, Leslie. *Anglo-Saxon Psychologies: The Vernacular and Latin Traditions* (Toronto: University of Toronto Press, 2011).
Loomis, C. Grant, *White Magic: An Introduction to the Folklore of Christian Legend* (Cambridge, MA: The Medieval Academy of America, 1948).
Lucas, Peter J., 'On the Incomplete Ending of *Daniel* and the Addition of *Christ and Satan* to MS Junius 11', *Anglia*, 97 (1979), 46–59.
Lucas, Peter J., 'Loyalty and Obedience in the Old English *Genesis* and the Interpolation of *Genesis B* into *Genesis A*', *Neophil*, 76 (1992), 121–35.
McCulloh, John M., 'Did Cynewulf Use a Martyrology? Reconsidering the Sources of *The Fates of the Apostles*', *ASE*, 29 (2000), 67–83.
McIntosh, Angus, 'Wulfstan's Prose', *Proceedings of the British Academy*, 34 (1949), 109–42; repr. *British Academy Papers on Anglo-Saxon England*, ed. E. G. Stanley (Oxford: Oxford University Press, 1990), 111–44.
McLeod, Neil, *Early Irish Contract Law*, Sydney Series on Celtic Studies (Sydney: University of Sydney Press, 1992).
McNamara, Martin, *The Apocrypha in the Irish Church* (Dublin: Dublin Institute for Advanced Studies, 1975; repr. 1984).
McNamara, Martin. *The Bible and the Apocrypha in the Early Irish Church (A.D. 600–1200)*, Instrumenta Patristica et Mediaevalia 66 (Turnhout: Brepols, 2015).
Mac Eoin, G., 'The Date and Authorship of *Saltair na Rann*', *Zeitschrift für celtische Philologie*, 28 (1960), 51–67.
Mac Eoin, G., 'Observations on *Saltair na Rann*', *Zeitschrift für celtische Philologie*, 39 (1982), 1–27.
Magennis, Hugh, *Images of Community in Old English Poetry*, CSASE 18 (Cambridge: Cambridge University Press, 1996).
Marafioti, Nicole, *The King's Body: Burial and Succession in Late Anglo-Saxon England* (Toronto: University of Toronto Press, 2014).
Marafioti, Nicole, 'Seeking Alfred's Body: Royal Tomb as Political Object in the Reign of Edward the Elder', *Early Medieval Europe*, 23 (2015), 202–28.
Marsden, Richard, *The Cambridge Old English Reader* (Cambridge: Cambridge University Press, 2004).
Marx, C. William, *The Devil's Rights and the Redemption in the Literature of Medieval England* (Cambridge: D. S. Brewer, 1995).
Meaney, Audrey L., 'Old English Legal and Penitential Rituals for "Heathenism"', in *Anglo-Saxons: Studies Presented to Cyril Roy Hart*, ed. Simon Keynes and Alfred P. Smyth (Dublin: Four Courts Press, 2006), 127–58.

Medieval Ireland: An Encyclopedia, ed. Seán Duffy (New York: Routledge, 2005).

Michelet, Fabienne L., *Creation, Migration, and Conquest: Imaginary Geography and Sense of Space in Old English Literature* (Oxford: Oxford University Press, 2006).

Milfull, Inge B., *The Hymns of the Anglo-Saxon Church: A Study and Edition of the 'Durham Hymnal'*, CSASE 17 (Cambridge: Cambridge University Press, 1996).

Mittman, Asa Simon and Susan M. Kim, 'Locating the Devil "Her" in MS Junius 11', *Gesta*, 54 (2015), 3–25.

Morey, James K., 'Adam and Judas in the Old English *Christ and Satan*', *SP*, 87 (1990), 397–409.

Morey, James K., *Book and Verse: A Guide to Middle English Biblical Literature* (Urbana, IL: University of Illinois Press, 2000).

Murdoch, Brian, *The Medieval Popular Bible: Expansions of Genesis in the Middle Ages* (Cambridge: D. S. Brewer, 2003).

Neckel, Gustav, 'Sigmunds Drachenkampf', *Edda*, 13 (1920), 122–40; 204–9.

Nelson, Janet L., 'A King Across the Sea: Alfred in Continental Perspective', *Transactions of the Royal Historical Society*, 36 (1986), 46–68.

Nelson, Marie, '*The Battle of Maldon* and *Juliana*: the Language of Confrontation', in *Modes of Interpretation in Old English Literature: Essays in Honour of Stanley B. Greenfield*, ed. Phyllis Rugg Brown, Georgia Ronan Crampton, and Fred C. Robinson (Toronto: University of Toronto Press, 1986), 137–50.

Neville, Jennifer, *Representations of the Natural World in Old English Poetry*, CSASE 27 (Cambridge: Cambridge University Press, 1999).

Ní Mhaonaigh, Máire, 'The Learning of Ireland in the Early Medieval Period' in *Books Most Needful to Know: Contexts for the Study of Anglo-Saxon England*, ed. Paul Szarmach, Old English Newsletter Subsidia 36 (Kalamazoo, MI: Medieval Institute Publications, 2016).

O'Brien O'Keeffe, Katherine, 'Body and Law in Late Anglo-Saxon England', *ASE*, 27 (1998), 209–32.

O'Brien O'Keeffe, Katherine, 'Guthlac's Crossing', *Quaestio*, 2 (2001), 1–26.

O'Brien O'Keeffe, Katherine, *Stealing Obedience: Narratives of Agency and Identity in Later Anglo-Saxon England* (Toronto: University of Toronto Press, 2012).

Ó Carragáin, Éamonn, 'How did the Vercelli Collector Interpret *The Dream of the Rood?*', in *Studies in English Language and Early Literature in Honour of Paul Christophersen*, ed. P. M. Tilling, Occasional Papers in Linguistics and Language Teaching 8 (Colerain: The University of Ulster, 1981), 63–104.

Ó Corráin, Donnchadh, 'Nationality and Kingship in Pre-Norman

Ireland', in *Historical Studies XI: Nationality and the Pursuit of National Independence (Papers Read before the Conference Held at Trinity College, Dublin, 26–31 May 1975)*, ed. T. W. Moody (Belfast: Appletree Press, 1978), 1–35.

Ohlgren, Thomas, 'The Illustrations of the Cædmonian Genesis: Literary Criticism Through Art', *Mediaevalia et Humanistica*, 3 (1972), 199–212.

Orchard, Andy, 'Crying Wolf: Oral Style and the *Sermones Lupi*', *ASE*, 21 (1992), 239–64.

Orchard, Andy, 'On Editing Wulfstan', in *Early Medieval Texts and Interpretations: Studies Presented to Donald G. Scragg*, ed. Elaine Treharne and Susan Rosser (Tempe: ACMRS, 2003), 311–40.

Orchard, Andy, 'Re-editing Wulfstan: Where's the Point?', in *Wulfstan, Archbishop of York: The Proceedings of the Second Alcuin Conference*, ed. Matthew Townend, SEMA 10 (Turnhout: Brepols, 2004), 63–92.

Orchard, Andy, 'Wulfstan as Reader, Writer, and Rewriter', in *The Old English Homily: Precedent, Practice, and Appropriation*, ed. Aaron J Kleist, SEMA 17 (Turnhout: Brepols, 2007), 157–82.

Overing, Gillian R., 'On Reading Eve: *Genesis B* and the Readers' Desire', in *Speaking Two Languages: Traditional Disciplines and Contemporary Theory in Medieval Studies*, ed. Allen J. Frantzen (Albany: State University of New York Press, 1991), 35–63.

Pelle, Stephen, '*Ræd*, *Unræd*, and Raining Angels: Alterations to a Late Copy of Ælfric's *De Initio Creaturae*', *N&Q*, 53 (2010), 295–301.

Picard, Jean-Michel, '*Princeps* and *principatus* in the Early Irish Church', in *Seanchas: Studies in Early Irish Archaeology, History and Literature in Honour of Francis J. Byrne*, ed. Alfred P. Smyth (Dublin: Four Courts, 2000), 146–60.

Portnoy, Phyllis, '"Remnant" and Ritual: The Place of *Daniel* and *Christ and Satan* in the Junius Epic', *ES*, 75 (1994), 408–22.

Portnoy, Phyllis, 'Ring Composition and the Digressions of *Exodus*: The "Legacy" of the "Remnant"', *ES*, 82 (2001), 289–307.

Pratt, David, 'Problems of Authorship and Audience in the Writings of King Alfred the Great', in *Lay Intellectuals in the Carolingian World*, ed. Patrick Wormald and Janet L. Nelson (Cambridge: Cambridge University Press, 2007), 162–91.

Priebsch, Robert, *The Heliand Manuscript Cotton Caligula A VII in the British Museum: A Study* (Oxford: Clarendon Press, 1925).

Rabin, Andrew, 'The Wolf's Testimony to the English: Law and the Witness in the "Sermo Lupi ad Anglos"', *JEGP*, 105 (2006), 388–414.

Raw, Barbara, 'The Construction of Oxford, Bodleian Junius 11', *ASE*, 13 (1984), 187–207.

Raw, Barbara, 'The Probable Derivation of Most of the Illustrations in Junius 11 from an Old Saxon Genesis', *ASE*, 54 (1976), 133–48.

Regan, Catharine A., 'Evangelicalism as the Informing Principle of Cynewulf's *Elene*', *Traditio*, 29 (1973), 27–52.

Remley, Paul G., *Old English Biblical Verse: Studies in Genesis, Exodus and Daniel*, CSASE 16 (Cambridge: Cambridge University Press, 1996).

Revard, Stella Purce, *The War in Heaven: Paradise Lost and the Tradition of Satan's Rebellion* (Ithaca, NY: Cornell University Press, 1980).

Reynolds, Andrew, *Later Anglo-Saxon England: Life and Landscape* (Stroud: Tempus, 1999).

Robbins, Frank Egleston, *Hexaemeral Literature: A Study of the Greek and Latin Commentaries on Genesis* (Chicago: University of Chicago Press, 1912).

Roberts, Jane, 'The Old English Prose Translation of Felix's *Vita sancti Guthlaci*', in *Studies in Earlier Old English Prose*, ed. Paul E. Szarmach (Albany: State University of New York Press, 1986), 363–79.

Robinson, Fred, 'God, Death, and Loyalty in *The Battle of Maldon*', in *The Tomb of Beowulf and Other Essays on Old English* (Cambridge, MA: Blackwell, 1993).

Rosenwein, Barbara H., *Negotiating Space: Power, Restraint, and Privileges of Immunity in Early Medieval Europe* (Ithaca, NY: Cornell University Press, 1999).

Rumble, Alexander R., 'The Laity and the Monastic Reform', in *Edgar, King of the English   959–975: New Interpretations*, ed. Donald Scragg (Woodbridge: Boydell, 2008), 242–51.

Sawyer, Peter H., *Anglo-Saxon Charters: An Annotated List and Bibliography*, Royal Historical Society Guides and Handbooks 8 (London: Roman and Littlefield Publishers, 1968).

Schabram, H., *Superbia: Studienzum altenglischen Wortschatz*, vol. 1, *Die dialektale und zeitliche Verbreitung des Wortguts* (Munich: Wilhelm Fink, 1965).

Scheil, Andrew P., *The Footsteps of Israel: Understanding Jews in Anglo-Saxon England* (Ann Arbor, MI: University of Michigan Press, 2004).

Scowcroft, R. Mark, '*Leabhar Gabhála* Part I: The Growth of the Text', *Ériu*, 38 (1987), 79–140.

Scowcroft, R. Mark, '*Leabhar Gabhála* Part II: The Growth of the Tradition', *Ériu*, 39 (1988), 1 –66.

Scragg, Donald G., 'An Old English Homilist of Archbishop Dunstan's Day', in *Words, Texts, and Manuscripts: Studies in Anglo-Saxon Culture Presented to Helmut Gneuss on the Occasion of his Sixty-Fifth Birthday*, ed. Michael Korhammer (Cambridge: Cambridge University Press, 1992), 181–92.

Scragg, Donald G., 'Napier's "Wulfstan" Homily XXX: Its Sources, its Relationship to the Vercelli Book and its Style', *ASE*, 6 (1977), 197–211.

Seymour, J. D., 'The Book of Adam and Eve in Ireland', *Proceedings of the Royal Irish Academy*, 36 (1921–4), 121–33.

Seymour, J. D., 'Notes on Apocrypha in Ireland', *Proceedings of the Royal Irish Academy*, 37 (1926), 107–17.

Sharma, Manish, 'A Reconsideration of the Structure of *Guthlac A*: The Extremes of Saintliness', *JEGP* (2002), 185–200.

Shepherd, Geoffrey, 'Scriptural Poetry', in *Continuations and Beginnings: Studies in English Literature*, ed. Eric Gerald Stanley (London and Edinburgh: Nelson, 1966), 1–36.

Shippey, T. A., 'Winchester in the Anglo-Saxon Period and After', in *Winchester: History and Literature: The Proceedings of a Conference in Celebration of the 150th Anniversary of the Founding of King Alfred's College Held on 16th March 1991*, ed. Simon Barker and Colin Haydon (York: King Alfred's College, 1992), 1–21.

Shook, Laurence K., 'The Burial Mound in *Guthlac A*', *MP*, 58 (1960), 1–10.

Shook, Laurence K., 'The Prologue of the Old-English *Guthlac A*', *Mediaeval Studies*, 23 (1961), 294–304.

Sievers, Eduard, *Der Heliand und die angelsächsiche Genesis* (Halle: M. Niemeyer, 1875).

Siewers, Alfred K., 'Landscapes of Conversion: Guthlac's Mound and Grendel's Mere as Expressions of Anglo-Saxon Nation-Building', *Viator*, 34 (2003), 1–39.

Simms, Katherine, *From Kings to Warlords: The Changing Political Structure of Gaelic Ireland in the Later Middle Ages* (Woodbridge: Boydell, 1987).

Sisam, Kenneth, 'Anglo-Saxon Royal Genealogies', *Publications of the British Academy*, 39 (1953), 287–348.

Sleeth, Charles R., *Studies in Christ and Satan*, McMaster Old English Studies and Texts 3 (Toronto: University of Toronto Press, 1982).

Smith, Anthony D., *The Ethnic Origins of Nations* (Oxford: Blackwell, 1986).

Smith, Scott T., 'The Edgar Poems and the Poetics of Failure in the *Anglo-Saxon Chronicle*', *ASE*, 39 (2010), 105–37.

Smith, Scott T., 'Faith and Forfeiture in the Old English *Genesis A*', *MP*, 111 (2014), 593–615.

Smith, Scott T., *Land and Book: Literature and Land Tenure in Anglo-Saxon England* (Toronto, University of Toronto Press, 2012).

Sowerby, Richard, *Angels in Early Medieval England* (Oxford: Oxford University Press, 2016).

Stafford, Pauline, *Unification and Conquest: A Political and Social History of England in the Tenth and Eleventh Centuries* (London: Edward Arnold, 1989).

Stanbury, Sarah, 'In God's Sight: Vision and Sacred History in *Purity*', in *Text and Matter: New Critical Perspectives of the Pearl-Poet*, ed. Robert Blanch, Miriam Youngerman Miller, and Julian Wasserman (Troy, NY: Whitson, 1991), 105–16.

Stanley, Eric, '*Staþol*: A Firm Foundation for Imagery', in *Text, Image, Interpretation: Studies in Anglo-Saxon Literature and its Insular Context in Honour of Éamonn Ó Carragáin*, ed. Alastair Minnis and Jane Roberts (Turnhout: Brepols, 2007).

Stenton, F. M., *The Latin Charters of the Anglo-Saxon Period* (Oxford: Clarendon Press, 1955).

Stephenson, Rebecca, *The Politics of Language: Byrhtferth, Ælfric, and the Multilingual Identity of the Benedictine Reform* (Toronto: University of Toronto Press, 2015).

Stephenson, Rebecca, 'Scapegoating the Secular Clergy: The Hermeneutic Style as a Form of Monastic Self-Definition', *ASE*, 38 (2009), 101–35.

Stodnick, Jaqueline, 'What (and Where) is the *Anglo-Saxon Chronicle* About: Spatial History', *John Rylands University Library Manchester*, 86 (2004), 87–104.

Szarmach, Paul E., 'Ælfric as Exegete: Approaches and Examples in the Study of the *Sermones Catholici*', in *Hermeneutics and Medieval Culture*, ed. P. Gallacher and H. Damico (Albany, NY: SUNY Press, 1989), 237–47.

Szarmach, Paul E., 'The (Sub-) Genre of *The Battle of Maldon*', in *The Battle of Maldon Fact and Fiction*, ed. Janet Cooper (London: The Hambledon Press, 1993), 43–61.

Ten Brink, Bernhard, *History of English Literature*, vol. 1, trans. Horace M. Kennedy (New York: Henry Holt and Company, 1883).

Thornbury, Emily, *Becoming a Poet in Anglo-Saxon England* (Cambridge: Cambridge University Press, 2014).

Thorpe, Benjamin, *Caedmon's Metrical Paraphrase of Parts of the Holy Scriptures in Anglo-Saxon: with an English Translation, Notes, and Verbal Index* (London: Society of Antiquaries of London, 1832).

Trilling, Renée R., *The Aesthetics of Nostalgia: Historical Representation in Old English Verse* (Toronto: University of Toronto Press, 2009).

Trilling, Renée R., 'Sovereignty and Social Order: Archbishop Wulfstan and the *Institutes of Polity*', in *The Bishop Reformed: Studies of Episcopal Power and Culture in the Central Middle Ages*, ed. John S. Ott and Anna Trumbore Jones (Burlington, VT: Ashgate, 2007), 58–85.

Tyler, Elizabeth, *Old English Poetics: The Aesthetics of the Familiar in Anglo-Saxon England* (Woodbridge: York Medieval Press, 2006).

Van Meter, David C., 'The Ritualized Presentation of Weapons and the Ideology of Nobility in *Beowulf*', *JEGP*, 95 (1996), 175–89.

Vickrey, John, 'Adam, Eve, and the *tacen* in Genesis B', *PQ*, 72 (1993), 1–14.

Vickrey, John, 'Some Further Remarks on *selfsceaft*', *Zeitschrift für deutsches Altertum und deutsche Literatur*, 110 (1981), 1–14.

Vickrey, John, 'The Vision of Eve in Genesis B', *Speculum*, 44 (1969), 86–102.

Walsham, Alexandra, *The Reformation of the Landscape: Religion, Identity, and Memory in Early Modern Britain and Ireland* (Oxford: Oxford University Press, 2011).

Wartnjes, Immo, 'Regnal Succession in Early Medieval Ireland', *Journal of Medieval History*, 30 (2004), 277–410.
Wehlau, Ruth, 'The Power of Knowledge and the Location of the Reader in *Christ and Satan*', in *The Poems of Junius 11: Basic Readings*, ed. R. M. Liuzza (New York and London: Routledge, 2002), 287–301; repr. from *JEGP*, 97 (1998), 1–12.
Wehlau, Ruth, *The Riddle of Creation: Metaphor Structures in Old English Poetry* (New York: Peter Lang, 1997).
Wentersdorf, Karl P., '*Guthlac A*: The Battle for the *Beorg*', *Neophil*, 62 (1978), 135–42.
Whitbread, L. G., 'Wulfstan Homilies XXIX, XXX and Some Related Texts', *Anglia*, 81 (1963), 347–64.
Whitelock, Dorothy, 'Archbishop Wulfstan, Homilist and Statesman', in *Transactions of the Royal Historical Society*, 24 (1942), 25–45.
Whitelock, Dorothy, 'The Authorship of the Account of King Edgar's Establishment of the Monasteries', in *Philological Essays: Studies in Old and Middle English Literature in Honour of Herbert Dean Meritt*, ed. J. L. Rosier (The Hague: Mouton, 1970), 125–36.
Wilcox, Jonathan, 'The Dissemination of Wulfstan's Homilies: The Wulfstan Tradition in Eleventh-Century Vernacular Preaching', in *England in the Eleventh Century: Proceedings of the 1990 Harlaxton Symposium*, ed. Carola Hicks, Harlaxton Medieval Studies 2 (Stamford: Paul Watkins, 1992), 199–217.
Wilcox, Jonathan, 'The Wolf on Shepherds: Wulfstan, Bishops, and the Context of the *Sermo Lupi ad Anglos*', in *Old English Prose: Basic Readings*, ed. Paul E. Szarmach (New York and London: Garland, 2000), 395–418.
Wilcox, Jonathan, 'Wulfstan's *Sermo Lupi ad Anglos* as Political Performance: 16 February 1014 and Beyond', in *Wulfstan, Archbishop of York: The Proceedings of the Second Alcuin Conference*, ed. Matthew Townend (Turnhout: Brepols, 2004), 373–96.
Willard, Rudolph, 'The Blickling-Junius Tithing Homily and Caesarius of Arles', *Philologica: The Malone Anniversary Studies* (1949), 65–78.
Williams, Ann, 'Land tenure', in *The Blackwell Encyclopedia of Anglo-Saxon England*, ed. Michael Lapidge, John Blair, Simon Keynes, and Donald Scragg (Malden, MA: Blackwell, 2001).
Withers, Benjamin C., 'Satan's Mandorla: Translation, Transformation, and Interpretation in Late Anglo-Saxon England', *Insular and Anglo-Saxon Art and Thought in the Early Medieval Period* (2011), 247–70.
Woolf, Rosemary, 'The Devil in Old English Poetry', *RES*, 4 (1953), 1–12.
Woolf, Rosemary, 'The Fall of Man in *Genesis B* and *The Mystère d'Adam*', in *Studies in Old English Literature in Honor of Arthur G. Brodeur*, ed. Stanley B. Greenfield (New York: Russell and Russell, 1973), 187–99.

Woolf, Rosemary, 'Saints' Lives', in *Continuations and Beginnings: Studies in Old English Literature*, ed. E. G. Stanley (London and Edinburgh: Nelson, 1966), 37–66.

Wormald, Francis, 'Late Anglo-Saxon Art: Some Questions and Suggestions', in *Studies in Western Art: Acts of the Twentieth International Congress of the History of Art*, ed. M. Meiss and I. E. Rubin, 4 vols (Princeton: Princeton University Press, 1963); repr. *Francis Wormald: Collected Writings*, II, Studies in English and Continental Art of the Later Middle Ages, ed. J. J. G. Alexander, T. J. Brown, and J. Gibbs, 2 vols (London: Harvey Miller, 1984), 19–26.

Wormald, Patrick, 'Archbishop Wulfstan: Eleventh-Century State-Builder', in *Wulfstan, Archbishop of York: The Proceedings of the Second Alcuin Conference*, ed. Matthew Townend (Turnhout: Brepols, 2004), 9–27.

Wormald, Patrick, 'Æthelwold and his Continental Counterparts: Contact, Comparison, Contrast', in *Bishop Æthelwold: His Career and Influence*, ed. Barbara Yorke (Woodbridge: Boydell, 1988), 13–42.

Wormald, Patrick, 'Archbishop Wulfstan and the Holiness of Society', in *Anglo-Saxon History: Basic Readings*, ed. David A. E. Pelteret (New York: Garland, 1999), 191–224.

Wormald, Patrick, 'Celtic and Anglo-Saxon Kingship: Some Further Thoughts', in *Sources of Anglo-Saxon Culture*, ed. Paul Szarmach (Kalamazoo, MI: Medieval Institute Publications, 1986), 151–83.

Wormald, Patrick, '*Lex scripta* and *verbum regis*: Legislation and Germanic Kingship from Euric to Cnut', in *Legal Culture in the Early Medieval West: Law as Text, Image, and Experience* (London: Bloomsbury, 1999), 1–48.

Wormald, Patrick, *The Making of English Law: King Alfred to the Twelfth Century. Vol. 1 Legislation and Its Limits* (Oxford: Blackwell, 1999).

Wormald, Patrick, 'Oaths', in *The Blackwell Encyclopedia of Anglo-Saxon England*, ed. Michael Lapidge, John Blair, Simon Keynes, and Donald Scragg (Malden, MA: Blackwell, 2001).

Wrenn, C. L., *A Study of Old English Literature* (London: Harrap, 1967).

Wright, Charles D., 'Apocryphal Lore and Insular Tradition in St. Gall Stiftsbibliothek 908', in *Irland und Christenheit: Bibelstudien und Mission*, ed. Próinsías Ní Chatháin and Michael Richter (Stuttgart: Klett-Cotta, 1987), 124–45.

Wright, Charles D., '"fægere þurh forðgesceaft": The Confirmation of the Angels in Old English Literature', *MÆ*, 86 (2017), 22–37.

Wright, Charles D., 'From Monks' Jokes to Sages' Wisdom: *The Joca monachorum* Tradition and the Irish *Imacallam in dá Thúarad*', in *Spoken and Written Language: Relations between Latin and the Vernacular in the Earlier Middle Ages*, ed. Mary Garrison and Marco Mostert (Turnhout: Brepols, 2013), 199–225.

Wright, Charles D., '*Genesis A* ad Litteram', in *Old English Literature and the Old Testament*, ed. Michael Fox and Manish Sharma (Toronto: Toronto University Press, 2012), 121–71.

Wright, Charles D., *The Irish Tradition in Old English Literature*, CSASE 6 (Cambridge: Cambridge University Press, 1993).

Wright, Charles D., 'Jewish Magic and Christian Miracle in the Old English *Andreas*', in *Imagining the Jew in Anglo-Saxon England*, ed. Samantha Zacher (Toronto: University of Toronto Press, 2016), 167–93.

Wright, Charles D., 'More Old English Poetry in Vercelli Homily XXI', in *Early Medieval English Texts and Interpretations: Studies Presented to Donald G. Scragg*, ed. Elaine Treharne and Susan Rosser (Tempe: ACMRS, 2002).

Wright, Charles D., 'An Old English Formulaic System and its Contexts in Cynewulf's Poetry', *ASE*, 40 (2011), 151–74.

Wright, Charles D., 'The Three Temptations and the Seven Gifts of the Holy Spirit in *Guthlac A*, 160b–169', *Traditio*, 38 (1982), 341–3.

Wright, Charles D., 'Vercelli Homilies XI–XIII and the Anglo-Saxon Benedictine Reform: Tailored Sources and Implied Audiences', in *Preacher, Sermon and Audience in the Middle Ages*, ed. Carolyn Muessig (Leiden: Brill, 2002), 203–27.

Wright, Charles D., 'Vercelli Homily XV and *The Apocalypse of Thomas*', in *New Readings in the Vercelli Book*, ed. Samantha Zacher and Andy Orchard (Toronto: University of Toronto Press, 2009), 150–84.

Zacher, Samantha, *Preaching the Converted: The Style and Rhetoric of the Vercelli Book Homilies* (Toronto: University of Toronto Press, 2009).

Zacher, Samantha, *Rewriting the Old Testament in Anglo-Saxon Verse: Becoming the Chosen People* (London: Bloomsbury, 2014).

Zangemeister, Karl and Wilhelm Braune, 'Bruchstücke der altsächsichen Bibeldichtung aus der Bibliotheca Palatina', *Neue Heidelberger Jahrbücher*, 4 (1894), 205–94.

Index

Note: n. after a page reference indicates a note on that page.
Page numbers in **bold** refer to figures.

Abbo of Fleury 258–9
Acta Cyriaci 172–3
Adam 12, 14, 36, **37**, 38, 46, 75, 89, 101–2, 117, 166, 207
  creation of 77
  fall of 97–103, 250–1
  rights over lands 96
  and Satan 79–80
  sin 83–4
  territorial inheritance 76
Ælfric of Eynsham 1, 2, 2–3, 12, 17, 202, 204, 218, 236, 252, 262
  account of the fall of Satan 245–50
  Catholic Homilies 3
  De Initio Creaturae 3, 277–8
  fall of the angels narrative 237–9, 245–50, 278–9
  Heptateuch 9
  Letter to Sigeweard 3, 59, 237, 248–50
  Letter to Wulfgeat of Ylmandun 237–8, 246–8
  'Preface to *Genesis*' 1, 237
  replacement doctrine 250–1, 252–3
  Vita S. Æthelwoldi 135
  Wulfstan of York, Archbishop and 239, 244–5

Ælfthryth, Queen 129
Ælfwine 48–9
Æthelred I, King 58, 238, 239
Æthelred II 48–9, 50
Æthelwold 7, 90, 124, 128, 128–9, 136, 138–9, 143–4, 144–5, 147–8, 265, 276
Alcuin 1, 2, 4, 9, 115, 123, 261
Aldhelm 115, 123, 142
  Carmen de Virginitate 115, 276
  De laudibus virginitatis 177
Alfred, King 12, 23, 25, 27–9, 44, 45, 74, 86, 127, 128
  Preface to Augustine's *Soliloquies* 59–60, 71–3, 90, 102, 182
Ancrene Wisse 276
Andreas 16, 160, 162, 174–80
angelic creation 13, 34, 38
angelic orders, hierarchies 5
angelic rebellion and the fall of the angels 1–2, 4–5, 13, 58, 103, 123, 160, 241–6
  Ælfric of Eynsham and 237–9, 245–50, 278–9
  as charm 160–3, 172–3, 178, 180–7
  charter references 47–51, 130, 139–42, 144–7
  in *Christ and Satan* 207–14

Index

crimes 25
and the fall of man 99
Genesis A account 32, **33**, 35, 36, 39–46
Genesis B account 84–99
in *Guthlac A* 184–6
influence 275–9
Irish versions 77–83
as a legal clash 83
New Minster Charter and 130, 139–45
in patristic theology 5–10
political iteration 3–4
and pride or *ofermod* 8, 74, 95, 105n.14, 243, 247
punishments 26, 42–3
Sigewulf's questions 1, 2
sin 60
Wulfstan of York and 236, 237–9, 241–6, 278–9
angelology 180–6
angels, loyalty to God 3
Angli, land of 6–7
Anglo Saxon Chronicle 30, 134, 232–4
Antichrist 17, 201, 234, 236, 243, 252, 257–8, 262, 264
apocryphal texts 84
Ascension theology 205
Asser 23
Athanasius 161, 188–9n.21
Augustine of Hippo 5, 6, 7–8, 9, 34, 36, 236, 249
  De Catechizandis Rudibus 3, 39
  De Civitate Dei 26, 140–1, 253, 262
  De Genesi ad Litteram 123
  Enchiridion ad Laurentium 26, 140–1, 253, 262
  replacement doctrine 26, 29, 252, 253, 262, 263

Baldwin, Abbot 52
Baptism, liturgy of 173
Battle of Maldon, The 99

Bazire and Cross Homily 1 203
Bazire and Cross Homily 4 206–7
Bazire and Cross Homily 5 218
Bazire and Cross Homily 6 219
Bede 3, 4, 12, 15, 115, 119–24, 136, 201, 252–3, 264, 275
  Commentary on the Epistle of Jude 6 76, 119–20
  Epistola ad Ecgbertum 119, 120–2, 157–9
  In Genesin 8
  Historia ecclesiastica 6–7, 52
  In Lucae Euangelium Expositio 141, 253–4
  Martyrologium 164
  'On Tobias' 7
Benedictine Reform, the 3–4, 12–13, 15, 54–5, 69n.137, 86, 99, 117, 124, 124–6, 130, 147, 159–60
  aims 147–8, 151n.38
  concerns 232
  origins 133–4
Beowulf 30, 40, 53–4, 65n.70, 170, 170–1, 174, 214–16
Bible 2, 14, 76
birthright 79–80
Blickling Homily 4 115–16, 117, 119, 263, 276
Blickling Homily 19 175
Boniface 8
Book of the Secrets of Enoch, The 5
boundaries 197, 202–7, 218–19
bounds, beating the 205
Bretha Nemed 80
Byrhtferth of Ramsey 127–8, 132–3
  Enchiridion, 118
  Vita S. Oswaldi 134

Cædmon 3
catechetical *narratio* 139
charms 160–1, 163, 181, 186–7
charters 12, 29, 30, 31, 46–51, 119, 131, 140

Christ
 in *Christ and Satan* 210, 214–19
 and Satan 8–9, 17, 199–201, 213
 as sovereign figure 57
 Temptation of 204, 214–17, 220–1
Christ and Satan 17, 32, 57, 103, 107n.38, 197–202, 278
 Christ in 210, 214–19
 fall of the angels narrative 207–14
 final episode 214–19
 and liturgical practice 202–7, 220–2
Christian identity 7, 99, 103, 148, 254, 264–5, 275
Chrysostom, John 122–3
Church, the, unity of 120
Church leaders, negligence 116–17
clerics
 Bede on failures of 119–24
 corruption 114–16
 duties 122–3
 fallen 122–4
 punishments 147
 secular 118–19, 127, 129, 131–48, 232, 254, 265
Cnut, King 49–50, 50, 239, 240, 260, 262
Codex Wintoniensis 145
compensation 44–6
confiscation 12, 28, 30, 47
Constantine, Emperor 163, 168
creation narratives 26–7, 38, 51–2, 139
Cross, the, power of 171–2, 174
Cynewulf 7, 16, 162
 Elene 16, 117, 160, 163, 168–74
 Juliana 16, 160, 163–8, 170

Death of Edgar, The 146
demons 157–9, 164–8, 177–8, 180–7
devils, idle speech 180–6
Devil's Account, The 165

Dhuoda, *Handbook for William* 6
Di Astud Chor ('On the Securing of Contracts') 82–3
disinheritance 76, 201
Doomsday 202

Eadwig 128
ecclesiastical hierarchy 55
ecclesiastical possessions 120–1, 148
Edgar, King 15–6, 54–5, 57–8, 86, 117–18, 122, 124, 127–9, 131, 133–4, 135–6, 144, 146, 147, 148, 184, 232, 234, 265
Edward the Elder, King 127
Edward 'the Martyr', King 232–3
Enlarged Rule of Chrodegang, The 133
Enoch 76
Epiphanius of Salamis, Bishop 9
Evagrius 181
Eve 14, 36, **37**, 38, 46, 77, 89, 96, 117, 166
 exiting paradise 101–2
 fall of 75, 97–103, 250–1
 sin 83–4
 temptation of 85
 vision of 100–1
Exeter Book 9, 181, 201

fasting 206
Felix, *Vita Guthlaci* 181, 201
Florence of Worcester 51
forfeiture 27–9, 36, 47
free will 247–8, 252
Freolsboc to Ciltancvmbe 145–6

Genesis 1
Genesis A 9, 13, 14, 23, 28, 76, 85–6, 87, 117, 139, 200, 235, 278
 account of the angelic rebellion 39–46
 creation narrative 38, 51–2

Index

creation of humankind 36
destruction of Sodom and
  Gomorrah 54, 57
fall of the angels illustration 32,
  33, 35, 36
heavenly space 25–6
land descriptions 51–5
and legal practices 38–46
and replacement diplomas 46–51
replacement doctrine 26–7, 38,
  43–4
Satan's crime 59
sources 38–9, 64n.59
and space 30–8, 51–60
Genesis B 9, 12, 13, 14–15, 32, 60,
  73–5, 83, 166, 182, 199, 200,
  278
  fall of the angels in 84–99
  and the fall of man 97–103
  problems and peculiarities of
    76
  Satan in 73–5, 83–4, 88–99, 212,
    213
gield 44–6
Gildas 4, 261, 263, 264
God
  angels loyalty to 3
  command to Adam 46
  creation of hell 41–2
  creation of humankind 27, 36
  fiat lux command 10, 34
  and Lucifer 78, 89–90
  relationship to Satan 92–3
  response to angelic rebellion
    93–4
  sovereignty 90, 97, 236, 250–1
Gospel of Nicodemus, The 76
Gregory the Great, Pope 5–7, 24,
  102, 138, 147
  Dialogues 23–5, 52, 180
  Homiliae in Evangelia 26, 141
  Pastoral Care 114–15
  replacement doctrine 26, 29,
    252, 253
Grimbald 72

Guthlac, St 157–60, 180–7
Guthlac A 16, 46, 158–9, 162,
  180–7
Guthlac B 181

habitations, creation of meaning
  through 71–3
hagiography 179–80
Haimo of Auxerre 7, 141
heaven 12, 24–6, 40–1, 83, 202,
  249–50
  Genesis A representations
hell 39, 41–2, 75, 95, 96–7, 197–8,
  199–200, 202, 218–19, 221, 279
hermeneutic Latin 133, 276
homelands 197–222
  boundaries 199–200, 218–19,
    220–2
  Christ and Satan fall of the
    angels narrative 207–14
  in *Guthlac A* 181–2, 197
  and liturgical practice 202–7
horror vacui 51–60
Hrabanus Maurus 3
Hymn for Vespers of the Feast of
  All Saints 142–3

idle speech, of devils 180–6
inheritance 148, 206
  co-heirs 108n.44
  seniority 75, 78, 80–1
  sibling rivalries 77–84
  Irish vernacular adaptations 75–84
Isaiah 75, 92

Jeremiah 258
Jews 4, 169–70, 174
John the Saxon 72
John XII, Pope 135–6
Judas Cyriacus 16, 168–74
Judgement Day 17, 117, 127, 222
Junius Manuscript 11, 25, 27, 31,
  32, **33**, **35**, **37**, 46, 47, 85, 86,
  88, 98, 99, 103, 197–9, 202,
  221–2

'King Edgar's Establishment of
    Monasteries' 132
kingship 13, 128, 147, 201
knowledge, recovery of 168–74
Konungs Skuggsjá 255–6

Lactantius 9
land
    care and maintenance 82
    charters 13–14
    classifications 50, 101
    in *Guthlac A* 182
landholding, obligations 57
Last Judgment 57, 180, 182, 199
law codes 12, 44
Le Goff, Jacques 11, 29
Leabhar Breac ('Speckled Book')
    80, 197
Lebor Gabála Érenn ('Book of the
    Taking of Ireland') 14, 75, 76,
    77, 81–2, 82, 87, 108n.44
Lefebvre, Henri 11, 12, 15, 29, 31,
    47, 124, 248
legal precedent, sacral narrative
    as 30
Leofsige, ealdorman 50
Liber Vitae 59
Life of Gregory the Great 6–7
Life of Oswald, The 146
Lucifer *see* Satan
Luke 5–6, 56

man, fall of 83, 88, 97–103
Martin of Braga 3, 7, 97
martyrdom 161–8, 186
migration myth, the 4
Milton, John 1, 200
missionary activity 87
monasteries
    code of conduct 126
    neglect 54–5
    property 121–2, 125–6

Napier 30 241, 241–3, 243,
    270n.52

narratio 3, 29, 139
New Minster Charter, the 15–16,
    17, 55, 118, 126, 128, 138,
    146–8, 254
    author 124, 129
    critical attention 129–30
    fall of the angels motif 124,
        139–45
    hermeneutic Latin 133, 276
    iconography 130
    martial associations 142–4
    replacement doctrine in 140–5,
        232
    and spiritual identity 133
    theological dimension 139–40
Northumbrians 6
Nunnaminster 129

oaths and oath-breaking 23, 47,
    62n.17, 90, 255–6
obedience 43, 252
Odo of Cluny 3
*Old English Dialogues of Solomon
    and Saturn, The* 19n.4
Old Minster Charter, the 118, 126,
    145–7

Passio S. Iulianae 164
Patrick, St 197
patristic theology, fall of the angels
    in 5–10
Paul's Epistle to the Romans 97
Pirmin of Reichenau 3, 245
Populus Israhel tradition 4
pride 7–9, 74–5, 242–3, 247, 257,
    266
Prudentius 142
Pseudo-Augustine 56
Pseudo-Dionysius 5
pseudo-Wulfstan 241, 241–3, 245
punishments 26, 27–9, 42–3, 82, 147

reciprocity 211
Regularis Concordia 13, 54–5, 118,
    125, 126

Index

religious values, decay of 120
replacement diplomas 46–51
replacement doctrine, the 2, 6–7, 26–8, 38, 43–4, 97, 124
   as legal transaction 27–9
   New Minster Charter and 140–5, 232
   and sovereignty 29–32
   as worldly strategy 29
   Wulfstan of York and 234, 235–6, 243, 250–1, 252–7, 261–7
resettlement 27, 46–51
Resignation 9
retainers, duties 41
Rogation homilies 225n.36
Rogationtide 17, 199–200, 202, 202–7, 217, 218, 219, 220–2, 231, 255, 279
Roman law 31, 170–1
Rome 136
royal authority 134–5
royal lordship 23
Rule of St Benedict 12–13, 90, 125–6, 132

sacral narrative as legal precedent 30
saints 16–17, 157–63
   bodily protection 174–80
   non-verbal weapons 163, 167–8
   recovery of knowledge 168–74
   revelation of the devil's persecutions 163–8
   and salvation 180–6
Saltair na Rann ('Psalter of the Quatrains') 14, 75, 77–80
salvation 26, 180–6
salvation history 174–80, 186, 243–5
Satan 9, 25, 29, 276–8
   and Adam 79–80
   Ælfric's account of fall 245–50
   aspirations 73–5
   and Christ 8–9, 17, 199–202, 213

Christ and Satan fall of the angels narrative 207–14
   claim of innocence 97
   crime 14–15, 59, 74–5, 82–3, 211
   and the fall of man 97–103
   fall of the angels illustration 32, 33, 34, 36
   final defeat 199–201
   forfeiture of space 11
   in *Genesis B* 88–99, 212, 213
   Irish accounts 75–6
   measurement of hell 197–8, 199–200, 218–19
   oath-breaking 255–6
   pride 9, 242–3, 247, 257
   punishment 94–5, 199, 209
   punishments 17
   rebellion 14, 77, 90–4
   relationship to God 92–3
   renunciation of 178–9
   seniority 80–1
   status 78–9, 82
   Temptation of Christ 204, 214–17, 220–1
   Wulfstan's account of fall 244–6, 247
Sawyer 342 58
Sawyer 362 27, 29
Sawyer 817 57–8
secular authority 147
seeing 100–1
Senchas Már 80
seniority 75, 78, 80
servants, obedient 183
sibling rivalries 77–84
Sievers, Eduard 85
Sigeric, Archbishop of Canterbury 47
Sigewulf 1, 2, 115
sin demons 177–8
Smith, Anthony 11, 58
Solomon and Saturn 160, 162–3, 165
source analysis 9

sovereign authority 4, 10, 13,
    29–32
  and territorial possession 46–51
sovereign duties 46–7
sovereignty 4, 76, 90, 92–3, 201
  and biblical authority 14
  God 90, 97, 236, 250–1
  and land 49
  and replacement doctrine 29–32
  separate 114–15
  and space 12–13, 29–32, 124,
    251–2
space 10–12, 15
  appropriation of 211
  bounded 220–2
  Genesis A and 30–1, 51–60
  heavenly 24–6
  idle 30–1
  organisation of 200
  production of 47
  Satan's forfeiture of 11
  and sovereignty 12–13, 29–32,
    124, 251–2
spiritual identity 132–3
stability 29
stewardship 30
Stowe Missal, the 173

Tacitus 65n.76
Tatwine 8
territorial competition 75
treason 27–9, 45, 66n.86

vanity 115, 276
Vercelli Homily 4 221
Vercelli Homily 8 221
Vercelli Homily 9 221
Vercelli Homily 10 16, 30, 55–7,
    148
Vercelli Homily 12 204
Vercelli Homily 19 74
Vercelli Homily 21 242, 243
Vercelli Homily 23 157–8, 186
vernacular literatures 3
Vespasian A. VIII **138**

Viking raids 17, 29, 231, 233–4,
    236, 239, 240, 252, 254, 256,
    257, 257–62
Visio Pauli 116, 127
Vita Adae et Evae ('The Life of
    Adam and Eve') 75, 76, 77,
    207
Vita S. Dunstani 135
Vita tripartita Sancti Patricii
    197
Vitae Patrum 161

Werferth 27, 43
  Dialogues translation 23–5, 52,
    275
wicked kings, the twelve abuses
    of 82
Winchester 55, 117–18, 119,
    124–17
  charters 15–16
  expulsion of the secular clerics
    127, 129, 131–48
  new Christian community 144
  New Minster 127, 128, 129
  Old Minster 127
  see also New Minster Charter,
    the; Old Minster Charter, the
wisdom, quest for 71–3
women, adornments 115
Wulfgeat 51, 237–8, 268n.20
Wulfhere, Ealdorman 27–9, 62n.17
Wulfstan of Winchester, *Vita S.
    Æthelwoldi* 134–5
Wulfstan of York, Archbishop 3,
    7, 239–40
  account of the fall of Satan
    244–6, 247
  Ælfric of Eynsham and 239,
    244–5
  appeal for penance 231
  central theme 254–7
  concerns 231–2
  and the fall of the Britons
    257–67
  homilies 17, 240–1

Institutes of Polity 243
overview of salvation history 243–5
path to salvation 265–7
replacement doctrine 234, 235–6, 243, 250–1, 252–7, 261–7
Sermo 6 39, 234, 235, 241, 243–5, 249, 250–1, 252, 257–8, 261, 262, 263–4, 266

Sermo 10 243
Sermo Lupi ad Anglos 17–18, 231–67
and the source of evil 234
sources 245
treatments of fall of the angels 236, 237–9, 241–6, 278–9

Zangemeister, Karl 85

EU authorised representative for GPSR:
Easy Access System Europe, Mustamäe tee 50,
10621 Tallinn, Estonia
gpsr.requests@easproject.com

www.ingramcontent.com/pod-product-compliance
Lightning Source LLC
Chambersburg PA
CBHW071400300426
44114CB00016B/2129